Modern in the Middle

Susan S. Benjamin
Michelangelo Sabatino

Foreword by Pauline Saliga

Modern in the Middle

Chicago Houses 1929–1975

The Monacelli Press

Contents

Coda

The Authors and Their Homes

Pauline Saliga

Foreword

As I'm writing this foreword, one thought repeatedly comes to mind—*at last*—and with apologies to Etta James: at last this book has come along. And by that, I'm not referring to the length of time it took the authors to research and write *Modern in the Middle,* because they spent just as much time as they needed to produce this insightful manuscript. Instead, I'm referring to the decades of foundational work that had to be undertaken before this history of the best modern houses in Chicagoland even could be written.

From the 1980s to the 2000s, architectural historians, critics, journalists, architects, preservationists, oral historians, and others delved into the question of how midcentury modernism manifested in the Chicago area; how it looked and was experienced, who its innovators were, and what the highpoints were. Bit by bit the architects, their stories, and their remarkable buildings were "rediscovered," and their careers were explored through a wide variety of oral histories, publications, and exhibitions. I was involved with two of these research and presentation projects when I was an associate curator in the Department of Architecture at the Art Institute of Chicago; I interviewed Mies disciples George Danforth and A. James Speyer for the Chicago Architects Oral History Project, begun in 1983, and a year later I worked on an innovative series of exhibitions, envisioned by the curator of architecture John Zukowsky, called "Architecture in Context." They presented drawings and analysis of remarkable, but little-recognized, Chicago modernists such as Paul Schweikher and William Ferguson Deknatel.

On other fronts, important new research and monographs of the period defined different types of modernism in Chicago—Beaux-Arts modernism, Miesian structuralism, Wrightian organicism, Walter Netsch's Field Theory of rotated squares, and Bertrand Goldberg's innovative concrete mixed-use projects. And, as houses of the era approached the fifty-year mark, the point at which they could be considered for landmark status, there was an explosion of new research and interest in the topic, particularly recently in popular publications such as *Crain's Chicago Business* and *Curbed Chicago,* which regularly feature in-depth articles about modern houses in the news. In addition, important special interest groups such as Landmarks Illinois, Preservation Chicago, the Chicago chapter of Docomomo US, and Chicago Bauhaus and Beyond gave the public ample opportunities to learn about Chicagoland modernism and to fall in love with it.

Two uniquely qualified individuals undertook writing *Modern in the Middle*. First, Susan Benjamin, MA, has worked since 1978 to nominate hundreds of homes and other structures for local and national landmark status. She founded Benjamin Historic Certifications in 2004, and her firm has written more nominations to the National Register of Historic Places than any other firm in the state of Illinois. The coauthor, with architect Stuart Cohen, of two books on residential architecture, *Great Houses of Chicago, 1871–1921* (2008) and *North Shore Chicago: Houses of the Lakefront Suburbs, 1890–1940* (2004), and a contributor of essays to numerous other books on North Shore architecture, Benjamin is well versed in the history and significance of the region's architectural legacy. While documenting and analyzing historic structures in the Chicago region, Benjamin encountered dozens of well-designed, innovative residences of the modern era, which, for purposes of this book, are defined as 1929 to 1975. Many of these buildings have only recently become eligible for landmark status as they turned fifty years old and are now considered "historic." Over the years, Benjamin assembled a long list of the residences in the Chicago-area that formed the core inspiration for *Modern in the Middle.*

After years of collecting research on Modern Chicagoland homes, Benjamin met and began collaborating with a scholar who had the historical insights to help Benjamin turn an excellent idea into a published book. This coauthor, Michelangelo Sabatino, PhD (Professor + Director PhD Program, College of Architecture, Illinois Institute of Technology) had the scholarly perspective to analyze this unique strain of modern residential architecture within larger modern design trends in the US and the world. Sabatino is the author of numerous books and essays on the history of modern architecture and planning in Europe and the Americas, including *Avant-Garde in the Cornfields: Architecture, Landscape, and Preservation in New Harmony* (with Ben Nicholson, 2019), *Canada: Modern Architectures in History* (with Rhodri Windsor Liscombe, 2016), and his SAH Alice Davis Hitchcock award-winning *Pride in Modesty: Modernist Architecture and the Vernacular Tradition in Italy* (2011). These together with his forthcoming books *Making Houston Modern: The Life and Architecture of Howard Barnstone* (with Barrie Scardino Bradley and Stephen Fox, 2020) and *Carlo Mollino: Architect and Storyteller* (with Napoleone Ferrari, 2020) are evidence of Sabatino's broad perspective on the subject and his ability to reaffirm the rightful place of Chicago modern residential design, given the area's stellar architecture schools, architects, and clients.

Benjamin and Sabatino have embraced the abundance of research that was decades in the making (while generating yet more), distilled it down to the essence of what Chicago modern residential architecture is, and curated a selection of the most exemplary modern houses in the region. Even though all these houses can be described as modernist, together they make an eclectic mix of styles and inspirations. Some rely on European precedents such as the École des Beaux-Arts or Alvar Aalto, while others reveal elegant designs that extend the work of Mies van der Rohe, and some manipulate the barriers between indoors and outdoors to embrace their natural settings in deference to Wright. Regardless of the architect's approach to design, all of the residences collected in this book are outstanding, and the period photographs that the authors secured raise this book to a work of design art, itself. And, of course, the research and writing of these historians is an artful enterprise in its own right.

Benjamin's essay "Frank Lloyd Wright and Ludwig Mies van der Rohe: The Giants in the Room" takes a deep dive into the influences of architectural educators. The author details vastly different design teaching philosophies from the late nineteenth century to the 1950s, from the École des Beaux-Arts system of training architects, to the organic theories Frank Lloyd Wright taught at Taliesin, and the structuralist theories Ludwig Mies van der Rohe taught at Illinois Institute of Technology. Benjamin brings into focus the multiplicity of design choices from which modern Chicago architects could choose. And, in fact, all three influences can be found throughout the selection of houses included in *Modern in the Middle*.

As Sabatino details in his essay "Modern Houses for Modern Living in Chicago" the first round of studies on Chicago modernism were focused on major commercial and institutional commissions and the architects and engineers who reshaped the Chicago skyline. Starting in the 1980s and continuing through today, research on and interest in lesser-known Chicago modernists skyrocketed. His essay analyzes the more recent literature and primary source material and focuses on residential commissions, often by less well-known designers who reshaped the region's streets, cul-de-sacs, and neighborhoods. The students of Wright, Mies, Danforth, Netsch and others developed a modern aesthetic in the region through both humble and spectacular design solutions that shape the way we live.

To Susan Benjamin, who initiated this study, and Michelangelo Sabatino, who provided the national and international context for this important group of buildings, we thank you. Your research, documentation, interpretation, and analysis of Chicago's modern residential architecture is a beautifully packaged gift to us all, which helps place modern Chicago and suburban houses in their rightful place. But the genius of this book is that it focuses on individual structures, setting the stage for studies to follow on entire urban and suburban developments that reshaped the region in the 1950s, '60s, and '70s. Now, new generations of architectural historians, homeowners, preservationists, architects, and citizen historians will be inspired to research the intriguing modern homes in subdivisions and planned communities, as these developments approach and pass their fiftieth anniversaries and become newly historic.

Michelangelo Sabatino

Modern Houses for Modern Living in Chicago

The modern house can be said to have acted as a receptacle of seemingly infinite capacity for new ideas. Despite the vast and complex building programmes of this age, the house's relative importance probably stood higher in the first half of this century than at any other time in history.

Sherban Cantacuzino, *Modern Houses of the World*

Frank Lloyd Wright's compact yet porous Robie House—completed in 1910 for Lora Hieronymus and Frederick C. Robie, an entrepreneur and his family in the Chicago neighborhood of Hyde Park—is a highpoint in a seminal episode of architecture in America that historians have long coined as the Prairie School.[1] Since the late nineteenth century, Wright and a group of other architects pioneered an approach in the "Middle West" based on a new dialogue with nature (i.e., prairie landscape) and tradition that eschewed explicit references to classicism and historicism.[2] German émigré architect Ludwig Mies van der Rohe arrived in Chicago in 1938, nearly three decades after the completion of the Robie House, on the eve of World War II, when the tenets of the Prairie School no longer yielded the same fascination despite ongoing interest in organicism among newer generations of architects. After only a decade in his new adopted city, Mies began designing the Edith Farnsworth House (p. 162), a glass-and-steel one-story pavilion sited along the Fox River in nearby Plano, completed in 1951. Together, the Robie and the Farnsworth houses, albeit with entirely different approaches to the integration of modern materials and building technology, established Chicago and its surrounding cities and villages (Chicagoland) as a laboratory for architectural innovation in residential architecture during the first half of the twentieth century.[3] Yet, as the contents of our book *Modern in the Middle: Chicago Houses 1929–1975* reveal, there are many more exemplars in this multifaceted history about modern domestic architecture, which begins on the eve of the Great Depression and ends when the Watergate scandal was just winding down, than a handful of iconic houses.

Our book has four areas of focus: a two-part introduction, a portfolio of 53 houses ranging from 1929 to 1975 selected primarily on the basis of their architectural, cultural, and social significance, a coda that includes a discussion about post-1975 houses that reveals the ways in which Chicago architects revised the modernist

Opposite: Robie House with four-story modernist McGiffert House (1959), originally a dormitory for the Chicago Theological Seminary, behind.

Hiroshi Sugimoto blurs Miesian precision in his *Farnsworth House*, 2001.

11

legacy and a concluding discussion (written with Serge Ambrose) about Chicago's preservation community and ongoing challenges for the preservation of modern houses. Historic photographs are an important tool for telling our story about modern houses and interiors as they appeared at the time of completion. Many of the historic photographs of houses featured in *Modern in the Middle* were taken by Hedrich Blessing—Chicago's leading architectural photographers, from 1929 when the studio opened until its closing in 2017.[4] Although other photographers, including Richard Nickel, and non-native Chicagoans such as Harry Callahan (who taught at the Institute of Design), Julius Shulman, Balthazar Korab, and Ezra Stoller (who was born in Chicago), traveled to Chicago on assignment, Hedrich Blessing's decades-long commitment was paralleled by none. Unfortunately, a number of interesting modern houses were not photographed by these individuals and remained virtually unknown.

Modern Houses in America

The July 1939 issue of *Architectural Forum* dedicated the entire volume to "Modern Houses in America." The opening editorial reads: "It is thirty years since Frank Lloyd Wright built the Coonley house, fourteen years since Le Corbusier's pavilion disrupted a Paris fair, nine since Mies van der Rohe produced the Tugendhat plan. Long enough, one might think, for the modern house to come of age in an epoch of swift development. But the new dwellings in the 1939 U. S. landscape are still predominantly traditional."[5] Out of the seventeen featured houses that cumulatively demonstrate the coming of age of American modern residential design, two were designed by Chicago-based architects for cities and villages that are part of the greater Chicago metropolitan area. These houses include George Fred Keck's Irma Kuppenheimer and Bertram J. Cahn House in Lake Forest (1937 p. 84) and Philip B.

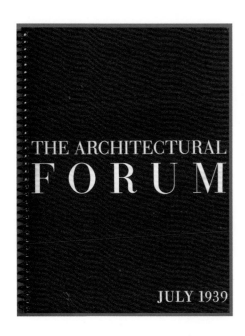

THE ARCHITECTURAL
FORUM

JULY 1939

Maher's own house (with Madeleine Michelson Maher, his spouse at the time) in Lake Bluff (1938 p. 94).[6] The third house was designed by Chicago-based architect William F. Deknatel for Marie Celeste McVoy and Walter J. Kohler Jr. in Kohler, Wisconsin (1937).[7] In the Cahn House, Keck used large picture windows and glass block for his one-story crescent-shaped pavilion. Maher's elegant two-story L-shaped volume also made abundant use of "glass block walls," plus large panes of glass, in order to take advantage of the views of Lake Michigan. Cumulatively, these three modern houses reveal how different generations of Chicago-based architects during the 1930s—who were at the time in their thirties and forties—were rethinking residential architecture in response to a rapidly modernizing American society still grappling with the challenges of the Great Depression. Rather than view organic principles associated with the Prairie School in opposition to modern functionalism or rationalism (e.g., the International Style), most of these architects absorbed cues from *both* traditions throughout the course of their careers. It is with this exchange of ideas and approaches in mind that *Modern in the Middle* examines significant modern houses for modern living designed by architects like the ones discussed in the July 1939 issue of *Architectural Forum* that are both well-known and lesser-known within the local, national, and international context.

In recent years the genre of general-audience and scholarly books focused on twentieth-century houses located mainly in Europe and the Americas has grown exponentially.[8] The twentieth-century temporal framework allows most

The Architectural Forum (July 1939) theme issue: "Modern Houses in America."

Main entrance to Frank Lloyd Wright's (Addie) "Queene" Ferry and Avery Coonley House (1907) Riverside, in 2019.

authors some freedom to present a more diversified multi-generational history of residential architecture by including a range of arts and crafts, art deco, secessionist, and classically-inspired houses that constitute important trajectories in the decades leading up to the rise of a more narrowly defined modern movement by militant critics.[9] Several authors have chosen to focus on the cultural and contextual specificity of the modern house in America.[10] In addition to a number of gatherings such as the Congrès Internationaux d'Architecture Moderne (CIAM, International Congresses of Modern Architecture) held in Europe on the theme of houses and housing, the popular book *The Modern House* (1934; subsequent editions in 1935, '37, '43, '44, '48, '51, and '56) written by English architect F. R. S. Yorke is one of the earliest international surveys to focus exclusively on the "individual villa type of house."[11] Alongside a handful of American exemplars that include Richard Neutra's Leah Press and Philip M. Lovell House in Los Angeles (1929), F. R. S. Yorke presents two houses by Chicago-based architect Howard T. Fisher who established the company General Houses, Inc. Fisher promoted his "economical and efficient houses of a large variety of types" making it possible "to purchase a completely equipped and permanent home as modern as tomorrow."[12] Significantly, a reproduction of a Fisher drawing forms the basis of the book's first edition dustcover.

Insofar as the process of designing and realizing houses relates to clients and architects, many publications aim for a general readership as well as for professionals and scholars that focus on the popular genre of houses by individual twentieth-century American architects such as Joseph Esherick, Louis Kahn, Harry Weese, and William Wurster to name a few.[13] By eschewing a monographic format focused on a single architect in favor of a chronologically ordered cross-section of houses designed by a variety of architects of different generations, *Modern in the Middle* traces the growth of a phenomenon that helped shape America's contribution to modern architecture. Building upon the efforts made by architects, historians, and preservationists in the recent past, we explore the contributions of remarkably diverse generations of Chicago professionals (born in the US and trained nationally and-or internationally, and foreign-born and trained internationally) who contributed to a significant corpus of modern residential buildings. The houses discussed cover a range of sizes (larger houses coexist alongside mid-size and modest-sized ones) commissioned by a range of generally middle and upper-middle-class clients. Recognizing the importance of oral history, whenever possible, we have interviewed architects, commissioning clients, and current homeowners.[14]

In selecting the houses we have endeavored to correct the omission that was summarized on the dustcover of the book *Mid-Century Architecture in America* (1961) to which Chicago-based architect Philip Will Jr. (originally Perkins, Wheeler & Will; now Perkins + Will) contributed: "Some of the architects—such as Edward Stone, Philip Johnson, Eero Saarinen, Pietro Belluschi, and the firm of Skidmore, Owings & Merrill—are well known, but much of our best architecture has been created by relative unknowns, and their work is well represented."[15] Unfortunately, despite the best efforts of architects, journalists, and historians as well as various advocacy and preservation groups to focus on lesser-known yet talented architects, there is a continuing desire to publish articles and books about "masters"

Opposite: F. R. S. Yorke's *The Modern House* (1934) with drawings of General Houses, Inc. models on dustcover and within book.

"House for Miss Ruth Page," in Hubbard Woods, Howard T. Fisher Architect, General Houses, Inc. *Architectural Record* (April 1933), later demolished.

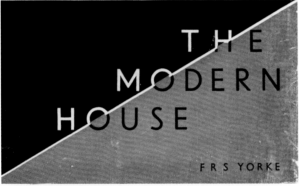

Frank Lloyd Wright and Ludwig Mies van der Rohe who are extensively researched instead of tackling those that might require entirely new frameworks of interpretation.

In the July 1939 issue of *Architectural Forum* cited earlier, the editorial introducing the seventeen houses asserts that change is in the air: "There are the recent polls, which show a consistent consumer opinion of 40 odd percent favorable to the modern house, some four times the figure of a few years back," and goes on to assert that "The modern house today is no longer the frigid white symbol of a small cult, and in changing it has immeasurably broadened its appeal."[16] Without explicitly identifying an architect, building, or country, the editors' reference to "frigid white symbol of a small cult" seems to target a certain modern architecture of the late 1920s through the early 1930s. Some of these buildings were on display at *Modern Architecture: International Exhibition* (exhibition 15) held at the Museum of Modern Art (MoMA) in New York in 1932, and later that year shown in the galleries of the Sears flagship State Street store in Chicago's Loop.[17] The curators and authors of the accompanying catalogue revised it as a book entitled *The International Style: Architecture Since 1922*; they single out three Chicago-based architects whose work is also discussed in this book: Howard Fisher, George Fred Keck, and Henry Dubin.[18] Despite the fact that an entire section was dedicated to Frank Lloyd Wright, this traveling exhibition seems to have contributed to the American public's understanding (or misunderstanding) of modernism as "frigid white" buildings that all looked alike regardless of client, climate, or site.[19] Following the *Modern Architecture* (aka *International Style*) exhibition (1932), Henry-Russell Hitchcock and Philip Johnson looked to bolster the "American" dimension of modern architecture by presenting at MoMA the *Early Modern Architecture: Chicago 1870–1910* exhibition (1933), which featured photographs of tall buildings and houses such as H. H. Richardson's Frances Macbeth and John Glessner House (1886) and Emily Eames and Franklin MacVeagh House (1885), Dankmar Adler & Louis Sullivan's (with their junior draftsman at the time, Frank Lloyd Wright) Helen Douglas and James Charnley House (1892), Frank Lloyd Wright's Edith Henry and William H. Winslow House (1893), and George Maher's Amanda Buchanan and James A. Patten House (1902).[20]

FROM MASONRY TO STEEL

One of the first Europeans to use international in association with modern architecture was German architect Walter Gropius who authored a survey book entitled *International Architecture* (1925) for the Bauhausbücher series; in his foreword Gropius wrote: "Shared traits common to all countries can be identified in the specially selected works presented, over and above their various individual and national idiosyncrasies. This kinship, which is also apparent to non-experts, is an indication of their future-oriented significance and the harbinger of a fundamentally new form of design drive, represented in all cultivated countries on Earth."[21] In addition to grain elevators, the only American buildings selected by Gropius among his "international" exemplars were Wright's Robie House and Larkin Administration Building (1903, demolished 1950).

One year after the MoMA International Style exhibition, Chicago hosted the hugely popular A Century of Progress International Exposition (1933–34) that did much to distract Depression-era citizens from their daily challenges. George Fred Keck's House of Tomorrow (1933 interiors and furniture by Irene K. Hyman and Leland Atwood; 1934 redesign without Keck) and Crystal House (1934) drew considerable interest. The range of model houses on display at the "Home and Industrial Arts Exhibit" promoted the use of both modern and traditional building materials: Keck's high-tech Crystal House juxtaposed with Andrew Rebori's House for Brick

Cover, *Mid-Century Architecture in America* (1961).

1933 MoMA *Early Modern Architecture: Chicago 1870–1910* exhibition.

Advertisement appearing in the *Chicago Daily Tribune* on June 12, 1932.

Opposite: Century of Progress Crystal House (1934) with Buckminster Fuller's Dymaxion Car parked inside.

Manufacturers' Association of America (1933).[22] In a bid to correct the perceived shortfalls of Chicago's exposition, which in his opinion was not modern enough, Philip Johnson launched his own polemical counter exhibition in 1933 entitled *Work of Young Architects in the Middle West* at MoMA in 1933:

> It seems appropriate in the year that Chicago is the cynosure of architectural eyes that there should be an exhibition of work of men whose attitude toward architecture is newer and younger than that of those in charge of designing the buildings for the Century of Progress Exposition. Some of these young men are working for the Exposition but their work will be lost in the midst of the official architecture which dominates the main pavilions.

> This exhibition is a logical successor to the International Exhibition of Modern Architecture held by the Museum in 1932. The young generation, now beginning their independent practice, have broken away from academic design. They have not as much opportunity to build as their predecessors, but more to observe and study. As a result this exhibition consists mainly of projects, but projects which show not only research into new problems but great strides away from the Beaux Arts classical (not to mention the Beaux Arts "modernistic").[23]

As Europe became increasingly politically unstable during the late 1930s, a number of modern artists and architects immigrated to American cities ranging from Boston and New York to Chicago and Los Angeles.[24] Shortly after his arrival to the US, Walter Gropius designed, between 1937 and 1938, a house for his spouse at the time Ise Frank and adopted daughter Ati in Lincoln, Massachusetts just outside of Boston. It was among the seventeen houses discussed by the editors of the July 1939 issue of *Architectural Forum;* despite a flat roof and simple massing, most of the primary materials (wood for the structure and cladding) and building techniques used were typical of the traditional New England "saltbox."[25] Gropius, like many of the protagonists of the so-called International Style, understood it as an evolving approach based on a shared understanding of "universal technical achievements."[26] The rejection of a static definition of International Style is confirmed later on by Swiss architect, historian, and critic Sigfried Giedion when he wrote in *A Decade of New Architecture,* published in 1951:

> Since around 1900, when F. L. Wright adapted the free ground plan of early American tradition to modern needs, the single family house has everywhere provided the greatest range of opportunity for modern architects and has given rise to many of the best examples of contemporary architecture.
>
> Even a few examples are enough to show the wide variety of ways in which a common vocabulary has been employed in different regions—extending from Finland to South America, and it is to be hoped that the unfortunate and misleading designation of an "International Style" will now finally disappear.[27]

Not by coincidence, the Gropius House is among the examples discussed by Giedion (along with houses by Chicago-area architects Winston Elting, George Fred Keck, Ralph Rapson, Paul Schweikher, Robert Bruce Tague, and Harry Weese), in his overview covering the years 1937–47. Decades later, the American architectural historian and critic William Jordy offers the following insight: "If, however, one interprets Hitchcock and Johnson very narrowly—more narrowly than they would wish—and if one seeks the outstanding buildings designed after 1932 which continue in the image of the Style described in their book, few are to be found."[28] More recently, architectural historian Sandy Isenstadt has convincingly discussed the emergence of a "Modern in the Middle," and Gwendolyn Wright, a pioneering scholar on domestic architecture in Chicago and the US, asserted: "Hybridity rather than purity seemed the fitting expression of American culture, unpredictable amalgams of tradition and innovation, local and universal, personal and collective."[29]

It is against the backdrop of an evolving debate shaped by complementary and sometimes competing ideas about modern architecture that the houses in *Modern in the Middle* are presented and analyzed. Although the focus of the book is on houses, we understand

that a variety of different building types ranging from schools to religious buildings played important roles in creating livable neighborhoods while promoting acceptance of modern architecture. For example, the Katherine Dummer and Walter T. Fisher House (1929, p. 58) introduced modern architecture to Winnetka nearly a decade before Perkins, Wheeler & Will collaborated with Eliel and Eero Saarinen to design the Crow Island School (1940). In Glencoe, along with A. James Speyer's Marian Short and Stanley G. Harris Jr. House (1950, now demolished, p. 156) and the Keck & Keck-designed Forest Crest Subdivision of twenty-two houses (1951–52), stands Minoru Yamasaki's Reform synagogue completed in 1964 for North Shore Congregation Israel.

Inside the Modern House

Ise Gropius relaxing on second-floor terrace of Gropius House (1938) Lincoln, Massachusetts, photographed by Robert Damora in 1947.

Crow Island School (1940) Winnetka designed with the collaboration of Perkins, Wheeler & Will and Eliel and Eero Saarinen.

While this book focuses primarily on modern houses and their architects, when research is available, the authors have endeavored to acknowledge the contributions of landscape architects and interior designers. As far as interior design and furniture are concerned, it is worth recalling that Chicago was an important regional center for the production and sale of furniture and household objects before and during the time period covered by this book.[30] The American Furniture Mart, opened in 1924, and the Merchandise Mart, opened in 1930—both of which contained wholesale showrooms—were located in prominent buildings. Noted American furniture designer Edward Wormley wrote in the early 1950s: "Twice

yearly in Chicago, a Home Furnishings Market is held for store buyers from all over the country to inspect, at one time, the industry's newest products. Much of the activity there is centered in the Merchandise Mart (excepting the Pentagon, the world's largest building)" with its slightly over four million square feet of floor space.[31] From 1950 to 1955 the Merchandise Mart and MoMA collaborated to host Good Design Exhibitions in Chicago and New York City. In the postwar years, small yet highly influential retail stores such as Baldwin Kingrey (established by architect Harry Weese, his spouse, Kitty Baldwin Weese, and mutual friend Jody Kingrey) made it possible for consumers to purchase affordable designed objects and furniture, by Alvar Aalto, Harry Bertoia, and Charles and Ray Eames, for their homes.[32] Along with interior and industrial design, parallels in the arts (painting, sculpture, textiles, and graphic design) that shaped the backdrop for the design and realization of the modern houses discussed in this book are also taken into account.[33] An example is the modern house designed by A. James Speyer in Highland Park (1953) for textile designer Ben Rose and his

Herman Miller Furniture Company showroom by designer Gilbert Rohde, 1939, Merchandise Mart.

A. James Speyer's *Good Design Exhibition*, Merchandise Mart, 1954, in collaboration with MoMA.

GOOD DESIGN

As shown in the Good Design Exhibition at The Merchandise Mart, Chicago, chosen by The Museum of Modern Art, New York.

Ben Rose's Textile and Wallpapers showroom, Merchandise Mart (c. 1953).

Merchandise tag, *Good Design Exhibition,* 1954.

spouse, Frances Landrum, a weaver and his business partner (p. 190).[34] Samuel Marx also designed a number of modernist interiors and houses.

Chicago is a particularly interesting city to study the impact of principles of the so-called International Style émigrés that arrived from Europe to establish them-selves as academics/architects because Wright and the Prairie School architects had already developed a uniquely "American" architecture with an international following. By understanding the trajectories of Ludwig Mies van der Rohe in Chicago, Rudolph Schindler and Richard Neutra (both of whom worked in Chicago) in Los Angeles, Gropius in Cambridge/Boston, and Eliel Saarinen (after a sojourn in Chicago) in Bloomfield Hills, Michigan, we see how the arrival of émigrés offered opportunities for exchanges that contributed significantly, along with other aspects of everyday American culture, toward a new approach to designing modern houses.[35]

It is worth noting that a number of these émigrés held important leadership roles within educational institutions. In 1938, Mies was appointed director of the Department of Architecture at the Armour Institute of Technology (subsequently the Illinois Institute of Technology, IIT). In 1932 Gropius was appointed chair of the Department of Architecture at Harvard University's Graduate School of Design established a year earlier. Like Gropius, Eliel Saarinen (who became president and

Baldwin Kingrey Store, 105 East Ohio St. (Michigan Square Building) photographed by Ferenc Berko following 1952 renovation. The store opened in 1947 and closed in 1957.

"Loja" Gesllius and Eliel Saarinen House and Studio (1930), dining room, Cranbrook Academy of Art, Bloomfield Hills.

would head the Department of Architecture and Urban Design of the Cranbrook Academy of Art from 1932-46) designed his House and Studio (1928–30) as a personal pedagogical manifesto.[36] Incidentally, the design competition held in 1922 for a new *Chicago Tribune* headquarters tower drew the attention of a number of modernist architects, including Gropius and Saarinen, both of whom eventually immigrated to the United States.[37] Eliel Saarinen's submission won second place.

Two important books published in the early 1940s and co-written by architect James Ford and sociologist Katherine Morrow Ford—*The Modern House in America* (1940) and the companion volume *Design of Modern Interiors* (1942)—acknowledge the changes to the American house and its interiors:

> Then came the hegira to America. In their relative youth came Belluschi, Lescaze, Neutra, Schindler, and Soriano, each prior to 1930. In more recent years arrived such already established leaders as Gropius—the founder of that pioneering school, the Bauhaus—and his associates, Breuer and Moholy-Nagy; also Mies van der Rohe from Germany, Saarinen from Finland, and Ruhtenberg from Sweden.
>
> These men have been quick to catch the spirit of America, to appraise its opportunities for new rationales and mediums, and for new uses of materials. They are now making their own performance essentially American. They and their students are producing, not an "international style," but a new American architecture, cosmopolitan in spirit, but native both in form and detail—a genuine expression of American individuality.[38]

The Fords' anthology includes, among others, the same Chicago-based architects (Deknatel, Keck, and Maher) discussed in the July 1939 issue of *Architectural Forum*. In a subsequent publication written by Katherine Morrow Ford and Thomas

H. Creighton entitled *The American House Today: 85 Notable Examples Selected and Evaluated* (1951) the authors reflect on the dissemination of modern houses beyond the East and West Coasts:

> So it was not until the late thirties and early forties that anything which could be reasonably called a contemporary movement in architecture had developed in the United States. In contrast to the choice of material available for this book, when one of the present authors collaborated on a book about residential architecture in 1940 it was a matter of discovering unrecognized talent, of searching for little-known work.[39]

Together, these three books did much to document modern residential architecture and interiors in America.

It is not surprising that as battles were raging in Europe for a war that was jump-started by the rise of nationalist ideologies, increasingly the focus turned to modern architecture with "American individuality" and more importantly, the single-family house, since it promoted the traditional family nucleus. Parallels exist in the realm of interior and industrial designers; for example, American designer Russel Wright is well known for his informal yet artistic and functional American Modern dinnerware series that he launched in 1939.[40]

Advertising the Modern House

Along with professional journals and anthologies organized around themes or types, the houses discussed in *Modern in the Middle* were occasionally selected to be part of marketing publications and shelter magazines aimed at architects, builders, and homeowners.[41] For example the Rosalie Brown and Robert Hosmer Morse House in Lake Forest (1932, p. 68) appeared early on in a marketing brochure by Rolscreen® (now Pella).[42] William (and Harold) Pereira's Charles Dewey Jr. House (1940, p. 118) in Lake Bluff was featured on the cover of George Nelson and Henry Wright's *Tomorrow's House: A Complete Guide for the Home-Builder* (1945). A number of

Cover, *Design of Modern Interiors* (1942).

Cover, *The Modern House in America* (1940).

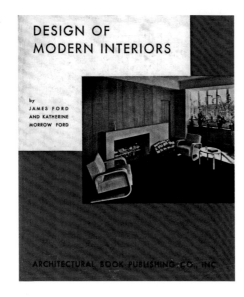

Chicago houses including Schweikher and Elting's Gertrude Stevens and Philip S. Rinaldo Jr. House (demolished) in Downers Grove (1942) and William Deknatel's Ellen Newby and Lambert Ennis House in Evanston (1942, p. 132) were featured in *Windows in Modern Architecture* by Geoffrey Baker and Bruno Funaro (1948).[43] From the 1930s onwards fixed picture windows (as well as awning and casements windows) were frequently showcased in residential architecture advertisements as they were seen as key to the pursuit of "spaciousness" in the modern American house.[44] The Libbey-Owens-Ford Glass Company (Toledo) published a brochure on "Glass—As an Architectural Medium in 9 Small Modern Houses at the Century of Progress 1933–34," and they used the Vine Itschner and Herbert Bruning House (1936, p. 76) in an adver-

tisement about Insulux Glass Block published in *Architectural Record* (November 1938).[45] Companies also featured modern amenities in their advertising campaigns such as appliances in "The Modern Kitchen is All-ELECTRIC!" advertisement by General Electric featuring the Walter Gropius House in Lincoln, Massachusetts and air conditioning such as "The Frigidaire Air Conditioned House" at the Century of Progress Exposition.[46]

While glass was most often associated with modernism, the materials and building technologies deployed in the houses discussed in *Modern in the Middle* are quite diverse, and they range from radically innovative to traditional. Architect Henry Dubin's "fireproof" Battledeck House in Highland Park (1930, p. 64) abandoned wood as a conventional structural building material in favor of a hybrid steel and load-bearing common-brick-and-concrete-block system. The first house designed by Howard T. Fisher in 1935 for Ellen Borden and Adlai E. Stevenson II in Libertyville was prefabricated (steel panels) and was replaced by another more conventionally built wood house designed by Perkins, Wheeler & Will (1938, p. 104). During the years that saw the realization of these houses, a previous generation of architects combined traditional materials with modern simplicity: Barry Byrne designed the William McDermott House (1928) in Glencoe and Andrew Rebori (with artist Edgar Miller) designed the Fisher Studio Houses (1936) on Chicago's Near North Side and the Illana Herzig and Philip L. Weintraub House (1941) in the North Park neighborhood of Chicago.[47] Paul Schweikher and Theodore Warren Lamb's brick masonry Flora and David B. Johnson House (1936) in the neighborhood of

Brochure, Russel Wright's *American Modern* by Steubenville, designed in 1937 and launched in 1939.

Bruning House (1936) by Keck featured in "Modern to the minute..." advertisement for Insulux Glass Block by Owens-Illinois, *Architectural Record* (November 1938).

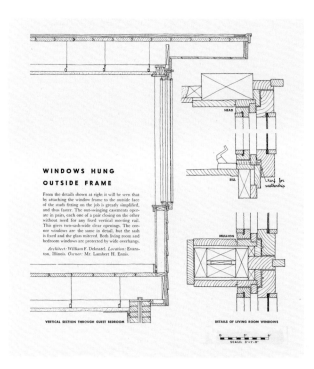

Details of the Ennis House
(1942) Evanston, published
in Geoffrey Baker & Bruno
Funaro's *Windows in Modern
Architecture* (1948).

Plan, Keck & Keck's Duncan
House (1941) Flossmoor,
Architectural Forum (August
1943).

Jackson Park Highlands reveals a debt to the aesthetics of Eliel Saarinen's Cranbrook campus.[48] Decades
later, Mies van der Rohe's design for a house for
Robert Hall McCormick III and his spouse at the time
poet Isabella Gardner (1952, p. 184) in Elmhurst was
conceived as a prefabricated glass and steel modular
pavilion that could be easily replicated.[49] While Mies's
students deployed steel construction in a number of
modern houses discussed in *Modern in the Middle,* the
American residential building industry has remained
mainly conventional; elsewhere in America, despite
their best efforts, many architects who participated
in the Case Study House program, whose epicenter
was mainly Los Angeles, were unable, despite the
vigorous campaign by *Arts & Architecture* magazine,
to convince the majority of Americans that modern
houses should be built of steel.[50] Conversely, thanks to
George Fred Keck, who was in the forefront of passive
solar experimentation, Chicagoland houses received
a considerable amount of national and international press from the 1940s–60s.[51]
(See the Minna Green and Hugh D. Duncan House, 1941, p. 130).

Throughout the late nineteenth and twentieth centuries, the definition of "modern
architecture" has shifted considerably depending on the country and language.
The use of concepts such as modernization, modernity, and modernism adds
some clarity since these terms differentiate among technical, philosophical, and
aesthetic innovations. For example, as early as 1895, Otto Wagner published his
lectures in a volume entitled *Modern Architecture.*[52] Even Frank Lloyd Wright
who took issue with the term "modern" delivered a series of lectures at Princeton
University in 1930, subsequently published as *Modern Architecture.*[53] Within this
evolving landscape of definitions, the questions that beg asking are: Which are
Chicago's most significant modern houses? Is designing and building modern
houses for Chicago different from other major cities
in the US and beyond? What makes a single-family
house modern? Does a house need to be built of glass
and steel or glass, brick, and wood with an open plan
to be modern or can it combine tradition with innovation? Why did nature and site play such a consistently
important role in the design of modern houses? What
role did suburban expansion play in encouraging the
development of the modern house in Chicago? We
have set out to address these and other questions
through a discussion about individual houses as well
as shared forces that made the modern house a reality.

Chicagoland: Neighborhoods, Cities, and Villages

The cities and villages surrounding Chicago and its neighborhoods were considered part and parcel of its metropolitan identity early on as is evident from a number of guidebooks produced from the late nineteenth century to the first decades of the twentieth century.[54] In recent years scholars based in Chicago have focused considerable efforts on studying this city's suburbs in the context of American domestic architecture and urbanism.[55] Scholars based outside Chicago have also contributed their insights on the history of suburbs in Chicago, America, and beyond.[56] While the *World's Columbian Exposition* of 1892–93 brought plazas and parks for Chicago's citizens, as early as the 1850s railroads had created an extensive network that connected the city and its neighborhoods with the burgeoning suburbs; the future expansion of the city was set in motion. The majority of the houses discussed in *Modern in the Middle* are located either in neighborhoods, cities, or villages established in the nineteenth century.[57] For example, the Portfolio section of this book opens with the Katherine Dummer and Walter T. Fisher House (1929) designed by Howard T. Fisher for the North Shore village of

Winnetka and closes near the Ruth Nelson and Robert J. Freeark House (1975, p. 258) designed by John Vinci and Lawrence Kenny in the western suburban Village of Riverside. Winnetka, like Riverside, differs from postwar subdivisions that are often associated with "sprawl" insofar as these independent villages were established during the nineteenth century as railroad suburbs.[58] Riverside was planned by Frederick Law Olmsted and Calvert Vaux in 1869, replete with winding streets and modern conveniences for the time.[59] After World War II, newly established villages such as Park Forest to the south of Chicago were designed around the automobile while bringing affordable single- and multi-family housing to returning GIs.[60] Developed by Nathan Manilow, Carroll F. Sweet, and Philip M. Klutznick, designed by city planner and landscape architect Elbert Peets with the Chicago firm of Loebl, Schlossman and Bennett, Park Forest provided fodder for William H. Whyte's best-selling book *The Organization Man* (1956). The mass consumption of the automobile and the construction of infrastructure to support it did much to increase access to new and more established cities and villages in and around Chicago.[61]

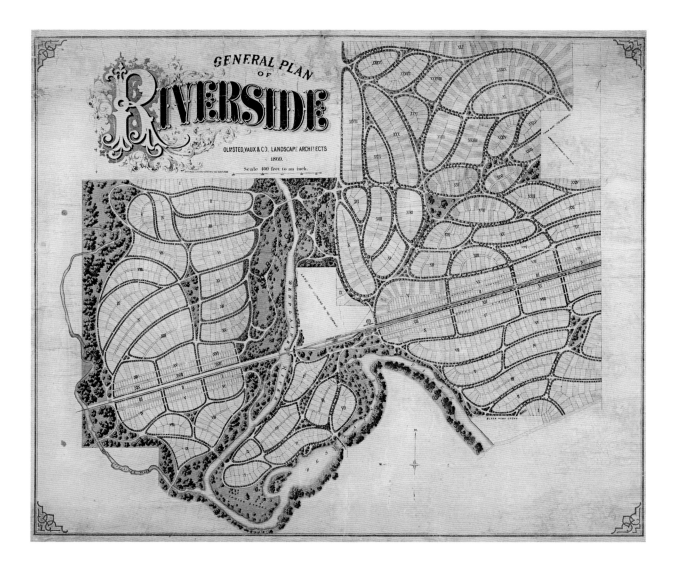

"General Plan of Riverside,"
Olmsted, Vaux & Co. Landscape
Architects, 1869.

Opposite: Elbert Peets, Site
Planner with Loebl, Schlossman
and Bennett Architects and
Engineers, "Park Forest – Cook
and Will Counties, Illinois,"
February, 2, 1950.

The network of neighborhoods, cities, and villages discussed in this book are linked together by trains, buses and cars. They range from the North Shore City of Evanston to the Village of Lake Bluff, established during the nineteenth century, Oak Park and Riverside to the west, and Olympia Fields and Flossmoor to the south. During the temporal arc taken into consideration for *Modern in the Middle*, these neighborhoods, cities, and villages witnessed the realization of a range of modern houses. Just as the designs of modern houses differed, so too did the social fabric of the communities in which they were located. What they share in common is the fact that architects and their adventurous clients introduced modern architecture in places where none existed. Thus, the network of suburban cities and villages provided many opportunities for experimentation in modern residential architecture, at least until the 1970s. These areas still had available affordable and desirable parcels of land unlike within the city itself which had been taken up by nineteenth- and early-twentieth-century houses or mid- and high-rise apartment buildings.

Many of the single-family modern houses discussed in this book are sited on standard residential lots or large parcels of land. They functioned as primary residences for their owners who commuted daily to Chicago for work and were generally not secondary/seasonal houses.[62] The exceptions discussed include the following secondary houses: the Mies-designed Farnsworth House (1951) in Plano, the Keck-designed Cahn House (1937) and the Zimmerman, Saxe & Zimmerman-designed Morse House (1932) both in Lake Forest, the Harry Weese-designed Kitty Baldwin and Harry Weese House (1957, p. 216) in Barrington, and the Stanley Tigerman-designed Iris Smith and Paul Goldstein House (1975, p. 262) in Harvard, Illinois.

During the 1930s a number of iconic modern houses realized in Europe were referred to as villas, and they functioned as weekend retreats: recall Le Corbusier's Villa Savoye (1931) at Poissy on the outskirts of Paris and Alvar Aalto's Villa Mairea (1939) in Noormarkku, Finland.[63] A number of houses in Europe located in the suburbs of the great cities were also referred to as villas even though they functioned as primary residences: see for example the Villa Müller (1930) in Prague by Adolf Loos. In America, the usage of the term *villa* was not common, especially in relation to modern architecture.[64] The most iconic pair of weekend houses in

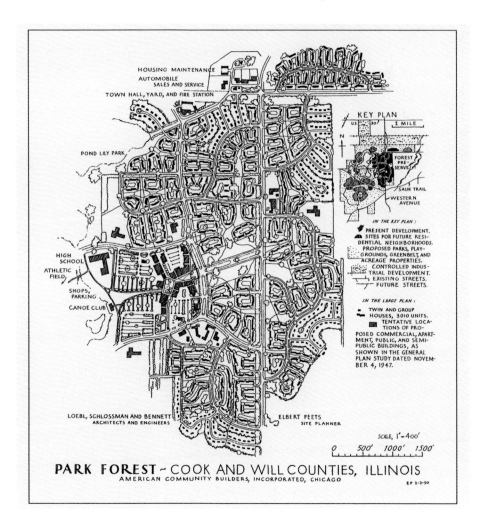

America commissioned by the same patron in two different parts of the country are described as houses instead of villas: Fallingwater (1936) in Mill Run, Pennsylvania was designed by Frank Lloyd Wright for the Liliane and Edgar Kaufmann family and the Kaufmann Desert House in Palm Springs, California (1946) designed by Richard Neutra.[65] The acclaimed International Style house was designed in 1938 by Edward Durell Stone for A. Conger Goodyear and his spouse at the time, Mary

Martha Forman, on Long Island and conceived as a weekend retreat for the industrialist and art collector who was appointed as MoMA's first president in 1929.[66] On the East Coast, during the postwar years, the town of New Canaan along with Cape Cod and its surrounding areas became preferred sites for New Yorkers and Bostonians, clients and architects in search of either primary or secondary houses.[67] While Philip Johnson's Glass House completed in 1949 functioned as a weekend retreat, architects like Marcel Breuer and Eliot Noyes designed houses for themselves during those same years in New Canaan and in so doing established it as a progressive enclave for modern architecture.[68] From the early 1930s when Albert Frey and A. Lawrence Kocher realized their acclaimed Aluminaire House (1931) well into the 1980s, Long Island also functioned as a place where a host of architects designed primary and secondary modern houses for themselves and for their affluent clients.[69]

Throughout the nineteenth and twentieth centuries, Chicagoland witnessed a remarkable production of vernacular builder-designed mass-produced single-family houses alongside one-off architect-designed exemplars: vernacular residential types range from the Chicago bungalow and Sears Roebuck & Co.'s "Modern Homes" mail-order houses to Lustron (prefabricated enameled steel) and "midwestern ranches and splits."[70] The rising popularity of the single-family modern house for the middle class during these post-war years (for example, Park Forest in south suburban Chicago) provided Chicagoans with alternatives to multi-family living characterized by two-and three-flats as well as the ubiquitous courtyard apartments that continued to be built until the 1930s.[71] This said, Chicagoans also continued to demonstrate a strong affinity for living in apartment buildings. In fact, throughout the twentieth century, apartment towers (and hotels) along the shore of Lake Michigan offered residents and tourists opportunities to enjoy impressive views of the city and lake.[72] After World War II, Chicago architects pioneered modern steel, concrete, and glass tall buildings for residential use, including such noteworthy examples designed by Mies such as Promontory Apartments (1949), 860–880 Lake Shore Apartments (1951), and 900–910 Esplanade (1956); Bertrand Goldberg's celebrated Marina City (1968); and George Schipporeit and John Heinrich's Lake Point Tower (1968); and the mixed-use John Hancock Center (1969) designed by Bruce Graham and Fazlur Khan (SOM), reinforced a trend to live in high-rise multi-unit buildings. The middle and upper-middle class residents of the buildings could afford an urban lifestyle. Elsewhere in the city during the 1950s through the 1970s, apartment towers were being constructed as public housing, and became associated with segregated housing for the African American poor and have been gradually razed due to dysfunctional and biased policies that led to challenging living conditions.[73]

Night view of Ludwig Mies van der Rohe's 860-880 North Lake Shore Drive Apartments c. 1961.

The title *Modern in the Middle* assumes multiple meanings in order to describe a complex story about modern houses. The most obvious reference to "middle" relates to geography. Once the West began to be inhabited by pioneer settlers, writers began to describe Chicago as the geographical "middle" of the continental United States. Often referred to as a midwestern city, it has also been called "mid-continental," "mid-America," or "middle American."[74] Whereas labels such as Third Coast, Second City, or Inland (also the title of an influential journal the *Inland Architect* established in Chicago in 1883) don't include "middle," they nevertheless associate location to Chicago's identity over time.[75] By alluding to geography in the title, we lay bare our conviction that the modern architecture produced in Chicago was place-specific in the broadest sense of this term. Place specificity is understood here as both physical and non-physical manifestations, including climate and sociocultural milieu.[76] In recent decades the historiographical debate surrounding the revision of modern architecture has introduced such place-specific concepts as "critical regionalism."[77]

Although the range of houses discussed extends from large, the Katherine Dummer and Walter T. Fisher House (1929) in Winnetka, to small, the Doris L. and Thomas A. Mullen House (1936, p. 78) in Evanston, "middle" also refers to the income status of many of the clients (middle- and upper-middle class) who commissioned

the houses and appropriated the modern movement born in Europe that was typically associated with housing for the working class.[78] Overall, the clients who commissioned the modern houses discussed in this book generally tended to be professionals who identified with progressive values.[79] Although many had some wealth, they were not the super-affluent who had commissioned the nineteenth- and early twentieth-century mansions along Prairie Avenue, the Gold Coast, Lake Shore Drive, and areas of the North Shore.[80] We have endeavored to discuss a number of the modern houses designed by architects for their own families, especially since they tend to fall into the category of middle-class professionals. Examples include Caroline Sinclair and Philip Will Jr.'s House (1937, p. 92) and Sheila Adelman and David Haid's House (1969, p. 240) both in Evanston as well as Doris Curry and Jacques Brownson's House (1952, p. 176) in Geneva and Kitty Baldwin and Harry Weese's House (1957, p. 216) in Barrington. Other modern houses discussed in *Modern in the Middle* highlight significant clients including labor activist Ralph Helstein, medical doctors Aaron Heimbach, Edith Farnsworth and Gustave Weinfeld, and sociologist Hugh Dalziel Duncan. Present among clients are president of Formfit Company Sigmund Kunstadter, cofounders of Johnson Products Company George E. and Joan Henderson Johnson, and Charles "Cork" Walgreen III, professor Lambert Ennis, journalists Lloyd and Kathryn Dougherty Lewis, artist Ruth Van Sickle Ford and her spouse engineer Sam Ford, and designers Henry P. Glass and Ben Rose. Architect Walter Netsch designed the house he shared with his spouse, elected-official Dawn Clark Netsch, in Chicago's Lincoln Park neighborhood (1974).

Other related meanings of "middle" that overlap herein are allusions to the positioning of Chicago's post–World War II production of houses as part of a broader trend of *middle of the century,* hence "mid-century." While the chronological arc of this book starts with the late 1920s and continues to the mid-1970s, the 30s through 60s typically associated with the midcentury years do indeed cover a substantial period of the book's time frame.[81]

What is particularly striking of the period investigated is the relative dearth of research available regarding single-family houses designed by women, Hispanic, Asian, and African American architects in Chicago. Not until the late 1960s to the early 1970s did gender, racial, and sexual-orientation imbalances in the profession begin to change.[82] The Ruth Koier and Laurence Sjoblom House by Jean Wiersema Wehrheim (1960, p. 220) is one of the Chicago area's few modern houses designed by a woman architect before the 1970s. Interior designer Marianne Willisch's independent work and her collaboration with Keck & Keck is worth noting.[83] Also troubling to our contemporary outlook is the fact that when the houses were first published, they tended to credit only the male as the client. We have endeavored to include the name of the spouse/domestic partner in association with the houses even when they have not been included in historic records. Whenever possible we have attempted to correct gender and racial imbalances. A number of modern houses discussed in the book are located in Chicago's southern suburbs, recently the focus of renewed inquiry: worth noting is the prominent African American IIT architecture graduate ('48), John W. Moutoussamy whose one-story house (1954, in Chatham, p. 200) was designed for his spouse, Elizabeth Hunt, and children.

Our Chicago focus shares much with a host of place-specific scholarship, focused on cities and states (or provinces) throughout the United States and Canada.[84] George A. Larson and Jay Pridmore's *Chicago Architecture and Design,* now in its third edition, deserves mention for providing an intelligent and inclusive overview first published in 1993.[85] Although there is no single book about Chicago's modern residential architecture from the 1930s through the 1970s, the 2010 book on mid-century modernism in Chicago seen through the eyes of photographer Julius Shulman brings attention to important and less-studied houses.[86] The contribution of art deco architecture, interiors, and design during the interwar years has also been recently

CULTURE & DEMOCRACY

The struggle for form in society and architecture in Chicago and the Middle West during the life and times of Louis H. Sullivan

HUGH DALZIEL DUNCAN

Cover, Hugh Dalziel Duncan, *Culture and Democracy* (1965).

John W. Moutoussamy against the backdrop of Theodore K. Lawless Gardens (1970) Chicago, in upper photo from "Architecture's New Wave" *Ebony* (June 1971).

Opposite: Grand Opening of Walgreens (September 22, 1947) on 757 Michigan Ave and Chicago.

Towering above Chicago's black South Side, clean-lined Theodore K. Lawless Gardens moderate income housing development is an award-winning project of architect John W. Moutoussamy, partner in Chicago firm of Dubin, Dubin, Black and Moutoussamy.

Interior courtyard of Friendship House designed by Robert Traynham Coles is shielded from blighted ghetto area of Lackawanna, N. Y. Firm, founded by Coles eight years ago in Buffalo, will design a $25 million state university recreation complex outside city.

Continued on Next Page 33

studied.[87] Specifically, in the Midwest, a number of studies focusing on modernism have been published about cities and states ranging from Minnesota to Michigan.[88]

International Style vs Organic Modernism

Chicago's motto *urbs in horto* ("city in a garden") describes the special relationship of its inhabitants with nature as a source of beauty and well-being.[89] In an article entitled "The Threat to the Next America" published in the April 1953 issue of *House Beautiful* magazine by its editor Elizabeth Gordon, a Midwesterner with an undergraduate degree from the University of Chicago, established an antagonistic relationship between the organicism of Louis Sullivan and Wright and the International Style associated with Mies and a number of European émigrés.[90] Gordon begins her article by taking aim at Mies, by citing him but not mentioning him by name: "There is a well-established movement, in modern architecture, decorating, and furnishings, which is promoting the mystical ideal that 'less is more.'"[91] Later on, likewise without naming Edith Farnsworth, Gordon writes: "I have talked to a highly intelligent, now disillusioned, woman who spent more than $70,000 building a 1-room house that is nothing but a glass cage on

stilts."[92] Rather than viewing Wrightian organicism as antithetical to International Style modernism associated with Mies and his former students, the houses featured in *Modern in the Middle* demonstrate how even IIT-trained architects in Chicago were exposed to notions of "organic architecture."[93] Wright boldly engaged nature by way of siting of the buildings (house, studio, school) at Taliesin, located just outside Spring Green, Wisconsin: "I knew well that no house should ever be on a hill or on anything. It should be of the hill. Belonging to it. Hill and home should live together each the happier for the other."[94] Mies took on a more abstract approach: "Nature, too, shall live its own life. We must beware not to disrupt it with the color of our houses and interior fittings. Yet we should attempt to bring nature, houses, and human beings together into a higher unity."[95] While Wright tended to perforate walls with groups of windows (both horizontal and vertical) to allow light to enter and the viewer to frame and visually engage with the outdoors, Mies used large windows or floor-to-ceiling glass walls to let in light and provide expansive and uninterrupted views. Furthermore, the glass-and-steel flat-roof pavilions designed by Mies and IIT graduates share more in common with Wright's Usonians than might first appear especially since both were one-story and both relate to nature.[96] During an interview, Mies stated thus about his views on nature and its colors: "The Farnsworth house has never I believe been really understood. I myself was in that house from morning to evening. Up to then I had not known how beautiful the colors in nature can be. One must deliberately use neutral tones in interiors, because one has every color outside. These colors change continuously and completely, and I have to say that simplicity is splendid."[97] Well before Gordon began her campaign depicting Wright and Mies as polar opposites, Mies's enthusiastic reaction to the exhibition and publication of Wright's Wasmuth portfolio (1910) in Berlin demonstrates his reverence.[98]

Cover, *House Beautiful* (April 1953).

Emblematic of a synthesis of lessons regarding nature and organicism learned from Wright and Mies by Chicago architects is Paul Schweikher's House (1938, p. 96) and additions (1949) in Schaumburg (previously Roselle). Schweikher used natural materials (unfinished redwood) interior paneling and exterior siding and employed large panes of glass. In addition he seems to replicate the House and Studio mixed-use model used by Wright in Oak Park.[99] The Frances and Ben Rose House designed by A. James Speyer, the first graduate student to train with Mies upon his arrival at Armour, designed the steel-framed one-story main house with vertical cypress infill boards painted brown to complement the wooded setting. Edward Humrich combined Wrightian with mid-century modernist cues in his numerous houses, including the Eleanor Gray and Saul Lieberman House (1956) designed for the planned community of Graymoor Residential Park in Olympia Fields.[100] Perhaps more than anyone else, it was landscape architect Alfred Caldwell who understood how a shared appreciation of nature united Wright and Mies.[101] To be sure, the proximity to Mies and Wright buildings in Chicago's neighborhoods and suburban villages and cities served as a catalyst for younger architects in the city. For example, Ralph Rapson, speaking about his commission for the Adele Bretzfeld and Willard

Gidwitz House (1946, p. 136) in Hyde Park admitted that the proximity of the site to Wright's Robie House just a few blocks away prompted him to "work at that level."[102] Whereas Mies' exerted considerable influence upon future generations of architects who he trained at Chicago's Armour Institute (now IIT) and who chose to remain in the city to work, Wright continued to educate his own Fellows at the School of Architecture at Taliesin he founded in Wisconsin in 1932 and in Arizona in 1937.[103]

In addition to Wright's explicit advocacy for organic architecture (and the more abstract organicism of Mies), from the 1930s onwards, Finish architect Alvar Aalto becomes increasingly known to American architects with his compelling output of architecture and industrial design that combined functionalism-rationalism with organicism. Aalto's first built project in the US was the Finnish Pavilion for the World's Fair held in 1939 in New York. In 1938, MoMA presented an exhibition *Aalto–Architecture and Furniture*. [104] In his foreword to the catalogue, John McAndrew, the curator of Architecture and Industrial Art, writes about the changes to the debate since the 1932 *Modern Architecture: International Exhibition*:

> Six years ago when the Museum of Modern Art opened the first exhibition of modern architecture in this country, attention was focused on the fundamental qualities of the new "International Style." The work of Gropius, Mies van der Rohe, Oud, Le Corbusier and others was shown to have been conceived with a basically functionalist approach, and to have been carried out with a common set of esthetic principles.
>
> Since then, modern architecture has relinquished neither the functionalist approach nor the set of esthetic principles, but both have been modified, particularly by the younger men who have since joined the established leaders. Among those none is more important than Aalto.

As is clear from McAndrew's description, modern architecture was evolving and expanding its breadth beyond the narrow confines of one style or the other. This dynamic transforming scenario certainly applies to the houses discussed in *Modern in the Middle.* By absorbing cues from an International Style (associated with Mies and other Bauhaus émigrés such as Walter Gropius) with an organic architecture (associated with Wright's Prairie School), architects of different generations designed innovative modern houses best exemplified in the one-story pavilion type that diversified the residential architecture of neighborhoods, cities, and villages throughout the Chicagoland area. As the pages that follow will demonstrate, while approaches to material, structure, and program changed in response to different sites and clients, architects shared a common interest in designing modern houses for modern living. Over the course of the decades discussed in this book, architects and clients negotiated the relentless ebb and flow of ideas about modern architecture as they contributed to Chicago's unique place in the history of twentieth century architecture.

36

Susan S. Benjamin

Frank Lloyd Wright and Ludwig Mies van der Rohe: The Giants in the Room

Frank Lloyd Wright (1867–1959) and Ludwig Mies van der Rohe (1886–1969) are the "masters" who directly or indirectly influenced nearly every subsequent Chicago modern residential architect of note.

Because of Wright's established reputation in Chicago dating from his Prairie School years, his presence was persistently felt—sometimes his ideas were embraced, sometimes rejected, considered old school, but rarely ignored. Mies brought a fresh perspective captivating many young architects when he settled in Chicago in 1938. Despite their nearly two-decade age difference and their very different cultural backgrounds—Wright from small town Wisconsin; Mies a non-English-speaking German émigré—they became the giants in the room. Wright's architecture—blending into the surrounding landscape and utilizing natural materials—and Mies's cooler structuralist aesthetic represent two very different strains of thought. But it can be argued that their approaches coexist in several of Chicago's great modern houses.

The impact Wright and Mies had on the development of the modern house in Chicago and environs from the 1930s through the 1970s is outsized relative to their actual output there. Frank Lloyd Wright built little in the Chicago area during this period, designing only two of his wood, brick, and glass houses that he named

Frank Lloyd Wright at Taliesin, Spring Green, Wisconsin, photographed the year Mies visited him there, 1937.

Ludwig Mies van der Rohe with model of S. R. Crown Hall (1953), a column-free, 120' x 220" space supported by exterior steel structure.

Opposite: Charles F. Glore House (1951) Lake Forest, view from living room toward staircase.

Usonians, the Kathryn Dougherty and Lloyd Lewis House (1939, Libertyville, p. 112) and the Elizabeth Castle and Robert Muirhead Farmhouse (1951, Hampshire, p. 174) plus a handful of larger more costly houses, including the Dolores Mummert and Charles F. Glore Jr. House (1953, Lake Forest), based on the Usonian example.[1] Mies van der Rohe designed just two houses in Illinois: for Dr. Edith Farnsworth (1951, Plano) and for Isabella Gardner and Robert Hall McCormick III (currently on the campus of the Elmhurst Art Museum). But the talented cadre of residential architects whose careers overlapped and followed those of Wright and Mies would take their ideas—sometimes in narrow interpretations of their respective schools of thought, but moreover synthesizing aspects of each—and would extend their influence throughout the region for generations to come.

A tension between extremes, like those of Wright's and Mies's architecture, has historically been characteristic of Chicago architecture. In 1880s Chicago, as tall buildings were being constructed, there was a dichotomy between the Victorian past and the modernist future. As the birthplace of the modern skyscraper, its architects developed the building type that would come to define America's urban streetscape in the twentieth century and beyond. In 1884, William Le Baron Jenney designed the ten-story Home Insurance Building, considered the first tall building in which the masonry envelope is totally supported by its underlying iron and steel frame.[2] The building's brick and terra cotta ornament, however, draws from historical sources. Those who worked in Jenney's office, talented members of the "Chicago School"—Louis Sullivan, William Holabird, Martin Roche, and Daniel Burnham—designed similar metal frame buildings camouflaged in brick, stone, and terra cotta. Victorian era ornamental treatments coexisted with modern construction methods.

This, however, was changing. The architects of Chicago's skyscrapers were divorcing ornamentation from historic precedent, and in residential contexts applied ornament was beginning to disappear altogether. Louis Sullivan graced his tall buildings, like that which housed Schlesinger & Mayer Department store (1899, 1904) at the corner of Madison and State Streets, with ornament (especially at the first two floors) that was based on natural motifs, not Classical, Romanesque, or other historical precedents.[3] Famously, Sullivan was Frank Lloyd Wright's early employer, his beloved "Lieber Meister," whose influence on his disciple during this transitional era was incalculable.[4] Wright's Prairie School houses incrementally shed ornamentation with historical references. By 1910, his Lora Hieronymus and Frederick C. Robie House exhibited no overt connection to historical architecture and was totally free of applied ornament.

Home Insurance Building (1885) Chicago by William Le Baron Jenney, demolished and replaced by the Field Building (1931).

Opposite: Schlesinger & Mayer Department store. Photographed immediately after construction of sections designed by Louis H. Sullivan (1904).

Chicago Residential Architecture after the Prairie School

Wright departed for Berlin in 1909 to oversee the publication of a portfolio of his work by the Ernst Wasmuth Press (1910). He maintained a Chicago presence but his notable work from this later period was generally elsewhere: the Imperial Hotel in Tokyo (1915, demolished 1968) and the concrete-block houses in and around Los Angeles in the early 1920s. With Wright as well as Walter Burley Griffin and Marion Mahony Griffin gone, there was no cohesive group of architects designing Prairie houses; in addition, preferences were changing, and interest in the Prairie School was waning. Chicago's residential architecture began to undergo a shift in fashion towards more traditional styles. There was a resurgence in patriotism after World War I that attracted clients to Colonial architecture, and European styles took on increased cachet—especially for those drawn to the conformity and respectability associated with historical architecture.[5] Even architects of the Prairie School—Wright's followers—were creating Colonial, Tudor, or French-inspired houses.[6] George Fred Keck, who would innovate passive solar designs in the mid-1930s, was designing historical revival houses in the early 1920s.

The Draw of European Modernism

By 1930, many young Chicago architects were attracted to the dramatic work of European modernists whose ideological and theoretical platforms largely rejected historical precedent. Bertrand Goldberg, for example, left Chicago to study with Mies van der Rohe, then director of the Bauhaus in its final location in Berlin. Even those who received formal Beaux-Arts training, like Paul McCurry (when he studied at Armour Institute from 1922–26) were curious and explored progressive architecture in France, Germany, Holland, and Belgium. Because the Museum of Modern Art's seminal 1932 *Modern Architecture: International Exhibition* subsequently traveled to Chicago, young local architects in attendance were exposed to the creative ferment on the continent, or they could learn about the show's pared-down International Style architecture from its widely read catalogue.[7]

The 1930s: Frank Lloyd Wright Reenters the Midwest Scene

Frank Lloyd Wright, who had an extraordinary knack for reinventing himself, enjoyed a second act in the Midwest in the 1930s. In 1932, the same year as the *International Style* exhibition, Wright and his spouse at the time Olgivanna established the Taliesin Fellowship, a community of apprentices who lived, studied, and worked with Wright at Taliesin in Spring Green, Wisconsin.[8] It provided

an immersive and hands-on atmosphere, where the relatively small number of apprentices devoted much of their time to designing and working on the Taliesin property. As Wright's commissions picked up in the mid-1930s, apprentices were also dispatched to supervise Wright's projects. The Fellowship expanded to Taliesin West in Scottsdale, Arizona, upon its establishment in 1937.

Many former Fellows like John Lautner in Los Angeles, Mark Mills in Monterey, Aaron Green in San Francisco, and Fay Jones in Arkansas would go on to have prominent national careers. Curiously, few Fellows established independent architectural practices in the Chicago area; exceptions were Dennis Blair and William Deknatel. Donald Kalec, Taliesin Fellow and longtime professor at the School of the Art Institute, coauthored with John Garrett Thorpe *The Plan for Restoration and Adaptive Use of the Frank Lloyd Wright Home and Studio* (1978), in nearby Oak Park, and authored a book on the Home and Studio in the early 1980s.[9]

Although Wright's Wisconsin school trained relatively few of Chicago's more progressive architects and its impact was minimal, his own architectural direction had a huge influence on the city's architects. In 1936, at the age of sixty-nine, Wright began designing Usonian houses, affordable homes constructed of natural

Taliesin Fellows surrounding Wright, Spring Green, Wisconsin, 1937.

Opposite: Jacobs I House (1937) Madison, Wisconsin, back of house shortly after construction.

materials—in the Midwest, typically built of wood and brick. These were modern, flat or layered roofed houses, geared to the needs of informal family living, easy to maintain, and comfortable to live in.[10] There was no attempt to create, by association with tradition, a false or elevated image of the owner's status.

Wright's first Usonian was the 1500 sq. ft. Katherine Wescott and Herbert Jacobs House (Jacobs I, 1937) in Madison Wisconsin, south of Taliesin.[11] Like other Usonians, his Lewis House (1939) and his Muirhead Farmhouse (1951) (a job supervised by Allen Lape Davison, a Taliesin apprentice) had no plaster, no painted crown molding, or baseboards. Nothing feels additive or extraneous in a Usonian house. The typical Usonian was modest in size, had an open plan and built-in furniture (book shelves and closets to take advantage of every inch of space), and a carport. The front of these houses generally had few windows to the street, but many glazed openings that faced and framed views of a more private rear garden.

Usonian houses were promoted in publications along with Wright's iconic Fallingwater (1935) in Bear Run, Pennsylvania, for Liliane and Edgar Kaufmann and the Johnson Wax Administration (1936) building in Racine, Wisconsin for Herbert F. Johnson Jr.—the projects that rebuilt his reputation and brought Wright a fresh dose of fame. Regaining popularity, he was featured on the January 17, 1938 cover of *Time*, with his eyes cast upward toward a rendering of Fallingwater in the background. That same month *Architectural Forum* published a special issue on Wright, featuring Hedrich Blessing photographs of Fallingwater, Taliesin (1890s–1950s), Wingspread (1938–39) for Herbert F. Johnson Jr. and his spouse at the time Esther Jane Tilton in Racine, Wisconsin, and a double-page spread on the Jacobs I House.[12] In his introduction to the publication that included these eye-catching and inventive works, Wright wrote, "I would rather solve the small

house problem than build anything else."[13] Wright devoted a considerable amount of his time in subsequent years doing just that. The Museum of Modern Art's 1940 retrospective on Wright's work that contained photographs, drawings, and models included illustrations of his Usonian houses.[14] The Lewis House was published in the January 1948 issue of *Architectural Forum*.

Like their Prairie School predecessors, Wright's Usonian houses were "organic," a term that he defined and redefined throughout his lifetime.[15] His principles of organic architecture were first published in an article, "In the Cause of Architecture" in *Architectural Record,* March, 1908.[16] In summary, these were: simplicity and

repose, windows, doors and furnishings treated as part of a structural whole, an open plan, harmony with the site, and color derived from the surrounding fields and woods. He prized above all a deep connection with nature.[17] With broad overhangs and horizontal detailing, his late nineteenth- early twentieth-century Prairie School houses were integrated into Chicago's generally flat terrain. Usonian houses, like their Prairie School predecessors, were intended to be in harmony with their setting, whether sited along a riverbank like the Lewis House or located on gently rolling farmland like the Muirhead Farmhouse. Overhangs extended well beyond walls and the building envelope took multiple, not always rectangular shapes. Exterior and interior spaces flowed into one another, with the edges of his

Fallingwater, Lilian and Edgar Kaufmann House (1937) Mill Run, Pennsylvania. Widely recognized photograph by Hedrich Blessing shortly after completion.

houses blurring the distinction. A clear order, where every part is related to the whole, was also central to the philosophy of the Usonians. A consistent module typically determined the location of walls, cabinetry, windows, and overhangs. The Muirhead Farmhouse, for example, has a four-foot grid, etched in the concrete flooring, which is repeated throughout.

Wrightians: The Master's Influence Spreads

Although he designed only a handful of Usonian Houses and Usonian-inspired larger houses in the Chicago region—and, in nearby Rockford, the Phyllis Carman and Kenneth Laurent House (1951)—the qualities found in Wright's Usonian houses became popular almost immediately among architects who admired Wright and were influenced by his recent work.

One of these architects was Edward Humrich (1902–1992), whose numerous wood, brick, and glass houses were intimately related to their site, many nestled in a forested setting in the northern Chicago village of Riverwoods. Designed in the Wrightian idiom, many were long and low, featuring broad overhangs.

A second architect in this vein was Edward Dart (1922–1975). In 1949, a young Dart was on his way back from a job interview with his future employer Paul Schweikher when he drove past several Frank Lloyd Wright houses, including the Lewis House in Libertyville and one of Wright's most significant Prairie School houses, the Cecilia Berry and Ward W. Willits House (1902) in Highland Park. At the Cora Gilman and William A. Glasner House (1905), sited on the brow of a ravine in Glencoe, he knocked on the door. The owners graciously gave him a tour that he summarized as "wonderful."[18] Thoroughly enamored, in 1949 he undertook a pilgrimage to Taliesin to meet Wright, who shook his hand in dismissive silence. Despite this, his regard

for the master would be expressed in many of his houses, including the first house he designed for himself in 1951 that reflects Wright's influence.

A third was William Deknatel (1907–1973). Although educated at the École des Beaux-Arts and exposed to European modernism through a two-year stint with André Lurçat, Deknatel embraced Wright's aesthetic. Employing natural materials, his Ellen Newby and Lambert Ennis House (1942, p. 132), with pierced overhangs and broad overlapping horizontal planes, reflects its flat Midwest setting.

1937–38 Mies Arrives on the Scene

Although Mies had been exposed to Wright's work in Berlin in 1910 while still in his early twenties and was impressed by Wright's Prairie School architecture, many years were to pass before he actually met Wright. Early in 1937 Helen Lansdowne Resor approached Mies about designing a large summerhouse for her spouse, Stanley B. Resor, and family near Jackson Hole, Wyoming.[19] On his trip west to meet Helen Resor, Mies stopped in Chicago and, with architects William "Bill" Priestley, Gilmer V. Black, and Bertrand Goldberg, drove several hours northeast to visit Wright at Taliesin.

Frank Lloyd Wright and Ludwig Mies van der Rohe visiting Johnson's Wax Company Building, Racine, Wisconsin, 1937.

Opposite: Taliesin, Spring Green, Wisconsin, Hill Tower (1911) photographed 1937.

Wright welcomed him. Taliesin Fellow Edgar Tafel received the initial request for Mies to visit, to which Wright responded: "By all means, bring him up."[20] Given that both Walter Gropius and Le Corbusier had approached Wright for meetings in the early 1930s and were summarily—and rudely—turned down, it seemed like a remarkable achievement.[21] But Wright was impressed with Mies's Barcelona Pavilion and the Tugendhat House in Brno that he had seen in publications and genuinely admired him. Tafel recalled that Wright viewed Mies "as an individualist, not as part of a foreign school or movement."[22]

The two enjoyed an instant connection. Mies stood out on the terrace at Taliesin, and, viewing the expansive rolling landscape, exclaimed, "Freedom, this is a kingdom."[23] Mies biographer Franz Schulze wrote that Mies applauded the siting of the buildings and motioned with his hands to acknowledge the interpenetrating masses he had until then only known from books.[24] The two architects got along so well that Mies's intended one-day visit turned into a four-day stay, with a stop on the way to tour the construction of Wright's Johnson Wax building in Racine. Once back in the Chicago area, they visited Wright's Unity Temple in Oak Park, the (Addie) "Queene" Ferry and Avery Coonley House (1907) in Riverside, and the Robie House.

After the visit, Tafel observed that "the greatest difference between Mies and Mr. Wright we felt was that while Mies dedicated his entire life to the search for one style, refining, and purifying, Mr. Wright kept evolving, growing and developing new styles." He said Wright's favorite phrase was "What we did yesterday, we don't do today. And what we do tomorrow will not be what we'll be doing the day after."[25]

When Mies settled in Chicago in 1938 to assume the directorship of the Department of Architecture at Armour Institute of Technology (in 1940 to become the Illinois Institute of Technology—IIT), an inaugural gala was held on November 20 in his honor. Wright was chosen to introduce him to Chicago's architectural community. His speech showered Mies with praise while self-servingly taking credit for the appointment: "Ladies and gentlemen, I give you Mies van der Rohe. But for me there would have been no Mies—certainly none here tonight. I admire him as an architect, respect and love him as a man. Armour Institute, I give you my Mies van der Rohe. You treat him well and love him as I do. He will reward you." [26] It was probably a good thing that Mies's English was minimal.

Mies in Chicago: His Ideas Defined

The general themes that Mies first described in his acceptance speech at the 1938 gala expressed his fundamental principles. Order and a "clear understanding of ... materials"—brick ... wood, concrete, and steel—to give each thing what is suitable to its nature."[27] To these principles, Gene Summers, an important member

of Mies's IIT-trained employees, later added "structure," stating the one thing Mies felt must be present in architecture—the refinement, the development, and the expression of structure.[28]

After Mies's arrival in Chicago, his reputation grew quickly through his prominent US projects: the campus plan for IIT and his design for its architecture school, S. R. Crown Hall; iconic high rises like 860–880 Lake Shore Drive; and the Farnsworth House.

In the Farnsworth House, as in his other buildings, Mies developed *his* vision of organic architecture, a view seemingly quite unlike Wright's definition of organic. Mies's steel-and-glass Farnsworth and McCormick houses capture views of nature through large panes of glass and stand proud, not echoing the surrounding land-scape. His work embodied a rationalist and structuralist approach to organic architecture.[29] The concept of the organic, in the sense of interrelation and order, dominated his work. Every element in a building designed by Mies is intimately related to every other, as are the parts of a human body. Myron Goldsmith, Mies's student and a distinguished architect in his own right, stated it this way: "(A) building should be a coherent work of structural art in which the detail suggests the whole and the whole suggests the detail."[30] Phyllis Lambert, an architect and the founder of the Canadian Centre for Architecture, also studied under Mies and recalled,

> in the 1960s Mies continued to affiliate himself with the pursuit of the organic but explained that, for him, organic architecture was something different than it was for Wright.[31] For Wright it meant that buildings grow out of the ground, whereas for Mies it pointed to the

relationship between the tip of a finger and the finger as a whole, the finger to the forearm, and so on—a proportional relationship of parts to the whole as well as amongst parts of a whole to one another.[32]

In his first draft of the curriculum for the Armour Institute, Mies wrote, "The goal of an Architecture School is to train men who can create organic architecture," adding that "such men must be able to design structures constructed of modern technical means to serve the specific requirements of existing society."[33] The curriculum was to become standard design pedagogy: students learned drafting, then the use of building materials, and finally learned the fundamental principles of construction before undertaking building design.[34] This approach would come to dominate instruction at IIT, then influence the architecture of subsequent graduates of IIT following Mies's retirement in 1958.

George Danforth was Mies's first draftsman in the US and succeeded him as director of the School of Architecture from 1959–75. Danforth recalled that even though Mies was not doing a lot of teaching, his presence was still strong. When Danforth took the lead, he saw his position as one of "continuing the program and encouraging its continued development, growth, and expansion as times demanded other things of architectural education within the framework of Mies's tenets. You don't replace a man like that at all."[35]

Mies's goal was to create a program that would endure. IIT, under Mies and subsequent deans, served as training ground for numerous talented Chicago architects, many of whom went on to gain national recognition. According to Kevin Harrington, Professor Emeritus of Architectural History, Mies always wanted the school to create excellent craftsmen and women, and encourage those with true gifts to make the expression of technique an act of high art.[36]

Miesians: His Influence Spreads

The influence of Mies and his curriculum arguably had a greater effect, if measured in built works, than that of the Taliesin Fellows, largely because IIT-trained practitioners primarily designed large, high-profile projects, not just houses. Jacques Brownson (1923–2012), Gene Summers (1928–2011), and Myron Goldsmith (1918–96) are chief among them.[37] Brownson, who received his MS from IIT in 1954, designed the widely acclaimed 31-story Chicago Civic Center (today the Richard J. Daley Center) in 1965, while working for C. F. Murphy Associates. Less well-known is his steel-and-glass house (p. 176) in Geneva, designed in 1952 as his IIT master's thesis.[38] Brownson later joined the faculty at IIT.

Numerous IIT graduates who practiced—including Brownson, A. James Speyer, David Haid, Clarence

Krusinski, Edmund Zisook, H. P. Davis "Deever" Rockwell, and John Vinci—designed houses featured in this book based on Miesian order, sensitivity to materials, and a structuralist aesthetic: though noteworthy, their residential work tends to be lesser known than Mies-inspired Chicago skyscrapers. A. James Speyer (1913–86) enrolled at IIT in 1939 specifically to study with Mies and became his first graduate student as well as a lifelong friend and colleague. Beginning in 1946, he taught architectural design and opened a private practice focusing on residential architecture.[39] He subsequently enjoyed a long and distinguished career as curator of twentieth-century painting and sculpture at the Art Institute of Chicago until his death in 1986.[40]

Clarence Krusinski (1940–) received his Bachelor of Architecture at IIT in 1963, after Mies had retired from teaching, but became immersed in his philosophy. Krusinski worked for PACE Associates, the firm that had collaborated with Mies on S. R. Crown Hall and 860–880 Lake Shore Drive. He also worked in the office of Schipporeit-Heinrich, whose principals, George Schipporeit and John Heinrich, were IIT graduates who designed one of the most brilliant Miesian structures in Chicago, Lake Point Tower.

IIT graduate John Vinci (1937–) has designed many late modern buildings like the Ruth Nelson and Robert J. Freeark House (1975, p. 258) and the Arts Club of Chicago (1997), where he installed the staircase from the club's previous Mies-designed interior after its demolition. Vinci has also been deeply dedicated to historic preservation, where he is recognized as a pioneer and has overseen the restoration of numerous Chicago landmarks, including an early restoration of Frank Lloyd Wright's Robie House, Wright's Home and Studio, Burnham and Root's Monadnock Building, and Adler & Sullivan's Chicago Stock Exchange Trading Room (parts of which were relocated prior to the demolition of the building and installed at the Art Institute of Chicago).

Other young Chicago architects who were not trained at IIT still embraced Mies's approach. Harry Weese (1915–1998), who studied at Cranbrook Academy and received his BA at the Massachusetts Institute of Technology, viewed Wright as "too romantic and not totally honest."[41] He looked to the European modernists, holding Alvar Aalto, Le Corbusier, and Mies in high regard. To Weese, Mies exemplified the hopes and dreams of his generation.[42] Commenting that he and his contemporaries saw the

Lake Point Tower (1968) Chicago by Schipporeit & Heinrich, with 2.5 acre private wooded Skyline Park designed by Alfred Caldwell (1968) photo c. 1970.

formal teachings of the École des Beaux-Arts as "petering out," Weese admired the clarity and technique in Mies's architecture.[43] Although, there is little of Mies's specific influence in Weese's houses, his rectangular Corten steel and mirrored glass Time-Life Building, built in 1969 on Chicago's near north side, has a familial relationship to the architect who inspired him. Even late in his life he acknowledged, "I haven't been able to change the world like Mies, but I'd like to."[44]

Bertrand Goldberg (1913–97) attended Harvard for two years, but once he left to learn the lessons of the Europeans directly, attending the Bauhaus at age nineteen in the early 1930s and going on to work for Mies in Berlin, he commented, "the arrival at Mies's office was for me the moment when my career was really beginning seriously."[45] Goldberg was dismissive of Wright's romanticism early on.[46] When Goldberg got older, he was more reflective and forgiving of Wright, illustrating a key difference between the two masters: "Mies's message was a universal message for a universal person. Frank Lloyd Wright was designing for individuals and for their individual changing experiences."[47]

Like Weese, Ernest (Tony) Grunsfeld III (1929–2011) also trained at MIT and briefly worked in the offices of Skidmore, Owings & Merrill, George Fred Keck, and Bertrand Goldberg before opening his own office. He developed a large residential practice, especially on Chicago's North Shore. Mies's influence on Grunsfeld was clear. His Nancy Franklin and Julius Epstein House (1969) in Northfield is an elegant black steel-and-glass pavilion that is a tribute to Mies's design influence.[48]

Wright and Mies: Their Opinion of Each Other

Despite their admiring initial interactions at Taliesin and their shared interest in creating an organic architecture, neither Mies nor Wright bought into the other's aesthetic. Mies stated in 1960 that Wright was a "great genius," but also that "these Wright things don't belong to our time."[49] Mies biographer Franz Schulze points

Opposite: Epstein House (1969) steel-and-glass designed by Ernest "Tony" Grunsfeld and pool house. Chicago Bauhaus & Beyond open house, 2019.

William McDermott House (1928) Glencoe by Barry Byrne, modern design with art deco influences, photo 2002.

out that "Wright recognized Mies as the best practitioner of modern architecture but wanted no part of the movement, admitting his own struggle 'hard against it.'"[50]

Wright may have had disdain for Mies's brand of modernism but he was very much in the forefront of creating residential architecture that was new and exciting in the 1930s to the 1950s, which was in its own way modern.

A drive down Chicago area streets—urban and suburban alike—continues to reveal surprises, whether the houses were designed by well-known architects or not. Numerous modern houses embedded in traditional neighborhoods or in postwar subdivisions harken back to the work of the two masters. In some cases they may be a blend of recognizable features and allusions to their philosophies. Whether the houses are predominantly Wrightian, nestling into their site, built of warm woods and soft Chicago brick, or Miesian, rectilinear with crisp edges, expanses of glass, and clearly expressed structure, the influences are evident, often traceable, and inevitably compelling.

DUBUQUE, IOWA

MADISON

ROCKFORD

BELOIT

JANESVILLE

Homer Grooman

Katherine Dummer and Walter T. Fisher House — Anne Green and Henry Dubin House — Rosalie Brown and Robert H. Morse House — Irene Tipler and Paul McCurry House — Vine Itschner and Herbert Bruning House — Doris L. and Thomas H. Mullen House — Rosalie Strauss and Gustave Weinfeld House — Irma Kuppenheimer and Bertram J. Cahn House — Josephine Topp and De Forest S. Colburn House — Caroline Sinclair and Philip Will Jr. House — Madeleine Michelson and Philip B. Maher House — Dorothy Miller and Paul Schweikher House — Ellen Borden and Adlai E. Stevenson II House — Lucile Gottschalk and Aaron Heimbach House — Kathryn Dougherty and Lloyd Lewis House — Charles Dewey Jr. House and Beach House — Marjorie Horton and Winston Elting House — Marjorie Candler and William Ganster House — Minna Green and Hugh Duncan House I — Ellen Newby and Lambert Ennis House — Adele Bretzfeld and Willard Gidwitz House — Eleanor Knopp and Henry P. Glass House — Florence Pass and Erne Frueh House I and II — Maggie Sheahan and Le Roy Binkley House — Ruth van Sickle and Albert Sam Ford House — Marian Short and Stanley G. Harris Jr. House — Wilhelmina Plansoen and Edward Dart House I — Edith Farnsworth House — Rachel Brin and Ralph Helstein House — Elizabeth Castle and Robert Muirhead Farmhouse — Doris Curry and Jacques Brownson House — Maxine Weil and Sigmund Kunstadter House — Isabella Gardner and Robert Hall McCormick III House — Walter Frazier and William Moulis House — Frances Landrum and Ben Rose House — Susanne Weese and Robert Drucker House — Elizabeth Hunt and John W. Moutoussamy House — Margaret Montgomery and Howard Raftery House — Priscilla Huffard and H. P. Davis Rockwell House I — Alice Lieberman and J. Marion Gutnayer House — Kitty Baldwin and Harry Weese House — Ruth Koier and Laurence Sjoblom House — Donald Wrobleski House — Joan Henderson and George E. Johnson Sr. House — Priscilla Huffard and H. P. Davis Rockwell House II — Ming Djang and Chung Kuo Liao House — Sheila Adelman and David Haid House — Donna Parr and Charles Walgreen III House — Margaret Berman and Paul Lurie House — Dawn Clark and Walter Netsch House — Arlene and Richard Don House — Ruth Nelson and Robert J. Freeark House — Iris Smith and Paul Goldstein House

Portfolio

Katherine Dummer and Walter T. Fisher House

View east toward front entrance terrace.

Prominent architectural historians have praised the Walter T. Fisher House from the time it was first constructed. Henry-Russell Hitchcock who, with Philip Johnson, would go on to curate the hugely influential 1932 *Modern Architecture: International Exhibition* at the Museum of Modern Art, wrote in the February 1930 issue of *The Arts* that "it is nearly the first [house] in America to which the most rigid international standards of contemporary architectural criticism may be applied."[1]

In November 1929, *Architectural Record* featured the house with photos and floor plans; its architect Howard Taylor Fisher commented about how traditional house design compared poorly to the emergent modernism:

*Nota bene: All dates correspond to completion of houses.

The house, among all the important tools of the twentieth century, is unique in the inefficiency and clumsiness of its design. The age that has produced the ocean liner, the skyscraper and the zeppelin has as yet done but little toward solving one of the most important and basic needs of mankind…. Of all the productions of our present day, the house alone is considered in terms of the past. We do not ride in Louis XIV stage coaches, or wear Elizabethan ruffles—why then should we live in imitations of Cotswold cottages or French eighteenth-century chateaux?[2]

Howard Fisher was only 26 years old when he wrote his perspective about the inadequacy of borrowed styles from the past.

Although Howard Fisher graduated Harvard with a Bachelor of Science in 1926, his son Morgan Fisher recalls that his father, hating the Beaux-Arts education he was receiving at its School of Architecture from 1926–28, dropped out to design a house for his brother and sister-in-law Walter and Katherine Dummer Fisher.[3] At the time their new home was built, the Harvard-educated Walter was a member

South facade: eating porch, sleeping porch, third-floor screened porch.

Entrance terrace: open windows to play room.

of his father's law firm, Fisher, Boyden, Bell, Boyd, & Marshall. From 1929–31, he was a trustee of the University of Illinois. Subsequent civic service included a term as chair of the Illinois Commerce Commission from 1949–53. Katherine Fisher graduated from Radcliffe College, married Walter in 1915, and raised their children at the house. With an abiding interest in early childhood education, she organized a developmental education program in 1932 for Winnetka first-graders.

Though the architectural community admired the house and appreciated its sophistication, neighbors did not initially understand its ingenuity. One neighbor, not realizing she was speaking to the architect's wife, Marion Hall Fisher, said, "Oh, you live near the ocean liner."[4]

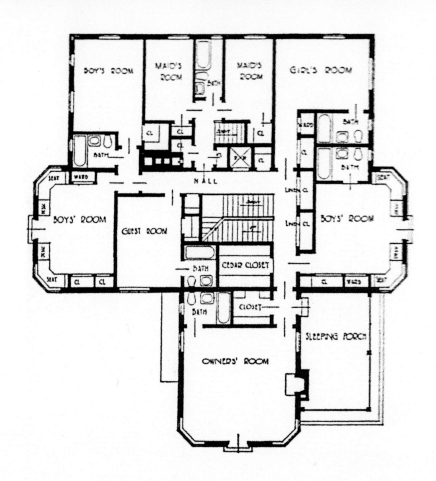

BOY'S ROOM

MAID'S ROOM

MAID'S ROOM

GIRL'S ROOM

BATH

WARD

BATH

BATH

CL

CL

CL

BATH

BOYS' ROOM

SEAT WARD

SEAT

CL CL

GUEST ROOM

HALL

LINEN CL

LINEN CL

BATH

CEDAR CLOSET

BATH

CLOSET

BOYS' ROOM

SEAT

WARD

SEAT

CL WARD SEAT

SLEEPING PORCH

OWNERS' ROOM

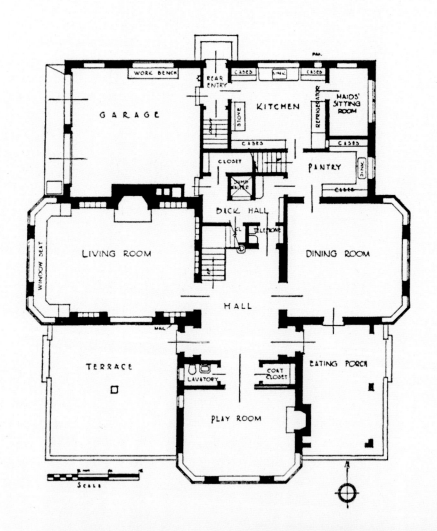

WORK BENCH

CASES

SINK

CASES

PAN.

REAR ENTRY

GARAGE

STOVE

KITCHEN

REFRIGERATOR

MAIDS' SITTING ROOM

CASES

CASES

CASES

CLOSET

PANTRY

DUMB WAITER

SINK

BACK HALL

CL TELEPHONE

WINDOW SEAT

LIVING ROOM

DINING ROOM

HALL

MAIL

TERRACE

LAVATORY

COAT CLOSET

EATING PORCH

PLAY ROOM

SCALE

The house was extraordinary compared to the nearby 1920s Colonial Revival houses
in Winnetka. It stands three stories, without cornices, window moldings, or applied
ornament. The major rooms have casement windows that wrap the corners on the
diagonal and are flush with the walls—maximizing fresh air and beautiful views.

With its planar surfaces, crisp geometry, and sparseness of detail, the Fisher House
bears a familial resemblance to European modern housing of the International
Style: the work of Le Corbusier (in France and Germany), Mies van der Rohe (in
Germany), J. J. P. Oud (in Holland and Germany), and émigré Richard Neutra (in
Los Angeles). Its warm red brick exterior, however, sets the Fisher House apart
from European counterparts and places it in a Chicago idiom.

The Fisher House has a cruciform plan, with wings extending into the landscape.
Rather than a prominent brick fireplace at the home's core (as is often found in
Frank Lloyd Wright-designed houses), it has an open staircase leading from the
first floor to the roof at the center, allowing hallways to be infused with light.

Function rather than style was the major design consideration, with a plan created
to meet the living requirements for a family of two adults, six children, and two
servants. There are four major rooms on the first floor: living room, dining room,
kitchen, and a large playroom.[5] The home's child-oriented design celebrated
enjoyment of sports activities, with a shuffleboard court on the roof terrace and
two squash courts with viewing gallery in the basement.

The Fisher House, located in the Hubbard Woods area of Winnetka, embraces
nature and the outdoors with terraces, porches, and roof decks. The front door is
accessed from a large brick terrace. There is an eating porch, a sleeping porch off
the master bedroom, and, on the third floor, several additional outdoor spaces:
a living porch, sleeping porch, and sun terrace with a prominent brick fireplace.

The third floor functions as an outdoor suite that included a dumbwaiter to convey food; today an elevator replaces it. The ocean-liner analogy referenced by the neighbor was perceptive; projecting porches with slatted wood handrails recall decks on a ship, bringing to mind the metal railings found on Le Corbusier's Villa Stein (Garches, 1928) and, later, Villa Savoye (Poissy-sur-Seine, 1930), although Fisher's choice of wood, rather than steel, compliments the natural brick.

The interior spaces were colorful, cheerful, and inviting, anything but Spartan, despite the simplicity of the house. Cabinets under the windows and tables, designed by Fisher, were painted green on the outside and red on the inside. Furniture upholstery mirrored the cabinet colors.[6] The slightly rough walls provided contrast with a tint of yellow. Cork tile floors with a warm patina resembling stone continue throughout the house. An ornamental glazed ceramic drinking fountain was built into a niche in the front hall.

A few years after the house was completed, Howard Fisher designed a flat-roofed, prefabricated metal house, subsequently demolished, for his sister-in-law, the highly acclaimed dancer Ruth Page. Located nearby, it was the first produced by General Houses, Inc., a prefabrication company Fisher established in 1932. In this new venture, Fisher built custom houses using standardized windows, doors, plumbing parts, and other elements produced by various manufacturers to be assembled on site on top of the building's foundation. The process resembled a car manufacturing assembly line. Using standard, prefabricated parts reduced building costs. Models were described in a formula. In Model K2H40, the K represents the basic house design, 2 is a subdivision of the design, H stands for a hall entrance, 4 indicates there are four beds (in two bedrooms), and 0 means there is an optional extra room.[7] For marketing purposes, the houses were also given names such as the "Elmhurst," the "Barrington," and others after established Chicago suburbs.

The work of Howard Fisher—along with that of George Fred Keck and Paul Schweikher—was featured in the exhibition *Work of Young Architects in the Middle West* at the Museum of Modern Art in April 1933. The show included photographs of the Ruth Page House and the steel house with a flat roof that General Houses, Inc., built as a model house for the 1933 Century of Progress.

Howard Fisher's firm served as training ground for many distinguished architects, including Lawrence Perkins, Philip Will, and Edward Larrabee Barnes. In 1956, Fisher built a modernist house for himself near the iconic home he designed for his brother Walter. Six years later, after working in architecture and planning for decades, Howard Fisher returned to Harvard to teach at the Graduate School of Design; he developed SYMAP, a computer program that produces sophisticated statistical maps.

The Fisher House is being restored and sensitively updated by the current owners, Karen and Jeff Watts. —SSB

Anne Green and Henry Dubin House

South (street) facade with the Dubins' son, Arthur.

The "Battledeck House" marked a turning point in the history of modern residential architecture in Chicago. Influenced by the work of Le Corbusier, architect Henry Dubin of Dubin & Eisenberg introduced the modernist European sensibility of the 1920s to Chicago and its suburbs. Dubin's own home was built during the same period that Le Corbusier designed the Villa Stein and the Villa Savoye for the Parisian suburbs of Garches and Poissy respectively. All three houses reflect the popular practice of building on vacant parcels in established suburban areas within a relatively short commute of major city centers.

Dubin chose the Ravinia section of the North Shore city of Highland Park, a community favored by noteworthy architects Robert E. Seyfarth and John Van Bergen and landscape architect Jens Jensen and naturalist May T. Watts.

Dubin designed his house in 1929, just before the onset of the Great Depression. It was to be a modest, fireproof (or at least fire-safe) home for his small family.[1] He described himself as being of moderate means and social activity, and their house was to provide ample space for sleeping, studying, and socializing—a place for living "as understood by one specially trained in the appreciation of such things."[2]

64

Although Dubin was trained in the Beaux-Arts style and his practice in the 1920s was dominated by Tudor, Spanish, and other period-style commercial buildings, his home was to be above all functional and livable—more a "machine for living in."[3] The house was a manifesto for his vision. Indeed, Dubin was quoted as saying, "Modern architecture is not a mantle hung on a framework to suit the whims of the hanger. It is a principle of aesthetics, based on new materials and methods of construction."[4] This vision was shared by some of Dubin's contemporaries; architects Howard Fisher, George Fred Keck, and the Bowman Brothers were also looking for better, cheaper, and faster ways of construction[5]

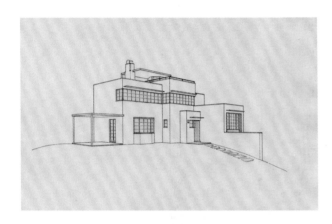

Henry Dubin had traveled to Europe in 1926–27, met with Le Corbusier, and visited the Bauhaus in Dessau. Its modernist teachings and Le Corbusier's machine aesthetic had a profound influence on the design for his house. Dubin's grandson architect Peter Dubin confirms the connection by way of a letter in his possession with the name Le Corbusier written above Jeanneret and addressed to Chez Monsieur Stein. Le Corbusier's 1928 letter introduces his new friend Henry Dubin to Michael Stein (Gertrude Stein's brother), asking that he give Dubin a tour of Villa Stein (also known as Villa Garches), which Le Corbusier had recently completed. Accompanying the letter is a map Le Corbusier drew with directions from his studio in Paris to Stein's house.[6]

Dubin clad his house with clinker brick, not a finished hard face brick, and gave it a flat roof—a novelty in Highland Park. Accessed by a winding steel staircase, the flat roof was more than a nod to the Modern aesthetic; he designed a terrace "for the enjoyment of sunbaths and the cool breezes above the mosquito zone."[7] Views are toward a ravine to the south but as splendid as those from the deck of a ship. There was never an attempt to follow any particular style. A prominent ribbon of windows spans across the facade. The house was to be free of dormers, gables, and bays, lacking any applied ornament, and expressing in form what came to be known, after 1932, as the International Style. With the intention of being white-washed, this brick home bore a family resemblance to the European villas featured in the 1932 Museum of Modern Art exhibition of the same name. Resembling a piece of cubist sculpture, the house rests prominently on its wooded lot, even today looking quite unlike its neighbors.

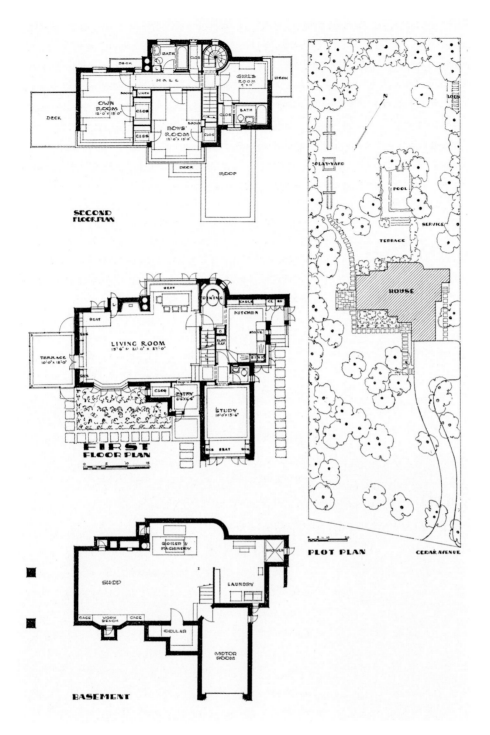

Known as the Battledeck House because of its association with ship construction, the house is made up of a system of beams and plates welded together to form a continuous unit. This technique allowed it to be not only fireproof but also economical by being easy to assemble and speedy to erect.[8] Little work was required in the field. Whole sections were fabricated in the shop, then hoisted into place and anchored into the brick masonry.[9] In keeping with the importance of fire prevention, windows are steel casements with exterior sills of aluminum and interior sills of grey slate. (Some casements are located on corners to provide cross ventilation.) Hoods over the windows are also slate. The use of wood was kept to a minimum, reserved for doors, interior trim, and built-in furniture.

Dining alcove.

Staircase adjacent to the
front entrance.

Function dominated design considerations. A study over the "motor room" (garage) features prominently in the massing of the house. With its adjacent bathroom, the study doubled as a guest room. The semicircular family dining room would not provide enough dining space for entertaining, so a rectangular table was nestled adjacent to it with seating in an L-shaped window bay. The living-dining space consists of "one large room for lounging and entertaining."[10] Floors are of variegated Vermont slate in the living-dining area, cork in the bedrooms and study, and rubber tile in the kitchen. Thoughtfully designed built-ins minimize clutter. Radiators are cleverly concealed behind flush cast aluminum grills. Lighting fixtures in the major rooms consist of flat panels of frosted glass supported by simple bands of brushed nickel. The Dubins' interior furnishings, however, were surprisingly traditional.

A profusely illustrated article by Henry Dubin in the August 1931 issue of *Architectural Forum* showcased the house, and it was awarded honorable mention in the *House Beautiful* Fifth Annual Small House Competition in 1931.

Henry Dubin's sons M. David Dubin, FAIA (1927–2013) and Arthur D. Dubin (1923–2011) joined the family firm established by their father and structural-engineer uncle Eugene Dubin (1908–1998). Arthur viewed the Battledeck House as "a watershed between the Beaux-Arts way of viewing architecture and a whole new way that came to be known as Modern, using materials in a different way, and being concerned with the design as regards to function."[11]

The house is listed on the National Register of Historic Places. Its current owners Lydia Hankins and Ted Chung are undertaking a meticulous rehabilitation directed by the firm Johnson Lasky Kindelin Architects.[12] For example, the porch that opens off the living room is now sympathetically enclosed. —SSB

Rosalie Brown and
Robert H. Morse House

The monumental house built for Col. Robert H. and Rosalie D. Brown Morse demonstrates how twentieth-century architects absorbed cues from different yet complementary approaches ranging from classicism, art deco, and the International Style.[1] Despite its stately size (twenty-four rooms), the three-story, flat-roofed house was designed as a second residence for the client and his family in the North Shore city of Lake Forest, on the golf course grounds of the

Knollwood Club, founded in 1924. The Clubhouse was designed by Howard Van Doren Shaw and the premier golf course by the UK-based firm of Colt and Alison. The Morse House was built on one of the several lots sold to finance the club.

To commission a house for leisure during the height of the Depression era (and the challenging Prohibition years) speaks to the financial prowess of Col. Robert H. Morse. He became president and general manager of Fairbanks, Morse & Company in 1931, a year before the completion of his new Lake Forest house; headquartered in Chicago, Fairbanks, Morse & Company was a prominent manufacturer that produced a wide range of machines (engines, locomotives, pumps), and in so doing helped steer the industrial growth of America.[2]

The firm selected to design the house, Zimmerman, Saxe & Zimmerman, was tied to the Lake Forest elite through previous architectural commissions. Founding partner William Carbys Zimmerman died in 1932 in the same year the Morse House was completed. The design of the house was thus likely carried out in collaboration with Zimmerman's son and partner, Ralph Waldo Zimmerman, and son-in-law, Albert Moore Saxe.[3]

With its bold and asymmetrical massing, the Morse House contains some elements typically associated with the International Style. However, upon closer examination

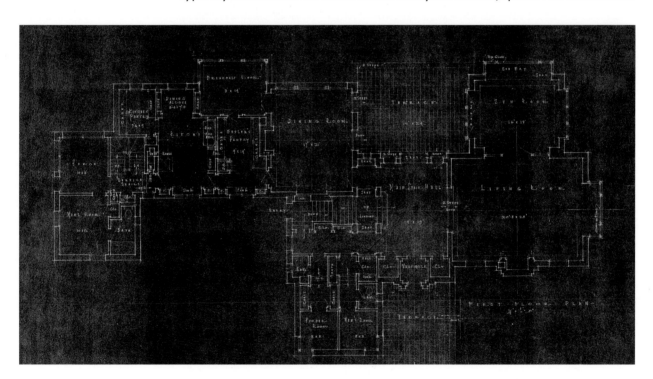

of the elevations, the plan, and the ornate interiors, the design reveals a formality and luxury that is more akin to classically derived art deco that was popular in America following the landmark Exposition Internationale des Arts Décoratifs et Industriels Modernes held in Paris in 1925.

The house was built with materials common to the modern building industry, such as reinforced concrete for the foundations, load-bearing brick walls (covered in salmon-colored stucco), steel beams throughout, and different types of windows (awning, casement, and picture). While it shares some similarities with the early modern Anne Green and Henry Dubin House (p. 64) and Katherine Dummer and Walter T. Fisher House (p. 58), the stucco exterior renders the volume more abstract because it conceals the tactile materiality of the brick that is so dominant in these two other modern houses. It was fitted with bathroom fixtures produced by Crane Co., established in Chicago in 1855, which manufactured plumbing products in one of the city's most modern factories.[4] The house was featured shortly after it was completed in an advertisement for window screens by the Rolscreen Company (later renamed Pella, in Iowa).

Numerous windows reinforce the relationship with the surrounding country qualities of the Knollwood Club golf course. Not surprisingly, C. D. Wagstaff and Co., considered among America's foremost golf course designers at the time, was the landscape architect of the Morse House. Several balconies and roof-top terraces afford views and access to the outdoors from a number of vantage points, to enjoy sun and fresh air. These strategies for wellbeing were also reflected

Rolscreened home of C. S. Teal, Washington, D. C.
A. H. Sonnemann, Architect

Rolscreened home of Col. Robt. H. Morse, Chicago, Ill.
Zimmerman, Saxe & Zimmerman, Architects

Page 14

Advertisement, "In Behalf of Beautiful Windows," Morse House, lower image, for Rolscreen Company (1936).

Living room with modern chrome steel furniture.

in the groundbreaking modern design of the nearby Lake County Tuberculosis
Sanatorium in Waukegan by William Ganster and William Pereira (1939).

Current owners Laureen and Bruce Grieve wrote the nomination that led to the
house's inclusion on the National Register of Historic Places in 2000 as the Robert
Hosmer Morse House.[5] Working with preservation architect Chris Wahlberg, they
have proven to be thoughtful stewards throughout the entire process. —MS

Irene Tipler and Paul McCurry House

Front entrance protected by cantilevered slab; glass block window provides lighting for interior dressing table.

Paul and Irene McCurry's house in the Beverly neighborhood of Chicago is strikingly modern—crisp and geometric, bold and dramatic in its simplicity. Yet, Paul D. McCurry had very traditional architectural training. Ink plan drawings of their 1935 house, symmetrical and meticulously detailed, reveal Paul McCurry's early indebtedness to the Beaux-Arts teaching at the Armour Institute, from where he graduated over a decade before Mies van der Rohe was hired as director of architecture, and the curriculum vastly changed. At the time McCurry entered in 1922, morning classes were held in the Armour Institute 1890s Romanesque main building in the Douglas neighborhood near the future site of Mies van der Rohe's Illinois Institute of Technology buildings. Afternoons were spent at the Art Institute, where students became skilled draftsmen and renderers. Also, access to the Art Institute's Burnham Library enabled the architecture students to spend substantial time with its resources, including the European avant-garde architectural journals such as *L'Architecture d'Aujourd'hui (AA)*.[1] Although the Beaux-Arts curriculum

Garage setback to allow for corner windows. Entrance to McCurry's office with sign: "Paul D. McCurry architect,"

Paul McCurry's drawings of first and second floors.

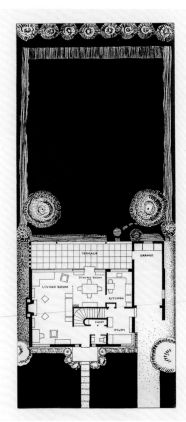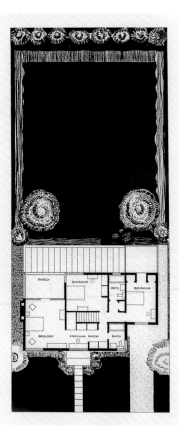

was strictly followed during McCurry's years at Armour, he and his fellow students shared a common fascination with European architecture that was more modern.

Two years after his graduation in 1926, Paul McCurry spent a year exploring Germany, Holland, France, and Italy. Admittedly, he was a young man interested in adventure, but architecture never was far from his mind. In Amsterdam he was particularly impressed with the country's brick buildings, with their new forms and shapes far removed from classic concepts. He saw these buildings dependent on solids and voids and textures, interacting to create a favorable aesthetic impression.[2] Back in Chicago, McCurry retained his interest in modernism. He had seen the exhibition of Bauhaus work held at the Arts Club of Chicago in 1931 and was aware of the 1932 *Modern Architecture: International Exhibition* at the Museum of Modern Art through publications.[3]

Early in his career, McCurry had worked for architect and writer Thomas Tallmadge (1876–1940), who came out of the Prairie School, from 1926–28; for architect Andrew Rebori (1886–1966), a Beaux-Arts-trained architect beginning to explore a simplified approach to design, from 1929–30; and for Holabird & Root in 1930, which during this period was designing the Chicago Board of Trade Building, the iconic art deco skyscraper at the foot of LaSalle Street in the financial district. In the early 1930s, while in the office of D. H. Burnham Jr. (1886–1961), McCurry drew preliminary plans for the Century of Progress Exposition.

Because of the Depression, like so many of his colleagues, McCurry found himself out of work, and in 1933, after receiving a master's degree in education from the University of Chicago, he took a job teaching high school and remained a teacher for thirteen years. His spouse, Irene Bell Tipler McCurry, received a bachelor's degree at the University of Chicago and a master's of art from Columbia College and taught art in the Chicago public school system.[4]

Dining area with west-facing windows and entrance to rear yard.

Irene McCurry's dressing table lit by glass block window facing front of house.

McCurry never gave up the idea of practicing architecture and became his own client, building an International Style house. The young married couple purchased a typical 50-by-125-foot lot in an undeveloped area of Beverly and began construction in 1935. With blind walls on the sides—much like a townhouse—their new home had a central front entrance and, at the rear, a garden entrance opening off of the dining room. A second-floor terrace above the rear of the garage, and a sunroom, within the envelope of the house, faced the back yard. The McCurrys created the light and bright house they wanted, using a sizable amount of glass block to admit light while maintaining privacy. The large glass block opening at the front of the house provided an even level of light for Irene's dressing table.

The only nod to tradition in the house is its roofline. The flat roof is finished by a slim projecting band, topping a row of abstracted dentils. McCurry's house was published in the January 1938 issue of *American Home.* The article describes it as "smart in its formal appearance, lightness of volume—no longer awkwardly bulky or mediocre due to extraneous ornamental detail."[5]

While teaching, McCurry practiced architecture out of the house, installing a sign in front and incorporating a private entrance to his office next to the garage. The space became a breakfast room in 1946, when he returned to practicing architecture and joined Schmidt, Garden, and Erickson, a firm specializing in hospital design. He remained there thirty years.

Paul McCurry, as president of Chicago Chapter, American Institute of Architects, presenting Gold Medal to Ludwig Mies van der Rohe.

The McCurry's home, constructed of Chicago common brick laid on top of a base of black silica brick, is a very early Chicago-area International Style house—built a year before Keck's Herbert Bruning House in Wilmette, about two years before Keck's Bertram and Irma Cahn House in Lake Forest, and three years before Philip Maher's house in Lake Bluff. Like these homes, his house was simple, geometric, and painted white. At the time, McCurry knew of no other comparable style house in Chicago.[6] He describes it as consisting "mostly of really very simple shapes, practically without ornament, very much functional in character, and functional aspects of the house determining, to some degree, the character of the exterior, the visual aspect of the exterior."[7]

When Mies van der Rohe became director of architecture at Armour Institute, beginning in 1938, Paul attended his welcome dinner. As might be expected, given his enthusiasm for the International Style, McCurry praised Mies, saying, "I think the thing that makes him a great architect is his extraordinary sensitivity to proportion. This type of skill is timeless, ageless, and can be applied to any building that was ever built. It has to be visually a delight to look at."[8] He felt Mies "made an enormous contribution in terms of the exploration of the use of steel and glass; in terms of his ability to reduce the spatial requirements of buildings to relatively simple geometric shapes."[9]

Paul McCurry served as president of the Chicago Chapter of the American Institute of Architects and, in that capacity, presented its 1960 Gold Medal to Mies. In 1968, he was elected to the College of Fellows of the AIA. McCurry understood the aesthetics and timelessness of good architecture, eloquently expressed his feelings on the subject, and created its expression in his own modern home.[10] Both his daughters, Margaret McCurry, FAIA, and Marian Tweedie, became architects.

The McCurrys moved out in 1955. Subsequently, the house has been altered over time by the replacement of the original Hope's steel windows with wood windows, the removal of much of the glass block, and stripping the white paint. —SSB

Vine Itschner and Herbert Bruning House

South-facing street facade
with glass block stair tower
and entrance porch.

George Fred Keck, who was known as Fred, had designed several Colonial-, Tudor-, and French revival-style houses during the 1920s, which could be considered as "bread and butter" jobs. Not until the 1933–34 Century of Progress Exposition where his House of Tomorrow attracted considerable attention, did Keck acquire a residential clientele drawn to modernism. His first clients for a modern home were Herbert and Vine Bruning, who asked "that the finished structure be of such a character 'that the children would not be ashamed of it when they reached the age of reason' — i.e., that it be simple, permanent, and economically maintained."[1] This was his first important residential commission, one that received immediate recognition in *Architectural Record*.[2]

Keck had carte blanche to design everything from the site plan to the curtains.[3]
He created a house in the International Style, indebted to European modernism,
with a flat roof, planar surfaces, and geometric massing—devoid of ornament.[4]
Herbert Bruning's fifteen-room house, with an open plan, was built in 1936, at a cost
initially reported as $30,000 but later as $54,000.[5] Success as vice president of
his family manufacturing company allowed Bruning to afford a house that enabled
Keck to explore his architectural ideas.[6] Keck utilized the most up-to-date construction methods in the Bruning House such as a Stran-Steel frame that carried
light Truscon steel floor decking covered with lightweight concrete.[7] (Incidentally,

Stran-Steel had also exhibited houses in the Century of Progress, the Stran-Steel
Garden Home and the Good Housekeeping Stran-Steel House.) The exterior curtain
walls are finished in reinforced cement stucco.

The Bruning House was Keck's first passive solar house, a concept that would shape
his approach to residential architecture and build his reputation. Keck sited the
house after carefully studying the path of the sun and its angle on the twenty-first
day of December, March, June, and September, on the equinoxes and solstices.
All of the major living areas were oriented toward the west where roof decks,
screened porches, and paved terraces were located. A lightweight, concrete slab
roof was designed to hold a thin layer of water to cool the house by evaporation.
To further control temperature, the windows were double glazed, a technology
introduced by Owens Corning in 1935. Perhaps the most forward-looking aspect of
the home was its window unit designed to incorporate external aluminum Venetian
blinds that were raised or lowered by a metal bead chain and opened or closed by
a worm gear—both operated from the interior. Glass block, commonly found in
1930s houses, was used to create this home's most dramatic feature, a two-story,
semi-cylindrical tower that backlights the black terrazzo staircase and illuminates
the combination stair hall, living room, and library. —SSB

Bertrand Goldberg   Evanston   1936

Doris L. and Thomas H. Mullen House

Bertrand Goldberg (known as "Bud") is regularly lauded for the iconic cylindrical towers of Chicago's Marina City; as Blair Kamin, architecture critic for the *Chicago Tribune,* wrote for Goldberg's obituary, "Marina City is as much a symbol of Chicago as the historic old Water Tower."[1] Goldberg, however, receives little attention for the houses he designed between 1935, when he created a small house in Wood Dale, Illinois, for a single 28-year old Bostonian woman, and 1959, when he began work on the Marina City mixed-use residential and commercial complex. Historic preservationist Jeanne M. Lambin points out that these houses are "an oft-over-looked aspect of his career."[2]

At age 23, Bertrand Goldberg designed a modest house for Thomas and Doris Mullen in the North Shore suburb of Evanston. As young professionals in the arts—Thomas was an editor at a trade magazine and Doris wrote for magazines—they typify many clients who commissioned modern houses.[3] Goldberg never veered from a modernist approach and was clever in the way he explained to residential clients that his firm did not do Colonial houses. Rather than stating outright that they would have a "modern house," he presented a plan and allowed the process

to evolve naturally without showing them an elevation "for at least two months!"[4]

The Mullen home is L-shaped in plan with the main two-story section an unadorned 25-foot cube. Alison Fisher compares its shape to a stripped-down American Foursquare.[5] But that is where any relationship to traditional architecture referencing ends. The house, with its common brick chimney, is sheathed in horizontal wood boards and topped by a slim but deep wood overhang. This flat-roof house looked quite out of character in its conservative Evanston neighborhood of Colonial- and Tudor-inspired cottages. With no applied ornament, the home's design ingenuity stems from the modulation of rectangular elements.

Living and dining areas separated by fireplace.

Terrace between main block of house and one-story rear wing.

Although the house is small at 1,200 square feet, the open plan creates a perception of spaciousness. An imposing brick fireplace separates the approximately 20-by-13-foot living room from the small dining area, but an adjacent terrace accessible from tall glazed doors extends the space. Upstairs, one bedroom is 10 feet by 12 feet; the other, at 10 feet by 25 feet, incorporates a sitting area. A sliding screen, inspired by Japanese architecture, can provide privacy. Since the house was built on a slab with no basement, built-ins are necessary and plentiful.

The Mullen House was constructed around the same time as Frank Lloyd Wright's first fully developed Usonian design, the Katherine Westcott and Herbert Jacobs House I in Madison, Wisconsin. Both reflect a design solution for affordable housing in Depression-era America. They are comparable in size, use of wood, a prominent brick fireplace, and flow of space. The Mullen House was built at a cost of $5,265.

Bertrand Goldberg studied under Ludwig Mies van der Rohe at the Bauhaus and worked in his office. That said, Goldberg did not refine a particular design approach as had Mies. Each house Goldberg designed was different, reflecting the needs and budget of his clients. His early houses, like the Mullen House, were composed of geometric volumes. He later abandoned the rectilinear approach he had learned from Mies and, in his multifamily housing, espoused a more personal vision, as exemplified by Marina City.

Like Henry Dubin and Howard Fisher, Bertrand Goldberg was enamored with prefabrication and mass production in order to provide low-cost housing. In 1939, he formed Standard Houses Corporation to design prefabricated housing units and built five identical four-room plywood houses in the Chicago suburb of Melrose Park. Priced at only $2,995, the houses made with plywood walls, ceilings, wardrobes, and cabinets sold out in one day. Units were manufactured in a size easily transported in a truck that would accommodate 4-by-8-foot plywood sheets. Ironically, these houses were simplified Cape Cods. In 1952, Goldberg designed a more luxurious house for John Snyder in Shelter Island, New York to demonstrate that prefabrication and the use of plywood need not be perceived as a stigma.[6] Goldberg's approach to materials contrasted sharply with that of Mies, whose Tugendhat House, completed in 1930 for the wealthy Tugendhat family, incorporated chrome-steel, marble, onyx, and rare woods—a variety of precious materials.

Although acknowledging that the Depression of the 1930s carried with it "a certain amount of hopelessness," Goldberg describes a hopeful environment of new ideas and a new world, "You also see things that were new—a new mathematics, new scientific things, new ways of looking at Shakespeare, new hospital treatments, new automobiles…. Not new models or not a new style, but I mean really innovatively new, with major contributions to offer to respective divisions of interest."[7] In the Mullen House, Goldberg subtly integrated construction advances—the use of Douglas fir plywood panels and Celotex, an acoustical product made of sugar cane fiber—in a small affordable home for a middle-class American family.

Floor plans showing main block of house and one-story wing.

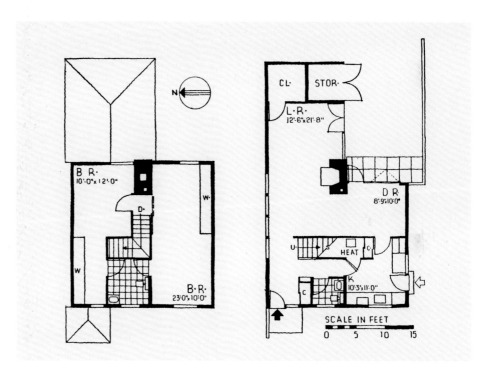

The Mullen House was featured almost immediately after construction in *The 1940 Book of Small Houses,* a handbook profusely illustrated with photos and plans for the prospective homebuilder published by the editors of the *Architectural Forum.*[8] The Mullen House was one of a relatively small number of houses in the book not derived from historical styles. The modern house designed by Harwell Hamilton Harris for John Entenza, editor of *Arts & Architecture,* is illustrated; and the Mullen House is singled out as "a small house of unusual interest."[9]

The original location for the home was next to the Northminster Presbyterian Church at 2501 Central Street in Evanston. When the church built its new south facade in 1951, the house was moved to its present location a few blocks away. The house was designated an Evanston Landmark in 2002. Its owner Margaret McRaith has lovingly cared for the house. —SSB

James F. Eppenstein   Highland Park   1936

Rosalie Strauss and
Gustave Weinfeld House

In the 1920s and early 1930s, James F. Eppenstein studied at Cornell and the University of Michigan before attending the École des Beaux-Arts in Paris and Harvard, both of which had a traditional curriculum. Despite his training—like many of his contemporaries who had been exposed to modern architecture in their time abroad—Eppenstein was eager to design modern buildings when he returned to Chicago. The year after he received his Master of Architecture degree from Harvard, he opened his own office and shortly thereafter designed the Weinfeld House in the Ravinia section of Highland Park.

Front entrance, terrace over two-car garage.

His clients Dr. Gustave F. and Rosalie Strauss Weinfeld were establishing their careers in pediatric medicine and early childhood education. Dr. Weinfeld was an associate professor in the Department of Pediatrics at the University of Illinois Medical School, started a private practice, and began publishing articles in professional journals, magazines, and books.[1] He was a proponent of nurturing infants via self-demand feeding and traveled the area giving lectures.[2] Rosalie Weinfeld taught at the Ravinia Nursery School where she became its director for 42 years and was "always open to new ideas."[3]

Like many clients for modern houses, Rosalie and Dr. Weinfeld embraced progressive ideas in their home as well as in their respective professions. Eppenstein's design met their basic needs, providing a house to accommodate a growing family as well as a "cook" and "nursery maid."[4] Primary elements were textbook International Style, with flat roofs, bands of windows, a vertical strip of glass block, and absence of applied ornament. But he also experimented with the streamlined *moderne* aesthetic, the aerodynamic styling that characterized fast new transportation—automobiles, trains, planes, and ships—that had also made its way into architecture. Eppenstein used the curvilinear form, a popular allusion to speed, over entrances to the Weinfeld home.

Of the many houses and interiors that Eppenstein designed, the Weinfeld home and his own home were particularly daring. For the Astor Street home he shared with his spouse, Louise, an author of children's books, and daughters, Eppenstein remodeled a Queen Anne, tucked between historic townhouses on a typical 25-by-110-foot Chicago lot. All ornament was removed, and the new facade consisted only of planar stucco walls with horizontal bands of windows and a third-floor recessed terrace.[5] Both the Weinfeld House and the Eppenstein House remain standing.

Eppenstein experimented with passive solar design, and one of his houses was featured—with architects George Fred Keck, William Deknatel, and others—in a promotional booklet on solar houses published by Libbey-Owens-Ford Glass Company.[6] In 1941, he designed a luxurious and colorful "smartly-styled" fast train, the Electroliner, for the North Shore Line that connected Chicago with Milwaukee.[7] As much an interior designer as an architect (he was a member of the American Institute of Decorators), James Eppenstein periodically wrote an advice column "What's Your Decorating Problem?" for the *Chicago Tribune*.[8] He also designed furniture and owned US Patents for furnishings that included a cantilevered ashtray, an extension table, and a convertible sofa bed.[9] —SSB

Streamline moderne canopy over rear entrance.

Living room interior designed by James Eppenstein.

George Fred Keck   Lake Forest   1937

Irma Kuppenheimer and Bertram J. Cahn House

Like millions of others, Irma (Mrs. Bertram J.) Cahn attended the 1933–34 Century of Progress International Exposition, where she visited the House of Tomorrow designed by George Fred Keck. But unlike anyone else, she came home desiring a summer house even more progressive than it, which she described as the "house of the day after tomorrow."[1] She envisioned a home that would be comfortable, low maintenance, and suitable for informal living—a servantless house that could be closed or opened easily with nothing that would deteriorate when it was unoccupied.[2]

Mrs. Cahn had been taking a class at the University of Chicago from preeminent historian Louis Gottschalk and happened to tell him what she was looking for in a house. Gottschalk was a neighbor of architects George Fred and William Keck in a three-unit cooperative apartment in Chicago's Hyde Park/Kenwood neighborhood, and the professor arranged a dinner party where the Cahns could meet Fred. Her vision launched Keck on the design of an extraordinary passive solar house.

At the time Irma and Bertram Cahn planned their house, he was president of B. Kuppenheimer & Co., a men's clothing business dating from before the Chicago Fire of 1871. The house was to be built on a forested thirty-one-acre property belonging to her father, Jonas Kuppenheimer. A large house existed on the property where her family spent summers and whose grounds were designed by Jens Jensen. The original house was demolished to make way for Mrs. Cahn's dream, but her new home was carefully sited high on a bluff to retain views of the adjacent meadow, a signature Jensen design feature.

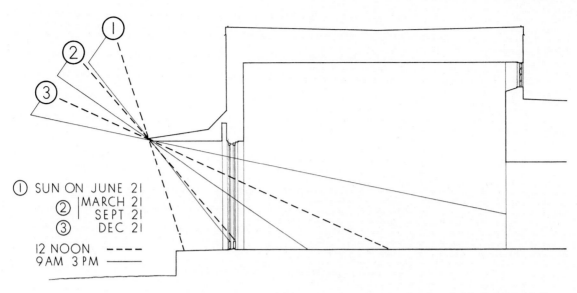

LIVING ROOM SECTION SHOWING
ORIENTATION FOR SUNLIGHT

① SUN ON JUNE 21
② |MARCH 21
   | SEPT 21
③ DEC 21

12 NOON ----
9AM 3PM ____

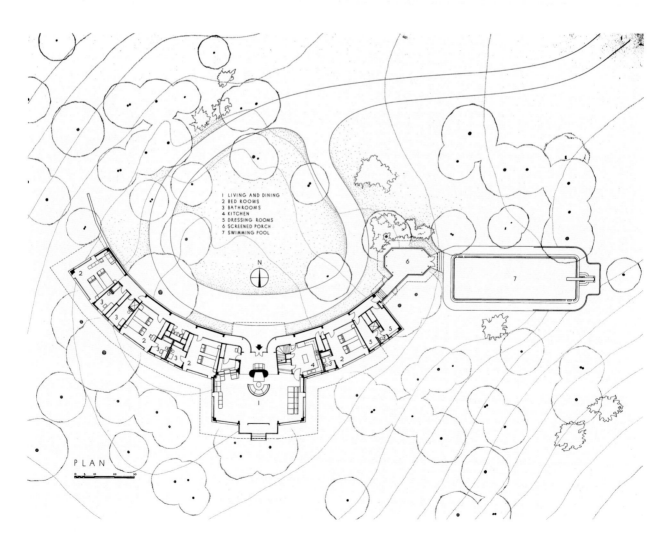

1 LIVING AND DINING
2 BED ROOMS
3 BATHROOMS
4 KITCHEN
5 DRESSING ROOMS
6 SCREENED PORCH
7 SWIMMING POOL

N

PLAN

Opposite top: Section diagram of sunlight path into living room during equinoxes and solstices.

Opposite bottom: Site plan. South facing windows on convex side of house provide light and views.

Interior hallway illuminated by sections of glass block facing driveway.

Irma Cahn had some specific design needs resulting from a horseback-riding accident when she was a young girl that left her with a limp. There could be no stairs, floor rugs, or lamp cords to trip over. Because she was a heavy smoker, her spouse wanted the house to be fireproof. Furniture contained built-in ashtrays, and tables had aluminum surfaces. To meet the Cahn's requirements, Keck designed a one-story, steel-frame house sheathed in stucco. Completed in 1937 at a cost of $125,000, it had four bedrooms, six baths, and a screened porch overlooking a swimming pool.

The house was crescent shaped with the north-facing concave curve embracing a circular drive to create an entrance court. To ensure privacy from the drive, Keck designed a hallway running the length of the interior curve to serve as a buffer between the other spaces. Glass block windows along the hallway's exterior wall allowed for the exchange of light while maintaining privacy. The living room and bedrooms were positioned in the rear of the house, which followed the convex curve; all the walls had large clear glass glazed walls facing south. Electric windows that could recede into the basement—like those found in Mies van der Rohe's Tugendhat house in Brno—were planned but deemed too expensive and eliminated from Keck's design.[3] The Cahn House did incorporate features on the cutting edge of Keck's experimentation in passive solar design. Broad eaves and external, chain-driven Venetian blinds shaded the glass openings, protecting the interior of the house from overheating in the summer, while allowing the sun to penetrate and warm the interior in the winter. The living room projected out from the southern curve of the house, with three glazed walls providing both morning and afternoon light as well as dramatic views of the meadow.

The interior was kept sparse, with built-in cabinetry and furniture. The living room was the home's most dramatic space, with a high ceiling painted cobalt blue, walls and furniture in yellow, and black rubber flooring. Instead of a separate formal dining room, square tables could be reconfigured for bridge games or to accommodate dinner guests in the open space. Dining chairs would also function as movable seating elsewhere in the room. The major fixed piece of furniture was a semi-circular sofa, with cobalt blue striped upholstery, facing the fireplace.

Mrs. Cahn wanted to be able to read from anywhere. To accomplish this without any lamps, eighteen recessed pinhole ceiling lights were installed that could illuminate any area of the room. Because of the hard surfaces in the combined living and dining room, its acoustics were excellent for listening to live string quartets or recorded music. Loudspeakers on casters could be tuned by remote control. Irma Cahn commented, "We like the house because it is spacious, colorful, bright, restful, and in harmony with the surrounding landscape."[4] It also met the Cahn's request for a turnkey, low-maintenance home that looked modern and accommodated a casual lifestyle for a family that could easily afford more lavish living. Their taste for modern architecture was atypical for wealthy Lake Forest residents who generally preferred houses based on traditional historic styles.

The Cahn House was included along with numerous other International Style homes in *The Modern House in America*, published in 1940.[5] Although the house remains standing, it has suffered substantial alterations. —SSB

Swimming pool at east end of house, adjacent to screen porch.

Living room color scheme:
bright yellow walls and blue
upholstered furniture with built
in armrests and ashtrays.

Bedroom with built-in furniture.

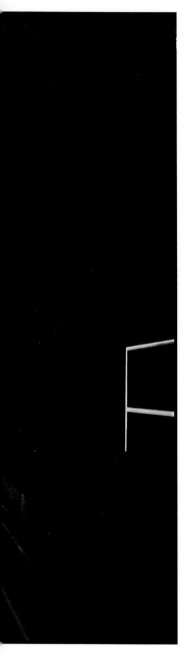

Josephine Topp and De Forest S. Colburn House

Like his friend and esteemed colleague Bertrand Goldberg, architect Gilmer Vardiman Black was enamored with European architecture; Goldberg once described Black's home for Josephine Topp and De Forest Smith Colburn as "kind of a cubist house."[1] The house for the Colburns was, above all, to be functional, to meet the needs of a couple, with no children living with them, who desired an open plan. Le Corbusier's definition of a house as "a machine for living in" describes it appropriately.[2] Longtime fans of modernism, the Colburns later had an apartment at Mies van der Rohe's iconic 860 Lake Shore Drive.

The Colburn House was sited on Green Bay Road, a major north-south road that connects the North Shore towns and follows a ridge that historically served as a Native American trail. The street side of the house contained the garage and utility room on the first floor, and servant's room on the second, buffering the family living spaces from traffic noise. The opposite side, where living areas were located, captured views to the Skokie Valley. Floor-to-ceiling windows on the first floor opened onto a terrace. The second-floor bedrooms accessed a deck that spanned the entire width of the house. Simple pipe railings formed the edge of this outdoor room.

West-facing living area and deck overlooking Skokie Valley.

The Colburn House was fireproof—built of concrete and, on the interior, featured a winding staircase with travertine treads and risers and aluminum rails. Concrete was the logical building material, given that De Forest S. Colburn was Vice President of Marquette Cement Manufacturing Company.

Gilmer Black worked at various times during the 1930s with Goldberg. He apprenticed on a design for the North Pole Mobile Ice Cream shop and worked with him on a prefabricated housing development in the Chicago suburb of Melrose Park.[3] Black, along with William "Bill" Priestley, accompanied Goldberg when he drove Mies van der Rohe to Taliesin to meet Frank Lloyd Wright in 1937.[4] Black was a free

Winding staircase with travertine stairs and aluminum railings.

Southeast corner with south-facing entrance facade; east-facing service area.

spirit, according to Goldberg, who indicates that they connected "in the wonderful days of friendship that we all had around jazz" and were part of a group that on Monday nights attended all-night events.[5]

The Colburn House was published several times. It was described in the *Chicago Daily Tribune* in minute detail, singled out as "a fascinating example of our very modern International architecture."[6] The house was selected by the American Institute of Architects as one of 150 of the finest buildings erected in the US and featured in a traveling photographic exhibition, which included Chicago's Adler Planetarium and Philip Maher's 1301 Astor Street apartments, circulated to colleges and galleries throughout the country.[7] In 1937, Black's work—along with that of Richard Neutra, Eero Saarinen, Marcel Breuer, Russel Wright, and numerous others—was featured in *Architectural Forum's* Domestic Interiors Special Issue, "devoted to the American reaction to the European Modernism."[8] The owner, photographer Howard Kaplan, takes great pride in his house. —SSB

Caroline Sinclair and Philip Will Jr. House

Founded in 1935, Perkins, Wheeler & Will arrived on the national stage when, in 1939–40, the firm partnered with Eliel and Eero Saarinen in the design of the Crow Island School. The architectural embodiment of progressive education, Crow Island was extensively published and received numerous awards. In 1956, the school was selected by fifty architects and scholars as twelfth among all buildings and first among all schools in an architectural poll to name the "most significant buildings in the past 100 years of architecture in America."[1] Perkins indicates that the basic plan was primarily designed by Will and that it launched their firm's specialization in school design, which over the years evolved into an international design firm with 2,500 employees.[2]

The firm Perkins Wheeler & Will had many award-winning buildings (built prior to Philip Will's 1971 retirement), including Indian Lake School in Barrington, Illinois (1947), Keokuk High School in Keokuk, Iowa (1954), International Minerals and

Chemical Building (1960) in Skokie, Illinois, and First National Bank of Chicago Headquarters (1969) in Chicago.[3] Lawrence B. Perkins had known Phil since their college days at Cornell and had worked with him on many award-winning projects. In the obituary tribute to his friend, Perkins revealed that Phil Will, even with many achievements, felt his own home was "one of his most prized designs."[4] He lived there with his spouse Caroline Sinclair Will and their two children.[5]

Philip Will's house was one among many proto-modern and modern houses designed by the firm during the 1930s–40s, including the Ellen Borden and Adlai Stevenson II House (1938, p. 104) and the Ruth and Hilmer V. Swenson House (1941,

Opposite: South-facing view of house from street.

Living room area fireplace wall.

Dining area of living-dining space.

p. 324). Modernist designs were still a challenge due to broadly entrenched, and slowly changing tastes. Perkins admitted, "All during our young career every job was a fight or a choice between traditional or modern. Modern had to prove itself. The safe thing to do for a house client was the colonial that they asked for, rather than the hopefully fresh clarity we felt we were expressing with modern."[6]

Will's house embodied the informal lifestyle popularized by Frank Lloyd Wright in his Usonian houses and practitioners such as Paul Schweikher, Harry Weese, Bertrand Goldberg, and other progressive Chicago architects. The Will House is a split-level, with living-dining and master bedroom on the first floor, bedrooms on the second level, and above that, a family room opening onto a roof deck. With horizontal board and batten siding, bands of windows, and sheltering rooflines, the house is a descendant of Prairie School houses of the early years of the twentieth century. Its lengthwise orientation on a long, narrow corner lot recalls the siting of Wright's 1909 Robie House—but translated into wood and glass with bands of tall corner windows that flood the interior with light. The house was published in the October 1939 issue of the *Architectural Forum*.[7]

In addition to his architectural achievements, Will served as president of the Chicago Chapter of the American Institute of Architects from 1946–1950 and as its national president from 1960–62. —SSB

Philip B. Maher   Lake Bluff   1938

Madeleine Michelson and Philip B. Maher House

Architect Philip Maher's International Style house is an anomaly; his architecture typically demonstrates a chic refinement of traditional architecture. Maher designed a handful of buildings—on North Michigan Avenue in the mid-to-late 1920s, including Blackstone Shops (1925, later expanded for Saks Fifth Avenue), Farwell Building (1928), Women's Athletic Club (1928), Jacques Building (1929) and two fashionable high-rise apartments on Chicago's Astor Street in the early 1930s at 1260 N. Astor St. (1931) and 1301 N. Astor St. (1932)—that brought him recognition.[1] These buildings and two houses in Wilmette he designed in the mid-1920s were inspired by historic French and Italian architecture. The Astor Street apartments, Women's Athletic Club (WAC), and Jacques Building all incorporate art deco flourishes.

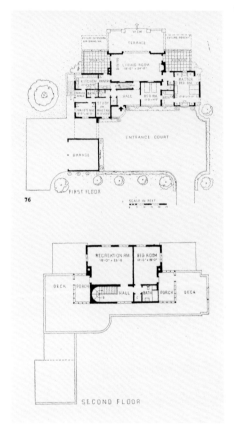

The house that Maher designed for himself and his first spouse, Madeleine Michelson Maher, is particularly interesting, if not radical, because his father, George W. Maher, was a Prairie School contemporary of Frank Lloyd Wright. The Philip Maher house, however, pointedly avoids referencing the Wrightian tradition.

Philip Brooks Maher was born in Kenilworth, Illinois. He served in Paris during World War I and traveled in Europe after the war. Maher attended the University of Michigan where he received Beaux-Arts training; when he returned to Chicago two years later, he resumed a partnership with his father. After George Maher died in 1926, Philip Maher established his own office. With the exception of his own modern house, Maher embraced architectural eclecticism and largely rejected progressivism. As the Depression deepened opportunities were lean for almost all Chicago architects, and he worked for the Public Works Administration in Chicago, designing public housing. Over the course of his career, he designed relatively few single-family houses. For the design of his home in the late 1930s, Maher was free from constraints imposed by clients who often preferred variants—even sleek variants—on classical European architecture. Maher's lakefront house was flat-roofed and brick (a material Chicago architects favored) similar to the 1930 International Style Battledeck House (p. 64) that Henry Dubin built for his family. The Maher House stood seventy feet above lake level, making it vulnerable to cold winter winds. For privacy, most light entered through glass blocks that spanned the entrance-court, where the front hall and bedrooms were located. On the side with views of Lake Michigan, there was a single 18-foot window lighting the 18-by-34-foot living-dining area. The second floor could be closed to save on heating costs. Porches were located on both levels in this simple and economically conceived home. Also, decks extend across the entire front and sides of the house. Comparisons to the design of a ship seem inevitable due to its location.

Master bedroom with west-facing corner and glass-block window.

Floor plans.

Maher's house was one of only sixty-four selected by James and Katherine Ford for their 1940 book *The Modern House in America,* where he was in the company of Richard Neutra, Walter Gropius, Edward Durell Stone, Marcel Breuer, and Chicagoans George Fred Keck and William Deknatel.[2] Like the other houses illustrated, Maher's home expressed the period's general simplicity of form and drive toward a more informal lifestyle—designed with spaces devoted to outdoor living, assuring closeness to nature under ideal weather conditions.

Despite its design pedigree and prime lakefront location, the Maher House was demolished sometime prior to 2008, when an architectural survey of the estate areas of Lake Bluff found that two large single-family houses had replaced it. —SSB

Dorothy Miller and
Paul Schweikher House

Opposite: View from east-west
entrance path toward studio
and Franz Lipp–designed
landscape in background.

Courtyard with Japanese
dry garden between the
Schweikhers' bedroom wing
and living room wing.

Of all his Chicago work, architect Paul Schweikher loved his own home best. In an interview in 1984, when asked about what pleased him most about the house, Schweikher reminisced about the smell of redwood after a rain, the warmth of the wood, the comfort in the low eaves, and the "feeling that the house belonged to the person in the sense of its scale–relatedness."[1]

Schweikher's 2,400-square-foot home was his workplace as well as his refuge. Originally farmland (in the village that was then Roselle) when Schweikher acquired the seven-acre property, suburbia eventually surrounded it with shopping malls and housing developments. Constructed of Chicago common brick, redwood

board-and-batten siding, and glass, the structure is surrounded by a landscape designed by Franz Lipp within a wooded setting.

The Schweikher House elegantly synthesizes Wrightian and International Style features. Frank Lloyd Wright built his first Usonian house in 1937, slightly before Schweikher created his own home in 1938. Neither Wright's houses of the period nor Schweikher's house were imitative: vestiges of historic architecture are gone. Eschewing synthetic materials, the architects shared a devotion to: warm natural elements, rooms laid out to accommodate informal patterns of living and entertaining, and a close relationship between building and site. Schweikher expressed admiration for Wright, whom he considered "among the super great in force and imagination"; "I pored over his stuff in disbelief."[2] What had impressed him most in Wright's work was the beauty of the overhang and the extension of one space into another—"walls that allowed the passing viewer to look through, if not go

through."[3] This flow of interior space, extending to the outside under protective overhangs, characterizes the Schweikher House. Exterior brick paths transition to interior flooring in the home's entrance hall.

The influence of Wright's work on Schweikher's home has long been acknowledged—not only by the architect himself but also by others. Peter Blake, who served as professor of architecture at Catholic University and former editor of *Architectural Forum,* maintained that of all the Wright-influenced houses built in the Midwest before and after World War II, Schweikher's was "one of the best."[4] Architect Will Bruder looked beyond the formal and material characteristics of Wright's work to note the house's bond with the Wrightian spirit. He asserted that the affinity had less to do with simple mimicry and more to do with the fact that both men were searching for a new architectural form to shelter a changing modern American lifestyle.[5]

Schweikher differentiated the use of space inside the house through the manipulation of ceiling heights or structural members in a Wright-inspired fashion. Visitors enter a low-ceilinged entrance hall that opens onto a brightly lit, one-and-a-half-story living room with an alcove marked by a wooden crossbeam forming an intimate dining area. A massive brick fireplace dominates the living room as it does in many of Wright's houses. The particular configuration of Schweikher's fireplace predates Wright's very similar design for the 1939 Usonian house (for Kathryn Dougherty and Lloyd Lewis in Libertyville, p. 112). Schweikher identified his use of "brick as a mass" that created "a contrast" and "the sense of strength, and the relatedness of brick as an enclosure for controlled fire"; when asked about the similarity between the two fireplaces, Schweikher replied, "Any skilled eye would see a strong difference."[6] Incidentally, Schweikher's carpenter had reported to him during construction "that we had a visit from a number of people, both designers and draftsmen, who said they came from Taliesin."[7]

Schweikher was equally influenced by European modernists. Although Ludwig Mies van der Rohe did not settle in Chicago until after Schweikher completed his home, the influential German architect's buildings were already well known in

North-facing front entrance next to interior brick wall with wood-enclosed radiator and sculpture niche. Brick path resembling *engawa* outside door.

Living room fireplace with vertical glass strip between walls and built-in bench seating.

Opposite: Current ground floor plan showing additions.

the United States. After receiving his Bachelor of Arts from Yale University in 1929, Schweikher went to Europe on a Charles Arthur and Margaret Ormrod Matcham Traveling Scholarship. He visited the Weissenhof Estate, an exhibition of housing built in Stuttgart under Mies's direction in 1927 as well as his Tugendhat House of 1929–30 in Brno. Schweikher also visited Mies's German Pavilion for the 1929 Barcelona International Exposition, which struck the young architect as a superb piece of sculpture as well as architecture. He especially revered Mies's sensitivity to proportion and use of exquisite materials for "that miraculously beautiful building."[8] It turns out their respect was mutual: Mies particularly admired Schweikher's house. The two were to become friends. Early in their friendship, Mies appeared uninvited at Schweikher's doorstep to see his house.[9]

Other architectural traditions also impacted the form and finishes of Schweikher's house. American vernacular architecture interested him, and although not immediately apparent, the American barn influenced the home's construction. Its builder—local carpenter Emil Spohrleder—had been building barns most of his life, and as Schweikher notes, "the detail was almost all typical farmhouse."[10]

Japanese architecture was another profound influence on the design; Schweikher first sketched the house in November 1937 onboard a ship returning from Japan. Schweikher programmed the entry sequence to be a ceremonial experience, guided through a long, straight driveway, past the carport, under a sheltered walkway to the entrance. Beyond, in the Franz Lipp-designed rear garden, are two rows of fruit trees, framed by the house and studio. The view is carefully crafted. Constantly aware of "joinings" (where a wall meets the ground) and

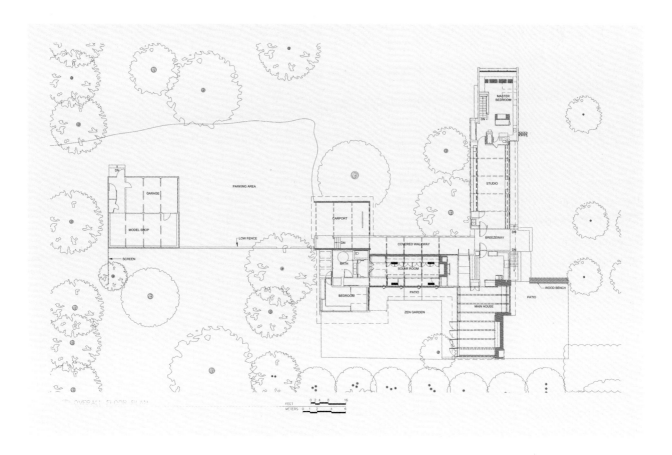

textural meetings, Schweikher wouldn't allow the house to butt up against the ground directly, so he created a path around much of it at the depth of the overhang, recalling an *engawa,* a veranda-like strip of wooden flooring that surrounds traditional Japanese houses.[11] Adjacent to the glass walls of the living room and bedroom sitting area is a gravel *karesansui,* or dry garden, raked to look like waves of water. Modeled after the famous rectangular garden from Ryōan-ji in Kyoto, this feature was designed to be viewed from inside the house, providing a place for contemplation.

In 1949, Schweikher built several additions: a bedroom for Paul Jr. to the west, an office attached to the drafting studio with a small bedroom and bath below, and a separate garage/model shop.[12] The studio—a large rectangular space with an entrance opposite the front door of the house—served as a drafting room with his personal office beyond, overlooking a winding creek. The bedroom and bath

Paul Schweikher's drafting room, with east-facing windows.

Opposite: Courtyard with Japanese dry garden; west-facing living room windows and broad overhang protecting glazed south wall of Schweikhers' bedroom sitting area.

beneath the office housed at different times apprentices—including Ralph Rapson, Edward Dart, and Irving W. Colburn—while in Schweikher's employ. In 1947, the house was featured in articles in *Architectural Forum* and *Nuestra Arquitectura*.[13]

Paul and Dorothy Miller Schweikher sold the house in 1952, when he became chair of the Department of Architecture at Yale, in New Haven, Connecticut. The purchasers of the house were Alexander Langsdorf Jr. (1912–96) and Martyl Suzanne Schweig Langsdorf (1917–2013). A physicist working on the Manhattan Project at the University of Chicago, Alexander collaborated with Enrico Fermi to develop technology that was used to create the first atomic bomb and famously joined seventy of his colleagues in petitioning President Harry S. Truman never to deploy it.[14] Martyl, a renowned artist, explored the themes of technology and landscape in her paintings. In 1947, she designed the legendary emblem of the Doomsday Clock for the cover of the *Bulletin of the Atomic Scientists*.

Wishing to move from Chicago to be closer to Langsdorf's work at Argonne Laboratory, the Langsdorfs investigated the western suburbs. Martyl almost gave up looking, refusing to settle for the "ordinary" or "mundane." Her daughter Sandie Shoemaker recalls that her mother needed a "visual fix." When Martyl, who drove the decision, saw the Schweikher House, she fell in love with the architecture and its beautiful surroundings. In terms of investment and care, "the house … became like a third child."[15]

North and east wall of Schweikher's drafting studio with breezeway between studio and house.

View from the Schweikher's bedroom sitting area south, under overhang toward courtyard with Japanese dry garden.

Cover, *Bulletin of the Atomic Scientists* (June 1947) image design by former owner Martyl Langsdorf.

Schweikher and his work influenced a generation of young architects, including Ralph Rapson, who became head of the School of Architecture at the University of Minnesota. He called his teacher and sometime-colleague a "native giant among architects [and] … a man of the highest principles and integrity." He added that "[t]his is reflected in his architectural work and quite naturally reaches its highest form in his own home. It is a beautiful and significant structure that most certainly deserves protection." Rapson's praise was articulated in a 1986 letter supporting the addition of Schweikher's home and studio to the National Register of Historic Places.[16]

The home and studio were threatened with demolition while it was owned by the Metropolitan Water Reclamation District of Greater Chicago, a municipal entity charged with protecting and improving water quality. Rapson and others, including architects Bertrand Goldberg and Peter Blake as well as architectural

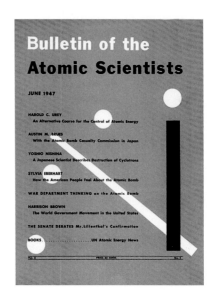

historians William Jordy (Brown), David Van Zanten (Northwestern), and Vincent Scully (Yale), successfully advocated for the building's preservation. In 1987, the property was listed on the Register, even though it was less than fifty years old at the time—an honor bestowed only on younger buildings of special significance. Today this remarkable structure and site is owned by the Village of Schaumburg, an excellent steward, and is administered as a house museum, The Schweikher House, by the Schweikher House Preservation Trust. —SSB

Ellen Borden and Adlai E. Stevenson II House

Widely admired today as a consummate statesman, Adlai Stevenson II (1900–1965) had two successive family homes, each built in a style that was unconventional for the time, unaffected by traditional architectural convention. Stevenson was a 35-year-old attorney at the beginning of his political career when he and his spouse Ellen Borden Stevenson moved to Libertyville. Located on forty rural acres thirty-nine miles from downtown Chicago, their house would be physically remote from the pressures of his professional world. When he purchased the property, formerly used for grazing and lumbering operations by German settlers, it was only accessible by canoe on the nearby Des Plaines River or by horseback. He often referred to it as The Farm. Its modern style comes as a surprise in an area that was

South-facing side facade, Adlai's study.

populated by working farms or gentleman's farms modeled after French country houses or Colonial mansions. Few owners of rural country houses, even those who considered themselves sophisticated, favored modernism.

Designed in 1938 by the fledgling firm of Perkins, Wheeler & Will, this quietly modern house reflects Stevenson's modest character. Simple and unpretentious, its horizontal character was emphasized by low-pitched slate roofs with broad overhangs, wide second-story windows tucked under the roofline, and horizontal wood boards. Its architectural treatment echoes the flatness of the surrounding grounds and connects the Stevenson House to the area's Prairie School heritage. A back porch and terraces offer views across the lawn to the Des Plaines River. The dining room had a mirrored wall where those who sat facing it could be immersed in the reflection leading down to the river.

The cool, unadorned block-like form of Adlai's house, with its geometric shapes, broad corner windows, and upstairs terrace, also references the International Style. Its simple interior with little embellishment provided an informal atmosphere where Stevenson could relax with his family or even welcome heads-of-state, offering comfort and hospitality.

Three years earlier, in 1935, Adlai and Ellen had hired (for their first house) Howard T. Fisher who had designed the Katherine Dummer and Walter T. Fisher House (p. 58) and subsequently founded General Houses, Inc., a design-build prefabricated housing company, one of several that emerged during the Depression. Stevenson had attended the 1933–34 Century of Progress Exposition and been impressed

East facade, front facing road.

Adlai Stevenson with Robert Kennedy and other guests in front of back porch.

by the steel house that General Houses exhibited. This first house, constructed by General Houses, Inc., was a two-story, flat-roof geometric composition. It was entirely sheathed in sleek vertical steel panels. To the Stevensons, the materials and aesthetic of their new steel house was tied to a bright future promised by a machine age of prefabrication. They proudly referred to it as their "mechanical house."[1] Their new home was purportedly fireproof. On the night of January 13, 1938, however, the prefabricated steel house burned. Although a neighbor ran in to rescue what he could, irreplaceable family papers and memorabilia were lost.

Adlai and Ellen Stevenson wanted to rebuild immediately and approached Howard Fisher about building a more "conventional house." Fisher replied, "No, we aren't equipped to do that" and recommended Perkins, Wheeler & Will (there was a connection, however; Wheeler had been chief draftsman for General Houses, Inc., and both Lawrence Perkins and Philip Will had been employed there too).[2] Soon after the fire, E. Todd Wheeler went to assess the condition of the house and found a "mess—twisted steel—and there was really nothing left."[3] Only the foundation could be salvaged, but Wheeler later remarked, "Phil Will designed them a very nice house."[4] A new, modestly larger home was built, featuring a dining room to accommodate the frequent entertaining that the Stevensons enjoyed and a large paneled study with a fireplace to provide Adlai with additional space to focus on work and accommodate his library. In between posts in Springfield and Washington DC, prior to the couple's divorce, the Stevensons reared their sons in a country setting.

Front of Howard Fisher–designed steel house (1935) that burned in 1938.

Rear of steel house.

Adlai Stevenson's diplomatic and political career notched many accomplishments. He served two terms as Illinois Governor, twice challenged Dwight D. Eisenhower for the US presidency, and held the position of US Ambassador to the United Nations from 1961 until his death in 1965. Beyond his devotion to government service, Stevenson was known for his eloquence and wit.[5]

When he was running for President in 1955, Stevenson hosted the Governor's Conference, providing a series of luncheons and dinners at Libertyville for several state Governors. His son Adlai III recalls that the Governors met in the large porch overlooking the lawn to the river. Over the years, there were many distinguished visitors to the Farm—including journalist and political commentator Walter Lippman, Eleanor Roosevelt, and (then presidential candidate) Robert Kennedy.

During his time between assignments and positions, Stevenson always returned to the Farm, his home base.

The Farm currently houses the Adlai Stevenson Center on Democracy, which leases the property from the Lake County Forest Preserve District. The house has excellent stewards who supervise continuous restoration. Its adjacent barn, designed by architect Stanley Anderson, features an exhibition on the history of the Farm and the significance of Adlai Stevenson. The property is a National Historic Landmark. —SSB

Lucile Gottschalk and
Aaron Heimbach House

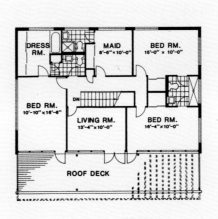

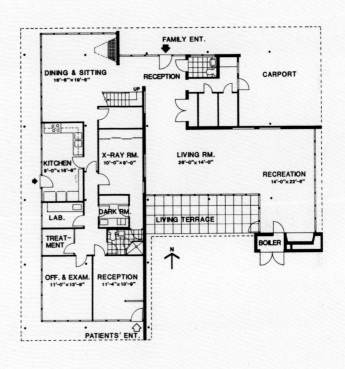

The house for Dr. Aaron and Lucile Gottschalk Heimbach in the city of Blue Island,
south of Chicago, is one of a handful of single-family houses designed by Bertrand
Goldberg. After starting his own independent practice with the commission of the
Harriet Higginson House (1935) in the city of Wood Dale (northwest of Chicago),
he designed this family residence and physician's office. This mixed-use live-work
building type was relatively rare, even though architects like Paul Schweikher (for
whom Goldberg had worked early on) had recently completed his house and studio
in 1938. While Goldberg's designs for multi-unit housing are among his most iconic
contributions to Chicago's post–World War II built environment, in recent years
his single-family houses have begun to receive more attention.[1]

Dr. Aaron Heimbach was part of a local family of established entrepreneurs in Blue
Island. Designed for himself, his spouse at the time, Lucile Gottschalk Heimbach,
and son Richard D. (who would follow in the footsteps of his father to become

a physician), this two-story, flat-roof house clad in Chicago common brick occupies a corner lot and has a distinctly urban quality.[2] While Goldberg would eventually become known for his exuberant curvilinear concrete volumes, the Heimbach House owes a considerable debt to International Style rationalism. A carport and living room with large windows separated by a monumental chimney are part of a rectangular volume that is set back from the street on a lawn; the one-story office wing (which contains a lab, dark room, and x-ray room) extends out to the sidewalk so as to make it more accessible and visible to patients from the street. The second story is set back farther from the street to ensure greater privacy for the family and contains bedrooms, a maid's room, baths, living room, and an enclosed outdoor roof deck facing south.

In 1997, Tom Hawley and Tommy Mandel purchased the house. In 2004, they began an extensive, multiyear preservation project involving repointing and masonry repair, reglazing, and a full upgrade of the heating and electrical system. In 2009, the Heimbach House was the recipient of the Landmarks Illinois Richard H. Driehaus Foundation Preservation Award. It has also received local Blue Island landmark status in 1991.[3] This is an inspiring example of stewardship of Chicago's modern heritage, especially in light of the recent demolition of Goldberg's Prentice Women's Hospital that occurred despite vocal protests. —MS

Kathryn Dougherty and Lloyd Lewis House

The Usonian house that Frank Lloyd Wright designed in 1939 for his friends Lloyd Downs Lewis and Kathryn Dougherty Lewis in Libertyville is a split-level, but one that is vastly different and more spatially complex than those built later through-out the Chicago region after World War II. In Chicago, split-level houses were layered back on the city's standard 25-by-125-foot lot. In the suburbs they typically sprawled laterally with a two-story section on one side and a one-story section on the other. Unlike either of these two split-level types, the Lewis House rests on a five-acre wooded site on the bank of the Des Plaines River in Libertyville, on land not hemmed in with zoning restrictions, located near Adlai Stevenson's farm.

House from across the Des Plaines River.

Although many of the clients for Wright's Usonian houses were young couples with children—such as Herbert and Katherine Jacobs in Madison, Wisconsin or Paul and Jean Hanna in Palo Alto, California—Lloyd and Kathryn Lewis were older, established professionals (both journalists) who were raising the daughter of a deceased friend when they engaged Frank Lloyd Wright to design their house. Born in 1891, Lloyd Lewis had a distinguished career as a journalist and an author. He began as a reporter first for the *North American* in Philadelphia before relocating to work for the *Chicago Herald* in 1915. After his Naval service in 1918, Lewis was publicist and advertising director for Balaban and Katz, owners of a large chain of movie theaters, before joining the *Chicago Daily News* in 1930, where he worked

Projecting balconies and overhangs with pierced rectangular openings.

his way from drama reviews to sports to managing editor. Lewis was coauthor, with Henry Justin Smith, of *Chicago: The History of Its Reputation* (1929). Lewis also published best-selling historical works on President Lincoln and Gen. William T. Sherman.[1]

The site that the Lewises selected for their house, like the location of Mies van der Rohe's Farnsworth House adjacent to the Fox River, is prone to flooding. It is likely that because of this, the house was raised on brick masonry walls, positioning the main living areas—the living room, office ("sanctum" on the plans), dining area and kitchen—two stories above the ground.[2] The bedroom wing, containing

two bedrooms opening off the "gallery" and bathrooms, is one-and-a-half stories. Extending from the living room is a cantilevered terrace clad in horizontal cypress boards, with a permanent screen enclosure (a necessity in this mosquito-prone location) supported by a slender steel framework in Wright's signature Cherokee red paint.

Barriers between the exterior and interior of Usonian houses are "diffuse." This ambiguity of where the building's corners and exterior walls are located is totally contrary to a Miesian approach, where the placement of corners and walls is based on precision and clarity. Like other Wright Usonian houses, the Lewis House reaches out to the surrounding landscape. He consistently blurs the relationship between exterior and interior spaces, creating a push-pull of interlocking volumes. In addition to the cantilevered living room balcony accessed by multiple patio doors, a shallow balcony spans the length of the bedroom wing with smaller balconies off the dining area and office. Several levels of flat roofs, many pierced with rectangular openings reinforcing the ambiguity between the built and natural environment, shelter the house. These projecting roofs extend the house into nature. Vines were planted to cover the piers, walls, and screens of the house, further blending the relationship.

Even though automobile production had slowed during the Depression years, the Lewis House has a two-car carport. The house is entered via a loggia beneath the living room and adjacent to terraced flowerbeds marked by square brick piers. Off the loggia, the entrance door leads directly to a stairway that extends up a half-flight to the bedroom wing; it reverses for another half-flight to the spacious

Dining area.

Front entrance on lower level.

Opposite: Floor plan.

living-dining area. A lowered ceiling creates a more intimate space for dining within Wright's informal open plan. All of the interior wood walls in the house are angled "sandwich wall construction," plywood pressed between overlapping boards of cypress.[3]

Flooring consisted of a concrete slab poured over a crushed stone bed. Wright would typically mix Cherokee red powder into the top, finish layer of concrete. Floors were scored following the module that governed the design of the house, with vertical metal fins imbedded in the concrete marking the location of walls, which could be slatted into the floors—Wright's variant of tongue and groove joinery. This practice is a standard detail, common to Usonian houses. The prominent brick fireplace, with its adjacent bench seating, is at first glance similar in size and configuration but not identical to that in the earlier (1938) Schweikher House (p. 96) living room.[4] Their similarity reflects a design feature common to Chicago's contemporary modern houses.

The Lewis House, like Wright's other Usonian houses, followed a typical design process. Wright would create a drawing, sometimes reusing design elements from previous Usonians in fresh new ways. The design would then go to his chief draftsman John H. Howe, who would complete more finished drawings, assigning details to other apprentices. At critical stages in the design process, Wright would

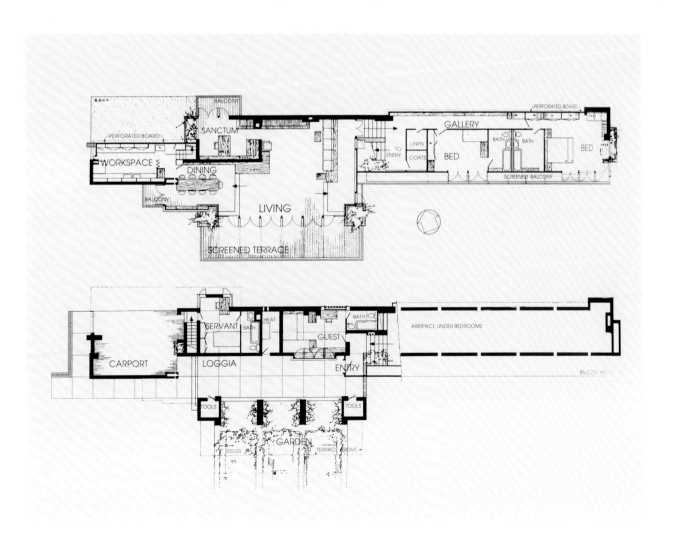

sign off by initialing the drawings. Presentation drawings would be initialed in a small red box, his signature symbol. When construction started, one of the apprentices served as Wright's representative in the field, sometimes acting as General Contractor. Necessary modifications would be approved by Wright, who was always in control of his projects, overseeing the jobs with personal engagement and discipline.[5]

In addition to the house, Wright designed a Farm Unit in 1943, creating a mini gentleman's farm like the many that historically were located in surrounding Lake County. The Lewises had previous experience with sheep ranching in Colorado and Utah in the late 1920s.[6]

Lewis retired in 1945 to continue his historical research and writing full-time but died in 1949, having enjoyed a decade in his comfortable home on the Des Plaines. He is credited for establishing a superb collection of manuscripts from writers with midwestern roots at the Newberry, Chicago's independent research library. This was possible because of his personal relationships with such luminaries as poet Carl Sandburg, playwright Sherwood Anderson, author Sinclair Lewis,

Living room fireplace wall, dining area topped by lowered ceiling with clerestory windows.

Opposite top: Living room with door to balcony providing views to Des Plaines River.

Opposite bottom: Playwright Marc Connelly, Kathryn Dougherty Lewis, and Frank Lloyd Wright at luncheon to honor memory of Lloyd Lewis.

and statesman Adlai Stevenson. An ardent Chicagoan, he was described in the *Encyclopedia of Chicago* as "A gifted raconteur, rich in friendships with the great literary, artistic, political, and sports figures of his time."[7]

According to a press release, over six hundred attendees honored him at a memorial luncheon.[8] After his death, Kathryn Lewis wrote a series of articles for the *Chicago Sun-Times* about her trip around the world in 1955. Kathryn Lewis sold the property in 1960, and the house remains standing. —SSB

Charles Dewey Jr. House and Beach House

Embedded in a forested area on the shore of Lake Michigan, the Charles Dewey Jr. House and its beach house were designed by William Pereira with his brother Harold Ernest "Hal" Pereira. Dewey's choice of a modernist design is somewhat curious; he grew up nearby in a stately 1913 Classical Revival house designed by popular society architect David Adler, who was famed for his meticulously detailed country houses based on historic precedent. Dewey's father was a banker and politician who served as Assistant Secretary of the Treasury from 1924–27. Dewey, who was in his late twenties when he built his home, was an investment advisor in the gas and oil industries. During World War II, he served with the Office of Strategic Services in China and was awarded the Medal of Freedom.[1]

Southwest corner of house and front entrance.

Architect William Pereira's work has received significant attention in California, where he moved in 1938, but considerably less so in his native Illinois. In 1938, Pereira together with his brother Hal designed Chicago's streamlined Esquire Theater, and William Pereira and William A. Ganster designed the International Style Lake County Tuberculosis Sanatorium.[2]

When 390 wooded acres to the south of the sanatorium were being developed near the prestigious Shore Acres Country Club (designed by David Adler in 1923) between Lake Bluff and the Great Lakes Naval Training Station, Dewey purchased six acres for his home and engaged Pereira.[3] The development was announced in

Beach house with view from Lake Michigan looking up at bluff.

the *Chicago Daily Tribune,* which also featured Philip Maher's International Style house then under construction nearby.[4]

Dewey's stylish International Style brick-and-glass house with a flat roof was featured in 1945 on the lower-right corner of the cover of *Tomorrow's Houses: How to Plan Your Post-War Home Now* by industrial designer George Nelson and Henry Wright, managing editor of *Architectural Forum.*[5] The book is copiously illustrated with photographs of modern houses from all over the United States, focusing on practical planning, the use of low-maintenance modern materials, and clean design in the service of meeting "every requirement of contemporary living."[6]

Front entrance.

Opposite top: Cover of *Tomorrow's House* showcasing Dewey House on the lower right.

Opposite bottom: Living room with band of windows and porch facing Lake Michigan.

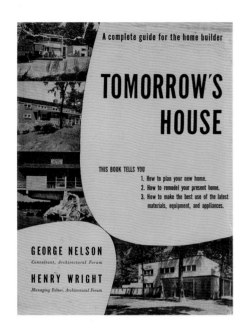

A practical guide, it features, in Illinois, the work of William Deknatel, Dubin & Dubin, James Eppenstein, Bertrand Goldberg, George Fred Keck, and Paul Schweikher, including office addresses for potential clients to contact them.

At the time of William Pereira's death at age 76 in 1985, he had led an international architectural firm, headquartered in Los Angeles, with a portfolio of high-rises, airports, department stores, and research facilities, as well as private homes.[7] He taught from 1949–1957 at the University of Southern California School of Architecture, counting Frank Gehry among his students. Pereira's brother also relocated to California, but Hal Pereira's career is associated more with his years as a successful art director at Paramount (receiving an Academy Award for the 1955 film *The Rose Tattoo* and twenty-three nominations) than his architecture, in which his primary interest was designing cinemas and theaters.[8]

The house continues to function as a single-family residence, although it has been altered. —SSB

Marjorie Horton and Winston Elting House

Rear view in winter from wooded ravine.

Located in the affluent city of Lake Forest, the house Winston Elting designed for himself and his spouse at the time, Marjorie Horton, and their family, shortly after completing the Sylvia Valha and Frances J. Benda House (1939, p. 320) in Riverside, blends modern attitudes toward massing, plan, and siting with organic materiality.

Elting trained as an architect at Princeton and subsequently spent three years in Paris at the École des Beaux-Arts; he grew up in the North Shore village of Winnetka, the site of the Crow Island School that opened the same year he completed his house. Elting's father, Victor Elting, was a prominent lawyer and long-time president of the City Club, Chicago's longest running civic forum; he had commissioned a new house in Winnetka (completed in 1908) by Arts and Crafts-architect Howard Van Doren Shaw.[1] Elting thus grew up amid affluence and an architecturally minded family with whom he traveled to Europe and visited important historic and contemporary sites. Victor wrote about a visit with his sons—Winston and John—to one of these sites:

Floor plans *Architectural Forum* (January 1941).

Work/guest room with drafting table.

"We chartered a big Fiat and a chauffeur named Joseph, and sailed away along the Riviera to Avignon. At Nimes is the marvelous aqueduct built by the Romans. It seemed one hundred feet high, and its great stones told an unbelievable story of the achievements of ancient engineering. The boys and I climbed up and walked over it, and reflected that the stones were there for Christ to have walked upon if he had gone to Nimes."[2]

Elting was among a group of architects who worked in the city but chose to design modern houses for themselves in the leafy villages and cities of Chicago's North Shore. He selected a lot on Walden Lane, part of the Harriet Hammond and Cyrus

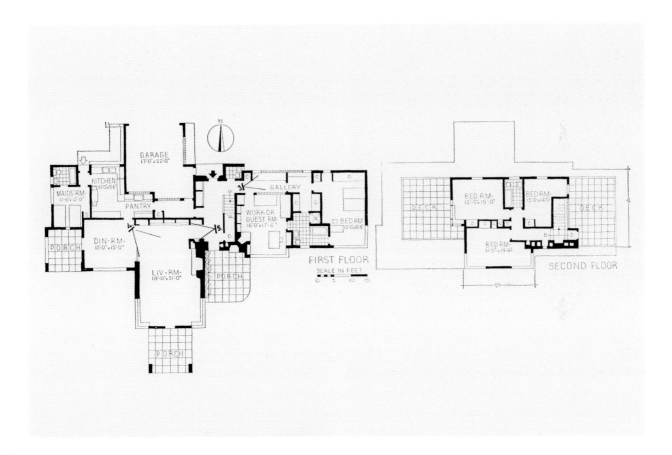

McCormick Jr. estate known as Walden; the original estate house was not dismantled until 1955, but lots were being sold by the 1930s.[3] The Elting House is sited close to the road giving it a uniquely urban quality despite the wooded setting. The Caroline Sinclair and Philip Will Jr. House (1937, p. 92) in nearby Evanston shares many affinities in terms of "urban" siting strategy and materiality with Elting's own approach.

Alternating between one and two storeys, this brick-and-redwood-clad, flat-roof house is planned according to orientation: utilitarian spaces like the two-car garage, service hall, kitchen, and entries face north; all the principal rooms including the dining and living room, bedrooms, porches, and decks open up to the southeast or west overlooking a wooded ravine. Large picture windows and corner windows are used throughout; a glass block wall is deployed for privacy in the "gallery" on the north facade. A number of indoor-outdoor spaces like the two screened porches that extend from the dining and living rooms encourage a direct experience with the surrounding nature defined by the ravine. The articulated massing with second-floor setbacks replete with sun decks gives the house a dynamic quality that emphasizes horizontality. The house features a monumental chimney that shares affinities with the one designed by Bertrand Goldberg in the contemporaneous Lucile Gottschalk and Aaron Heimbach House (1939, p. 108).

Gallery with built-in cabinets and glass block wall and window.

Ground floor main bathroom with Crane (Henry Dreyfuss) fixtures.

The Elting House was first published, shortly after completion, in *Architectural Forum,* and it is likely the second house designed by Elting on his own.[4] In the post-war years, Paul Schweikher tended to minimize Elting's own design contributions to the firm.[5] Despite this unfortunate behavior, the partnership of Schweikher and Elting received considerable attention during the 1950s in the professional and popular press.[6] A survey exhibition held in spring of 1949 at the Renaissance Society at the University of Chicago featured the work of Schweikher and Elting. Exhibition curator Meyric R. Rogers wrote: "The essential quality of their works as demonstrated here is its direct approach to the particular task and its use of the simplest materials to that end."[7]

The Elting House is extant albeit somewhat altered. The current owners James and Kathryn Govas have worked to keep the spatial organization intact even while changing some interior and external materials and finishes. —MS

William A. Ganster   Waukegan   1940

Marjorie Candler and William Ganster House

Rear of house, with major rooms projecting over wooded ravine.

William A. Ganster is arguably most associated with the International Style Lake County Tuberculosis Sanatorium that he designed in association with William L. Pereira.[1] Both architects graduated from the University of Illinois School of Architecture in 1930. The Sanatorium is their only known collaboration and was nationally recognized.[2] Ganster's residential architecture, however, is not as widely known, yet he designed several modern houses in Waukegan, including his own home.

The small house Ganster built for his spouse at the time Marjorie Candler was only 1,000 square feet and constructed in 1940 for $7,500, which included the lot.

126

Glass block exterior wall of master bedroom facing entrance courtyard.

Music alcove, created by bookcases screening front entrance, in living area.

A 1948 two-bedroom addition, providing a study and guest room, slightly expanded the house. Prior to construction of the addition, the area that today serves as an entrance courtyard, had a broad overhang that functioned as a carport.

Built of wood, common brick, and glass, the Ganster House is approached by stepping down to a front courtyard and walking past the exterior wall of the master bedroom to the front door. To allow for light yet privacy, the bedroom's court-facing wall is glass block with clerestory windows. The home's major public rooms, however, face the rear, with vast expanses of glass overlooking a deep wooded ravine with a flowing stream. Set far back from the street, the house is sensitively sited to capture views and visually expand the home's living and dining areas. Fixed panes of glass alternate with awning windows—maximizing light and ventilation.

The L-shaped interior living-dining space is screened from the front entrance by bookshelves that create a music area, where a piano was located. The décor includes a built-in TV set as opposed to the bulky consoles of the era, creating a streamlined modern look, an unusual presence because television was not widely available or popular until after World War II.[3] The dining area features a built-in buffet that separates it from the small kitchen, which feels larger because of the floor-to ceiling glazing facing the ravine. A prominent fireplace of Chicago common brick enhances the dining space. When Ganster lived there, the house was furnished with a dining table and chairs designed by architect Alvar Aalto.

The home's modest size, open plan, and use of natural materials draw a parallel to Frank Lloyd Wright's Usonian concept of affordable housing. A powerful and direct connection exists to Wright's work—specifically to Fallingwater, his 1936 house for the Kaufmann family in Bear Run, Pennsylvania. In the spring of 1938, Ganster's business partner, architectural engineer Arthur Hennighausen, received a set of working blueprints for Fallingwater from a representative of Hope's Windows.[4] The well-worn drawings have Hennighausen's notes about the installation of steel casement windows that had been used in Fallingwater and deployed again in Ganster's house, where steel awning and casement windows were installed. The margins of the Fallingwater drawings were "littered with persnickety instructions about where to hinge joints, conceal bolts and add friction pivots."[5] Hedrich Blessing's photograph of the Ganster House, up from the adjacent wooded ravine, echoes the studio's iconic view of Wright's imposing Fallingwater.

Many modern houses of the period have terraces, patios or, on the upper floors, decks. The Ganster House has an interior courtyard dominated by a massive brick chimney with a fireplace. Although recalling the more formal atria of Roman villas, this private space to lounge in and barbecue expresses the casual lifestyle that became ubiquitous in modern houses of the 1950s.

Corner of living room, showing awning windows.

Opposite top: Night view of dining area with Alvar Aalto–designed furniture.

Opposite bottom: Common brick fireplace wall across from dining area.

Ganster, who had grown up in Waukegan, designed three modern houses immediately south of his own home in 1941–42. A real estate developer who had been selling lots in the surrounding subdivision hired Ganster and Hennighausen to design a model home in the Colonial Revival style, which was still attracting home buyers. The buyers of lots south of the Ganster's house requested modern houses, though somewhat simpler than his own. The three homes create a small modern enclave at the ravine edge.

There have only been two owners of the house. In 1987, the Ganster family sold their home directly to Eileen and Dennis Peterson. Dennis Peterson had always known and admired the house, as his grandfather was the contractor who built it, and Dennis worked for the family construction company. He has commented that people either love the house and can't stop talking about it or, when they don't know what to make of it, become very quiet.[6] The house is treasured by the current owners and virtually unaltered. —SSB

Minna Green and Hugh Duncan House I

Southern window wall of house overhang angled to warm interior in winter and minimize sunlight in summer.

Opposite top: South wall of living room in winter; Minna sits inside while Duncan shovels snow outside.

Opposite bottom: North wall of living room with fireplace and study area.

The house that George Fred Keck designed and built in 1941 for sociologist Hugh D. Duncan and Minna Green, a social worker at Chicago's Hull House when they married, marked an important moment in his development of the passive solar house. After its completion Keck convinced Libbey-Owens-Ford and the Illinois Institute of Technology to undertake a yearlong study on how the sun could contribute additional thermal energy to the house's gas-fired hot-water radiant heated floor.[1]

Unlike Keck's earlier International Style houses designed for the wealthy Bruning (p. 76) and Cahn (p. 84) families in the mid-1930s, the Duncan House was an inexpensive wood frame building for a family of modest means, with only one bedroom and a study that could be separated by a curtain from the living room to create a second bedroom. It was built during the time that Hugh Duncan was working toward his PhD at the University of Chicago.

The design of the Duncan House I was linear, with the major spaces—the bedroom and combined living, dining, study, and kitchen—all facing south to capture sunlight. The walls on the southern exposure were floor-to-ceiling glass sheltered by a deep roof projection that took into account the seasonal angles of the sun. Wing walls consisting of vertical louvers extending seven feet onto the rear south-facing

terrace provided late afternoon shade in the summer months. Windows were double glazed to mitigate heat loss. The house was brightly lit and warm on sunny winter days. Only the terrace was fully exposed to the sun, and the house was comfortable in the summer.[2] The auxiliary rooms consisted of a bathroom and dressing room, accessed from the bedroom and the living area, and a storage room and workshop to the north of the living area.

Hugh Duncan was the perfect client for Keck. His interest in architecture flourished as his career progressed. He authored many books and articles, including *Culture and Democracy: The Struggle for Form in Society and Architecture in Chicago and The Middle West During the Life and Times of Louis Sullivan* and "The Chicago School: Original Principles" in *Chicago's Famous Buildings*.[3] Duncan became active in historic preservation and was instrumental in establishing Chicago's Commission on Architectural Landmarks in the late 1950s. Duncan's teaching career brought him to Carleton College, Rice University, and, in 1963–64, the Illinois Institute of Technology; Minna continued social work. He became a professor of Sociology at Southern Illinois University, Carbondale. They decided to build near Cobden, and architect Bruce Goff designed a curvilinear glass, wood, and fieldstone house on a wooded rural site in 1965. —SSB

William Deknatel   Evanston   1942

Ellen Newby and
Lambert Ennis House

The house William Deknatel designed for prominent Northwestern University English literature professor Lambert H. Ennis and his spouse, Ellen Newby Ennis, reflects Deknatel's training at the Taliesin Fellowship. Deknatel—along with his spouse, Geraldine, John H. Howe, and Wesley Peters—was among the charter applicants for membership at Wright's school when it was established in 1932. While in temporary quarters, he and his colleagues worked directly under Wright on construction of the Fellowship buildings.[1] This gave Deknatel hands-on experience with Wright before setting out to establish his own practice.

Garden facade, with doors to living room and dining room.

Deknatel was born in Chicago in 1907 at Hull House, a settlement house where his father was Jane Addams's volunteer secretary-treasurer and his mother a kindergarten teacher. He graduated from Princeton University in 1929, leaving the following year for Paris to attend the École des Beaux-Arts. It was here that he met his spouse Geraldine Eager, an interior design student. The couple returned stateside in 1932, and after spending two years at the Taliesin Fellowship, they returned to Paris in 1934 for two years in André Lurçat's office.

In 1937, Deknatel settled in Chicago and opened his practice. During the 1940s and '50s he designed a number of suburban houses that incorporated both Wrightian

and International Style elements. Geraldine often served as interior designer. William Deknatel's most prominent commission was for Celeste McVoy and Walter J. Kohler Jr., a member of the Kohler family whose company produced bathroom and kitchen fixtures and who served as Governor of Wisconsin from 1951–57. The modern estate house "Windway" in Kohler, Wisconsin was built in 1937–38 and reflects the collaboration with Geraldine for its interiors.[2] In 1939–1940, Deknatel designed *Good Housekeeping*'s "Better Living" House.[3]

Architect's perspective rendering of view from the garden. William Ferguson Deknatel. Lambert H. Ennis House, Evanston, Illinois, Elevations and Section, 1941.

North, street facade with front facing garage and front door beyond.

The design of the Ennis House, which was completed in 1942, bears a strong family resemblance to the Libertyville house Wright designed for Kathryn and Lloyd Lewis (p. 112) two years earlier. These houses of Chicago common brick, wood, and glass both "break the box," with interlocking volumes, several levels, and broad overhangs. But Deknatel designed a house that is distinctly different, suited to its suburban setting. Unlike the Lewis House, which stands adjacent to the Des Plaines River in a rural setting, the Ennis House faces the street in a small subdivision of the former estate of city planner Daniel H. Burnham, with a prominent garage and access from the front door to an office where Professor Ennis could meet with students without having them walk directly into the family living area. The backyard is strictly for family enjoyment, with French doors and bands of tall windows opening onto a raised stone terrace. Light and fresh air are plentiful. As homage to Wright, Deknatel embedded red concrete squares in the sidewalk that leads to the front door.

Accompanied by a photograph of the rear of the house and section drawings, an article on the windows of the Ennis House was featured in *Windows in Modern Architecture*.[4] Because they were hung to the outside face of the house, the outward-swinging casement windows could operate in pairs, each one of a pair closing on the other without need for any fixed vertical meeting rail. This allowed for two-window-wide clear openings.

Even though Wright's influence on the design of the Ennis House was profound, the home's openness, with walls of windows and glazed doors, is also characteristic of the International Style. Deknatel was influenced by his early professional experience in the office of André Lurçat, a French modernist architect who had been a founding member, along with Le Corbusier, Richard Neutra, Adolf Loos, and architectural historian Sigfried Giedion, of the Congrès Internationaux d'Architecture Moderne (CIAM, International Congresses of Modern Architecture). Lurçat's Hotel Nord-Sud in Corsica was shown in 1932 in the *Modern Architecture: International Exhibition* at the Museum of Modern Art.[5]

Study where professor Ennis met with students.

View into living room showing bands of tall windows that fully open.

Kitchen with natural wood cabinets and open storage for pots and pans on the dividing board and cutlery on the side of the island.

The Ennis House was published in the March 1947 issue of *Architectural Forum* in a story titled "Professor's House Features Separate-Access Study for Students."[6] It was also included in an exhibition catalogue on William Deknatel's and Paul Schweikher's architecture, *Architecture in Context: Avant-Garde in Chicago's Suburbs,* published by the Graham Foundation for Advanced Studies in the Fine Arts and the Art Institute of Chicago. The publication accompanied a 1984 exhibition and lecture series at the Foundation's headquarters in the historic Elsa Seipp and Albert F. Madlener House.[7]

Lambert Ennis was a distinguished member of Northwestern's faculty from 1936 until his death in 1954 at age 48. An authority on seventeenth-century English literature and nineteenth-century prose fiction, he was the author of *Thackery: The Sentimental Cynic,* published in 1950. The current owner, Barry Alberts, is a retired attorney and lecturer at the University of Chicago. He and his wife Susie have thoughtfully retained the integrity of the house. —SSB

Adele Bretzfeld and Willard Gidwitz House

Street-facing east facade with 2nd floor overhanging balcony and base walls below made of stone reclaimed from 1888 Victorian house previously on site.

Opposite: Front stair hall with flagstone floor and single stringer staircase with tube and cable railing.

An architect of enormous talent, Ralph Rapson is perhaps best known for the Tyrone Guthrie Theater in Minneapolis (1963), a building as progressive in its architecture as in its productions (now demolished). In Chicago he designed a progressive house for Willard and Adele Gidwitz in Hyde Park housing the University of Chicago and populated with traditional brick masonry houses by distinguished architects including Howard Van Doren Shaw, Henry Ives Cobb, and Benjamin Marshall. But Frank Lloyd Wright's 1909 Robie House, just a few blocks away, was the only nearby residence that had a major effect on him. Rapson stated fifty years later that the presence of Wright's house created pressure on him to "work at that level."[1]

After graduating from the University of Michigan in 1938, Rapson attracted the attention of Eliel Saarinen and was offered a scholarship to attend Cranbrook Academy of Art. While there, he worked in Eliel and Eero Saarinen's office.

When his Cranbrook fellowship ended, Rapson moved to Chicago. Barely making a living, he worked for a short time with Philip Will and picked up side work with George Fred Keck and Paul Schweikher. Rapson also connected with László Moholy-Nagy, who had founded the New Bauhaus in 1937 in the Marshall Field house on Chicago's Prairie Avenue.[2] Moholy-Nagy offered him a part-time job teaching and later made him head of the design curriculum. Visiting lecturers consisted of former Bauhaus colleagues Walter Gropius and Ludwig Mies van der Rohe, MoMA Director Alfred Barr, and architectural historian Sigfried Giedion. In 1941, while in Los Angeles on his honeymoon, Rapson called on Viennese émigré Richard Neutra, whose 1929 Lovell House had been featured in the Museum of

Modern Arts' 1932 *Modern Architecture: International Exhibition*.[3] Visiting several Neutra buildings while being squired around Los Angeles, Rapson was particularly impressed by Neutra's use of glass walls to increase the sense of space, fulfilling the modernist tenet of bringing the outside in.[4] By 1942, when Rapson opened his own office, he had enjoyed personal experience with a number of the country's greatest architectural talents.

Rapson's most important Chicago commission occurred in 1943, when Willard and Adele Gidwitz, members of the family that owned the Helene Curtis hair products and cosmetics company and major collectors of contemporary painting and sculpture, hired him to design a house. They had sought out Rapson as a young modernist architect of promise after attending an architectural exhibit at the Art Institute of Chicago.[5] Rapson brought on John Van Der Meulen, a classmate at the University of Michigan, to work on structural analysis.

The three-story Gidwitz House was a remodeling of an 1888 Victorian, though the alterations were so extensive that the term hardly applies. The foundation and stone chimney were retained and stones forming the first floor porch walls of the old house were recycled to provide facing for the first floor walls of Rapson's modern design— otherwise the building was completely rebuilt.

The dark stone base of the house resembles a hull of a ship; its upper floor spaces recall staterooms opening onto decks. Railings across the front second-floor deck are infilled with canvas panels. The entrance at the stone base is surrounded by large panes of glass that bring the outdoors in, as with Neutra's work. An exterior flagstone path continues inside to the stairhall, visually merging the front terrace with the hall floor. The house is notable for its easy flow between exterior and interior.

The staircase, visible from the front door, has no risers, only treads and steel cable railings that mimic rigging lines passing through wood blocks on a sail boat.

South facade with first floor raised deck and second floor balcony with railings and floor connected by metal panels.

The first floor interior features an open plan with living and dining areas separated by the massive stone fireplace, which is pierced by a rectangular opening that separates two sitting areas. The kitchen was designed with upper cabinets separated from the ceiling by a horizontal band of windows. The lower cabinets appear to float slightly off the floor as a result of a deeply recessed toe kick.

Several years after the house was constructed, Ada Louise Huxtable, then assistant curator in the Department of Architecture at the Museum of Modern Art, wrote to Rapson requesting information on the house for the museum's collection and requesting that Hedrich Blessing take photographs of the house for an upcoming traveling exhibition, "Three Post-War Houses," which circulated around the US and in Canada from 1948 to 1951.[6]

In 1945, at the same time the Gidwitz House was being constructed, Rapson designed Case Study House #4 for John Entenza's program for affordable and innovative postwar housing, only one of two architects who participated from outside California.[7] Rapson's submittal, which he called the "Greenbelt House" because of its park-like interior, measured 1,800 square feet and, unlike the others, was intended for an urban lot located between existing structures. With a nod to the era's fascination with futuristic modes of travel, Rapson drew a hovering helicopter piloted by a husband waving to his wife, who was below hanging clothes on the line. The house was published but not built.

Rapson moved to Cambridge, Massachusetts in 1946, setting up a practice and becoming an assistant professor at the School of Architecture and Planning at the Massachusetts Institute of Technology. In 1951, he was hired by the US State Department to design several embassies in Western Europe in collaboration with

Kitchen with cabinets that appear to float and large window facing back yard.

Living room with stone fireplace with rectangular opening located between two sitting areas.

John van der Meulen. Rapson served as Dean of the School of Architecture at the University of Minnesota between 1954 and 1984 and continued in private practice, designing numerous single-family homes, until his death, at age 94, in 2008.

Rian and Leon Walker purchased the Gidwitz House in 2003 and later visited Rapson, who provided sketches, work papers, and historic photos to them. Eager to restore the house at the time, Leon Walker comments upon reflection, "From the first moment when I toured the home, I knew that I could see my way to a satisfying end."[8] —SSB

Henry P. Glass   Northfield   1948

Eleanor Knopp and Henry P. Glass House

The passive solar house that industrial designer Henry P. Glass designed for his family of four, though relatively modest in size, included numerous innovative and practical space-saving features for a comfortable, efficient daily life and frequent entertaining.

Glass was born in 1911 in Vienna and reared by financially comfortable parents who admired art and architecture and had a taste for fine furniture.[1] Trained as an architect and engineer, his professional heroes included Viennese Secessionist architects Otto Wagner and Adolf Loos and Bauhaus directors Walter Gropius and Ludwig Mies van der Rohe.[2] When he finished his master's degree in architecture in 1936, Glass's first commissions were for private homes and interiors.

Glass had been arrested by the Nazis in 1938 and imprisoned at Dachau and Buchenwald. His spouse Eleanor (Elly), with the help of a lawyer uncle, convinced the Gestapo to release him. Once freed, Henry left for New York and arrived in early 1939; Elly soon followed. Although he knew little English, his portfolio of drawings spoke for itself, and industrial designer Gilbert Rohde hired Glass to work on pavilions for the 1939 New York World's Fair and to assist on design detailing for

Patio adjacent to large Thermopane windows with louvers for cross ventilation that could be closed by wood panels.

Opposite: Front of house showing butterfly roof. Eaves are angled to take advantage of sun angle to provide passive solar heat in the winter.

140

the Herman Miller furniture company. Glass also designed wrought iron "hair-pin" patio furniture for Russel Wright's American Way design program.

When work became scarce in New York after Pearl Harbor was attacked in December 1941, Glass moved to Chicago and found a job with the Stensgaard Display Company where he designed merchandising displays, exhibits, and store layouts as well as furniture for low-cost defense housing. Glass adapted to wartime material shortages by designing furniture from materials deemed non-essential for the war effort like plywood and Masonite that collapsed for storage, nested for more economical shipping, and often served multiple purposes.[3] He also designed

projects for the armed forces such as devices for cockpits in Navy fighter planes and Army camouflage kits. In 1946, he opened his own studio in the American Furniture Mart building for his industrial design and architectural practice.[4]

Glass attended night classes at the Institute of Design taught by architect George Fred Keck, who was then building passive solar houses. These new ideas inspired Glass to design his own passive solar home. He utilized large Thermopane windows spanning the entire south wall at the back of the house; broad angled eaves were designed to take advantage of the angle of winter sunlight and provide shade in the summer. Beneath the windows, louvers with interior screens for cross-ventilation could be closed by wood panels. Black asphalt tile flooring absorbed heat on the interior.

Multipurpose living space opening onto patio.

Glass focused on functionality in his family home. The main living area consisted of a living-dining space and kitchen. Three bedrooms, bathrooms, and a sewing room for Elly, a trained dressmaker, completed the floor plan. The house included space-saving built-ins, flexible movable furniture, and storage units that served as room dividers. The dining area included an opening for serving food from the kitchen to the dining table and a pass-through for serving from the kitchen to the patio picnic table. A living room cabinet swung open to become a bar for their frequent guests. A movie screen and audio speaker were embedded in the wall between the kitchen and the living-dining area, and a radio chassis and projector were built into the living room cabinets.

In the 1960s, Glass closed his American Furniture Mart studio and added a wing that included a drafting room, his office, a reception area, and a garage; its basement functioned as a display gallery for his work.

Sitting area showing movable furniture and multiuse built ins.

Henry P. Glass taught industrial design as a professor at the School of the Art Institute of Chicago from 1946–68, while leading an active product design practice that often focused on reducing waste in manufacturing. Glass received more than fifty mechanical and design patents. He credited Buckminster Fuller as the most significant influence on his career as a designer.[5] —SSB

Florence Pass and Erne Frueh House I and II

Robert Bruce Tague studied at the Armour Institute of Technology's School of Architecture (at the time it offered a joint Beaux-Arts defined program with the Art Institute of Chicago) where he earned his bachelor's in 1934 and his Master of Science in Architecture in 1935. Although Ludwig Mies van der Rohe did not radically conceptualize the curriculum until shortly after his arrival in 1938 (Armour would change to Illinois Institute of Technology in 1940), architecture students were exposed to new ideas through the 1933–34 Century of Progress exposition which showcased the work of some of Chicago's progressive architects including George Fred Keck who designed the House of Tomorrow (1933) and Crystal House (1934). Discussing his education, Tague later stated: "I was a rebel. I was a modernist.

Frueh House I in winter with rear patio.

Opposite: Frueh House II rear elevation with modular elements.

I didn't do their [Beaux-Arts] thing. In fifth year, Ray Schwab and I were teaching as assistant critics in the junior class, and we took over and really went to work with the guys. It was a pretty good class. For this one project, the dimensions were sent on to New York for national jury. Armour rated better than they had in years."[1] Tague completed his thesis under Keck's direction.[2]

Between 1949 and 1959, Florence and Erne R. Frueh, who had two daughters, commissioned two modernist houses (both of which are unfortunately no longer extant) in Highland Park. The first house was designed by Robert Bruce Tague, and the second was designed by Crombie Taylor in collaboration with Tague. Florence

trained as a classical pianist and Erne trained as a historian at the University of Chicago where they met. Mr. Frueh found employment in the textile manufacturing business.[3] Together, they cultivated a passion for the arts and an expertise for the history of art glass that culminated in an important coauthored book entitled *Chicago Stained Glass*.[4]

For Frueh House I, Tague designed a one-story, wood-clad L-shaped house that wrapped around a generous patio with mature trees. An understated street facade (with its one-car garage) clad in horizontal cedar boards deploys a continuous band of clerestory windows in the place of conventional picture windows to allow

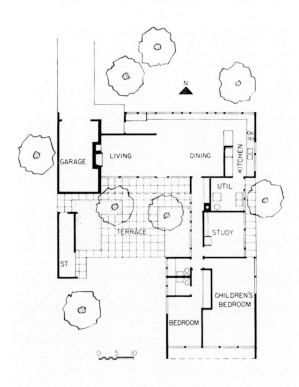

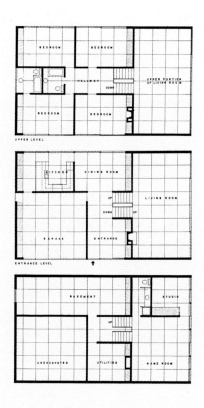

light to enter while maintaining privacy from the street. The only concession to spatial complexity in this otherwise restrained house is the double-height living room flanked with abundant glass on both sides (floor-to-ceiling on one side and clerestory on the other). Tague, like his colleagues of the Keck & Keck firm, brings together cues from Frank Lloyd Wright's Usonians—in particular referencing the street facade of Jacobs House I (1937) in Madison, Wisconsin—with Mies-inspired one-story pavilion simplicity. Upon reflection after many years in practice, Tague referred to the Frueh House as his most successful project.[5] The house received favorable reception in the architectural press shortly after

Frueh House I from street.

House I Plans in *Architectural Record* (November 1954).

House II plans.

it was completed in *Architectural Record* and was later included in the *Chicago Architects* exhibition and catalogue of 1976.[6]

A decade later the Fruehs commissioned Crombie Taylor, an architect who trained outside of Chicago but was an instructor and former acting director of the Institute of Design at IIT, to design a second, more spacious house on a different site, a prestigious lot with views to Lake Michigan and lakefront access.[7] Tague and Taylor connected as instructors at the Institute of Design, and Tague went on to be associated periodically with Taylor's practice for nearly a decade.[8] Although Taylor identified as a modern architect, he was equally interested in the recent

past, as evidenced by spearheading the groundbreaking restoration work of Adler & Sullivan's Chicago Auditorium Building (opened in 1889) during the mid 1950s.[9] Taylor shared many interests with Florence and Erne Frueh whose glass collecting increased beginning in the 1950s.[10] Frueh House II was an elegant two-story, Japanese temple-like brick-clad house with a gently pitched overhanging roof, with visual structural elements, and featured a below-grade level that hosted a studio and game room. The serene and sparsely furnished double-height living room relies on sliding glass doors that resemble *shoji* screens to frame the view of the wooded site.

The Tiffany lamps that hang in the dining room reflect the Fruehs's interest in historic glass that they shared with Taylor, who was also a collector and connoisseur. Taylor juxtaposed historic artifacts and art with modern and contemporary design. A. James Speyer—Mies's first graduate student in 1939—continued this approach with his apartment at Pearson Street (1965).[11] Frueh House II blends modernism with an interest in the "minimalism" of Japanese aesthetics, especially as it relates to the framing of nature from within the interior space. Recall that a year later, photographer Yasuhiro Ishimoto—a Japanese American who studied with Harry M. Callahan and Aaron Siskind at IIT's Institute of Design graduating in 1951—enlisted the support of architects Walter Gropius and Kenzo Tange to introduce his photographic essay about Katsura, the Imperial Villa in Kyoto.[12] Together with the Fruehs, Taylor embodied the ideal of progressive modernists who valued history and above all beauty over ideology, complexity over conformity.

Despite the architectural quality and the contributions to the arts of its owners, both of these houses were demolished: Frueh I in 2006 (after it had been listed as threatened by Docomomo US/Chicago) and Frueh II prior to 2006.[13] Their prestigious Highland Park address, and the modest footprints of both houses made them an easy target for profit-driven developers before the 2008 real-estate collapse. —MS

149

Maggie Sheahan and Le Roy Binkley House

Le Roy Binkley graduated from the Illinois Institute of Technology in 1944, during the years that Ludwig Mies van der Rohe was director of the architecture department. Mies's influence was profound; around the time construction was completed on the Farnsworth House, Roy Binkley built his own house, which his daughter Lisa Binkley Brunke aptly described as a "glass box," even with its two storeys.[1]

The 3,100-square-foot house that Roy Binkley built—for his spouse at the time Maggie Sheahan and their family—was an anomaly in historic Long Grove, an area settled by German immigrants in the middle of the nineteenth century and still farmland when Binkley purchased his five-acre site. Farmhouses and revival-style country houses were scattered throughout Lake County. The only other modern house in the area belonged to Binkley's business partner Dennis Blair, who had been a Fellow at Taliesin and whose work evolved from the Wrightian rather than Miesian tradition. Binkley had worked in the office of Paul Schweikher, who was also very much influenced by Wright.[2]

Sited at the edge of a hill, the approach from the driveway reveals the house as an almost solid wall, except for a plate glass opening next to the front entrance.

Two-story south facade with glazed modular openings warming the interior through solar gain and providing views of the countryside.

Detail of south-facing glass walls on first and second floors.

It appears to be only a single story. From the opposite vantage point it becomes evident that the house stands two storeys high. This southern facade features large floor-to-ceiling modular glass panels, so that all the interior spaces had unobstructed prairie views. A deep exterior overhang was positioned to permit solar gain in the winter and provide shade in the summer to both the upper floor, with four bedrooms and a bathroom, and the lower floor, with living, dining, and kitchen areas. The living room, a large open space, doubled as Brinkley's studio where he worked with draftsmen. Brick flooring on the lower level conveyed radiant heat. Binkley's daughter, Lisa Brunke, recalls that the house even on cold days became very hot.[3]

Roy Binkley never received the recognition achieved by many of his contemporaries even though he designed many elegant modern houses on Chicago's North Shore. He also designed modern houses near Weston, Connecticut where his sister Ann had lived.[4] Roy Binkley designed the Helen Lesser and Gene Federico House (1950) in Pound Ridge, New York.[5] He designed a house for Ernest Herrmann (1957) in Westport, Connecticut, which was purchased in 1975 by Winston and Ruby C. Allen; it was listed on the National Register of Historic Places in 2010 as the Allen House.[6] Roy Binkley had houses published, including his own, in *Arts & Architecture*. His house is extant.[7] —SSB

Bruce Goff   Aurora   1950

Ruth van Sickle and
Albert Sam Ford House

As the Century of Progress International Exposition was wrapping up in 1934, architect Bruce Alonzo Goff moved to the Chicagoland city of Park Ridge to work with artist Alfonso Iannelli. Goff's time in Chicago, from 1934–42, coincided with a highly productive time in his life during which he combined teaching with architectural practice.[1] Although the commission for the Ford House came after Goff moved away, he had made the acquaintance of Ruth van Sickle during his time as an instructor at the Chicago Academy of Fine Arts.

Ruth van Sickle Ford, an artist and former President-Director of the Chicago Academy of Fine Arts from 1937–60, worked in Chicago but chose to live in her

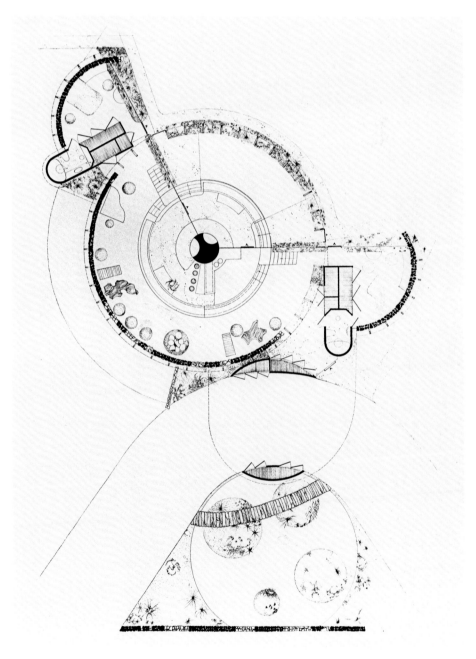

hometown of Aurora with her family.[2] Aurora is a city located to the west of Chicago on the CB&Q rail line and is traversed by the Fox River. Her spouse, Albert "Sam" Ford, was a civil engineer, and they had one daughter, Barbara. Goff's remarkable design for the single-family house combines modern building technologies with organic materiality and spatial articulation.

The Ford House occupies an acre lot in the Country Club Estates subdivision of Aurora. A monumental central dome 166 feet in circumference (partially clad in shingles on the exterior) defines the common living area flanked by two quarter-domes that contain bedrooms. The center of the dome encompasses the living,

kitchen, and dining areas, characterized by a central and circular hearth ("pit") with both interior and exterior usage. A mezzanine provided Ruth van Sickle Ford with a painting studio accessible to an exterior terrace. Goff combined modern materials such as standardized Quonset ribs and plate glass with Cannel-coal perimeter masonry walls embedded with glass cullets. Don Tosi, Goff's former student and employee, built the house.

Featured in the *Life* magazine article "The Round House," the Ford House is described as a "Quonset-hut mansion." The house has also been described as the Umbrella House, the Coal House, and Mushroom House.[3]

Outdoor section (balcony and dining) screened by Quonset ribs.

Opposite top: Second-story artist studio.

Opposite bottom: Living area with daughter, Barbara, in sunken living area, *LIFE* (March 19, 1951).

During the mid-1980s, Sidney K. Robinson—an educator, architectural historian, and architect—purchased the house.[4] Since then, Robinson has written extensively about the house and embarked on the restoration of various components.[5] It was listed on the National Register of Historic Places in 2016.[6] The Ford House received the 2019 Landmarks Illinois Richard H. Driehaus Foundation Preservation Awards for Stewardship.[7] —MS

Marian Short and
Stanley G. Harris Jr. House

A. James Speyer designed a relatively small number of houses. His career path led him, instead, to serve as curator of twentieth-century painting and sculpture at the Art Institute of Chicago beginning in 1961.[1] Prior to that time, he studied architecture at the Chelsea Polytechnique in London and the Sorbonne in Paris. In 1939, at age 26, Speyer enrolled at the Illinois Institute of Technology (IIT), a year after Ludwig Mies van der Rohe became its director of architecture, and was his first graduate student. In 1946, after serving in World War II, Speyer returned to IIT to teach architectural design under Mies. In an interview not long before his death, Speyer reiterated his admiration for Mies and the curriculum he introduced.[2]

Steel frame exterior with glazed panels forming exterior walls.

Dining area of living-dining space with exterior red brick knee wall.

Living area with drapery separating it from dining space. Fireplace incorporated into curved teak wall.

After returning to Chicago, Speyer designed a very handsome house of steel, brick, and glass in Glencoe for banker Stanley G. Harris Jr. and Marian Short Harris, his spouse at the time; it is no longer extant. It consisted of two connected one-story wings—one for living-dining, a large universal space, and the other to accommodate bedrooms. Mies's structuralist approach, as interpreted by Speyer, was immediately evident; the exterior of the house was a steel and glass grid painted, like the Farnsworth House, white. But Speyer personalized Mies's influence. Brick infill was deep red rather than cream-colored as in the Mies-designed IIT campus buildings. On the interior, the home's most notable feature was a curving wall that incorporated a fireplace. It terminated in a track that allowed the dining area to be curtained off. The wall was of teak, reminiscent of Mies's use of Macassar ebony, a similarly opulent material, to surround the dining area of the Tugendhat House in Brno.

Speyer's curatorial career included major exhibitions on the work of Constantin Brancusi, Jean Dubuffet, Alberto Giacometti, Henry Matisse, and Mies. James Wood, the Art Institute's director, summed up Speyer's professional contributions to Chicago, "He was a product and a primary source of what we see as Modern, and he realized it as an architect, a curator, and in his lifestyle."[3] —SSB

Wilhelmina Plansoen and Edward Dart House I

The first house Edward [née Edouard Dupaquier] Dart designed for his own family is characteristic of the home that young marrieds with modern ideas but not much money would build as a "starter house." The design fostered a simple, informal way of life. Unlike the ubiquitous Cape Cods that were built during the 1950s, there were no references to history. Prevalent modernist ideas—the use of natural materials, with interior and exterior detailing based on abstract geometry—governed the design of this flat-roofed house.

"Ned" (the nickname used by family and close friends) Dart married Wilhelmina Cornelia Plansoen in 1946. Wilma had graduated from Duke University and had been accepted at Columbia for a Master in Social Work, but World War II changed her plans.[1] To Wilma and Ned, the house was a dream. Their first home was a rented room on the second floor of an old house they called "Dirty Ida's" and their second a Quonset hut they lived in while Dart was attending the Yale School of Architecture.[2]

Edward Dart enjoyed the building process but had not thought about architecture as a career until after serving in World War II, during which he spent leisure time painting and drawing. At that point, he decided he would either be a commercial artist or architect, but another circumstance may have influenced his ultimate decision. His sister Susan was married to the grandson of architect Howard Van Doren Shaw, whom he met while stationed at Great Lakes Naval Base. After completing his service, Dart entered Yale.[3]

Dart's design philosophy first developed at Yale where many eminent modernists were visiting professors. They included Marcel Breuer, Richard Neutra, Pietro

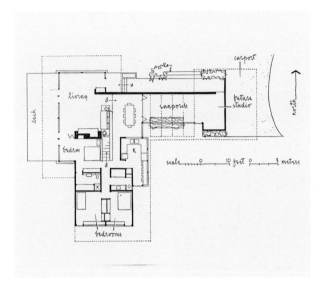

Opposite: Open cantilevered porch off of living room and bedroom, creating a raised outdoor living space.

Floor plan showing combined living room, dining room, and kitchen.

Exterior with carport on right and screen porch connecting to kitchen and bedroom wing.

Belluschi, Louis Kahn, Eero Saarinen, Edward Durell Stone, and Paul Schweikher. Following his 1949 Yale graduation, Dart briefly worked in New York for Stone, but ultimately settled in the Chicago area, where he took a job with Paul Schweikher at his studio in Roselle.[4] Edward Dart admired Schweikher—and his house—enormously.[5] The natural redwood, built-ins, Chicago brick fireplaces, walls of glass, and informal plan were impressive and conducive to the casual living that Dart would seek for the design of his own home.

After taking Dart to his interview with Schweikher, his sister Susan drove him to Frank Lloyd Wright's Lewis House (p. 112), a Usonian design in Libertyville. Dart was impressed and asked to see more of Wright's houses on the North Shore; and they set out for Wright's Prairie School houses dating from the early 1900s. After driving past the Cecelia Berry and Ward W. Willits House in Highland Park (1902) and going into the Cora L. and William A. Glasner House in Glencoe (1905), Dart wanted to go to Taliesin in Spring Green, Wisconsin, to meet Wright, which they did. Although Wright did not treat him graciously and the meeting was brief, Dart was entranced.[6] Wright's influence was heartfelt. In the design of his own home, Dart was inspired by the vocabulary of Wright's Lewis House, more relevant to its time than Wright's earlier Prairie houses.

What set the Dart House apart from typical 1950s houses was the manner in which Dart's superb design created a comfortable way of living. It was small, consisting of living room, kitchen-dining area, and three small bedrooms. Susan Dart described the one-story house as cozy.[7] On the exterior, the use of warm-hued natural materials—vertical wood boards and rose-colored Chicago brick—complemented the home's natural setting. On the interior, wood boards formed the ceiling; brick walls and wood built-ins divided the living areas.

Vast expanses of glass created a close relationship between the interior and exterior. A cantilevered deck extends from the living room. Protected by a deep overhang, the deck becomes an outdoor room to lounge and enjoy the surrounding countryside. Bedrooms had Dutch doors to the exterior. The screen porch features an interior sandbox and planting bed mirroring an exterior path and flower garden.

The interior was furnished inexpensively with canvas director's chairs, ladder-back chairs painted black, and a wood table that Dart designed and made of plain unstained wood with a hand-rubbed finish and butterfly inserts of walnut.

The house was published in a 1955 issue of *Progressive Architecture* with a four-page spread of Hedrich Blessing photographs.[8]

Bedroom with brick fireplace on other side of living room fireplace; double doors to patio.

Brick fireplace wall, living room.

Screen porch, with interior sandbox and planting bed mirroring exterior path and garden.

As Edward Dart's career grew, he designed two other houses for his family in the Barrington area, each progressively larger and more complex. In 1956, he built a concrete and glass split-level house, with flat roofs, glazed walls, and a prominent stone chimney. The house was published in *House and Garden* and *Architectural Record*.[9] In 1964, Dart purchased ten acres and built a multi-level house of common brick on the foundations of an old barn.

Edward Dart had a notable career. Having opened his office in 1951, he practiced independently for fourteen years. During that time, he designed eighty-eight buildings. In 1965, he joined the prominent Chicago firm of Loebl, Schlossman, and Bennett as a partner (which was then renamed Loebl, Schlossman, Bennett, & Dart), and in 1967 he was elected a Fellow of the American Institute of Architects. Many of his early commissions were houses, but he designed a variety of building types. Most of the accolades he received came for his beautiful human-scaled churches. He is particularly remembered for St. Procopius Abbey in Lisle, completed in 1970, which is considered one of his most notable designs. In 1970, he served as principal architect for Chicago's Water Tower Place on North Michigan Avenue. Dart died unexpectedly in 1975 at only fifty-three and is interred in the columbarium at St. Michael's Episcopal Church in Barrington—his first church commission.[10] —SSB

Ludwig Mies van der Rohe   Plano   1951

Edith Farnsworth House

The iconic glass-and-steel house designed by Ludwig Mies van der Rohe for Dr. Edith Farnsworth is among the most written about and photographed twentieth-century residential buildings. Architects of different generations in Chicago and beyond have adapted its combination of rigor and beauty by looking to principles rather than merely imitating form or technique. The reasons behind this enduring interest are interconnected: awe for the intrinsic architectural qualities and its out-of-the-ordinary response to site, as well as the controversial client-architect relationship that has generated intrigue among generalists and specialized observers.[1]

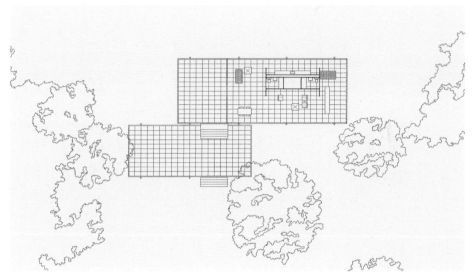

This single-story, free-standing pavilion was designed as a weekend retreat for Farnsworth, a Chicago-based medical researcher specializing in the study of kidneys, for a 62-acre site on the banks of the Fox River in Plano, a small city 60 miles west of Chicago.[2] Insofar as it was a house commissioned by a cultivated and nonconformist woman, she has generated interest among historians seeking to bring visibility to the fundamental role that women played during the twentieth century in shaping modern architecture and design.[3]

These contributions have also countered a barrage of unflattering characterizations of Farnsworth contained in first- and second-hand accounts over the years, articulated and shared mostly by men. Recall for example Lord Peter Palumbo, who purchased the house from Farnsworth in 1972, and who referred to her as a "difficult" and "ferocious" woman.[4] The first to come to Farnsworth's defense after she complained about the inadequacies of the house was Elizabeth Gordon, in an article entitled "The Threat to the Next America," published in the April 1953 issue of *House Beautiful,* the magazine she edited: "I have talked to a highly intelligent, now disillusioned, woman who spent more than $70,000 building a 1-room house that is nothing but a glass cage on stilts."[5]

In an *Architectural Forum* feature entitled "Houses—Architect & Client" published in 1951 shortly after Hedrich Blessing took the first series of photographs of the

Farnsworth House after completion, the writer observes that "Mies van der Rohe's house … is *modern* and *classical;* he has embraced industry, translated the steel skeleton frame into a house 'language,' provided impersonal but beautiful space to be personally arranged by those willing to live in the modern equivalent of the Doric order."[6] The writer then discusses differences between the Farnsworth and Philip Johnson's Glass House in New Canaan, Connecticut, describing the Glass House as "symmetrically balanced" and the Farnsworth House as "asymmetrical, dynamically balanced."[7] Unlike Johnson who painted the structural elements dark grey, Mies's choice of white painted steel echoes classical architecture while allowing for contrast with the surrounding nature throughout most of the seasons except after a winter snowfall. Unlike the Glass House, which rests on the ground, the Farnsworth's eight-inch wide-flanged white painted steel columns sustain both the ceiling plane and the floor, which is elevated five feet from the ground to accommodate the flood threshold of the Fox River; the historic measurements are now unreliable.[8] The elevation of the house confers an otherworldly dimension as it floats above the meadow. In addition to responding to the floodplain, Mies strategically sited the house in proximity to the monumental black sugar maple tree in order to exploit the shading capabilities of this "natural" architecture. These two responses to siting conditions alone speak to an architect who reacts to specific cues, despite the abstraction typically associated with the International Style that some critics claimed deprived architecture of a site-specific quality.

Living area with fireplace and central core clad with Primavera wood panels.

Galley kitchen, with steel countertop and base cabinets.

Unlike Johnson's frontal symmetrical entrance, the Farnsworth is accessed indirectly through a side entrance at the covered porch that is reached by way of the terrace and steps. The open-plan configuration (only the two bathrooms and utilities are concealed in the primavera wood-clad freestanding core flanked by a galley kitchen, "bedroom," and a living and dining area) confers a sense of airiness that is further reinforced by the unobstructed views on all sides of the rectangular floor plan. In the living area the hearth, as in most of Wright houses, plays a central role. Through a magisterial contrast of smooth and hard modern materials such as glass and steel, contrasted in part by the organic qualities of the travertine floor, Mies sets up a relationship with nature that is simultaneously deferential and participatory. The constant change of seasons made visible through the floor-to-ceiling glass "walls" ensures that the experience of this architectural space is always different for inhabitants and visitors alike.

The Edith Farnsworth House is one of three extant houses by Mies in America including the Isabella Gardner and Robert Hall McCormick III House in Elmhurst, Illinois (1952, p. 184) and the Rose Drapkin and Morris Greenwald House in Weston, Connecticut (1955; renovation and expansion completed by Peter Gluck in 1992). The Farnsworth House opened to the public in 2004, and is one of only three modern houses that belong to the portfolio of the National Trust for Historic

Porch seen from under Black Sugar Maple, Fox River bank side.

Primary entrance from covered porch into living and dining area.

Preservation sites together with the Glass House (1949; opened to the public in 2007) and Marcel Breuer's house in the Museum Garden designed for a MoMA exhibition (1949), which was relocated to Kykuit, the Rockefeller Estate in Sleepy Hollow, New York. Public access to Mies-designed houses in Plano and Elmhurst has done much to broaden awareness of his American domestic architecture among general and specialized audiences. Although the elevated piers confer a magical quality to the Farnsworth and often protect it from seasonal rising waters, the Fox River continues to threaten the very existence of this modernist master-piece that has already suffered damage from flooding in the past. The black sugar maple tree adjacent to the Farnsworth featured in so many photographs was removed in 2013 due to the risks to the house associated with its declining health. A new tree, propagated from the original by the Morton Arboretum in Chicago, has recently been planted so that future generations might enjoy it once it grows to maturity. —MS

Rachel Brin and Ralph Helstein House

The Helstein House is an anomaly among Chicago's midcentury modern houses.[1] Architect Bertrand "Bud" Goldberg designed it using the concepts of structural concrete associated with the concrete houses of Le Corbusier. The design is unique in a city with modern houses generally influenced by Wright's organicism or Mies's steel-and-glass structuralism. Its minimalist structure consists of concrete slabs supported by eight cylindrical concrete columns, their formwork expressed on the exterior. Inset glass panels punctuated by vertical strips of operable awning windows fill the area between the columns, allowing the refinement of steel and glass to provide a counterpoint to the brute surfaces of the concrete.

East-facing view of house from street; house located at back corner of the lot.

Opposite: Floor plans.

In 1933, Goldberg attended the Bauhaus at its third and final German location in Berlin. It was here, at the avant-garde school of design, that the American student absorbed a dedication to clarity of design and an industrial aesthetic that preferred modern materials. Goldberg's use of structural concrete in the Helstein House foreshadows his later exploration of the material's plastic nature in his iconic Marina City (1963–67), Prentice Women's Hospital (1975; demolished), and River City (1986).[2] The cylindrical forms used as supports in the Helstein House seem to have evolved into the cylindrical towers at Marina City and the Raymond Hilliard Center (1966), built as low-cost public housing.

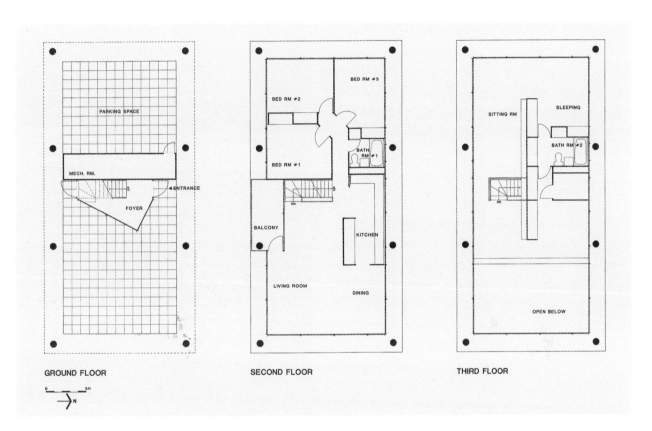

GROUND FLOOR

SECOND FLOOR

THIRD FLOOR

Goldberg had grown up in the Hyde Park neighborhood where the Helstein's new house was to be sited, a section of Chicago populated historically by independent thinkers and characterized by stellar examples of progressive architecture. To quote Tim Samuelson, Chicago's official Cultural Historian, "people who live in Hyde Park and Kenwood have never been afraid to speak their minds or, when they build, to raise eyebrows."[3] In addition to the iconic Prairie School Robie House (1910) by Frank Lloyd Wright, examples cited by Samuelson include poet Robert Herrick's house by Hugh M. G. Garden (1900), St. Thomas the Apostle Church by Barry Byrne (1924), the modern three-flat Keck-Gottschalk-Keck Apartments for University of Chicago professor Louis Gottschalk and architects George Fred and William Keck, designed by the Keck brothers (1937), and the Helstein House by Goldberg (1951). The latter took the form it did because architect and client were in sync with one another. Both were progressive thinkers: Goldberg was a modernist whose ideas were original and thoughtfully conceived, and the Helsteins had established themselves as social activists.

Ralph and Rachel had grown up in Minnesota, a state with a progressive political tradition of Farm-Laborites, but lived in Minneapolis, which in the 1930s and '40s had a strong anti-Semitic bias where Jewish people were routinely denied work, housing, community, and membership in service clubs.[4] Feeling a desire to help people, in 1942, Ralph Helstein began as general counsel for the Chicago-based United Packinghouse Workers of America (UPWA), which had become a predominantly African American organization.[5] Four years later he was elected its president and fought discrimination, leading the 100,000-member union to strike for increased wages; and they won. Rachel Brin Helstein, a graduate of the University of Chicago, had been an invited observer at the San Francisco founding of the United Nations in 1945 as President of the National Council of Jewish Women.[6] Goldberg designed, with input from the Helsteins, a thoroughly modern house, but one that aptly met the family's functional and social needs.[7]

The slab-and-column concrete construction of the Helstein House resembles Le Corbusier's 1914 Maison Dom-Ino that consisted of three rectangular concrete slabs connected by six square concrete columns. The Swiss-French architect's design allowed for a flexible floor plan and infinite expandability. When laid out horizontally, it became row houses; when stacked vertically, it morphed into a high-rise. The design incorporated a staircase, but no longer dependent on any particular location associated with engineering restrictions. With the prototype in mind, Bertrand Goldberg had the opportunity to build a skeleton of a house, something he had always wanted to do, while adapting it for the functional needs of the Helsteins.[8]

On the interior, rooms are oriented vertically as well as horizontally. A suspended steel staircase set within a glazed vestibule and incorporated within the frame of the building leads to the upstairs living space. The main floor accommodates three bedrooms, the kitchen, and living-dining area. Above is a master suite with bedroom and sitting area. A concrete screen-block balcony encloses a mezzanine overlooking the double-height living room. An outdoor terrace, also set inside the home's concrete framework, provides sheltered outdoor living space, making the area usable even in rain.

View from mezzanine toward two-story living-dining area.

Suspended staircase from ground level vestibule to upstairs living space.

Living room with mezzanine and
concrete screen-block balcony.

Goldberg's buildings express a commitment to technology influenced by the time he spent at the Bauhaus working under director Ludwig Mies van der Rohe. When he accompanied Mies, on his 1937 trip to Taliesin in Spring Green, Wisconsin, Goldberg met Frank Lloyd Wright and closely experienced his work. But Goldberg remained "lukewarm" about Wright's architecture: rather, he preferred the approach of industrialization and standardization that typified much European

Top floor sitting area.

modernism.[9] Goldberg explained, "Architecturally speaking, I never parted ways with Mies," meaning from "the discipline of creating an aesthetic out of the structure, the discipline of seeking an alliance with an industrial world."[10] That said, he veered from Mies's preference for orthogonal lines in exploring circular forms. Throughout his career, Goldberg experimented with new artistic approaches rather than refining a more singular path.

Goldberg's design for the Helstein House looked as radical as Mies van der Rohe's steel-and-glass Farnsworth House (p. 162), completed the same year. Their settings, however, could hardly have been more different. Mies's 1951 modern weekend home for Dr. Edith Farnsworth stands in a bucolic setting on the Fox River, whereas Goldberg's home for the Helsteins is sited in a historic urban neighborhood surrounded by nineteenth-century houses and brick apartment buildings. The Helstein House is still standing.

Over the years the Helstein home would welcome union leaders and civil rights activists.[11] As president of the UPWA from 1946–68, Helstein was widely recognized for his social activism. Illinois Union leader Robert Gibson describes Helstein as "a great intellectual in the labor movement" who "spent his whole lifetime working on behalf of the poor and underprivileged in our society."[12] In 1974, Helstein was honoree of the year at Chicago's annual Eugene V. Debs Dinner.

Helstein was a strong civil rights advocate and supporter of Dr. Martin Luther King Jr. His union contributed financially to the Southern Christian Leadership Conference (SCLC), and, in 1965, he personally marched in Selma with Dr. King. Helstein and a group of colleagues met with King once a month in New York to confer on policy decisions.[13] Dr. King inscribed a copy of his book *Where Do We Go From Here: Chaos or Community?:* "To my dear friend Ralph Helstein, for whom I have great respect and admiration and whose support I cherish very deeply, [signed] Martin."[14] —SSB

Frank Lloyd Wright   Hampshire   1951

Elizabeth Castle and Robert Muirhead Farmhouse

The Muirhead family, who were among the earliest settlers of Kane County, had farmed hundreds of acres there since 1860. By the mid-1940s, Robert, Elizabeth, and their five children had outgrown their old three-bedroom farmhouse. Robert and Elizabeth Muirhead needed a new farmhouse and dreamed that Frank Lloyd Wright would design it.

In 1948, they made their first visit to Taliesin. There they broached the idea of hiring Wright to design a home to accommodate their young family and serve as farm headquarters. Wright told the Muirheads that if they would write to him detailing their requirements, he would "see what he could do."[1] Mrs. Muirhead stated their budget as $24,000 plus the architect's fee and that her husband would like to do some of the work himself. In the end, there were cost overruns, but the Muirheads raised their spending limit in order to realize their dream.

Farmhouse and barn, 2015.

Opposite: Robert Muirhead Jr. along with his four sisters: Jean, Margaret, Ruth, and Mary.

The Muirheads were clients who did their homework. Mrs. Muirhead's letter to Wright was detailed and included snapshots and a sketch plan of their eight hundred gently rolling acres to help Wright generate a site plan. After figuring the cost of a stone house would be prohibitive, she wrote that their next choice would be common brick and cypress or redwood and that they might be able to get a good price on brick. They had seen photos of the interior of Wright's 1939 Kathryn Dougherty and Lloyd Lewis House (p. 112) in *Architectural Forum* and had driven to Libertyville, where they observed the exterior.[2] The Muirheads had also visited the second Usonian house Wright had designed in 1946 for the Herbert and Katherine Jacobs near Madison, Wisconsin, and shared their admiration of it with Wright.

Robert and Elizabeth Muirhead wanted separate living and dining rooms, to accommodate in part the unique requirements relating to farmstead use. The farmhands needed a place to wash up for meals somewhere near the back door. Wright designed a one-story linear Usonian spanning 180 feet, with a wing of children's bedrooms, a living room, and master bedroom in the core of the house and, accessed by an enclosed breezeway, the dining room, kitchen, and workroom for office and farmhand use.[3] The living room had a retractable screen for watching movies. Storage was a requested necessity—mainly for cooking equipment, sewing supplies, and bulk food items.

The Muirhead's home continues to accommodate farm and family needs. Owners Michael and Sarah Petersdorf, the Muirhead's granddaughter, have lovingly restored the home's chimneys, woodwork, brick walls, concrete floor (with radiant heat), and mechanicals. The house is open for public tours on specific dates by appointment.[4] —SSB

Doris Curry and Jacques Brownson House

Jacques Calmon Brownson has received praise for his civic buildings, especially as chief architect of the award-winning Chicago Civic Center (1965, renamed Richard J. Daley Center in 1976) during his time with C. F. Murphy Associates.[1] In the 1990s, Paul Gapp, architecture critic at the *Chicago Tribune,* listed it among the city's ten most important postwar works of architecture.[2]

Jacques Brownson started his undergraduate professional degree at IIT in 1941, shortly after the arrival of Ludwig Mies van der Rohe as the new director in 1938. Brownson acquired experience in the design-build process very early when his father agreed to build and sell a house with Brownson as apprentice builder in

View from woods of house with glass-enclosed living area on the right (above).

Opposite top: House under construction with steel structural frame.

Opposite bottom: Ground floor plan (IIT, MS thesis, June 1954).

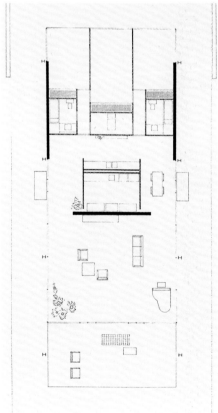

order to pay for his architectural education with profits from the sale.[3] Although the war intervened, upon his return to Chicago after serving with the US Army Corps of Engineers (from 1943–46), Brownson re-enrolled at IIT and in 1947 was awarded the opportunity to participate in the Build-It-Yourself House initiative sponsored by *Popular Mechanics* magazine.[4] Published in both the April and May issues of the magazine, the "modified Cape Cod" house that twenty-three-year-old Jacques, with the assistance of his spouse Doris, designed and built in his hometown of Aurora opened to the public in Spring 1947.[5] In the demonstration photographs published in the April 1947 issue, Jacques and Doris often appear working side-by-side to realize the house.[6] The sale of the *Popular Mechanics* Build-It-Yourself House in Aurora allowed the Brownsons to purchase property for their future modern house in nearby Geneva.

During the postwar years there was a growing trend among architects to live in Chicago-area villages and cities and either commute to work or establish home offices. Brownson designed and built a steel-and-glass one-story pavilion on a wooded site along the Fox River for Doris and their children.[7] The Brownson House lies flat on the ground—as does Philip Johnson's Glass House in New Canaan completed earlier in 1949, and unlike the elevated Edith Farnsworth House (p. 162) that was also under construction in nearby Plano. The pavilion effect was reinforced by the wooded setting in which hawthorn trees were planted with the guidance of landscape architect

Alfred Caldwell, Brownson's former teacher at IIT. Brownson wrote: "In a glass pavilion, the spectacle of nature is always before you."[8] The steel-framed roof plate is suspended from four rigid steel girders held up by black steel columns. In describing the spatial and material strategy of separating and demarcating living areas (defined by floor-to-ceiling glass walls) from sleeping areas (brick infill with windows) at the rear of the house. Brownson indicated that the "Geneva house is really two houses in one. If you look at the plan, it is separated very clearly by a wall that says that one part is very private, and the other part is the public space, which is the front part. It's a house in which the difference shows."[9]

A couple of years after completion of the house, Brownson submitted an overview of the design and building process—"A Steel and Glass House"—as part of the requirements for fulfilling his IIT Master of Science in Architecture degree in 1954. In the preface of his MS thesis Brownson writes: "It was my intention to explore the

architectural possibilities and the technical problems involved in building a house using industrial techniques and materials of the present time."[10] Also an educator, Jacques Brownson taught at IIT first as an instructor, then assistant professor (1948–59), and as professor and chairman of Architecture and Urban Planning at the University of Michigan (1966–68).[11]

The Brownson House was selected as one of "Eight Adventuresome Houses With New Ideas," in *Architectural Record: Record Houses of 1956*.[12] (This same issue of *Record Houses* also features the A. James Speyer designed steel-and-glass Frances Landrum and Ben Rose House in Highland Park (p. 190).[13]) An exhibition held in 2017 at the Geneva History Museum, *Inside & Out: Geneva's Faces, Places & Spaces* featured the Brownson House along with a number of notable dwellings designed by other prominent local architects including the Walter Frazier and William Moulis House (p. 188) and the Margaret Montgomery and J. Howard Raftery House (p. 204). In addition to exhibitions and professional journals, the Doris Curry and Jacques Brownson House received a considerable amount of attention from the popular press as well.[14]

Sold by the Brownsons in 1966, the house is currently in private hands and requires considerable restoration to return it to its original state. —MS

Maxine Weil and Sigmund Kunstadter House

George Fred Keck began as a solo architect in 1926; his brother William first worked as his draftsman but became a partner in 1946.[1] The Keck firm had served as training ground for several nationally recognized architects, including Ralph Rapson, Bertrand Goldberg, and Stanley Tigerman. Although Fred Keck's and subsequently Keck & Keck projects were regularly published from the 1930s–50s, their recognition as early visionaries in modernist design had dimmed by the 1970s; however, when images of Fred Keck's passive solar houses were included at the 1976 *Chicago Architects* exhibition, his architecture attracted considerable renewed attention.[2] He was described in *Inland Architect* as the "hit" of the show.[3] Tigerman later reveals in a homage to Fred Keck: "As (Stuart) Cohen and I researched and ferreted and

culled (the forgotten figures of Chicago's architectural heritage for the *Chicago Architects* exhibition) it soon became clear that Fred Keck was by *far* the major figure who had been overlooked by the polemicists of modernism… Keck's career was studded by modernist gems."[4] The Kunstadter House was one of these jewels.

The house was constructed on land that originally belonged to the acreage where Frank Lloyd Wright's Ward W. Willits House was sited. Sigmund W. Kunstadter, head of Formfit, a women's apparel manufacturer, and his spouse, Maxine, typified many clients who commissioned modern houses at the time. The Kunstadters collected art and contributed funds and works to the Art Institute of Chicago; Sigmund was a Governing Life Member during this commission (and later named a Life Trustee).[5]

Money wasn't spared for this solar house, constructed at the significant cost (at that time) of $100,000. The plan was rectangular, with modular wood-frame construction and floor-to-ceiling Thermopane windows facing south. Broad eaves allowed the sun to reach the interior during cold winter days but prevented it from doing so during the summer. The terrace and walkways, however, were sunlit even in summer months by large pierced openings in the overhangs. Wood louvers flanking the windows provided ventilation without impeding ravine views.

Long and linear like Keck's 1941 Minna Green and Hugh Duncan House I (p. 130), this home, which is eight bays wide, reflects the influence of Frank Lloyd Wright. The exterior was sheathed in vertical tongue-and-groove cedar panels stained a light gray, blending it into the forested setting. The north side of the house, which faced the street and where the kitchen, laundry, maid's room, and an art studio were located, had minimal windows. Gracious sunlit rooms were located at the back, where the family and guests could enjoy the home's wooded surroundings.

Front entrance with flat panel door flanked by floor-to-ceiling glazed openings.

Dining room with clerestory and band of windows under sideboard that offered glimpses of adjacent ravine.

Floors were of slate, cork, and vinyl over a radiant heating system. A massive rectangular limestone fireplace separated the living and dining areas. In addition to clerestory windows on the east side of the house, providing light to the kitchen and dining room, there was a band of windows under the wood sideboard in the dining room, affording views into the adjacent ravine. No detail was spared in creating this comfortable but elegant, award-winning design. Raymond W. Hazekamp, a pupil of Jens Jensen, designed the landscape.[6]

The American Institute of Architects recognized the Sigmund Kunstadter House with a 1953 Honor Award for Best Design by the Chicago chapter and with a 1955 National Award.[7] In 1956, the Kunstadters opened their modern home to fellow members of the Art Institute of Chicago's Society for Contemporary Arts to view their collection of "Tobeys, Klees, various examples of abstract sculpture, plus works by Fritz Winter and many others."[8]

Accolades for the house and its Keck & Keck design did not matter to the developer who purchased the property and demolished it in 2001-02.[9] The Kunstadter House was replaced in 2003 with a characterless McMansion. —SSB

Isabella Gardner and Robert Hall McCormick III House

The one-story Isabella Gardner and Robert Hall McCormick III House is one of two single-family houses designed for Chicago-area clients by German émigré architect Ludwig Mies van der Rohe after his arrival to the city in 1938.[1] Unlike the Edith Farnsworth House (1951, p. 162) in Plano that was elevated to accommodate flooding of the Fox River, the interlocking pavilions of the McCormick house, completed a year later, lay gently on the ground of a suburban lot in the city of Elmhurst with a landscape plan by Alfred Caldwell as part of Mies's overall scheme. The house was conceived as a prototype for affordable mass-produced modular homes, with the client Robert Hall McCormick III and Herbert S. Greenwald as codevelopers.

The history of twentieth-century residential architecture in the United States was shaped by a combination of low-tech and high-tech prefabrication prototypes.[2] Mail-order houses produced by Chicago-based companies like Sears, Roebuck & Co. ("Modern Homes") or Montgomery Ward ("Wardway Homes") typically deployed traditional materials such as wood and brick, whereas General Houses, Inc., the company Howard T. Fisher founded in Chicago in 1932, looked to steel to produce affordable modern counterparts. The 1933–34 Century of Progress Exposition displayed a number of innovative houses in a variety of materials for visitors to admire: George Fred Keck's Crystal House (with Buckminster Fuller's Dymaxion car proudly displayed in the garage) appeared along with General Houses, Inc., House, the Armco-Ferro Enamel House, the Stran-Steel Garden Home, and the Good Housekeeping Stran-Steel House.[3] A few years later Frank Lloyd Wright introduced his Usonians (with the Katherine Wescott and Herbert Jacobs House I (1937) typically considered the prototype), designed with middle-income families in mind, that used mainly traditional materials and construction methods.[4]

Robert Hall McCormick III was a commercial real estate executive and served as Vice President of the McCormick Management Corporation for many years. McCormick owned (in collaboration with developer Herbert S. Greenwald) the land on which the Mies van der Rohe-designed 860–880 Lake Shore Drive apartments were realized. Isabella Stewart Gardner, his spouse at the time, was a poet; and her

Opposite: Front facade of house on original suburban lot with surrounding trees.

View into living area with Barcelona chairs in the distance.

Ground floor plan.

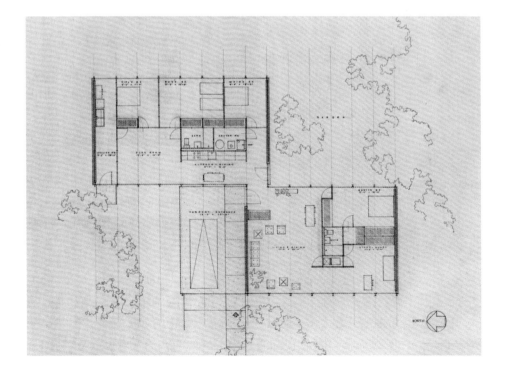

term as associate editor for *Poetry* magazine (1952–56) coincided with her time
in the new house; she wrote her first two books (*Birthdays from the Ocean* and
The Looking Glass) while living in the Mies-designed house.[5] After their divorce in
1959 they vacated the house, and it was eventually sold to Ray and Mary Ann Fick,
who lived there from 1963–92.

The two interlocking pavilions were sited with shorter blank brick-infill facades
facing north-south with the articulated glass facades facing east-west. The street
and backyard were visible from both children's and adults' wings. The adults' wing
grouped the living and dining room with the master bedroom and study, and the
children's wing grouped three bedrooms, a bathroom, and playroom with the
kitchen and laundry. The carport connected the two modules while providing
cover against weather for the tucked-away front door. Elmwood panels and cork
floors introduce an organic and sensuous contrast to the white-painted steel frame
(also visible as part of the ceiling) and windows framed externally with I-beams.

The period photos taken by Hedrich Blessing show interiors with design classics
such as a George Nelson daybed (first produced commercially by Herman Miller
in 1950) and Mies van der Rohe's Barcelona Chair (1929). Longtime resident and
former mayor of Elmhurst Ray Fick recalls:

> We became Miesian enthusiasts. We purchased as much of Mies's
> furniture as we could then afford. We might add that none of our fur-
> niture was manufactured by Knoll, the usual Mies furniture supplier.
> Ours was made by a special Chicago craftsman [Gerald R. Griffith]

Children's area, adjacent
to galley kitchen, has dining,
playroom, and bedroom with
Elmwood partitions.

whom Mies had authorized as the only other person to produce his furniture. (These purchases were arranged through Jodie Kingery, of Baldwin Kingery, the well-known modern furnishing store... of Chicago). We began to collect an architecture library containing everything written in the English language about Mies and his body of work.[6]

The careful selection of design that enhanced the architecture by the first and subsequent owners reflects the growing interest during those years for modernism and its cosmopolitan associations among the North American creative class.

Ray and Mary Ann Fick sold the McCormick House to the Elmhurst Fine Arts and Civic Center Foundation after having lived in it for nearly three decades. It was moved a half mile from its original location at 299 South Prospect Avenue to its current location in Wilder Park in 1994 and reopened in 1997 as part of the Elmhurst Art Museum with an attached addition by De Stefano + Partners.[7] The recent preservation initiative to disconnect the house from the rest of the museum in order to create a visual and experiential separation between the contemporary and "historic" modern architecture has been completed by Heidi Y. Granke, of Heritage Architecture Studio LLC and Berglund Construction. —MS

Walter Frazier and William Moulis House

House, historically painted black, as seen from the street.

Opposite left: Side of house with large glass openings that afforded views of garden and the Fox River.

Opposite right: View from entrance hall, past built in bookcases, down a staircase to the two-story living room facing the river.

The house that architect Walter Frazier called his "Black House" for the color of its exterior combines the formality of his Beaux-Arts training with the simplicity, planar wall surfaces, and large glazed openings more characteristic of a Miesian approach to the International Style.[1] It is a highly livable, yet elegant and—for its time—stylish home. The entrance is a recessed doorway, leading to a high-ceilinged living room after several steps down. Floor-to-ceiling windows open onto formal gardens and a spacious lawn fronting the meandering Fox River. The house has a dramatic color scheme and spatial sequence as well as views.

Frazier lived with his domestic partner artist William "Bill" Moulis who was a sought-after muralist. Moulin's mural commissions in Chicago included the Empire Room at the Palmer House and Jacques Restaurant. In New York his work was featured in the Starlight Roof at the Waldorf-Astoria and at the Philip Johnson-designed Four Seasons Restaurant in the Ludwig Mies van der Rohe-designed Seagram Building.

Walter Frazier, was born in nearby Aurora, like Geneva, a town on the Fox River west of Chicago. After spending time at the University of Illinois, he studied at the Massachusetts Institute of Technology. In 1919–1920, he moved to Paris and attended the École des Beaux-Arts. Despite his strict formal training there, Frazier was also influenced by the architecture of Le Corbusier, who had moved to Paris in 1917.[2]

In 1932 Frazier, while both he and Howard Raftery were living on Chicago's Gold Coast, expanded his solo practice to include Raftery as his partner. The houses designed by the firm of Frazier & Raftery were typically based on traditional styles,

though designed with a simplicity and flair that revealed a modern sensibility. Although Frazier & Raftery had designed a house in 1934 for Ann Steinwedell and Elliott Donnelley in generally conservative Lake Forest with traditional massing, in 1955 the firm created a new house for the Donnelley's that was pure International Style—with a slender structural frame, flat roof, and floor-to-ceiling windows.

Frazier & Raftery were among only a handful of local architects selected to design thirteen houses for the 1933–34 Century of Progress International Exposition— homes that represented progressive trends in the construction industry. With a goal of achieving "a renaissance in Home-building," houses in the Fair were designed to showcase modern and traditional materials used inventively.[3] Frazier & Raftery contributed the Masonite House, whose streamlined curvilinear forms and dramatic color scheme belie the use of a utilitarian pressed wood fiber material. Illustrious peers who designed houses for the exhibition included George Fred Keck (House of Tomorrow, Crystal House), Andrew Rebori (Brick House), Howard T. Fisher (General Houses Steel House), and Ernest A. Grunsfeld Jr. (Lumber House).

Elizabeth "Betsy" Moulis, sister-in-law of William Moulis, is the current and proud owner of the Frazier Moulis House. —SSB

Frances Landrum and Ben Rose House

Although textile designer Ben Rose has received worldwide recognition for his work, in the late 1940s, he and his spouse Frances Landrum, a weaver and his business partner, were building their business and could not yet afford a house compatible with their modern design sensibilities.[1] This all changed in 1952 when Rose received two large commissions: one for International Harvester to design fabric covers for refrigerator doors with matching window curtains and covers for window air conditioning units and another for the Packard Motor Car Company to design patterned linen upholstery for its cars. Once on firm financial footing, they set about commissioning a house.

The Roses held a competition, inviting three young local architects—Ralph Rapson, Bruce Tague, and A. James Speyer—to submit ideas. Speyer alone created a model of his design: this made a deep impression on the Roses, leading them to hire him. The model depicted a 5,000-square-foot house with a two-story central space.

Although financial considerations forced the Roses to scale back the design to a single story, they ended up with a spacious home, sited to take advantage of its ravine setting in the North Shore suburb of Highland Park.

A. James Speyer, who received his graduate architectural training at the Illinois Institute of Technology, absorbed Ludwig Mies van der Rohe's bare-bones philosophy. Like Mies's Farnsworth House, Speyer's design for the Roses' home is International Style. Accessed by perforated steel steps, the flat-roofed, steel-framed structure rests on pylons and appears to float above the home's wooded site.

The front facade is composed of eight rectangular modules of natural cypress boards laid vertically flanking a recessed entrance, two bays wide. Although the warm wood cladding ensures privacy on the west-facing street facade, the north, east, and south walls are floor-to-ceiling glass, opening the interior to its natural surroundings. With the exception of bathrooms, every room in the house has at least one wall of glass. The interior is filled with light, yet the proximity of trees makes it feel sheltered. Frances Rose likened the experience to being in "a tree house, because wherever you look, all you see are these gorgeous sculptural branches."[2]

The center of activity in the house is the spacious 25-by-40-foot living-dining space, with a high ceiling and Ben Rose-designed fabric curtains that could be drawn to

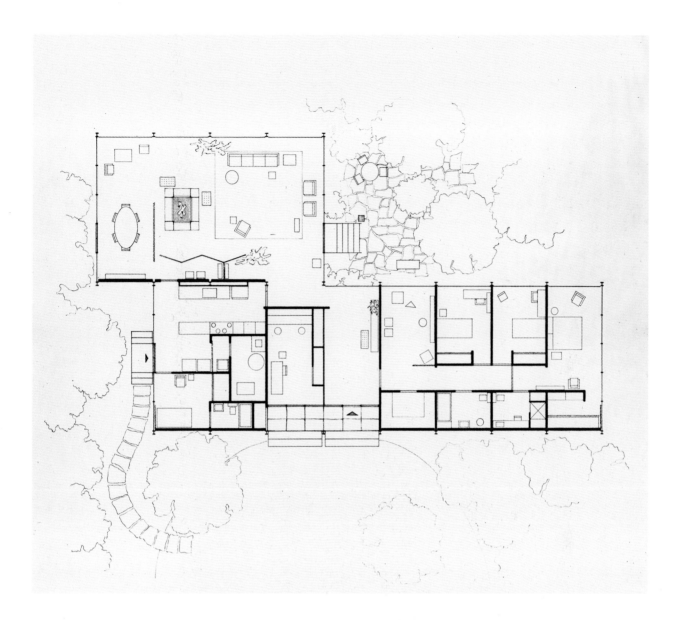

Opposite top: Exterior entrance to living room, facing wooded side lot.

Opposite left: Looking past open fireplace toward living room.

Opposite right: Dining area, separated from living room by drapery designed by Ben Rose.

Floor plan showing front hall and Ben Rose's studio, living-dining room, bedroom wing, and service area.

close off the eating area. An open fireplace, a steel-frame structure resting on a stone pedestal, stands in the middle of the room. As a central focus, it is analogous to the imposing brick fireplaces in Wright-inspired modern houses. Cork floors lend an element of warmth.

In its open plan and simplicity, the Rose home embodies the era's casual lifestyle. One of the only nods to formality is a servant's call bell located under the dining room table and a room designated for a servant, although the Rose family had none.

The living and dining room furniture was almost exclusively selected from the Chicago Merchandise Mart's Herman Miller and Knoll showrooms, which featured the work of midcentury masters including Charles and Ray Eames and Eero Saarinen. The Roses purchased bedroom furniture during a trip to Scandinavia and used Ben Rose's own textiles throughout.

Ben Rose won many awards for his fabric and wallpaper designs, which featured patterns of abstracted motifs.[3] Often based on nature, the shapes were derived from trees and rocks, and had names such as "Quartz" and "Cobblestones." Another design, "Terrain," featured an abstract interpretation of a topographical map. Rose frequently offered witty representations of animals; one of his most whimsical designs was "Kennel Plaid," composed of silhouettes of various dog breeds placed against loosely rectangular blocks following their silhouettes. Rose conceived his small-scale designs with the compact modern home in mind, and he maintained that the greatest contribution fabrics could make to gracious living in an age of individualism was to serve as background for an individual's personality.[4] Today, his fabric designs are preserved in the collections of the Art Institute of Chicago, the Cooper-Hewitt Museum of Design in New York, the Museum of Modern Art, and the Montreal Museum of Fine Arts.[5]

Steel-and-glass Auto Pavilion— built on stilts projecting over ravine (left).

Opposite top: Rose in his studio, adjacent to front entrance.

Opposite bottom: Sitting area of auto pavilion, with Mies van der Rohe MR leather side chairs.

A Corten-steel-and-glass pavilion built to house the couple's collection of classic modern cars is sited toward the back of the Roses' home. Designed in 1974 by David Haid, Speyer's first graduate student when he taught at IIT, this elegant structure stands on slender steel supports over the ravine. Recalling a single floor of Mies's Lake Shore Drive apartments, there is no applied ornament, only I-beams that hold the glass in place and create a play of light and shadow. The geometry of this rectangular steel International Style cage is classical in its discipline and order.

The large neutral space of the interior was designed to be totally flexible, serving as a second living room and a car exhibition area. Ben Rose's love affair with beautiful cars began in the early 1950s, when he first spotted a Porsche 356 convertible. Captivated by the purity of line characteristic of these high-design, aerodynamic

machines, he became a serious collector. His favorite was an exquisite 1927 Type 35B Bugatti, but he also owned a 1930 Alfa Romeo (purchased from the famous Italian racer Count "Johnny" Lurani) and a 1948 Cisitalia Coupe 202 Mille Miglia. Both Ben and Frances Rose raced their cars: he, the Bugatti, and she, a 100-point MgTC.[6]

The auto pavilion is perhaps best known for its role in the iconic 1986 film *Ferris Bueller's Day Off*. Director John Hughes had spent his teenage years in the Chicago suburb of Northbrook and frequently set his films in and around Chicago. In the now-famous scene, Ferris's friend Cameron accidentally crashes his father's bright red 1961 Ferrari 250 GT California through a plate-glass window of the fictional family's garage, actually the Rose Auto Pavilion. When questioned about why the Roses would allow the car to crash though the back wall (which had been temporarily replaced with break-away glass), Fran responded, "The producers promised they would wash the windows!"—no small incentive for the owners of a Miesian glass pavilion.[7]

The present owners Meghann and Chris Salamasick purchased the property from the Rose estate. They prize their house and have removed an unsightly garage addition as well as sensitively updating it to install double glazing that will make the house more energy efficient. —SSB

Harry Weese Wilmette 1954

Susanne Weese and Robert Drucker House

The Drucker House, located in the 170-acre Indian Hill Estates section of Wilmette (loaned caché from the nearby country club of the same name), was built in 1954 by Harry Weese early in his career. Like so many architects who went on to achieve considerable success, Weese began by designing homes for his family: "That's the only thing an architect can do when he starts out, because no one will trust him with anything bigger than that."[1] Weese's early houses, however, were always modern. Unlike many architects who evolved from designing in historical styles to modernism—such as George Fred Keck, who early in his career designed historical revival houses to get commissions—Weese never compromised his commitment to modernism by deferring to popular taste.[2] Even after gaining fame through large, high-profile projects such as the US Embassy in Accra, Ghana (1955–58), the Washington Metro (Washington DC, 1969–76), and the Metropolitan Correctional Center in Chicago (1971–75), Weese continued to design residences, more than eighty of them over the course of his career.[3]

Angled south facade with large windows from porch and bedrooms facing yard.

Opposite: Floor plan.

The house was built for Weese's sister Susanne and her spouse at the time, Robert Drucker. It is sited on a large lot in a mid-1920s neighborhood of curving roads, a subdivision conceived and partially funded by her father-in-law, Henry W. Drucker. Situated in an area of fashionable Tudor and Colonial-inspired houses, Sue's home still looks very much the avant-garde house on the block.

Bringing the outdoors in was a foremost priority to the family. Vast expanses of glass facing south and east flood the rooms with sunshine. Its bedroom wing, angled to the west, forms an obtuse angle to maximize the size and view of the spacious back yard. When the children were young, the ample yard accommodated

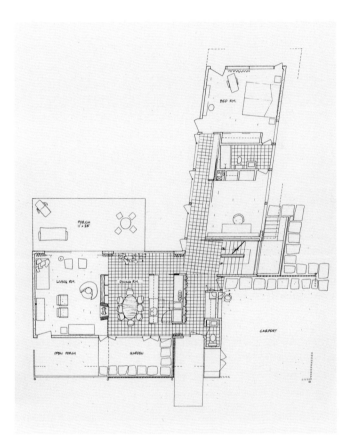

a large ice rink. Even with the extensive glazing, privacy was never compromised. In contrast to the sunny rooms on the south, a shaded terrace is located on the north side of the house, separated from the street by an enclosed screen of narrow vertical slats. Sue Weese Drucker Frank summarizes her experience by saying, "you could never feel morose in this house!"[4] In 1963, Ben Weese, a noteworthy architect in his own right, designed an addition to the house compatible with his brother Harry's design, to accommodate two more Drucker children.

An open plan, with walls that stop short of the ceiling, promotes easy communication and flexibility of use. Pocket doors open and close the bedrooms. A large children's room allows togetherness when wanted but could be divided by an accordion partition. Cleverly located built-in storage is distributed throughout, with bedroom drawers under closets and cabinets lining hallways. In the kitchen, cabinets have frosted glass doors to conceal pantry items, while those on the reverse side facing the dining room are clear

glass to show off glassware and china. The fireplace, with its cylindrical chimney, is open on two-sides, warming both the living and dining rooms. Every detail is thoughtfully conceived. Throughout the process, Harry and Sue Weese constantly conferred—a seamless architect-client relationship.

Even with its functionalism and comfort, the Drucker House is also about beauty. Geometry governs the design, with rectangular elements, both wide and narrow, repeated throughout. The staircase, comprised of open risers and slender metal railings, connects the second floor bedrooms, living areas, and both front and side entrances but also becomes a piece of sculpture. Backed by a wall of glass, the stairway adds an element of cheer.

Iconic modern furniture—with pieces by Alvar Aalto and Bruno Mathsson as well as by Weese himself—fill the house. While a student at MIT, Harry Weese had dreamed of opening a furniture store and gallery that would double as a salon for individuals interested in modern design. This happened in 1947, when he, his spouse, Kitty Baldwin Weese, and Jody Kingrey opened the store Baldwin Kingrey that built a fine reputation selling affordable modern designs directly to the public. The shop carried Alvar Aalto's Artek line of furniture from Finland, textiles by Alexander Girard, glass by Venini, and furniture by Bruno Mathsson and Charles and Ray

Eames. Baldwin Kingrey foreshadowed two other stores: Design Research, which opened in Cambridge, Massachusetts, in 1953 by Benjamin Thompson, cofounder of The Architects Collaborative (TAC), and Crate & Barrel, established in Chicago's trendy Old Town neighborhood in 1962 by Gordon and Carol Segal.

Living room with fireplace that opens into both living room and dining room.

Harry Weese embraced the modern aesthetic in the Drucker House with his devotion to simplicity, harmony, and clarity and rejection of applied ornament. He regarded Beaux-Arts as "petering out" and the work of Frank Lloyd Wright as a relic of the nineteenth century.[5] But he expressed great admiration for Ludwig Mies van der Rohe.[6] Scandinavian architecture, particularly the work of Erik Gunnar Asplund and Alvar Aalto, also influenced Harry. Asplund's 1917 Snellman House inspired Weese's angled wing on the Drucker House. Blair Kamin, architecture critic for the *Chicago Tribune,* remembers Harry Weese as "an eclectic, who thought about everything."[7] Harry Weese had the ability to absorb and synthesize a variety of influences, and he incorporated these in his unique modernist vision for Sue and Robert Drucker's home. Susanne Weese Drucker Frank, as of this writing, has been the sole owner and resided there for more than sixty years. —SSB

Kitchen with view toward yard.

Dining room, with open pass-through from kitchen.

View from living room toward open staircase.

John W. Moutoussamy   Chicago   1954

Elizabeth Hunt and
John W. Moutoussamy House

A Chicago native (with family roots in the French Caribbean), John W. Moutoussamy was part of a wave of veterans on the G. I. Bill who attended and graduated from the Illinois Institute of Technology with an architecture degree in 1948.[1] A few years after graduation, he purchased a 60-by-125-foot lot in the South Side neighborhood of Chatham and designed a one-story modernist house for his spouse Elizabeth Hunt (a later graduate of Harrington Institute of Interior Design) and their three children. Jeanne Moutoussamy-Ashe, one of his daughters, said "I loved growing up in my father's house. It was an accomplishment that, as a child, made me feel very special and, in time, very, very proud."[2]

Since the 1950s—as urban renewal initiatives in the near South Side displaced thousands of individuals and families who moved further south—the Chatham area of Chicago developed into an enclave for middle- and upper-middle class African American professionals. Notable inhabitants of Chatham have included gospel superstar Mahalia Jackson, civil rights attorney Lawrence E. Smith Jr. and his spouse, Virgie, who commissioned African American architect K. Roderick O'Neil to design their house (1964), and Joan Henderson and George E. Johnson Sr. (1963, p. 228).[3]

After training at IIT and working briefly for Mies van der Rohe, Moutoussamy went on to work for K. Roderick O'Neil.[4] Coincidentally, the first African American architect to be registered in Illinois (1939) was Walter T. Bailey. Shortly thereafter Moutoussamy joined the ranks of the renamed firm Dubin, Dubin, Black, & Moutoussamy; he became partner in 1966 and remained with the firm until his retirement. Moutoussamy was best known for his design of large-scale private and public buildings that include the Johnson Publications Company headquarters (1972) in Chicago's Loop district on Michigan Avenue and the middle-income multi-family housing known as Theodore K. Lawless Gardens (1970). In 2003, Arthur Detmers Dubin, a former partner, credited the Lawless Gardens as Moutoussamy's breakthrough:

> Yes, he was a protégé of Mies. And he became a licensed architect, and he did minor things; but this project, which later became the Lawless project, was an enormous venture. It was quite a nice building. And I don't know that this conversation should wander any more into affirmative action, because, we both know where it is today. It has a long way to go. But it's come a long way too. So let's leave it at that.[5]

Featured in an article entitled "Architecture's New Wave: Growing Demand Brings Surge of Contracts to Black Building Designers" published in Johnson Publishing Company's June 1971 issue of *Ebony,* Moutoussamy is photographed against the backdrop of Theodore K. Lawless Gardens:

> "Twenty years ago," says John W. Moutoussamy, a general partner in the predominantly white firm of Dubin, Dubin, Black & Moutoussamy in Chicago, "the black architect's advancement was limited to certainly not more than a 'low-middle' level, there being no reason in

the power sense to respond to black citizens. Now it is expedient for government to respond more to black political pressure. And as the interests of government expand greatly into what had been previously considered the province of private industry, these private interests, to get their share of business, find they must follow the moves of government. These factors, among others, make it possible now for more black architects to begin thinking in terms of responding to a wide market."

Street view with primary side entrance.

Thus, Moutoussamy was keenly aware of the growing political and economic impact that African Americans were developing in shaping the built environment.

Moutoussamy's family home was relatively modest in terms of square footage and materials: with a concrete block structure finished on the exterior with cream-colored brick (a material typical of most Mies-designed buildings on the IIT campus, including the Institute of Gas Technology Building, 1952). Although Chatham has a concentration of modern houses in the area of the Moutoussamy House, there are also many bungalows and builder's vernacular style houses. His house stood out with its flat roof and subtle differences such as locating the primary entrance on the side of the house. Natural ventilation was incorporated into the design thanks to louvers installed in the lower section of the windows.

Moutoussamy took out a loan in order to purchase the lot and build his single-story house. In an article that appeared in the *Chicago Daily News* in 1955, his efforts did not go without notice:

> The seven-room home of architect John Moutoussamy of 361 E. 89th Pl., is one of the new homes being financed by one of the Negro savings and loan associations. Moutoussamy has his studio in his home he designed for himself, wife, and three children. It has radiant heat imbedded in the floors, a bathroom and a powder room, and the walls are of finished concrete block. The ... house is located on a 60 by 125 foot lot.[6]

Despite Moutoussamy's growing status, like many of his African American peers, he had to overcome deep-seated structural inequities in the design and realization of the built environment in Chicago.

The house has undergone some alterations by its current owner to offset the perceived austerity of Mies's minimalism. —MS

Margaret Montgomery and Howard Raftery House

View of house from the street,
with linear sheltering overhang.

The Margaret Montgomery and Howard Raftery House, located immediately adjacent to and south of his business partner Walter Frazier's house, is a wood, brick, and glass home that owes its sensibility to Frank Lloyd Wright's Usonian designs. Set back from a busy road, the house is barely visible from the street. Its long, low roofline, with broad sheltering overhangs, mirrors the horizontal board-and-batten wood siding. Tall glass windows and doors afford expansive views of the Fox River.

On the interior, walls and ceilings are also wood, giving the feeling of a rustic lodge. The living room, like Wright-designed houses of the 1930s–50s, has a large fireplace whose brickwork extends to form a wall perpendicular to it and facing the extensive glazing through which the large lawn and river beyond can be seen. River views are even glimpsed through the kitchen. As in Wright's designs, the house has an open plan accessing a long gallery-hallway, with all the family bedrooms opening off it. Raftery's house is vastly different from Walter Frazier's more Miesian home and their firm's generally more formal design sensibility. Born on Chicago's North Shore in Evanston, Howard Raftery moved with his family to the river town of Geneva in 1911, where his architectural success began. After he received his degree in architecture from the Massachusetts Institute of Technology in 1925, he studied at the American Academy in Fontainebleau, France, and the American Academy in Rome. After receiving his license in 1932, Howard Raftery began working with Walter Frazier.[1] Raftery's spouse Margaret was an alumna of the Presbyterian Hospital School of Nursing in Chicago.

Kitchen with large glass opening, offering a vista toward the back of the house, facing the Fox River.

Informal family living space with view toward dining area facing river, office section of room.

Kate Raftery, Howard's mother, played a significant role in the career of Frazier & Raftery. A devotee of travel and the arts, she opened The Little Traveler, a shop in Geneva featuring items from all over the world. In 1939, she engaged the young artist William Moulis, who had studied at the Institute of Design with László Moholy-Nagy, to paint whimsical murals at her store. Moulis also painted murals for Chicago's fashionable Casino Club, designed by Frazier & Raftery in 1929. Moulis became Walter Frazier's life partner, where they lived next door to Raftery.

Current owners of the Raftery House are Kimberly and Joseph Lyons who find it to be very accommodating for their family of six. They "feel honored to live here and will always find inspiration in Raftery's vision."[2] —SSB

Paul Schweikher and Winston Elting   Flossmoor   1955

Priscilla Huffard and
H. P. Davis Rockwell House I

Paul Schweikher and Winston Elting   Flossmoor   1955

Schweikher and Elting became increasingly well known in and outside of Chicago due to a number of outstanding buildings including the houses they designed for themselves before the outbreak of World War II: the Dorothy Miller and Paul Schweikher House in Schaumburg (1938 and Additions 1949, p. 96) and the Marjorie Horton and Winston Elting House in Lake Forest (1940, p. 122).[1] During the postwar housing boom, their work was featured in the April 1947 issue of *Life* as part of a story about "Three Modern Houses: They are the Kind of Homes U.S. Now Can Have," alongside other architects that would also become of national consequence, Pietro Belluschi and Edward Durell Stone and Associates.[2] A 1949 exhibition of Schweikher and Elting's work held at the Renaissance Society at the University of

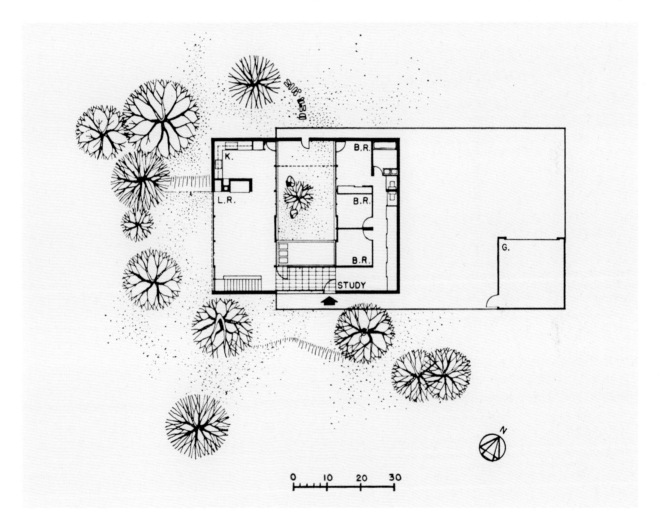

Chicago recognized their stature; it was only the second of a series of architecture exhibitions held there after the early one on Mies van der Rohe held in 1947.[3]

The house they designed for Priscilla "Cil" Huffard and H. P. Davis "Deever" Rockwell in Flossmoor, a historic village to the south of Chicago, demonstrates how architect-designed modernist houses elevated the overall quality of the predominant builder examples.[4] Schweikher described the design process for the Rockwell House I, without explicitly crediting Elting, as such: "The house, to me, is an odd mixture of the various attitudes that I had about wood construction, concrete construction, and steel. It has in it some of this orderly, rectilinear simplicity.

But I recall, and I see in the pictures that I look at of it now, that we were almost obsessed with the idea of separating the view from the circulation of air from outdoors to indoors so that an accentuation, a constant repetition, was the appearance of louvered openings alongside or next to the glass apertures."[5]

The approximately 2,500-square-foot courtyard house overlooking a wooded ravine was first featured in the theme issue of "Record Houses of 1956" as part of the rubric of "Twenty Houses for Family Living."[6] The emphasis on "family living" recalls the focus in American society on the traditional nuclear family as GIs returning home led to a boom in family life. The Rockwells had three small children at the

time of the commission. The house also appeared in a volume edited by the English writers and designers Monica Pidgeon and Theo Crosby entitled *An Anthology of Houses* (1960), which featured a selection of houses from around the world ranging from Canada to Japan.[7] Other examples from the USA included a courtyard house José Luis Sert designed for his family in Cambridge, Massachusetts and Craig Ellwood's Case Study House no. 18 in Beverly Hills, California. Pidgeon and Crosby summarized the Rockwell house:

View of interior courtyard
with reflecting pond, on left.

With houses on both sides, the site has a street level with it at the front and a ravine cutting diagonally across it at the back. The best exposure is south-west overlooking the ravine. The living room and the lower level fitted beneath it are placed to take advantage of the view and the sun. Bedrooms are closed to the street side, but opened to the central patio, louvres and curtains giving them ample privacy when needed … Except for the large glass areas overlooking the ravine, the exterior is brick veneer. The patio sides are light wood members, louvres, glass and a third one of brick with a service gate.[8]

Hans Wegner's Wishbone Chair (1949) near fireplace.

The authors also cited the Rockwells' own words: "the house is good to us—it lets us live with sky, sunlight and our woods. The inner courtyard is a serene centre from any point in the house. In the summer we eat in the court, the children play there. They swim in the pool. Even in winter when we can't be in it, the court remains the core of the house."[9]

The events following the design and completion of the house by Schweikher and Elting speak about the power of architecture to both improve and transform lives. Deever Rockwell, who had trained as an engineer at MIT, left his position at Inland Steel Company, to study architecture at IIT. Schweikher recounted how "somewhere toward the end of the construction period Deever came to me and said he was giving up his own profession and going to study to become an architect. He said that he attributed it all to his experience with me in building his house."[10] By the early 1960s, Deever and Cil Rockwell would choose nearby Olympia Fields for Rockwell House II (p. 232), which he would design.

Dining area looking into interior courtyard.

Opposite: View of south corner with entrance at the top of slope.

Schweikher left Chicago in 1953 to assume a new role as chair of the Yale School of Architecture. The last work he and Elting completed was the Faith United Protestant Church in Park Forest, an important postwar suburb planned by Philip Lutznick and Nathan Manilow's American Community Builders, to the immediate south of Flossmoor.

The Rockwells sold the house to Mary Jane and David Nelson who lived there with their two children until the early 1990s. Their son, David Nelson Jr., credits his experience living in the house with his decision to study architecture; he graduated with a Bachelor of Architecture from IIT in 1991. Unlike the Nelsons who made no substantial alterations to the house while living there, recent owners have added an unsympathetic addition. Following best practices in preservation and renovation can be a challenge when modern houses change hands because typically the knowledge behind design decisions is lost in the transfer of ownership. Unfortunately much of the rich heritage of modern houses in Flossmoor and other Chicago suburbs face this challenge as the search for authenticity often conflicts with contemporary desires of the new owners. —MS

Josef Marion Gutnayer   Wilmette   1957

Alice Lieberman and
J. Marion Gutnayer House

The home that J. Marion Gutnayer designed for his spouse, Alice Lieberman Gutnayer, and family pays homage to the Villa Savoye in Poissy, France. When in Paris during the early 1930s, Gutnayer had served as a draftsman in Le Corbusier's studio.[1] Like Le Corbusier's masterpiece, Gutnayer's home is built of concrete with much of the volume raised on pilotis, but unlike Le Corbusier's Savoye, he clads it in stone. Covered space under the second floor was intended to accommodate parking for automobiles and a boat, though the space allotted to the boat was later converted to an office. The living space above was accessed by a spiral staircase. The roof featured a terrace and roof garden.

Recent photo of west facade. House raised on pilotis with band of horizontal windows lighting library and living room.

Opposite: Gutnayer's design for the family holiday card, with a sketch of the front and side elevations.

Gutnayer referred to his house as a "'rocket ranch,' a one-level house raised to a position between the earth and the sky, accessed by a rocket-like tower."[2] Lit by a 40-foot band of windows, the interior features an open plan, with a master bedroom two steps up from and opening onto the living room—effectively creating a stage. A fireplace that combines rough-faced and polished marble is the room's central focus. Only natural materials are used throughout: walls and ceilings are wood; there is no drywall.

Gutnayer designed several one-story houses of wood, stone or brick, and glass. The sales brochure for his custom homes describes "the inventiveness and artistic use

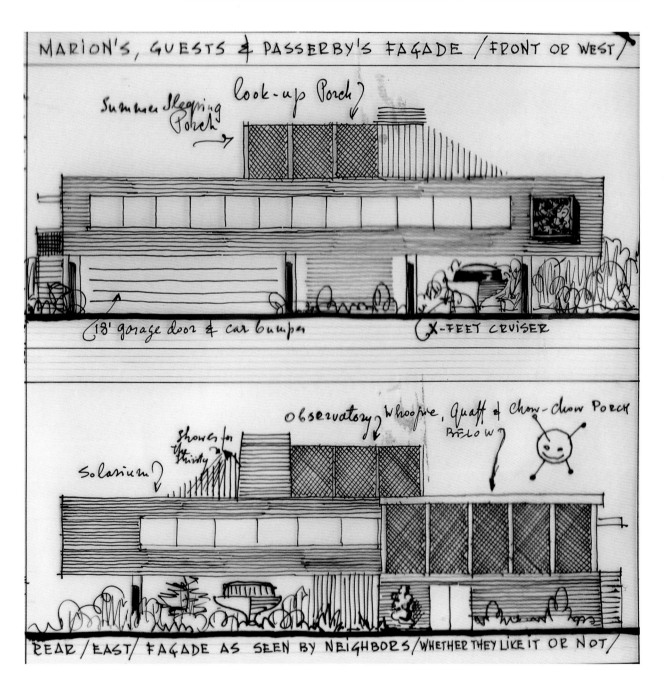

of material, textures, lights and shadows as an exterior skin of your happier and dignified life."[3] All of his buildings were designed using a modular system, as Frank Lloyd Wright did in his Usonian houses.[4] Gutnayer owned a copy of Wright's *Genius and the Mobocracy* that is filled with underscores.[5] Although Wright's influence prevails in many Gutnayer-designed houses, each is unique. Gutnayer's work integrates a variety of artful geometric treatments, including stained glass, patterned brickwork, and irregular rooflines.

The Gutnayers were frequent purchasers of fine art, with a collection that included paintings and drawings by Francis Picabia, Milton Avery, Jacques Lipchitz, and Fernand Léger.[6] Collecting was in his DNA; Gutnayer's father was a dealer and art collector in Warsaw before the Nazis looted his collection. His parents, like thousands of other Jews, were sent to the ghetto, then to the extermination camp Treblinka where they were executed. Before the war began, J. Marion Gutnayer had studied art history at the École du Louvre and graduated from the École Spéciale d'Architecture in Paris. He returned to Warsaw to visit his parents but escaped their fate by linking up with the Polish underground, arriving in the United States in 1946.[7] After opening an architectural

Opposite: Living room with view toward spiral staircase from ground floor and band of windows at the front.

studio in New York with his brother Henry, J. Marion moved to Chicago, where he practiced architecture for the rest of his career and served as assistant professor of architecture at the Chicago campus of the University of Illinois.

In 2008, Reed and Anne Hayden Stevens moved from Seattle to work at Northwestern University and purchased the Gutnayer House from the estate. They thoughtfully renovated the house based on Anne's research of contemporary buildings designed by Gutnayer.[8] —SSB

Opposite: Library, looking toward living area.

Master bedroom, up two stairs, separated from living room by bi-fold doors and adjacent to bench and fireplace. African masks and figures constituted much of the Gutnayer collection.

Harry Weese   Barrington   1957

Kitty Baldwin and Harry Weese House

The home that Harry and Kitty Weese built in Barrington was their second, con- structed at a time when America's postwar economy was thriving and Harry's career was becoming established. Harry Mohr Weese was educated at the Massachusetts Institute of Technology (with a year at Yale University) and Cranbrook Academy, founding Harry Weese & Associates after graduation. In the 1950s, he received many substantial commissions. His friend Eero Saarinen had recommended him to J. Irwin Miller (president then chairman of Cummins Engine Co. between 1947–77) for an interview. Miller, a patron of modern architecture, was instrumental in the selection of world-class architects to design major public buildings in Columbus, Indiana. Over the course of fifteen years, Miller selected Weese to design a

Pool facade of the "studio" designed with fanciful cat-ear gables.

Porch that, when glazed, served as a conservatory in the winter.

Approach to front entrance via sidewalk topped by arched grape arbor trellis.

series of buildings, including ones for the company, the First Baptist Church, and several schools.

Although there is great diversity among his numerous projects, Weese had a life-long interest in residential architecture. Beginning in 1936, with a family house he designed and helped build in Glen Lake, Michigan, Weese designed over eighty-two houses, until his death in 1998. Kitty Baldwin Weese, a designer and author of *Harry Weese Houses,* writes that his "houses were not only an exercise for all of Harry's design principles, but also a test for his multiple use spaces and his interest in designing for human needs. A house encompasses all aspects of design standards."[1]

Harry designed a wood-frame summer and weekend home for his family at the top of a hill on five acres of wooded property that had been in the Weese family since the 1920s. The walls of the "Studio," as the Weeses called their home, were clad with western red cedar tongue-and-groove boards. The V-shaped roof was suspended between twin wings with cat-ear gables. These "cat ear" gables contributed to Kitty's description of it as "medieval, whimsical, fanciful, and frolicsome."[2] Harry, with a great sense of wit, drew a cartoon cat face mimicking the configuration of the house.

The arched front door, located in the west wing, is reached by a long, arched vine-covered grape arbor. A sense of playfulness and a feeling for casual living prevails throughout the interior of the house. In the double-height living room, a seventeen-foot suspension bridge (reputed to sway slightly) connects bedrooms tucked under the eaves of each gable. A conversation pit below accommodates fifteen people (a feature that Eero Saarinen famously incorporated in the house he designed for Irwin Miller in Columbus, Indiana.)[3] A fireplace opens into both the living room and dining room—a design element that Harry had also included in the house he designed for his sister, Susanne Weese Drucker Frank (p. 196).

Built for a family with three young girls, the house has features particularly attractive to children. Although Kitty and Harry's bedroom is accessible by a staircase, one daughter would reach her room by a narrow catwalk adjacent to the stairs. The other two girls would reach their rooms from the bridge, a configuration that eliminated the need for a second staircase. On the outside, however, ladders descend from each bedroom balcony to a stone terrace in front of the swimming pool.

The house conveyed a sense of spaciousness that belies its total area of 1,600 square feet. Glass walls open from the living room to the terrace and the pool beyond. At the southeast corner of the first floor, a porch could be enclosed in glass to function as a conservatory in the winter. The modernist tenet of bringing the outdoors in mattered considerably to Weese, who once said, "Architecture is most at home below the trees within walking distance of the earth."[4]

Harry Weese's expression of structure in his house was as paramount to him as it was to Mies van der Rohe in the designs for his steel-and-glass skyscrapers. Even though Weese was not using industrial materials or building strictly in the Miesian mode, he admired Mies and likened him to a Buddha, asserting that for his cadre of architects, "all of us were influenced."[5] Harry described his own Time-Life Building in Chicago as "highly Miesian" but explains how he was "carrying Miesian logic to a further stage."

Living area conversation pit with dining area on other side of open fireplace and, above, suspension bridge connecting upstairs bedrooms.

View through glass walls of house, past dining area, living area suspension bridge toward pool.

218

Despite his respect for Mies, Weese's work was eclectic and followed no singular path. Betty J. Blum, head of the Chicago Architects Oral History Project, described him as "a maverick among his peers beholden to no greater fashion than his own conviction."[6] As an architect, Harry was an individualist, much like Walter Netsch and Bertrand Goldberg.[7] If there are some shared characteristics in Harry Weese's body of work, his biographer Robert Bruegmann says it is his tendency toward using natural materials and his interest in creature comfort.[8] He looked for inspiration to the Scandinavian modernist architects Alvar Aalto and Gunnar Asplund, who preferred wood over concrete or steel, unlike the International-Style European modernists.

Suspension bridge between bedrooms with view into living room conversation pit.

Dining area with table and bentwood chairs.

Weese's impressive body of work worldwide includes such significant buildings as the United States Embassy, Accra, Ghana (1955–58), the Frederick E. Terman Engineering Center at Stanford University, Palo Alto, California (1974–78), the design for the Washington DC Metro (1966–1976) and, in Chicago, the restoration of the Auditorium Theater (1964–67), designed by Adler & Sullivan in 1886.

The Harry and Kitty Weese house, with its slate floors, natural cedar plank interior walls, and conversation pit, creates a cozy setting and exudes fun. Their daughter Marcia Weese describes the home as a "fantastic wondrous house to grow up in."[9] In private ownership today, the house has reportedly been restored.[10] —SSB

Ruth Koier and Laurence Sjoblom House

The Sjoblom House perches on the edge of a ravine on ten wooded acres, a modern home of wood, brick, and glass designed in 1960 by Jean Wehrheim, a woman who happens also to have been a very talented modernist architect. Vertical board and batten grey cedar boards and floor-to-ceiling window mullions echo the tall, slender trees of the property, creating a pleasant organic harmony with nature.

Ruth Augusta Columbia Koier Sjoblom, a chemist at Argonne National Laboratory, and Laurence Richard Sjoblom, a mathematics professor at the University of Illinois, Chicago Circle Campus, sought a house that would accommodate their needs as they reached retirement.[1] The middle-aged Sjobloms, known as "Patti" and "Larry,"

Exterior showing glazed conservatory next to living room and balcony surrounding dining room and kitchen.

would be moving from a huge Victorian house. They were not entirely certain that a modern design would suit them. The Sjobloms engaged Jean and John Wehrheim who were practicing together; however, Jean Wehrheim handled the firm's residential work.[2]

Both in its intimate relationship with the surrounding landscape and its economy, the Sjoblom House recalls Frank Lloyd Wright's Usonian houses. Like Wright, Jean Wehrheim also viewed a house as a place where space flows naturally between exterior and interior rather than as a box with holes punched for windows. The Sjoblom House has a subtle T-shaped plan, with the living room, dining

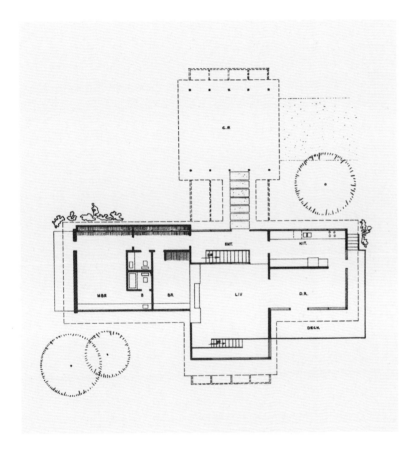

Floor plan.

Living room fireplace with adjacent floor-to-ceiling window.

Living room with glass wall view into plant conservatory.

room, kitchen, and master bedroom, all extending out to the landscape from a central fireplace. Wood decks and flat roofs with broad overhangs supported by exposed brackets further relate the house to the landscape.

The decks accessed from the dining room, kitchen, and master bedroom allow for extended living space with bucolic views. Broad floor-to-ceiling windows bring the outdoors in—almost sixty percent of the exterior walls are glass. The Sjobloms' niece Jennifer Sjoblom describes the house as a "magical oasis" because "it was a private sanctuary in the suburbs. Every detail and angle of the house was built with the intention of maximizing the connectedness to nature."[3]

All the major living spaces and master bedroom share the main floor, with a large recreation room and guest suite opening out on grade from the lower level; a two-car garage is connected to the house by a breezeway.

On the interior, a broad stacked-bond fireplace dominates the surrounding major living areas thus creating an informal open plan. Original furnishings were minimal so as not to detract from the architecture of the house or exterior views. Walls and ceilings are cedar. In some sections the flooring is brick laid in a basketweave pattern, and in others wide pine boards. Composed entirely of natural materials, with no painted surface treatments or stylistic references, all of the woodwork was stained and hand-rubbed by Larry Sjoblom. From the beginning the architect-client relationship was collaborative. Larry acted as general contractor. Wehrheim focused on keeping costs down: the proportions of the house were all based on multiples of six and building materials were all stock sizes.

Front entrance, across from staircase to lower level.

Opposite: Two car garage under kitchen and dining room.

The Sjoblom House received public recognition a dozen years after it was built, when, in January 1972, the house was featured in a *Chicago Tribune* article "Great Home is a Bargain," noting that it was built for $40,000. The author describes how the couple was attracted to the easy maintenance, convenience, and comfort this modern home provided.[4]

In 1977, more than a decade after the Sjoblom House was built, the *New York Times* published an article entitled, "The Last Profession to be Liberated by Women." Highly respected critic Ada Louise Huxtable expressed outrage: "Professionally speaking, women architects have yet to get out of the kitchen. They are chained, tied, and condemned to the house—to house design and house interiors in the name of design efficiency, *gemütlickeit,* and the family."[5]

In the 1960s, designing houses was just fine with Jean Wiersema Wehrheim. Encouraging women to pursue architectural careers, she was quoted in a 1966 *Chicago Tribune* article, "We have a natural inclination for homes.... Men seem to prefer big projects, like offices and public buildings, but I know what I am doing when it comes to designing a kitchen."[6] More recently, Chicago architect Cynthia Weese, FAIA, founding partner of Weese, Langley, Weese, and Dean Emerita, School of Architecture, Washington University in St. Louis, reaffirmed that doing residential work is "wonderfully satisfying, deeply personal."[7]

Following her graduation with a degree in architectural engineering in 1948 from the University of Illinois at Urbana-Champaign, Jean began with the architectural firm of Keck & Keck (where she met her spouse, John Wehrheim, also an architectural engineer) and received her license the next year. In the early 1950s the Wehrheims joined the York Center Community Cooperative, a residential subdivision in Lombard where they built their own home and established a professional office. He branched out to concentrate on commercial and industrial projects.

She established a successful independent residential practice in 1954, with her first commissions to design eight of the 80 houses built within the 85-acre co-op community. In the early years, she was also a general contractor on homes that she had designed.[8] A prolific architect, Wehrheim designed over 150 houses over her career, mostly in Chicago's western suburbs. She continued to work out of their Lombard home after John's death in 1962, which enabled her to care for their two young adopted children and permitted a flexible schedule.

In the late 1960s Wehrheim taught a course at the College of DuPage incorporating topics that included the interplay of space, functional yet artistic architectural principles, kitchen and bathroom planning, and solar orientation of a house on its lot.[9] Her own house and several others she designed incorporated passive solar design, which she learned during her stint at Keck & Keck.

Jean Wehrheim enjoyed success in her chosen field of residential architecture, yet she often felt that she wasn't taken seriously by contractors and was frustrated at her inability to command the same fee as a man.[10]

The number of women architects in practice was still at a low ebb in 1960, with an estimated 260 in practice in the United States.[11] Prior to that time, there were but a handful of Chicago women that enjoyed recognition. Marion Mahony Griffin, who worked for Frank Lloyd Wright from 1895 until 1909 (when he left for Germany) and produced elegant renderings for the 1910 Wasmuth Portfolio, was Chicago's most distinguished, joining a cadre of nationally accomplished women architects including Julia Morgan, Mary Colter, Louise Bethune, Theodate Pope Riddle, and others. Chicago's women architects included Elizabeth Martini, who initiated Chicago's Women's Architectural Club and the publication of its small journal *The Architrave,* and Mary Ann Crawford, who received acclaim for her beautiful Beaux-Arts drawings. After receiving her bachelor's and master's degrees from MIT, Crawford paved the way for women at the firm of Perkins, Fellows & Hamilton in the early 1930s but found it difficult to find work during the Depression and later accepted a full time job in social work.[12]

During the watershed decade for women's rights, eight Chicago women who had already begun to enjoy success in the field founded Chicago Women in Architecture (CWA) in 1974; they were Gertrude Lempp Kerbis, FAIA (Jean Wiersema Wehrheim's roommate at the University of Illinois), Carol Ross Barney, FAIA, Cynthia Weese, FAIA, Nancy Abshire, AIA, Gunduz Dagdelen (Ast) , Natalie de Blois, Laura Fisher, FAIA, and Jane M. Jacobsen. No women, however, were represented among the at least forty-five men in the *Chicago Architects* exhibition of 1976 that was installed to pay tribute to the many architects who had been passed over by historians of modern architecture.[13] In 1977–78, Chicago hosted two exhibitions and a series of panels focused on women in architecture. The venerable Architectural League of New York's 1977 exhibition "Women in American Architecture: A Historical and Contemporary Perspective" traveled to Chicago.[14] At the same time, Chicago Women in Architecture organized an exhibition "Chicago Women Architects: Contemporary Directions: Chicago Women in Architecture" at Artemisia Gallery, January 1978 that focused entirely on Chicago women architects who were

Door from balcony into kitchen and dining room.

largely unknown and not-yet-nationally known.[15] Jean Wiersema Wehrheim's 1960 residence for the Sjobloms was featured in the exhibition.

Despite its importance, when the house came on the market in 2017, its modern design was misunderstood—as these houses frequently are—and the listing agent marketed the house as a "teardown." Jennifer Sjoblom was appalled at the prospect of the demolition of the historic house and took over the listing, refusing to sell to someone who would demolish it. In 2011 the house was sold to a couple that appreciates modern homes. —SSB

Donald Wrobleski   Bannockburn   1960

Donald Wrobleski House

Nestled on a wooded site in the small Village of Bannockburn, architect Don Wrobleski's one-story home is a tribute to the modernist masters who influenced him. The 2,000-square-foot house is a pavilion of wood, Wisconsin fieldstone, and glass. Its exterior is clad in vertical boards of sawn red cedar treated with a bleaching oil. Wisconsin fieldstone was selected to form a low retaining wall separating the house from the parking area; the floor-to-ceiling fireplace repeats use of the fieldstone. Wrobleski chose fieldstone because of his fondness for the late 1930s and '40s houses of Marcel Breuer, and in this respect Wrobleski's house recalls a strong feature of New Canaan modernism. Many of his Chicago contemporaries demonstrated a preference for brick.

Exterior with low wall of fieldstone separating house from driveway.

Wrobleski employed glass cleverly and economically. Vast expanses of floor-to-ceiling Thermopane glass, consisting of standard-size picture windows turned 90 degrees result in a 4-foot-2-inch-by-8-foot module that is used consistently throughout the house. Walls of glass provide a flow of space between the interior and exterior, with rooms opening into secluded courtyards. A rear terrace is on axis with the 20-by-29-foot sunken living room. The house has exquisitely detailed woodwork, including quartersawn oak floors in a herringbone pattern and ceilings executed in quarter-sawn cedar, fine-tuned with a ⅛" bevel.

The glazed openings that face south illuminate the house with winter sunlight, yet an overhang keeps out the strong summer rays. The first modern house that Wrobleski had ever seen and admired was Keck & Keck's Maxine Weil and Sigmund Kunstadter House (p. 180) with its use of passive solar design.

Wrobleski trained at the Illinois Institute of Technology (IIT), although he was originally set to attend the Massachusetts Institute of Technology based on its reputation. After seeing newspaper articles on the 1947 Museum of Modern Art's exhibition on Ludwig Mies van der Rohe, his family felt that Don could receive an equally fine education at nearby IIT. Although he had only a handful of critiques from Mies, Wrobleski absorbed the importance of proportion and, like Mies, employed a module to govern design. Wrobleski was particularly impressed with

Bedroom with view of wooded rear yard.

Architect Don Wrobleski sitting on living room couch; visible are built-in bookcases and glass wall.

the teachings of A. James Speyer, whom he felt understood how people lived, and of Alfred Caldwell, who taught him construction. Classes on housing and solar orientation taught by Ludwig Hilberseimer had influenced Wrobleski as well. Studying philosophy at the University of Chicago rounded out his education.[1]

The Wrobleski House was featured in *Better Homes and Gardens 1968 Home Building Ideas,* a shelter magazine that billed itself as including "The Finest in New Home Design—Coast to Coast."[2]

Don Wrobleski continues to live in the home he designed. Virtually unaltered, it continues to reflect his design sensibility. —SSB

Joan Henderson and George E. Johnson Sr. House

The cofounders of the Chicago-based Johnson Products Company, Joan Henderson and George E. Johnson Sr., commissioned an architectural firm on Chicago's North Shore, Huebner & Henneberg, to design a modernist house in Chatham for their family. At the time the Johnsons engaged Huebner & Henneberg, the firm's stature was rising in modern residential architecture even though it is not widely known today. George E. Johnson Sr., who became identified as the "King of Black Haircare" arrived to Chicago in 1929 from Mississippi with his mother and three brothers; they were part of the first great migration.[1] Joan Henderson was born and lived in Chicago; she actively participated in the management of Johnson Products Company (which would go on to become the first black-owned business on the American Stock Exchange by 1971) and sponsored the popular "Soul Train" television show.[2]

Street view with covered entrance walkway.

The site the Johnsons chose for their new house was located a mile away from the Elizabeth Hunt and John W. Moutoussamy House (1954, p. 200) designed by John W. Moutoussamy, who was emerging at the time as the most prominent black architect in Chicago. The wave of modernist houses commissioned by African American entrepreneurs and professionals in Chatham during the 1950s and 1960s was in part a response to the divisive politics of urban renewal that prompted families to leave the near South Side for neighborhoods farther south.[3]

Detail of covered entrance walkway.

From 1950 to 1960, Chatham experienced a major shift in its racial composition, with African Americans comprising only 1 percent of the population in 1950 but 64 percent by 1960.[4] After resistance by some sellers, famed Gospel singer Mahalia Jackson was able to purchase a spacious Ranch-style house in 1957 and became one of a few African American residents in the predominately white neighborhood, despite threats of violence.[5] By the time the Johnsons commissioned their house, Chatham was an established African American neighborhood that appealed to upwardly mobile entrepreneurs and professionals as well as educators and municipal employees. Despite the number of architect-designed houses built in Chatham near the Johnson House at the time, the majority of the housing stock remains more conventional builder housing types such as bungalows, multi-unit flats, and Ranches.

Louis H. Huebner was a 1944 graduate of University of Illinois Urbana-Champaign with a Bachelor of Science in Architectural Engineering. He was a longtime resident of the City of Park Ridge to the northwest of Chicago (where he designed his first residence in 1950 as part of a wave of post–World War II housing boom).[6] Park Ridge was the enclave of creativity with the Kalo Arts and Crafts Community House (founded in 1900) and the studio of artist and designer Alfonso Iannelli.[7] Here, Bruce Goff designed two important houses for forward-looking clients: the Ruth and Frank F. Cole House (1939) was commissioned by the editor of the *Park Ridge Herald* and his spouse followed by a commission from local art teacher Helen Unseth (1940).[8] James C. Henneberg joined the firm in 1960 and worked with his partner Huebner to design the Johnson House in Chatham.[9]

In order to accommodate the program for four bedrooms, two-and-a-half bathrooms, living room, kitchen, and dining room, the Johnsons purchased and joined two lots. The master bedroom with en suite bathroom with its own suncourt are located at the front of the house with an additional three bedrooms with a bathroom at the rear of the house. The one-story, flat-roof, L-shaped patio house plan featured a post-and-beam wood-frame, exposed brick walls, and large windowpanes. The covered walkway, roof overhangs, and the freestanding, extended structural elements of the Johnson House evoke a West Coast–inspired informality. The covered walkway extends to the circular driveway and is flanked on one side by a two-car garage signaling automobile-friendly suburbs. A monumental honey locust tree likely planted when the house was completed has grown over the years and provides a distinctive natural canopy.

The West Coast atmosphere of the architects' built and unbuilt work may explain why the firm's projects (first credited as Huebner and later as Huebner & Henneberg) were extensively featured in the California-based magazine *Arts & Architecture* directed by John Entenza from 1940–62 (until he moved to Chicago to direct the Graham Foundation for Advanced Studies in the Fine Arts).[10] Even though the work of Huebner & Henneberg received wide coverage, the Johnson House unfortunately does not appear to be published, although a remarkably similar one referred to as a "house in Illinois" (with Theodore D. Brickman, Landscape Architect) appeared earlier in the *Arts & Architecture* June 1961 issue.[11]

By the mid-1970s, the Johnsons relocated to Glencoe (a community with a historic presence of African Americans) after they purchased the substantially larger 8,712-square-foot house that Tony Grunsfeld had designed for Chicago business developer Jerrold Wexler in 1963.[12]

View from street with surrounding houses.

Current owners Pamela Martin Orr and spouse Michael Orr bought the house in Chatham from her father, a builder, who had purchased it in the mid-1980s from George Johnson after it had suffered damage from a fire.[13] The Johnson House is one of the most distinguished modernist houses still standing that were owned or commissioned by African American professionals on Chicago's South Side; despite recent efforts, much research and recognition still remains to be accomplished in order to identify and protect the modern built heritage of this important area of Chicagoland's multifaceted identity.[14] —MS

Priscilla Huffard and
H. P. Davis Rockwell House II

Colloquially known as the "House on a Bluff," this modern pavilion has a symmetrical plan and four monumental exposed aggregate reinforced-concrete tapered columns holding up the roof, giving it an airy temple-like quality.[1] Architect Harry Phillips Davis Rockwell designed the house for his wife Priscilla and their four children in the village of Olympia Fields, a community in the southern suburbs of Chicago that developed around the Olympia Fields Country Club established in 1915. The Rockwell House is sited on the edge of a ravine overlooking Butterfield Creek. Writing about his design, Rockwell stated, "with gravel forecourt, walks, walls, steps and treatment of glass, the building partakes of the landscape while maintaining its architectural integrity. The use of berms and native planting has restored as much as possible the naturalness of the surroundings, the variety of vistas and spaces."[2] Having begun his career working for landscape architect Alfred Caldwell and subsequently Mies van der Rohe, Rockwell's inspired design pays homage to both mentors.

Front lawn with entrance to the main floor (upper level).

232

H. P. Davis "Deever" Rockwell obtained a degree in labor relations and mechanical engineering at MIT. Priscilla "Cil" Huffard graduated from Vassar College with a major in English. In 1949 the couple moved to Chicago, and he went to work for Inland Steel Company in East Chicago, Indiana. In 1955, Rockwell and his spouse commissioned a house in the southern suburb village of Flossmoor by the firm of Schweikher and Elting.[3] The building process inspired Rockwell to change career paths and enroll in the architecture program at IIT, where he graduated in 1957. By 1961 he joined Daniel Brenner and George Danforth, who were both teaching at IIT at the time, to form Brenner Danforth Rockwell, a partnership that lasted two decades (1961–81). Their most notable commissions at the time of Rockwell's house in Olympia Fields include the transformation of the Elsa Seipp and Alfred F. Madlener House into the headquarters of the Graham Foundation in Chicago (1963) and the conversion of a former bakery into the first location of the Museum of Contemporary Art Chicago (1967).

View from ravine of upper and lower levels.

Visible reinforced concrete structure with "glass corner window" and terrazzo floors.

George Danforth described the house as follows:

> It sits as a pavilion on the ravine and the lower part, which is in the ground, are the bedrooms, and the master bedroom is up in the glass pavilion. There are just four columns, concrete, with glass all the way around. There is a center core with a living and dining area within that and the master bedroom and Deever's drafting table.[4]

A critic writing in *Architectural Record* shortly after its completion provides a thoughtful overview of the house while noting (without explicitly identifying examples) a shift from steel-and-glass pavilions such as the Farnsworth House:

> A forceful, sculpturesque concrete frame for this elegant house in Olympia Fields, Illinois, makes a notable departure from the now classic glass pavilion. In spite of the massiveness of the structure, the light and open character of the main-floor pavilion is preserved by the use of tapered, faceted columns, and by the truncated pyramidal form of the podium set into the slope.[5]

Lower and upper level plans.

Study with "Deever" Rockwell's drafting table.

The concrete columns holding up the massive roof create a subtle tension between weightiness and airiness.

Deever and Cil eventually sold the house and moved to the East Coast in 2012.[6] In recent years the Rockwell "House on a Bluff" has changed hands a number of times, which has led to substantial visibility, especially within the world of online real-estate marketing. It has also received attention among midcentury architecture enthusiasts, thanks to a 2010 publication by Gary Gand with new color photography by Julius Shulman, whereas previous black-and-white images were taken by noted architectural photographer Richard Nickel.[7] While it has served as a permanent residence for all previous inhabitants, the new owners plan to use the house as a weekend retreat. —MS

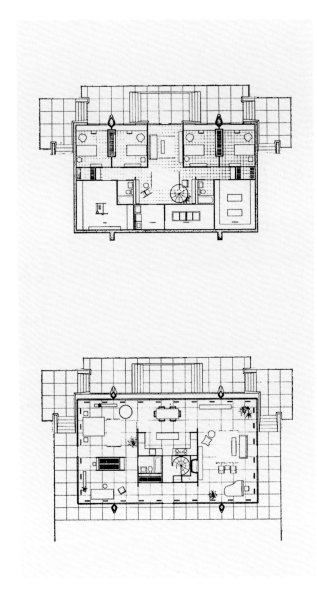

Lower and upper level plans.

Study with "Deever" Rockwell's drafting table.

Ming Djang and Chung Kuo Liao House

Commissioned by the Chinese American ophthalmologist Dr. Chung Kuo Liao and his spouse, Ming Djang, this two-story, prestressed concrete house (with brick infill walls) is sited on a wooded lot across from the historic Olympia Fields Country Club.[1] This flat-roofed structure was designed by Chinese American and IIT-trained Yau Chun Wong and R. Ogden Hannaford. Y. C. Wong (as he is generally known) earned a Master of Science in Architecture in 1951 at IIT and like Liao immigrated to America from Guangzhou (formerly known as Canton).[2] Hannaford earned a BA from Yale in 1939 before earning his Bachelor of Science in Architecture from IIT, where he was associate professor from 1960–86.[3] Both Wong and Hannaford had worked for Mies van der Rohe in the late 1950s.[4] In an interview, Wong candidly explained his challenges as a non-native English speaker and why he had partnered with Hannaford: "I knew my handicap, or my drawback, is my accent in talking to people, so I thought he would be a much better person to deal with clients and get jobs or whatever."[5]

Not unlike Mies's choice of white painted steel to set the Edith Farnsworth House (p. 162) off against the natural setting of the Fox River Valley, with the use of white painted prestressed concrete Wong evokes the classical underpinning of his teacher's masterwork. In fact, the pronounced pilasters, horizontal fascia, and symmetrical plan give the Ming Djang and Chung Kuo Liao House a distinctly

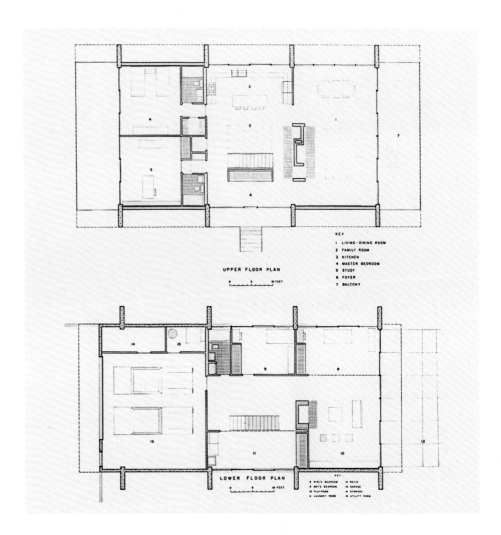

Opposite: Living room balcony (upper) and playroom patio (lower), facing wooded ravine.

Upper and lower level floor plans, *Arts & Architecture* (January 1967).

monumental, temple-like quality.[6] In order to accommodate the natural grade changes of the sloped site, Wong designed a below-grade level in which he located two bedrooms, a playroom, laundry, garage, storage, utility room, and an outside patio; the main floor has a master bedroom, study, foyer, and living-dining room with floor-to-ceiling windows opening up to a cantilevered balcony. Another balcony at the opposite end above the two-car garage also runs across the entire width of the house to ensure views from the bedroom.

In addition, Wong and Hannaford designed Liao's medical clinic in the city of Harvey, Illinois, south of Chicago, that also exploited the qualities of precast and prestressed concrete to avoid "load-bearing partitions to achieve a flexibility of space."[7] An article about the building in *Arts & Architecture* described it in the following terms:

> … roof slabs spanning 52' resting on two reinforced concrete edge beams, each 64' long and supported on three columns spaced 25' on center and cantilevered 7' at both ends. The enclosed space is 50' by 50', divided into four offices, a large waiting room and a drop-in area with separate entrance for patients who have received pre-examination medication…. The house, like the clinic, has precast and prestressed roof slabs resting on reinforced beams and piers and is similarly enclosed with glass and brick.[8]

Wong is best known for his widely published one-story brick 2,000-square-foot atrium houses (1961) in Hyde Park, Chicago.[9] In Olympia Field's in addition to the Priscilla Huffard and H. P. Davis Rockwell House II, 1964 (p. 232), the Graymoor neighborhood hosted a number of modernist houses including the Eleanor Gray and Saul Lieberman House (1956) by Edward Humrich, and others designed by Edward Dart and Keck & Keck.[10] Neighboring Flossmoor was also a site of experimentation by well-known architects during the postwar years: consider the Priscilla Huffard and H. P. Davis Rockwell House I (Schweikher and Elting, 1955, p. 206), the Minna

Green and Hugh Duncan House I (Keck & Keck, 1941, p. 130), and the Sylvia and Leo Levin House (Bertrand Goldberg, 1957).

During and shortly after World War II, Yau Chun Wong was among a group of students of Asian descent who trained at IIT, worked with Mies, and went on to establish independent practices, work with major firms, and/or teach in Chicago. Pao-Chi Chang, also Chinese-born, had lived in Shanghai before she earned her Master of Science in Architecture in 1954 and became an Associate Professor, teaching at IIT from 1973–93.[11] Japanese American Joseph Y. Fujikawa was born in Los Angeles but his education was interrupted twice during the war: first when, after several years at USC, he was sent to a relocation center in Colorado before appealing to Mies to attend IIT, where he earned his Bachelor of Science in Architecture in 1944; and then when he served in the Army translating Japanese before returning to earn his Master of Science in Architecture in 1953.[12] (See the Grace Yamada and Joseph Fujikawa House in Winnetka (1971), p. 296). Japanese American Arthur S. Takeuchi was sent to an interment camp in Idaho for several years; at IIT he earned both his Bachelor of Architecture in 1958 and his Master of Science in Architecture in 1959 and became an associate professor, teaching at IIT from 1965–2018.[13] Like Wong, these individuals continued to build upon, both in terms of teaching and practice, the pedagogical ideals embodied in the Mies van der Rohe curriculum he established shortly after arriving in 1938.[14]

The Ming Djang and Chung Kuo Liao House was sold in 1985, and the Liao family moved to neighboring Park Forest.[15] The prestressed concrete house appears to have weathered well through the years and stands as a testament to the integration of Chinese-born individuals who contributed to American design and society. —MS

Sheila Adelman and David Haid House

The one-story house that David Haid designed for his spouse at the time Sheila, and their daughters is set among a block of Victorian-era houses facing Stockham Place Park, located in Evanston, a city that borders the northern limits of Chicago. Since the early twentieth century, Evanston has attracted a considerable number of outstanding architects who have designed homes for themselves and their families while maintaining offices in the city; from the Arts-and-Crafts-inspired Lucy Perkins and Dwight H. Perkins House (1904) to the organic-modern Caroline Sinclair and Philip Will Jr. House (1937, p. 92), the history of Evanston's built environment is particularly rich with outstanding residential architecture.[1]

The award-winning Sheila Adelman and David Haid House was realized after the architect sold his adjacent Victorian-era house and designed a new and decidedly compact house on the side yard of his former residence.[2] Based on the modern pavilion type explored by Mies van der Rohe and his students, Haid's design cautiously opens to the street with a large window wall while the main entrance of the house is tucked into the side. A small courtyard off the master bedroom projects outward from the front facade enclosed by a brick privacy wall. Further south

House sited within Stockham Place Park neighborhood.

240

Rear patio and garage.

View of side courtyard looking into the house.

Ground floor plan.

on Michigan Avenue and a decade later in 1978, architect and interior designer George Larson designed a remarkable two-story house for his family that shares many characteristics with Haid's design, including the intelligent use of a compact lot and an understated facade behind which one finds elegant interior spaces.

Haid described the brief of his house thus:

> This house is on a 50' by 150' urban site in a neighborhood of large old houses. The problem was to provide adequate space for a family of five, maximum site utilization with privacy both indoors and

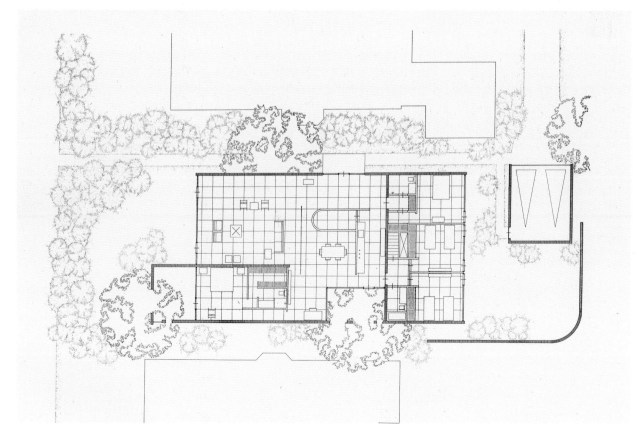

241

out, and preserve existing trees. The solution developed is a four bed-room house with three enclosed courtyards affording private outdoor spaces off various areas of the house…. The 77' 4" by 40' 4" roof is framed in structural steel using wide flange beams, girders and fascia members. The brick walls provide more than adequate support for the roof so columns were not utilized. The exterior glass walls are framed of welded steel bar stock sections and were completely shop fabricated as units, including the tubular steel doors which were fitted and installed in the shop. Interior finish materials are a suspended drywall ceiling, drywall on steel stud partition, a terrazzo floor and white oak cabinet work.[3]

At just under 3,000 square feet, the Haid House combines meticulous detailing and modern materiality with a plan that skillfully uses a limited amount of space to a host a variety of different functions. For example, in proximity to a galley kitchen, the dining room was visually separated from the living room by a floor-to-ceiling curtain.

Both David and Sheila Haid were from Winnipeg, a city defined by its modern architectural legacy. He had apprenticed as a cabinetmaker there.[4] Sheila worked as an industrial and clinical psychologist.[5] Haid started his architectural education at IIT in 1951 and studied with and worked for Mies van der Rohe on a number of

buildings, including Cullinan Hall of the Museum of Fine Arts Houston (1958); Reyner Banham remarked that, "next to Chicago itself, Houston must be the most Miesian city in North America."[6] After a couple of years of practice in Houston in the early 1960s with Cowell & Neuhaus, Haid returned to Chicago and established an independent practice, David Haid and Associates.[7] Shortly before designing his house in Evanston, Haid completed the award-winning Abraham Lincoln Oasis, Tri-State Tollway in South Holland, Illinois (1967) and would go on to design the Rose Auto Pavilion (1974, p. 190) in Highland Park.[8]

Following his death in 1993, the heirs sold the house to poet Deborah Cummins (former board member of the Poetry Foundation) and her spouse, Robert. They hired Powell/Kleinschmidt for a sensitive renovation in 2001 and lived there until 2011. Current owners, Elizabeth Solaro and Joseph Frank, purchased it and have taken a special interest in the history of the house: "I can't say that our house fits into the neighborhood. Newer houses were built to reflect their surroundings, while ours is an obvious, but quiet rejection. The Haid House all but disappears between much larger houses and is hidden behind naturalistic landscape that creates beautiful views through the window walls and also provides a little privacy."[9] —MS

Opposite: Living room, with Mies-designed furniture, looking outside towards Stockham Place Park.

Galley kitchen.

Owner's bedroom looking into walled courtyard that faces street.

Donna Parr and
Charles R. Walgreen III House

Clarence Krusinski designed an impressive home for Charles R. "Cork" Walgreen III who was thirty-three years old at the time and named president of the Walgreen Company (founded by his grandfather who had worked in a drugstore on Chicago's South Side, purchased it in 1901, and then set about expanding the company). Cork Walgreen knew the business well, having begun as a stock boy in 1952. After earning a degree in pharmacy from the University of Michigan in 1958, he worked his way up through the ranks. By 1975, six years after the house was completed, Walgreens had grown to more than 1,500 pharmacists in 633 stores.[1]

View toward front entrance, adjacent to study.

Clarence Krusinski established his architecture and interior design firm, Clarence Krusinski and Associates, in 1967. During his first year in practice, he received a call from Donna Parr Walgreen, Cork's spouse at the time, asking if he would like to be interviewed for the design of the family's Lake Forest house. He responded that he had not designed a lot of houses but would welcome the opportunity. When Krusinski proposed a Z-shaped, Mies-inspired Corten-steel-and-glass house, he was immediately hired. The predominantly steel-and-glass Walgreen House closely follows the design aesthetic of Ludwig Mies van der Rohe, a material palette most frequently associated with Chicago's modern skyscrapers, not single-family homes.

View from circular driveway to house from road.

Steel-and-glass curtain wall opening into sitting area of living room, dining room, breakfast room, and servant's bedroom. Garage beyond, past breezeway.

In residential architecture of the 1970s, Mies's influence was diminishing in popularity. Steel- or concrete-frame houses were generally unpopular for family living because they were perceived to be cold and lacking in privacy. Mies's Farnsworth House (p. 162), located along the Fox River as a weekend house, is the iconic example, but it was already twenty years old at the time. Exceptions include houses designed by two architects who each embraced Mies's influence when designing his own home: Jacques Brownson (1952, p. 176) and David Haid (1969, p. 240). Although David Haid created a steel-and-glass Auto Pavilion (1974, p. 190) for textile designer Ben Rose, it was designed for a collection of classic cars and receptions rather than as a home.

The Walgreen House was simple in design but grand in size at 11,000 square feet. Krusinski's Corten curtain-wall structure, consisting of eight modules of 34-foot bays, enclosed 5,500 square feet of column-free space, with an equal amount of square footage in the concrete-walled basement. Corten, which weathers to a mellow brown, was selected for its durability, color compatibility with the home's forested setting, and its low maintenance.[2] Bronze-tinted glass complemented the color of the weathering steel.

Built for a young family, the house was designed for easy care and comfortable living. It had the era's characteristic open plan, with only partial walls separating the major public rooms. The Z shape provided for living room, family room, and dining room in the long central portion with library and bedrooms in one wing and kitchen and maid's room in the other. There were no operable windows; only doors open to the outside. Air vents were located in the floor throughout the entire perimeter of the house, with terrazzo flooring in the main area and carpeting in the bedrooms.

Clarence Krusinski is a little-known Chicago architect, having spent much of his career in real estate development, but his design talent is clearly reflected in the Walgreen House. In 1959 Krusinski enrolled at the Illinois Institute of Technology (IIT) to study architecture. Although Mies had retired two years earlier, his design sensibility, which had formed the basis of the architecture school's curriculum, brought Krusinski into contact with such gifted teachers as Alfred Caldwell, a protégé of master Prairie School landscape architect Jens Jensen, and Walter Peterhans, a photographer and colleague of Mies at the Bauhaus and at IIT.

As an undergraduate and after graduation, Krusinski worked for PACE Associates (Planners, Architects, Consulting Engineers), the firm that had collaborated with Mies on S. R. Crown Hall (1956) at IIT and 860–880 Lake Shore Drive (1949–51). In 1965, Krusinski left PACE to join Schipporeit Heinrich, a five-person architectural firm that in the late 1960s designed Chicago's award-winning 70-story Lake Point Tower—a building reminiscent of Mies's 1922 project for a curvilinear skyscraper.[3] Both John C. Heinrich and George C. Schipporeit had studied with Mies at IIT and subsequently worked in his office. The firm, while Krusinski was there, also designed the 20-story curtain-walled State National Bank Building, Evanston's first high-rise, completed in 1969, after Krusinski had left the firm.

Opposite: View from yard at master bedroom toward terrace entrance to living room.

Hallway with dining room beyond. Living room sideboard on opposite wall.

Recognition for the rare and purely Miesian Walgreen house came immediately—it was widely published in newspapers as well as trade and professional journals. In 1972, the *Chicago Tribune* featured it as "Home of the Week."[4] The European press also took note, with an article in the December 1971 issue of *Bauen & Wohnen*. The house won an award for Krusinski's firm in the suburban homes division of the 17th annual Homes for Better Living program sponsored by the AIA and trade publications *House and Home* and *American Home Magazine*. It was the only Illinois project to win an award.

The house had successive owners, one of whom had been the perpetrator of a Ponzi scheme whose disgruntled employees had looted it. After having sat vacant, the house was purchased in 2013 for the land and replaced by a traditional house.[5] —SSB

Margaret Berman and
Paul Lurie House

When James L. Nagle (1937–), then a partner in Booth & Nagle, designed a home for clients in the suburb of Evanston, he had a clear brief: Paul and Margaret Lurie wanted a rectangular, flat-roof house.[1] They moved from an apartment in Chicago's Hyde Park neighborhood and were looking for a modern house that would be functional and meet the needs of a growing family. The result was an elegantly executed house built of steel, brick, and glass with a flat roof and no applied ornament.

In the article "Midwest Moderns," Nagle reflected on his career noting that his "houses have a distinct and consistent modern theme, but it is a modernism overlaid

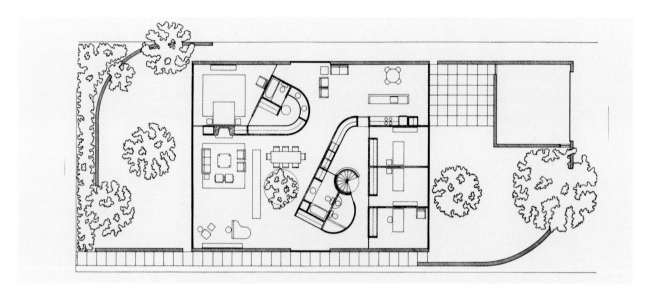

with adaptations to site, context, and program and tempered by attention to scale, materials, and detail and the desire to create an architecture that is more difficult to categorize. It is a modernism humanized."[2] These words aptly describe Nagle's design approach to the Lurie House.

Nagle acknowledged that he was very much influenced by Ludwig Mies van der Rohe's courtyard houses of the 1930s. These were compact, inward-looking designs like the atrium houses of ancient Greece and Rome; they had a single open plan, juxtaposed opaque and transparent planes, and interior spaces shaped by walls and storage units independent of structure. Nagle also admired the work of David Haid whose own home was a short distance from the Lurie House.[3] With its geometric order and careful attention to materials and detailing, the Lurie House reflects the spirit and, can be argued, the letter of Miesian modernism. Nagle described his designs using a musical analogy to illustrate their differences. Like a Mozart symphony, "Classics" such as the Lurie House are those that have a clear formal structure, a spatial organization or geometry, and careful attention to proportion.[4]

The Lurie House was created to respect the architecture of the neighborhood, which at the time was largely comprised of traditional homes, brick apartment buildings, and a sprinkling of newer houses. Nagle's intent was to relate the Lurie House to other houses nearby in scale and materials. The Lurie House almost completely fills the 60-by-140-foot side yard of an adjacent early twentieth-century brick house. To the west were one- and two-story modern houses with flat roofs. He complimented the surrounding buildings with a sensitive use of materials and a landscape designed by Joe Karr Associates.

Recent photo of bedroom hallway with circular staircase to basement, topped by a skylight.

Privacy was important to the Luries. Although the north and south walls of the house are glazed, tall curving brick walls separate the house from the back alley and the street, creating an intimate private outdoor dining terrace at the rear and a shallow secluded garden in the front. Masonry walls are all of oversize iron spot brick. Large bronze-tinted glass panels on the front and back of the house, along with the bronze-painted steel fascia, create a warm and understated color scheme.

Curving walls delineating the public and private spaces echo those on the exterior, while allowing light to flow from one side of the 3,200-square-foot house to the other. Light further enters the living room from a dramatic ten-foot-diameter skylight. A bar joist roof that spans fifty feet and ceiling heights of nine-and-a-half feet allow for a spacious interior and free plan with living areas delineated by furniture; only the bedrooms and baths are separated by walls, which are not structural.

Informal sitting area looking toward kitchen space and glass wall at rear of house.

Living room, view toward glass wall facing shallow garden and street.

Widely published in newspapers and architectural journals, the Lurie House was featured in the April 1975 issue of *Inland Architect,* illustrated in an April 1976 issue of the *Chicago Sun-Times Midwest Magazine,* and showcased in the December 1976 issue of *A + U (Architecture and Urbanism).*[5] More importantly, it was among the handful of houses illustrated in the catalog of the exhibition *100 Years of Architecture in Chicago* held at the Museum of Contemporary Art Chicago in 1976.[6]

Nagle's Miesian approach continues to resonate as other design sensibilities have become popular even within the context of the architect's own body of work. His design for the house has suited the Luries' lifestyle well over the decades.

Paul had been a founder of the Chicago Architecture Foundation, established in 1966 to buy and preserve H. H. Richardson's iconic Glessner House.[7] Margaret owned a popular Evanston shop and served on the Evanston school board (D202) for over twenty years; she currently serves on the city's public library board. Paul serves as a mediation attorney and has received acclaim for his photography. They continue to enjoy living in their modern house, adapting it to their evolving needs as empty nesters while retaining the features that make it distinctive. —SSB

Dawn Clark and Walter Netsch House

Two very accomplished Chicagoans lived in this unusual house. The owner-architect, Walter A. Netsch Jr., trained at the Massachusetts Institute of Technology and became a partner in the Chicago headquarters of Skidmore, Owings & Merrill (SOM) where he spent almost his entire career. Dawn Clark Netsch, his spouse, was a professor of law at Northwestern University and an Illinois State Senator.

Walter Netsch designed a home that expressed in microcosm an approach to design that he termed his "Field Theory."[1] A romantic as much as a theorist, he took the dense form of a chrysanthemum, abstracted its facets into squares, and rotated the squares from a central core as the basic geometry for his designs. He revealed that the idea of creating a forty-foot cube, running a diagonal through it, and rotating a square "came to me while I was sitting in Eero Saarinen's beautiful Dulles airport with my squared paper working on it while waiting for a plane back to Chicago."[2]

Although Netsch applied the theory to several public buildings, including an addition to the Art Institute of Chicago, this was the only time he ever applied it to a house.[3]

The Netsches' house had to meet three criteria. First, it had to accommodate the couple's growing art collection, which included large museum-quality pieces by some of the world's greatest modern artists, including Robert Motherwell, Jim Dine, and Claes Oldenberg. Second, the house had to be economical, and third, it needed to be built within Dawn's state senatorial district. Netsch also didn't want to purchase property that would require a building to be torn down.

The Netsches bought a 40-by-75-foot corner lot in Chicago's Old Town neighborhood, then a somewhat rough area but today associated with lovingly restored historic houses and stunning new townhomes. Bids for construction of the house came in at $125 per square foot even though the average rate was around $40 to $50. The house ultimately cost only $34 per square foot, mainly because Netsch used common materials that could be ordered from a catalog—brick, concrete block, wooden framing members, and patio doors. Eschewing standard double hung windows, glass doors were a particularly attractive solution. They were inexpensive and mimicked the shape of his paintings. The openings formed by

the edges of the patio doors framed scenes, including the adjacent St. Michael's Catholic Church and, when used as skylights, the top of the John Hancock Building a mile away.

The 3,000-square-foot townhouse evokes surprise. Its exterior is unadorned, dark red-brown brick, with sparse trim painted a deep chocolate brown. Windows are placed high, offering no glimpses inside. Tucked next to the garage, the front door is barely noticeable. In contrast to the dark exterior, the interior walls are white. Entrance is through a low-ceilinged foyer, which then opens into a triple-height living

View into dining space connected to kitchen.

Recent photo of living room with stairs up to sitting area that has large windows facing side street.

room flooded with light. From this universal space, smaller spaces unfold like a spiral into layers of rotating squares forming open rooms to accommodate living and dining areas, a kitchen, bedrooms, and bathrooms. The walls are standard 8-inch-by-16-inch concrete block that had a "fake joint in the middle," creating what appeared to be 8-inch square units; Netsch took advantage of this "to create a subtle rhythm across … the walls."[4] Diagonal stairs, with neither risers nor railings, were designed to cut through and access the various areas.[5] Wide steps were also designed like bleachers to accommodate audiences, including attendees at fundraising events for Dawn Clark Netsch's political campaigns.[6] Other than for bathrooms, the house has no doors.

The spatial progression in Netsch's house was conceptually similar to Frank Lloyd Wright's approach in his Prairie School and Usonian houses. The visitor enters through a compressed passage that opens onto a grander space. Netsch was a great admirer of Wright. He once commented, "Why isn't everyone filled with Frank Lloyd Wright buildings? They don't want to go to the trouble that Frank Lloyd Wright did in creating buildings. It takes genius to create a complex aesthetic idea. All I was doing was carrying on the tradition of Chicago."[7] Walter Netsch acknowledged that he had done what Wright advised architects to do: "Find a set of artistic principles and work within them to find one's own solution."[8]

Walter Netsch viewed his house as a study of specific problems and solutions, much like the modern Case Study houses commissioned and built in California from 1945–66 by *Arts & Architecture* magazine and designed by major architects of the time, including Richard Neutra, Charles Eames, and Ralph Rapson.[9] Although the

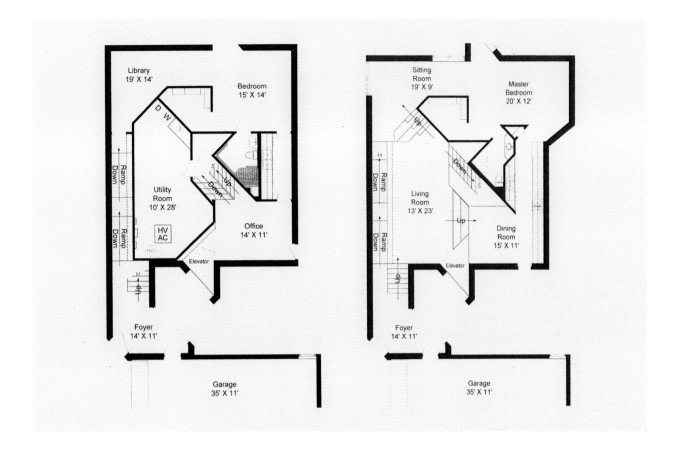

Library
19' X 14'

Bedroom
15' X 14'

Ramp
Down

Utility
Room
10' X 28'

HV
AC

Office
14' X 11'

Elevator

Foyer
14' X 11'

Garage
35' X 11'

Sitting
Room
19' X 9'

Master
Bedroom
20' X 12'

Ramp
Down

Living
Room
13' X 23'

Dining
Room
15' X 11'

Elevator

Foyer
14' X 11'

Garage
35' X 11'

Floor plans showing first and second levels and third and fourth levels.

Field theory illustrating rotating square from a central core like an abstracted chrysanthemum.

Case Study houses were intended to serve as examples of affordable post–World War II modern housing while the Netsch House was a design tailored to fit the needs of a particular owner, each set out test cases for new ideas of their times and continued this practical and experimental tradition in residential architecture.

Among Walter Netsch's distinguished, award-winning designs were the University of Illinois in Chicago, the United States Air Force Academy and Chapel in Colorado Springs, libraries at the University of Chicago and Northwestern University, Chicago's Inland Steel Building (with Bruce Graham), and the East Wing of the Art Institute of Chicago (now the Arthur Rubloff Building). Netsch was a Fellow of the American Institute of Architects.

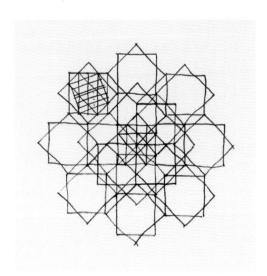

During her lifetime, Dawn Clark Netsch not only served as an Illinois State Senator and State Comptroller, she was also the first woman in the state to run for Governor of Illinois. After her death in 2013, current owners Will Forrest and Mark Smithe bought this unique home from the estate. They have been ideal stewards of the Netsch House and worked with Skidmore, Owings & Merrill (SOM) on plans for some sensitive updates, including the addition of stair railings and updating of baths and the kitchen, while retaining some of the original features, such as the cabinets. —SSB

Arlene and Richard Don House

Stanley Tigerman never designed buildings with a single-minded stylistic direction.[1] His works during the 1960s–70s were sometimes Brutalist—under the influence of his Yale professor Paul Rudolph—and sometimes Miesian. Tigerman recounted that he was drawn to Mies by "his work and his rigor, his intellect," and by how this "self-made" German émigré went on to become "the greatest architect of the twentieth century."[2] The "Metal and Glass House," as Tigerman referred to the house for Richard and Arlene Don, is unadorned, clad with repeating, similarly sized rectangular panels. The house, however, is an irregular shape, composed of walls that are flat surfaces, angles, and various types of segmented curves. It conveys the anticipated tension between opposites typical of Tigerman, a personal

Exterior of irregularly shaped house, clad with aluminum and grey-tinted glass panels.

departure from Ludwig Mies van der Rohe's structuralist aesthetic.

Tigerman's design for the Don House adapts Mies's open plan to the somewhat idiosyncratic requirements of his client. Richard Don requested a totally high-tech home. The house structure is a steel frame faced with rectangular aluminum panels and grey-tinted glass. The first features seen from the street are an astronomical observatory and a four-car garage with electric roll-up aluminum doors. Rear and side walls have several large glazed openings accessing terraces, facing Lake Michigan—elements expected in a modern house. But other features are less expected. The house was extensively computerized, though built at a time when electronic systems-control for houses was in its infancy. It was programmed to notify the owner if visitors arrive at the property and included a remote-controlled robot cart to shuttle laundry around.

The grey and silver tones of the house allow it to take on the changing colors of the sky, the lake, and the surrounding landscape.[3] There is a discipline about its orderly design but also a sense of mystery. It provides a curious twist on Le Corbusier's dictum that a house is *une machine-à-habiter*--a machine for living in. —SSB

View from driveway showing astronomical observatory and garages with electric roll-up aluminum doors.

Room with glazed wall providing lake views.

John Vinci & Lawrence Kenny   Riverside   1975

Ruth Nelson and Robert J. Freeark House

The Freeark House was designed for a relatively small lot in Riverside, a village in Chicago's western suburbs planned by Frederick Law Olmsted and Calvert Vaux in 1869.[1] The 3,400-square-foot, two-story house is adjacent to residential buildings designed by Prairie School architect William Drummond's Thorncroft Residence (1912) and a short distance from Frank Lloyd Wright's (Addie) "Queene" Ferry and Avery Coonley House (1907), Gardener's Cottage, and Playhouse.[2] Like Wright, John Vinci and Lawrence Kenny invert the conventional order of domestic architecture by locating the living room, kitchen, and master bedroom on the upper floor (the modern day equivalent of the historic *piano nobile*) and service-oriented spaces—additional bedrooms, a garage, and artist studio—on the ground floor. The modern square plan and industrial materials (glass, brick, and reinforced concrete) stand in contrast to the organic qualities of the meandering streets of Riverside that defy the relentless Chicago grid. This modern house was begun in 1971 and completed in 1975, during a time when a new appetite for the revision

Freeark House with Thorncroft and Coonley Houses to the left.

258

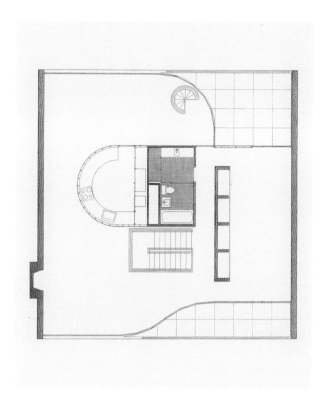

of modernism (i.e. "postmodernism") was beginning to change the mindset of new generations of clients and creating a backlash against Mies van der Rohe and his followers.[3] During the mid-1970s, there was also a gradual shift in interest among professionals toward Chicago, bringing them to reconsider leaving the suburbs in favor of urban dwellings.[4]

In 1970, Dr. Robert J. Freeark was appointed Chairman of the Department of Surgery at Loyola University Health System located in the village of Maywood, a short commute from Riverside. Prior to Loyola, in 1958 he became director of surgery at Cook County Hospital and during his tenure established the first trauma unit in the country and its Burn Center and Heliport in 1965. Ruth Nelson Freeark was an artist and several years after moving to Riverside, she and her spouse established the Riverside Arts Center in 1993.

Nelli Barr, a sculptor and teacher at IIT, the School of the Art Institute of Chicago, and the Evanston Art Center, introduced Vinci and Kenny to the Freearks. Chicago native John Vinci graduated from IIT in 1960 and worked for Skidmore, Owings and Merrill (SOM) and Brenner Danforth Rockwell for a number of years.[5] Lawrence Kenny also studied at IIT, earning a bachelor's degree in 1964 and a Master of Science in Architecture degree in 1968 under the direction of Myron Goldsmith. As a student he worked briefly at Mies's office and following graduation worked at SOM Chicago with Goldsmith on a city plan for Columbus, Indiana.[6] Vinci and Kenny were in practice together as John Vinci/Lawrence Kenny

Architects, in Chicago from 1968–77.[7] After Vinci designed a house for his parents in the Chicago neighborhood of West Elsdon, the Ruth Nelson and Robert J. Freeark House was Vinci (and Kenny's) first domestic architecture commission. They also collaborated on the preservation and adaptive reuse of historic houses such as H. H. Richardson's Glessner House and Wright's Robie House.

Living room looking out toward the Des Plaines River.

Although Vinci trained at IIT with a rigorous Miesian curriculum dedicated to disciplined experimentation with a focus on materials and structures, he gradually developed a penchant for preservation thanks to his experience (shared with photographer Richard Nickel) protesting the demolition of the Garrick Theater, designed by Adler & Sullivan. During the winter of 1960, the Laura Davis and Henry Babson Estate (1907), designed by Louis Sullivan and landscaped by Jens Jensen

Entrance foyer with concrete stair with steel railings.

in Riverside, was slated for demolition, and Vinci (with Nickel and others) worked to salvage pieces of the building.[8]

According to Vinci, the design of the Freeark House allowed him to assess his training critically. He explained his experience designing the Freeark in the following way: "And from that house I learned that you don't have to follow Mies religiously.

My work never adheres strictly to the module. If you look at my work and if you look at the house, I think you'll see that that's the beginning of that idea."[9]

In addition to Vinci and Kenny, Nelli Barr had introduced the Freearks to another architect, Willy (T. William) Fejer, who was also an IIT College of Architecture graduate, earning a bachelor's in 1964 and Master of Science in 1967.[10] Both firms were asked to produce a design concept, and in the end Vinci and Kenny's scheme was selected. Vinci, who took the lead during construction, relied upon his familial network of masons and contractors to realize the masonry component of the house: two windowless, monumental, load-bearing brick walls on the east and west sides of the house created privacy for the Freearks and their family. The upper floor of the north and south facades was defined by large floor-to-ceiling steel-framed windows with access to a backyard terrace and a balcony with views in the front toward Indian Gardens (an archaeological site) and the Des Plaines River. The reinforced concrete floating staircase in the entrance hall and a polished concrete floor on the ground floor confers a loft-like feeling to the space. The parquet wood floor adds warmth and elegance to the *piano nobile*. Currently, the house is owned by their daughter, Kim Freeark. —MS

261

Stanley Tigerman   Harvard   1975

Iris Smith and Paul Goldstein House

262

Opposite: View from rear
pond and wooded landscape.

Floor plans of the 15-by-65-
foot house reveal why it was
popularly referred to as the
"Hot Dog House."

The Goldstein House was built on ten acres as a weekend home for a young couple, Paul and Iris, from Chicago's Hyde Park neighborhood, an area that has long been home to progressive thinkers. Embedded in a rural area at the northwest corner of metropolitan Chicago, the Goldstein family's get-away was an eighty-mile drive, a place standing in stark contrast to Chicago's urban streetscape.

Stanley Tigerman's Goldstein House has enormous appeal as a study in contrasts. Just across from an apple orchard (containing trees planted by the Goldsteins), it appears closed at the front, a blank wall sheathed in vertical cedar boards, but open at the rear, which consists of glass and colored panels facing a wooded landscape that slopes down to a pond.

Upon arrival, only the orchard can be seen from the road, and the house is barely glimpsed through the geometric grid of one hundred thirty-two apple trees. The view from inside the house through the rear glass grid or from the adjacent terrace is bucolic and transfixing. The view back to the house (from the wooded side) appears as a painting.

The front entrance is centered, on axis with the orchard, so that at first encounter the house is symmetrical. The rear facade, however, is anything but; rather it is a tribute to Mondrian, with red, yellow, blue, and green rectangular shapes within a black grid. An artist as well as an architect, Tigerman's early paintings were

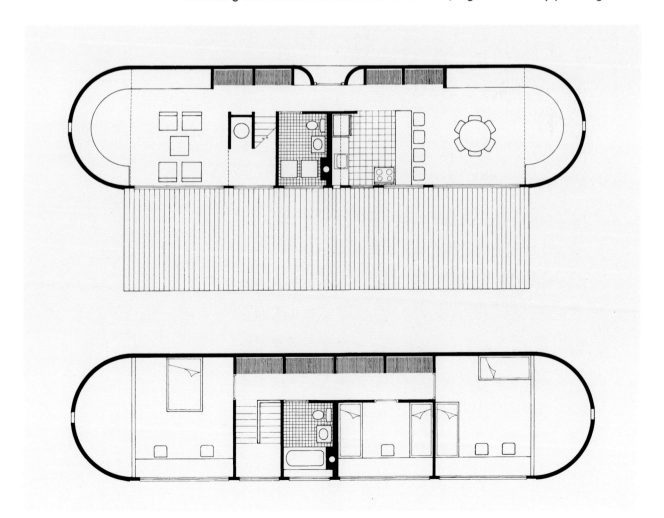

Site plan showing approach to house through geometric grid of apple orchard.

Opposite: Living room with no added millwork.

executed in a similar manner.[1] Iris Goldstein, who is an artist, recalls how she chose the colors and painted the back of the house; in addition, she painted all the interior ductwork and exposed electrical conduit black.[2] The late Paul Goldstein had a 33-year career as an attorney. In 1968, he represented the late comedian Dick Gregory in a civil rights case before the United States Supreme Court and won, establishing an important doctrine in First Amendment jurisprudence.

Since the Goldsteins needed to economize on the house, it had no interior or exterior millwork. Tigerman also suggested that the window and door openings be framed with butt-jointed lumber rather than mitered corners. Cost-saving measures extended to having open shelves rather than cabinets and interior doors only for bath and bedrooms but not closets.

There is a comfortable sense of balance to their slim 15-by-65-foot house. Tigerman wrote that he had "jumped aboard the van der Rohe bandwagon" in the 1950s, and that influence is not lost in the design, which has an inherent order. In both its plan and elevation there is a grid, though one that is disrupted.[3] Tigerman's world was about dichotomies, whether in architecture or in life.

The Goldstein House is also popularly known as the "Hot Dog House" because of its shape.[4] As a critic and a designer, Tigerman was often identified with postmodernism and was the rare figure to modulate the seriousness of architecture with humor. The house was widely published after its completion.[5] —SSB

Notes

Modern Houses for Modern Living in Chicago

1 — On the Robie House see: Donald Hoffmann, *Frank Lloyd Wright's Robie House: The Illustrated Story of an Architectural Masterpiece* (New York: Dover, 1984), Joseph Connors, *The Robie House of Frank Lloyd Wright* (Chicago: University of Chicago Press, 1984).

2 — H. Allen Brooks, *The Prairie School: Frank Lloyd Wright and His Midwest Contemporaries* (Toronto: University of Toronto Press, 1972). In 1908 Wright wrote: "We of the Middle West are living on the prairie. The prairie has a beauty of its own and we should recognize and accentuate this natural beauty, it's quiet level. Hence, gently sloping roofs, low proportions, quiet sky lines, suppressed heavy-set chimneys and sheltering overhangs, low terraces and out-reaching walls sequestering private gardens." First published as "In the Cause of Architecture," *Architectural Record* 23, no. 3 (March 1908) and republished in Frederick Gutheim ed., *Frank Lloyd Wright In the Cause of Architecture* (New York: Architectural Record, 1975), 53–119.

3 — Chicagoland is an informal term referencing the Chicago Metropolitan Area. The CMA consists of the City of Chicago (with 77 community areas and the various neighborhoods within these areas) and additional surrounding counties and suburban cities and villages.

4 — Robert A. Sobieszek, ed., *The Architectural Photography of Hedrich-Blessing* (New York: Holt, Rinehart and Winston, 1984). Tony Hiss and Timothy Samuelson, *Building Images: Seventy Years of Photography at Hedrich Blessing* (San Francisco: Chronicle Books, 2000).

5 — "Modern Houses in America," *Architectural Forum* 71, no. 1 (July 1939): 1.

6 — "Modern Houses," 12–15, 42–44.

7 — "Modern Houses," 50–53. See also: Thomas C. Reeves, *Distinguished Service: The Life of Wisconsin Governor Walter J. Kohler, Jr.* (Milwaukee: Marquette University Press, 2006), 9–10.

8 — David Dunster, *Key Buildings of the Twentieth Century Volume 1: Houses 1900–1944* (New York: Rizzoli, 1985); David Dunster, *Key Buildings of the Twentieth Century Volume 2: Houses 1945–1989* (London: Butterworth Architecture, 1990); Olivier Boissière, *Twentieth-Century Houses: Europe* (Paris: Finest SA / Pierre Terrail Editions, 1998); Anatxu Zabalbeascoa, *Houses of the Century* (Corte Madera, CA: Gingko Press Inc., 1998); Richard Weston, *Twentieth-Century Residential Architecture* (New York: Abbeville Press, 2002); Colin Davies, *Key Houses of the Twentieth Century: Plans, Sections and Elevations* (New York: Norton, 2006). An exception to these overviews with titles focused on the twentieth century are ones that explicitly refer to the modern or iconic house: Sherban Cantacuzino, *Modern Houses of the World* (London: Studio Vista, 1964); Phaidon Editors, *The Modernist House* (London: Phaidon, 2009) and Dominic Bradbury, *The Iconic House: Architectural Masterworks Since 1900* (New York: Thames & Hudson, 2009).

9 — The selections for these house anthologies demonstrate that the Modern Movement, an expression coined by architectural historian and critic Pevsner in this landmark study of 1936, was far from being a homogeneous body of works and attitudes, expanded or contracted according to the author's point of view. Nikolaus Pevsner, *Pioneers of the Modern Movement: From William Morris to Walter Gropius* (London: Faber & Faber, 1936). Charles Jencks, *Modern Movements in Architecture* (Garden City, NY: Anchor Press, 1973) famously repudiated Pevsner's singular definition.

10 — Kate Ellen Rogers, *The Modern House, U.S.A.: Its Design and Decoration* (New York: Harper & Rowe, 1962); Clifford Edward Clark Jr., *The American Family Home, 1800–1960* (Chapel Hill: University of North Carolina Press, 1986); Kenneth Frampton and David Larkin, eds., *American Masterworks: The Twentieth-Century House* (New York: Universe, 2002); Phaidon Editors, *The American House* (London: Phaidon, 2001). For broader discussion on American domestic architectures see: Lester Walter, *American Homes: The Landmark Illustrated Encyclopedia of Domestic Architecture* (New York: Black Dog and Leventhal, 2014); Jeffery Howe, ed., *The Houses We Live In: An Identification Guide to the History and Style of American Domestic Architecture* (London: PRC, 2003); Bernard Friedman, *The American Idea of Home: Conversations about Architecture & Design* (Austin: University of Texas Press, 2017).

11 — F. R. S. Yorke, *The Modern House* (London: Architectural Press, 1934), 1. Jeremy Melvin and David Allford, "F. R. S. Yorke and The Modern House," in *Journal of the Twentieth Century Society* 2 (1996): 28–40, (Theme issue "The Modern House Revisited"). See also Jeremy Melvin, *FRS Yorke and the Evolution of English Modernism* (Chichester, UK: Wiley-Academy, 2003).

12 — Cited from General Houses, Inc., "Century of Progress in Building Construction," 1–3, pamphlet courtesy APT. For an in-depth account of Fisher's contributions see John A. Burns, "K2H40: The Promise of Prefabrication," in H. Ward Jandl, John A. Burns, and Michael J. Auer, *Yesterday's Houses of Tomorrow: Innovative American Homes 1850 to 1950* (Washington: Preservation Press, National Trust for Historic Preservation, 1991), 156–167.

13 — Some monographs are: Kitty Baldwin Weese, *Harry Weese Houses* (Chicago: Chicago Review Press, 1987); Caitlin Lempres Brostrom, *The Houses of William Wurster: Frames for Living* (New York: Princeton Architectural Press, 2011); George H. Marcus and William Whitaker, *The Houses of Louis Kahn* (New Haven: Yale University Press, 2013).

14 — We have combined primary archival research and secondary resources with oral histories produced by Betty J. Blum, and others, since 1983 for the Chicago Architects Oral History Project (CAOHP) under the auspices of the Department of Architecture of the Art Institute of Chicago. Naomi Stead, Janina Gosseye, and Deborah van der Platt, *Speaking of Buildings: Oral History in Architectural Research* (New York: Princeton Architectural Press, 2019).

15 — Wolf von Eckardt, ed., *Mid-Century Architecture in America:*

Honor Awards of the American Institute of Architects, 1949–1961 (Washington, DC: American Institute of Architects, 1961).

16 — *Architectural Forum* 71, no. 1 (July 1939), 2.

17 — For announcement of the exhibition see: *Chicago Daily Tribune,* Sunday, June 12, 1932, 63. See also: Terence Riley, *The International Style: Exhibition 15 and the Museum of Modern Art* (New York: Rizzoli, 1992). See Barry Bergdoll, "Layers of Polemic: MoMA's Founding International Exhibition Between Influence and Reality" published in "An Introduction," 23–30 in Alfred H. Barr Jr., Henry-Russell Hitchcock, Jr., Philip Johnson, and Lewis Mumford, *Modern Architects* (New York: Museum of Modern Art with Norton, 1932; reprint: Lisbon: Babel, 2011).

18 — Alfred H. Barr Jr., *Modern Architects,* 22: Henry Dubin is incorrectly referred to as "Harry." Joanna Merwood-Salisbury, "American Modern: The Chicago School and the International Style at New York's Museum of Modern Art," in Alexander Eisenschmidt with Jonathan Mekinda, eds., *Chicagoisms: The City as Catalyst for Architectural Speculation* (Zurich: Park Books, 2013), 116–129.

19 — Neil Levine, "Abstraction and Representation in Modern Architecture: The International Style and Frank Lloyd Wright," *AA Files* 57, no. 11 (Spring 1986): 3–21.

20 — *Early Modern Architecture: Chicago 1870–1910* (New York: Museum of Modern Art, 1933) published in conjunction with an exhibition organized by Henry-Russell Hitchcock Jr. and Philip Johnson of the same title at the Museum of Modern Art, January 18–February 23, 1933.

21 — Walter Gropius, *International Architecture* (Zurich: Lars Müller Publishers, 2019), 5. (Originally published in German as *International Architektur* by Albert Langen Verlag München in 1925).

22 — Dorothy Raley, ed., *A Century of Progress Homes and Furnishings* (Chicago: M. A. Ring, 1934). See "Exposition Houses of Today and Tomorrow" in Lisa D. Schrenk, *Building a Century of Progress: The Architecture of Chicago's 1933–34 World Fair* (Minneapolis: University of Minnesota Press, 2007), 157–86; Brick Manufacturers' Association of America, *The Super-Safe Home of the Future* (Cleveland, Ohio: Brick Manufacturers' Association of America, 1933).

23 — Architects included in Johnson's exhibition are: Hamilton Beatty, Herbert C. Bebb, Howard T. Fisher, George Fred Keck, Hans Oberhammer, Robert Paul Schweikher, Joseph L. Winberg, and Conrad & Teare. See Philip Johnson's Foreword in *Young Architects in the Middle West: Exhibition 28* (New York: Museum of Modern Art, 1933) published in conjunction with an exhibition of the same title at the Museum of Modern Art, April 3–30, 1933.

24 — Stephanie Barron with Sabine Eckmann, eds., *Exiles + Emigrés: The Flight of European Artists from Hitler* (Los Angeles: Los Angeles County Museum of Art, 1997).

25 — Walter Gropius, *Scope of Total Architecture* (New York: Collier, 1962), 14: states "As to my practice, when I built my first house in the U.S.A—which was my own—I made it a point to absorb into my own conception those features of the New England architectural traditional that I found still alive and adequate. This fusion of the regional spirit with a contemporary approach to design produced a house that I would never have built in Europe with its entirely different climate, technical and psychological background." [*Scope of Total Architecture* was first published in 1943].

26 — Gropius, *Total Architecture,* 14: "I want to rip off at least one of the misleading labels that I and others have been decorated with. There is no such thing as an 'International Style,' unless you want to speak of certain universal technical achievements in our period which belong to the intellectual equipment of every civilized nation, or unless you want to speak of those pale examples of what I call 'applied archeology,' which you find among the public buildings from Moscow to Madrid to Washington. Steel or concrete skeletons, ribbon windows, slabs cantilevered or wings hovering on stilts are but impersonal contemporary means—the raw stuff, so to speak—with which regionally different architectural manifestations can be created. The constructive achievements of the Gothic period—its vaults, arches, buttresses and pinnacles—similarly became a common international experience. Yet, what a great regional variety of architectural expression has resulted from it in the different countries!"

27 — Sigfried Giedion, ed., *A Decade of New Architecture* (Zurich: Editions Girsberger, 1951), 65.

28 — William H. Jordy, "The International Style in the 1930s," *JSAH,* no. 24 (March 1965): 10–14, republished in Mardges Bacon, ed., *"Symbolic Essence" and Other Writings on Modern Architecture and American Culture* (New Haven: Yale University Press, 2005), 151–58. See also William H. Jordy, *American Buildings and Their Architects: The Impact of European Modernism in the Mid-Twentieth Century Volume 5* (Garden City, NY: Doubleday, 1970).

29 — Sandy Isenstadt, "Modern in the Middle," *Perspecta* 36, Juxtapositions (2005): 62–68, 71–72. Gwendolyn Wright, *USA Modern Architectures in History* (London: Reaktion, 2008), 125.

30 — "Great Chicago Furniture Mart to Open June 7: Called World's Largest Structure—Now Being Occupied by Furniture Exhibits for Midsummer Show," *Lumber and Veneer Consumer,* May 30, 1924, 13. Sharon S. Darling, *Chicago Furniture: Art, Craft & Industry, 1833–1933* (New York: Chicago Historical Society, in association with Norton, 1984). Jay Pridmore, *The Merchandise Mart: A Building Book from the Chicago Architecture Foundation* (San Francisco: Pomegranate, 2003).

31 — Edward Wormley, *The Dunbar Book of Modern Furniture* (Berne, IN: Dunbar Furniture Corp. of Indiana, 1953), 33. Marshall Field & Company, *The Story of the Merchandise Mart: The Great Central Market, Chicago* (Chicago: Marshall Field and Company, 1933). "Merchandise Mart," *Encyclopaedia Britannica,* accessed January 5, 2020, britannica.com.

32 — John Brunetti, *Baldwin Kingrey: Midcentury Modern in Chicago, 1947–1957* (Chicago: Wright, 2004). Lisa Napoles, "'A New Outlook' Baldwin Kingrey of Chicago," August 13, 2014, accessed September 10, 2019, docomomo-us.org.

33 — Elizabeth Kennedy, ed., *Chicago Modern, 1893–1945: Pursuit of the New* (Chicago: Terra Museum of American Art, 2004); Maggie Taft and Robert Cozzolino, eds., *Art in Chicago: A History from the Fire to Now* (Chicago: University of Chicago Press, 2018); Lynn Warren, ed., *Art in Chicago, 1945–1995* (Chicago: Museum of Contemporary Art, 1996); Robert V. Sharp and Elizabeth Stepina, eds., *1945 Creativity and Crisis: Chicago Architecture and Design of the World War II Era* (Chicago: Art Institute of Chicago, 2005).

34 — "Ben Rose," in Christa C. Mayer Thurman, *Rooted in Chicago: Fifty Years of Textile Design Traditions* (Chicago: Art Institute of Chicago, 1992), 24–33 published in conjunction with an exhibition organized by the Department of Textiles of the same title at the Art Institute of Chicago, February 12–July 27, 1997.

35 — It is worth noting that an exchange of ideas and know-how between the Americas and the "old world" started well before the 1930s. See for example: Jean-Louis Cohen, *Scenes of the World to Come: European Architecture and the American Challenge, 1893–1960* (Paris: Flammarion, 1995).

36 — Gregory Wittkopp and Diana Balmori, eds., *Saarinen House and Garden: A Total Work of Art* (New York: Abrams, 1995). See also Robert Judson Clark and Andrea P.A. Belloli, *Design in America: The Cranbrook Vision, 1925–1950* (New York: Abrams, in association with Detroit Institute of Arts and Metropolitan Museum of Art, 1983). Kathryn Bishop Eckert, *Cranbrook: An Architectural Tour* (New York: Princeton Architectural Press, 2001).

37 — Katherine Solomonson, *The Chicago Tribune Tower Competition: Skyscraper Design and Cultural Change in the 1920s* (Chicago: University of Chicago Press, 2001).

38 — James Ford and Katherine Morrow Ford, *The Modern House in America* (New York: Architectural Book Publishing, 1940), 14. (Re-issued as James Ford and Katherine Morrow Ford, *Classic Modern Houses of the Thirties: 64 Designs by Neutra, Gropius, Breuer, Stone, and Others* (New York: Dover, 1989); James Ford and Katherine Morrow Ford, *Design of Modern Interiors* (New York: Architectural Book Publishing, 1942).

39 — Katherine Morrow Ford and Thomas H. Creighton, *The American House Today: 85 Notable Examples Selected and Evaluated* (New York: Reinhold, 1951), 4.

40 — Donald Albrecht, Robert Schonfeld, and Paul Warwick Thompson, *Russel Wright: Creating American Lifestyle* (New York: Abrams, 2001). See also, Stewart J. Johnson, *American Modern, 1925–1940: Design for a New Age* (New York: Abrams, in association with the American Federation of Arts, 2000). Marilyn F. Friedman, *Making America Modern: Interior Design in the 1930s* (New York: Bauer and Dean, 2018).

41 — Richard Cheek, *Selling the Dwelling: The Books that Built America's Houses, 1775–2000* (New York: Grolier, 2013).

42 — The house was also fitted with Crane Co. plumbing fixtures manufactured in Chicago.

43 — Geoffrey Baker and Bruno Funaro, *Windows in Modern Architecture* (New York: Architectural Book Publishing, 1948), 72–73, 80–81.

44 — Sandy Isenstadt, *The Modern American House: Spaciousness and Middle-Class Identity* (Cambridge: Cambridge University Press, 2006).

45 — The houses featured in the LOF Glass Co. publication include: Lumber Industries House (architect Ernest Grunsfeld Jr), Tropical Home (architect Robert Law Weed), Common Brick House (architect Andrew N. Rebori), House of Today (Corbett, Harrison & MacMurray architects), Stran-Steel House (O'Dell & Rowland Architects), House of Tomorrow (architect George Fred Keck), Design for Living (architect John C. B. Moore), Masonite House (Frazier & Raftery architects), Armco-Ferro Enamel House (architect Robert Smith Jr.).

46 — *Architectural Forum* 71, no. 1 (July 1939): 72.

47 — Vincent Michael, *The Architecture of Barry Byrne: Taking the Prairie School to Europe* (Urbana: University of Illinois Press, 2013). An issue of the *Chicago Architectural Journal* 4 (1984) published by the Chicago Architectural Club is dedicated to Andrew Rebori with contributions by Wim De Wit, Joan E. Draper, and Raymond T. Tatum, 7–24.

48 — "Recent Work by the Office of Paul Schweikher and Theodore Warren Lamb, Associated Architects," *Architectural Forum* 71, no. 5 (November 1939): 350–366.

49 — *Mies van der Rohe: McCormick House* (Elmhurst, IL: Elmhurst Art Museum, 2018) published in conjunction with the exhibition curated by Barry Bergdoll titled *Mies's McCormick House Revealed: New Views* at Elmhurst Art Museum, June 10 August 26, 2018. The catalogue essay is by Bergdoll.

50 — Elizabeth A. T. Smith, *Blueprints for Modern Living: History and Legacy of the Case Study Houses* (Cambridge, MA: MIT Press, 1989); Elizabeth A. T. Smith, *Case Study Houses* (Köln: Taschen, 2013).

51 — Keck's experience building the Century of Progress houses indirectly served as a catalyst for his early solar houses in Chicago, the Sloan (1940) and Duncan (1941) Houses. Robert Boyce, *Keck & Keck* (New York: Princeton Architectural Press, 1993); Anthony Denzer, *The Solar House: Pioneering Sustainable Design* (New York: Rizzoli, 2013); Daniel A. Barber, *A House in the Sun: Modern Architecture and Solar Energy in the Cold War* (New York: Oxford University Press, 2016). Some important period publications include: Maron J. Simon, ed., *Your Solar House* (New York: Simon and Schuster, 1947) with Keck's "The Illinois State Solar House" designed with Libbey-Owens-Ford (1945) featured on 72–73.

52 — Otto Wagner, *Modern Architecture: A Guidebook for His Students to this Field of Art* (Santa Monica, CA: Getty Center for the History of Art and the Humanities, 1988).

53 — Frank Lloyd Wright, *Modern Architecture: Being the Kahn Lectures for 1930* (Carbondale: Southern Illinois University Press, 1987).

54 — For example: Everett Chamberlin, *Chicago and its Suburbs* (Chicago: T. A. Hungerford, 1874); Marian A. White, *Book of the North Shore: Homes, Gardens, Landscapes, Highways and Byways, Past and Present* (Chicago: J. Harrison White, 1910) followed by *Second Book of the North Shore: Homes, Gardens, Landscapes, Highways and Byways, Past and Present* (1911) and finally *Book of the Western Suburbs: Homes, Gardens, Landscapes, Highways and Byways, Past and Present* (1912). "Chicago" is included in the Federal Writers' Project of the Works Progress Administration, *The WPA Guide to Illinois* (1939) reissued with new introduction by Neil Harris and Michael Conzen: *The WPA Guide to Illinois: The Federal Writers Project Guide to 1930s Illinois* (New York: Pantheon, 1983), 187–302.

55 — Ann Durkin Keating, *Building Chicago: Suburban Developers and the Creation of a Divided Metropolis* (Urbana: University of Illinois Press, 2002); Ann Durkin Keating, *Chicagoland: City and Suburbs in the Railroad Age* (Chicago: University of Chicago Press, 2005); Ann Durkin Keating, ed., *Neighborhoods and Suburbs: A Historical Guide* (Chicago: University of Chicago Press, 2008).

56 — Kenneth T. Jackson, *Crabgrass Frontier: The Suburbanization of the United States* (New York: Oxford University Press, 1985); Robert Fishman, *Bourgeois Utopias: The Rise and Fall of Suburbia* (New York: Basic Books, 1987); John R. Stilgoe, *Borderland: Origins of the American Suburb, 1820–1939* (New Haven: Yale University Press, 1988); Robert A. M. Stern, David Fishman, and Jacob Tilove, *Paradise Planned: The Garden Suburb and the Modern City* (New York: The Monacelli Press, 2013). See his earlier study Robert A. M. Stern with John Montague Massengale eds., *The Anglo-American Suburb* (London: Architectural Design, 1981).

Special edition of *Architectural Design* to accompany the exhibition *Suburbs* at the Cooper-Hewitt Museum. Alan Gowans, *The Comfortable House: North American Suburban Architecture, 1890–1930* (Cambridge, MA: MIT Press, 1986).

57 — Dominic A. Pacyga and Ellen Skerrett, *Chicago, City of Neighborhoods: Histories & Tours* (Chicago: Loyola University Press, 1986).

58 — Robert Bruegmann, *Sprawl: A Compact History* (Chicago: University of Chicago Press, 2005).

59 — Victoria Post Ranney, *Olmsted in Chicago* (Chicago: Open Parks Project, 1972).

60 — See *Architectural Record* (May 1951) (reprint AR's Building Types Study n.174 Mobilization Housing) and Gregory C. Randall, *America's Original GI Town: Park Forest, Illinois* (Baltimore, MD: John Hopkins University Press, 2003).

61 — See David A. Spatz, "Roads to Postwar Urbanism: Expressway Building and the Transformation of Metropolitan Chicago, 1930–1975" (PhD diss., University of Chicago, 2010).

62 — Lewis A. Coffin, *American Country Houses of Today* (New York: Architectural Book Publishing, 1935) (reprinted as *American Country Houses of the Thirties with Photographs and Floor Plans* (Mineola, NY: Dover, 2007)); Mark Alan Hewitt, *The Architect and the American Country House, 1890–1940* (Yale University Press, 1990).

63 — James S. Ackerman, *The Villa: Form and Ideology of Country Houses* (Princeton, NJ: Princeton University Press, 1990). See also Wolf Tegethoff, *Mies van der Rohe: The Villas and Country Houses* (New York: Museum of Modern Art, 1985). On the villa, Le Corbusier, and modernism see Colin Rowe, *The Mathematics of the Ideal Villa and Other Essays* (Cambridge, MA: MIT Press, 1976), 1–28.

64 — The term was more used during the nineteenth century: A. J. Downing, *Cottage Residences; or A Series of Designs for Rural Cottages and Cottage Villas, and their Gardens and Grounds, Adapted to North America* (New York: Wiley, 1852). John Archer,

Architecture and Suburbia: from English Villa to American Dream House, 1690–2000 (Minneapolis: University of Minnesota Press, 2005).

65 — Edgar Kaufmann Jr., *Fallingwater: A Frank Lloyd Wright Country House* (New York: Abbeville, 1986). "Palm Springs Eternal: Richard Neutra's Kaufmann Desert House" in Alice T. Friedman, *American Glamour and the Evolution of Modern Architecture* (New Haven: Yale University Press, 2010), 74–107.

66 — Mary Anne Hunting, *Edward Durell Stone: Modernism's Populist Architect* (New York: Norton, 2013), 37–39.

67 — William D. Earls, *The Harvard Five in New Canaan: Midcentury Modern Houses by Marcel Breuer, Landis Gores, John Johansen, Philip Johnson, Eliot Noyes & Others* (New York: Norton, 2006); Jeffrey Matz, et al., *Midcentury Houses Today: New Canaan, Connecticut* (New York: The Monacelli Press, 2014). Peter McMahon, *Cape Cod Modern: Midcentury Architecture and Community on the Outer Cape* (New York: Metropolis, 2014).

68 — Joachim Driller, *Breuer Houses* (London: Phaidon, 2000); Bruce Gordon, *Eliot Noyes* (London: Phaidon, 2006).

69 — Caroline Rob Zaleski, *Long Island Modernism: 1930–1980* (New York: Norton, 2012).

70 — Joseph C. Bigott, *From Cottage to Bungalow: Houses and the Working Class in Metropolitan Chicago, 1869–1929* (Chicago: University of Chicago Press, 2001); Dominic A. Pacyga and Charles Shanabruch, eds., *The Chicago Bungalow* (Chicago: Chicago Architecture Foundation, 2001); Gwendolyn Wright, *Moralism and the Model Home: Domestic Architecture and Cultural Conflict in Chicago, 1873–1913* (Chicago: University of Chicago Press, 1980); Rosemary Thornton, *Sears Homes of Illinois* (Charleston, SC: History Press, 2010). See also Barbara Miller Lane, *Houses for a New World: Builders and Buyers in American Suburbs, 1945–1965* (Princeton: Princeton University Press, 2015), in particular, Chapter 4 "The Builder's of Chicago's Golden Corridor: Midwestern Ranches and Splits," 139–161.

71 — Daniel Bluestone, "Framing Landscape While Building Density: Chicago Courtyard Apartments, 1891–1929," *Journal of the Society of Architectural Historians* 76 no. 4 (2017): 506–31. Sidney Robinson, "The Postwar Modern House in Chicago," in *Chicago Architecture and Design, 1923–1993: Reconfiguration of an American Metropolis,* ed. John Zukowsky (Munich: Prestel, 1993), 200–217.

72 — Neil Harris, *Chicago Apartments: A Century of Lakefront Luxury* (New York: Acanthus, 2004); second edition (Chicago: University of Chicago Press, 2020).

73 — D. Bradford Hunt, *Blueprint for Disaster: The Unraveling of Chicago Public Housing* (Chicago: University of Chicago Press, 2010); Devereux Bowly, *The Poorhouse: Subsidized Housing in Chicago, 1895–1976* (Carbondale: Southern Illinois University Press, 1978); Ben Austen, *High-Risers: Cabrini-Green and the Fate of American Public Housing* (New York: Harper, 2018).

74 — Wayne Andrews, *Architecture in Chicago & Mid-America: A Photographic History* (New York: Icon Editions, 1973); Irving Cutler, *Chicago: Metropolis of the Mid-Continent* (Chicago: Geographic Society of Chicago, 1976).

75 — One of the most recent books that highlights Chicago's pioneering role in shaping American identity is Thomas Dyja, *The Third Coast: When Chicago Built the American Dream* (New York: Penguin, 2013).

76 — Although Chicago is best known for its prairie flatness, as one moves northward along Lake Michigan a gradual change in topography gives way to steep bluffs and ravines. To the south of Chicago, the prairie flatness gives way to sand dunes. For an overview see Joel Greenberg, *A Natural History of the Chicago Region* (Chicago: University of Chicago Press, 2002).

77 — For a summary see Liane Lefaivre and Alexander Tzonis, *Critical Regionalism: Architecture and Identity in a Globalized World* (Munich: Prestel, 2003). Vincent B. Canizaro ed., *Architectural Regionalism: Collected Writings on Place, Identity, Modernity, and*

Tradition (New York: Princeton Architectural Press, 2007).

78 — The Doris L. and Thomas A. Mullen House was published in the same year it was completed in: Editors of *Architectural Forum*, *The 1940 Book of Small Houses* (New York: Simon and Schuster, 1936), 44–45. Keck & Keck's Mabel and Sidney H. Davies House in Northfield, Illinois (1946) was included in William J. Hennessey ed., *America's Best Small Houses* (New York: Viking, 1949), 74–78.

79 — As was demonstrated by Leonard Eaton's pioneering study, differences between clients made real impact on the design outcome. See Leonard K. Eaton, *Two Chicago Architects and Their Clients: Frank Lloyd Wright and Howard Van Doren Shaw* (Cambridge, MA: MIT Press, 1969).

80 — Chicago's Gold Coast was filled with urban houses of note ranging from the Helen Douglas and James Charnley House (1892) to the Elsa Seipp and Albert F. Madlener House (1902). These urban houses were in sharp contrast to the free-standing nineteenth-century Beaux-Arts "mansions" that occupied large parcels of land on N. Lake Shore Drive such as the Palmer Mansion (1885) by Cobb and Frost or the various mansions on Prairie Avenue including the Glessner House (1886) by Henry Hobson Richardson along with those of Chicago's mercantile elite such as Marshall Field, Philip Armour, and George M. Pullman. See John Graf, *Chicago Mansions* (Charleston, SC: Arcadia, 2004); William H. Tyre, *Chicago's Historic Prairie Avenue* (Charleston, SC: Arcadia, 2008); Wilbert Jones, Kathleen Willis-Morton, Maureen O'Brien, and Bob Dowey, *Chicago's Gold Coast* (Charleston, SC: Arcadia, 2014).

81 — One of the first books to appear during those years that made explicit reference to middle is by John M. Jacobus, *Twentieth-Century Architecture: The Middle Years 1940–65* (New York: Praeger, 1966). Jürgen Joedicke, *Architecture Since 1945* (New York: Praeger, 1969). Wolf von Eckardt and Philip Will, eds., *Mid-Century Architecture in America: Honor Awards of the American Institute of Architects,*

1949–1961 (Baltimore: Johns Hopkins University Press, 1961).

82 — Susan F. King, "Only Girl Architect Lonely," in *Chicago Architecture: Histories, Revisions, Alternatives*, eds. Charles Waldheim and Katerina Rüedi Ray (Chicago: Chicago University Press, 2005), 129–142: Elisabeth Martini and her colleagues established the Chicago Woman's Drafting Club in 1921 that became the Women's Architectural Club in 1938 with its periodic publication *Architrave*. In 1974, eight women—including Gertrude Lempp Kerbis, Carol Ross Barney, Cynthia Weese, Nancy Abshire, Gunduz Dagdelen, Natalie de Blois, Laura Fisher, and Jane M. Jacobsen—established the Chicago Women in Architecture organization to support women architects and address challenges of underrepresentation in the field.

83 — Special thanks to Laura Herlocher for sharing her ongoing research on Willisch with me.

84 — For important studies focused on one city see: Thomas S. Hines, *Architecture of the Sun: Los Angeles Modernism, 1900–1970* (New York: Rizzoli, 2010) and Serena Keshavjee ed., *Winnipeg Modern: Architecture, 1945–1975* (Winnipeg: University of Manitoba Press, 2006). For state-based studies see: Jan Hochstim, *Florida Modern: Residential Architecture 1945–1970* (New York: Rizzoli, 2004).

85 — Jay Pridmore and George A. Larson, *Chicago Architecture and Design,* 3rd edition (New York: Abrams, 2018).

86 — See Gary Gand, *Julius Shulman: Chicago Midcentury Modernism* (New York: Rizzoli, 2010).

87 — Robert Bruegmann ed., *Art Deco Chicago: Designing Modern America* (Chicago: Chicago History Museum, 2018).

88 — Amy L. Arnold and Brian D. Conway, *Michigan Modern: Design that Shaped America* (Layton, UT: Gibbs Smith, 2016); Larry Millett, *Minnesota Modern: Architecture and Life at Midcentury* (Minneapolis: University of Minnesota Press, 2015).

89 — Julia S. Bachrach, *The City in a Garden: A History of Chicago's Parks* (Chicago:

Center for American Places, 2012). William Cronon, *Nature's Metropolis: Chicago and the Great West* (New York: Norton, 1992). Some examples of villages and cities named to evoke nature are: Highland Park, Oak Park, Riverside, River Forest, and many more.

90 — For an analysis of Gordon's career and contributions see Monica Penick, *Tastemaker: Elizabeth Gordon, House Beautiful, and the Postwar American Home* (New Haven: Yale University Press, 2017), 115–128.

91 — Gordon, *House Beautiful*, 126.

92 — Gordon, *House Beautiful*, 129.

93 — In the new architecture curriculum launched in 1938 by Mies at the Armour Institute (subsequently the Illinois Institute of Technology) he wrote in a section entitled "Planning and Creating" about "The obligation to realize the potentialities of organic architecture." See Rolf Achilles, Kevin Harrington, and Charlotte Myhrum, *Mies van der Rohe, Architect as Educator* (Chicago: Mies van der Rohe Centennial Project, Illinois Institute of Technology, 1986), 57. See also Alfred Swenson and Pao-Chi Chang, *Architectural Education at IIT, 1938–1978* (Chicago: Illinois Institute of Technology, 1980).

94 — Frank Lloyd Wright, "Taliesin," in Edgar Kaufmann and Ben Raeburn, *Frank Lloyd Wright: Writings and Buildings* (New York: Horizon, 1960), 173.

95 — Christian Norberg-Schulz, "A Talk with Mies van der Rohe," *Baukunst und Werkform* 11, no. 11 (1958), reprinted in Fritz Neumeyer, *The Artless Word: Mies van der Rohe on the Building Art*, trans. Mark Jarzombek (Cambridge, MA: MIT Press, 1991), 235.

96 — Wright's first Usonian was realized in 1937 for Katherine Wescott and Herbert Jacobs I in Madison, Wisconsin.

97 — Richard Padovan, "Machines à Méditer," in Rolf Achilles, Kevin Harrington, and Charlotte Myhrum eds., *Mies van der Rohe, Architect as Educator* (Chicago: Mies van der Rohe Centennial Project, Illinois Institute of Technology, 1986), 17–26. First quoted in Ludwig

Mies van der Rohe, "Ich mache niemals ein Bild," *Bauwelt,* 32 (August 1962): 884.

98 — Ludwig Mies van der Rohe, "Tribute," *College Art Journal* 6 (Autumn 1946): 41–42. Republished in H. Allen Brooks, ed., *Writings on Wright: Selected Comment on Frank Lloyd Wright* (Cambridge, MA: MIT Press, 1961), 129–30: Mies writes, "We young architects found ourselves in painful inner conflict. We were ready to pledge ourselves to an idea. But the potential vitality of the architectural idea of this period had, by that time, been lost. This, then, was the situation in 1910. At this moment, so critical for us, there came to Berlin the exhibition of the work of Frank Lloyd Wright. This comprehensive display and the extensive publication of his works enabled us really to become acquainted with the achievement of this architect. The encounter was destined to prove of great significance to the development of architecture in Europe. The work of this great master revealed an architectural world of unexpected force and clarity of language, and also a disconcerting richness of form. Here finally was a master-builder drawing upon the veritable fountainhead of architecture, who with true originality lifted his architectural creations into the light. Here, again, genuine organic architecture flowered." See also: Frank Lloyd Wright, *Frank Lloyd Wright: Eine Studie zu Seiner Würdigung* (Berlin: E. Wasmuth, 1911): English translation (New York: Dover Publications, 1982). Anthony Alofsin ed., *Frank Lloyd Wright: Europe and Beyond* (Berkeley: University of California Press, 1999). Even before Wright, we can trace the beginning of a dialogue with far reaching implications: see Leonard K. Eaton, *American Architecture Comes of Age: European Reaction to H. H. Richardson and Louis Sullivan* (Cambridge, MA: MIT Press, 1972).

99 — For an overview of Schweikher's career and architectural production see John Zukowsky and Betty J. Blum, *Architecture in Context: The Avant-Garde in Chicago's Suburbs: Paul Schweikher and William Ferguson Deknatel* (Chicago: Graham Foundation

for Advanced Studies in the Fine Arts and Art Institute of Chicago, 1984).

100 — Al Chase, "Luxury Homes Will Rise Near Olympia Fields: Graymoor is Name of 150 Acre Site," *Chicago Daily Tribune,* December 20, 1952, F-5: Graymoor was developed by Edward Gray and planned by Raymond William Hazekamp. See Edward Robert Humrich, Interview Maya Moran and Thomas Charles Roth, "The Architecture of Edward Robert Humrich," (MA thesis, University of Illinois at Chicago, 1993). Edward Robert Humrich, *Oral History of Edward Humrich / Interviewed by Maya Moran, Compiled Under the Auspices of the Chicago Architects Oral History Project, Ernest R. Graham Study Center for Architectural Drawings, Department of Architecture, the Art Institute of Chicago* rev. ed. (Chicago: Art Institute of Chicago, 2005), 15–16.

101 — Werner Blaser, *Architecture and Nature: The Work of Alfred Caldwell* (Basel: Birkhäuser Verlag, 1984); Dennis Domer, ed., *Alfred Caldwell: the Life and Work of a Prairie School Landscape Architect* (Baltimore, MD: Johns Hopkins University Press, 1997).

102 — Jane King Hession, *Ralph Rapson: Sixty Years of Modern Design* (Afton, MN: Afton Historical Society Press, 1999), 56.

103 — Werner Blaser, *After Mies: Mies van der Rohe, Teaching and Principles* (New York: Van Nostrand Reinhold, 1977); Alfred Swenson and Pao-Chi Chang, *Architectural Education at IIT, 1938–1978* (Chicago: Illinois Institute of Technology, 1980). Chicago's architecture schools include in addition to IIT, SAIC and UIC.

104 — Stanford Anderson, Gail Fenske, and David Fixler, eds., *Aalto in America* (New Haven: Yale University Press, 2012).

Frank Lloyd Wright and Ludwig Mies van der Rohe: The Giants in the Room

1 — In addition to these houses in the Chicago area, he designed the John O. Carr House in Glenview, Illinois (1950), the Margaret Soos and Louis B. Frederick House in Barrington Hills, Illinois (1954), and the Carl Post House, a prefabricated

house for the Marshall Erdman Company in Barrington Hills, Illinois (1956). The Allan Friedman House in Bannockburn, Illinois (1956) received their final plan revisions just before Wright's death.

2 — There is a thorough discussion of the construction of the Home Insurance Building in Frank A. Randall, *The History of the Development of Building Construction in Chicago* (Urbana: University of Illinois Press, 1949), 105–107. One of the best books on the history of the development of the skyscraper in Chicago is Carl W. Condit, *The Chicago School of Architecture: A History of Commercial and Public Building in the Chicago Area, 1875–1925* (Chicago: University of Chicago Press, 1964).

3 — The building was designed by Louis Sullivan for the retail firm Schlesinger & Mayer in 1899, and expanded by him in 1904. Carson Pirie Scott occupied the building for more than a century until 2006. Subsequent additions were completed by Daniel Burnham in 1906 and Holabird & Root 1961.

4 — The Frank Lloyd Wright issue of *Architectural Forum* 68, no. 1 (January 1938), noted by the editors as having been designed and written by him, was "dedicated to my beloved master Louis Henry Sullivan and Grand Old Chief Dankmar Adler."

5 — H. Allen Brooks, *The Prairie School: Frank Lloyd Wright and his Midwest Contemporaries* (Toronto: University of Toronto Press, 1972), 335–36: architectural historian Brooks questioned why the architecture of the Prairie School, which had been a "vigorous movement," came to an abrupt end after 1914/16. He noted that in the post-war years, it "no longer existed as a cohesive force or even as a diverse collection of individuals united by common ideals" and that "[a]ny semblance of a school had well nigh vanished." Although Brooks acknowledged the question "has long baffled the historian," he posited "that the Midwesterner increasingly rejected individuality in favor of conformity, that the client rather than the architect stipulated the change, and that the housewife, sooner and more readily than her husband, renounced the work of the Prairie School."

6 — Stuart Cohen, email to author, August 29, 2019: Cohen, FAIA, architect and architectural historian, has an additional perspective on why Wright's former pupils and colleagues abandoned working in the Prairie Style, noting that Wright expressed animosity toward his former "disciples" in several of his writings, including "In the Cause of Architecture" for the May 1914 issue of *Architectural Record*. Cohen commented, "In the face of such rage and scorn, why would Wright's disciples, pupils or colleagues continue working in this manner"?

7 — *Modern Architecture: International Exhibition* (New York: The Museum of Modern Art, 1932) published in conjunction with an exhibition organized by Philip Johnson and Henry-Russell Hitchcock Jr. of the same title at the Museum of Modern Art, February 10–March 23, 1932.

8 — Taliesin West, located in the desert in Scottsdale, Arizona, was not established by Wright as his winter home and school until 1937.

9 — Donald Kalec, *The Home and Studio of Frank Lloyd Wright in Oak Park, Illinois, 1889–1911* (Oak Park: The Frank Lloyd Wright Home and Studio Foundation, 1982). See also Zarine Weil, ed., Building a Legacy: The Restoration of Frank Lloyd Wright's Oak Park Home and Studio (San Francisco: Pomegranate, 2001).

10 — John Sergeant, *Frank Lloyd Wright's Usonian Houses: Designs for Moderate Cost One-Family Homes* (New York: Whitney Library of Design, 1976), 16.

11 — The name "Usonian" is a play on United States of North America and likely an attempt to set Wright's designs apart from houses of the Depression and post–World War II period— those rectangular clapboard boxes, with symmetrical floor plans, usually Colonial Revivals—bearing no relation to their surrounding site. Over 60 Usonian houses were built throughout the United States. Each house was immediately recognizable as having an intimate relationship with its setting. "Obituary--Katherine Jacobs," SF Gate, September 29, 1995, accessed November 8, 2019, sfgate.com: Katherine Wescott

Jacobs, Berkeley sculptor and coauthor, with her late spouse, journalist Herbert Jacobs, of the book *Building with Frank Lloyd Wright: An Illustrated Memoir* (Carbondale: Southern Illinois University Press, 1986).

12 — Kathryn Smith, *Wright on Exhibit: Frank Lloyd Wright's Architectural Exhibitions* (Princeton and Oxford: Princeton University Press, 2017), 111. It has been said that the impact of this publication, with a 12-page spread on Fallingwater, was greatly responsible for Wright's revived practice.

13 — Smith, *Exhibit,* 112.

14 — *Frank Lloyd Wright, American Architect* exhibition, November 13, 1940–January 5, 1941. The exhibition didn't incorporate the model house Wright had hoped to see built. His dream of building a model Usonian for the public to visit was to be realized, however, in an exhibition launched October 22, 1953, *Sixty Years of Living Architecture: The Work of Frank Lloyd Wright* that opened in New York on the site where the Solomon R. Guggenheim Museum was to be built. Wright designed a 1,700-square-foot, fully furnished, two-bedroom model, showcasing his solution for modest middle-class houses. A souvenir brochure containing a detailed description of the house, photos, and a floor plan, was distributed.

15 — Stuart Graff, "Organic Architecture and the Sustaining Ecosystem," July 11, 2018, Frank Lloyd Wright Foundation, accessed September 15, 2019, franklloydwright.org. This article originally appeared in "Perspective," *Frank Lloyd Wright Quarterly* (Winter 2018).

16 — Frank Lloyd Wright, "In the Cause of Architecture," *Architectural Record* 23 no. 3 (March 1908). The article is reprinted in Frank Lloyd Wright, *In the Cause of Architecture Frank Lloyd Wright,* ed. Frederick Gutheim (New York: Architectural Record Books, 1975), 53. In the section of the book "Organic Architecture Looks at Modern Architecture," 233: Gutheim notes that Wright's principles of organic architecture were actually written in 1894.

17 — Graff, *Ecosystem,* 5.

18 — Susan Dart, *Edward Dart Architect* (Evanston: Evanston Publishing, 1993), 136.

19 — "Mrs. Stanley Resor, Ex-Ad Executive, 77," *New York Times,* January 3, 1964, accessed September 18, 2019, nytimes.com: Mrs. Resor was a Museum of Modern Art director and vice president as well as director of the J. Walter Thompson Company of New York, a major advertising agency. Jennifer Scanlon, "Resor, Helen Lansdowne," in *American National Biography,* ed. Mark C. Carnes (Oxford and New York: Oxford University Press, 2005) accessed September 18, 2019, books.google.com: in 1908 she joined, as its sole copywriter, the Cincinnati branch of Thomson, where she met and later married Stanley in 1911.

20 — Edgar Tafel, *Apprentice to Genius: Years with Frank Lloyd Wright* (New York: McGraw-Hill, 1979), 65–66.

21 — Tafel, *Apprentice,* 66: reports that when Walter Gropius was in Madison on a lecture tour, he called about visiting Taliesin; Wright's brusque response was, "I'm very sorry. I'm quite busy, and I have no desire to meet or entertain Herr Gropius. What he stands for and what I stand for are poles apart." Tafel, 65: reported that whenever Mr. Wright read that the French architect Le Corbusier had completed a building, he would say, "Well, now that he's finished one building, he'll go write four books about it." Le Corbusier requested a visit with Wright when he visited the States in 1935, and was also refused.

22 — Tafel, *Apprentice,* 69.

23 — Franz Schulze and Edward Windhorst, *Mies van der Rohe: A Critical Biography, New and Revised Edition* (Chicago and London: University of Chicago Press, 2012), 183.

24 — Schulze and Windhorst, *Mies,* 183.

25 — Tafel, *Apprentice,* 70.

26 — Frank Lloyd Wright, *An Autobiography* (New York: Duell, Sloan, and Pearce, 1943), 400. Schulze and Windhorst, *Mies,* 191.

27 — Peter Blake, "A Conversation with Mies van der Rohe," in

Four Great Makers of Modern Architecture: Gropius, Le Corbusier, Mies van der Rohe, Wright: The Verbatim Record of a Symposium Held at the School of Architecture, Columbia University, March–May, 1961 (New York: Columbia University, 1963), 103. Schulze and Windhorst, *Mies,* 192.

28 — Gene Summers, *Oral History of Gene Summers / Interviewed by Pauline A. Saliga, Compiled Under the Auspices of the Chicago Architects Oral History Project, Ernest R. Graham Study Center for Architectural Drawings, Department of Architecture, the Art Institute of Chicago* (Chicago: Art Institute of Chicago, 1993), 15–16.

29 — Detlef Mertins, *Mies* (London: Phaidon, 2014), 237.

30 — Myron Goldsmith, *Myron Goldsmith: Buildings and Concepts,* ed. Werner Blaser (Basel: Birkhäuser Verlag, 1986), 24. Schulze and Windhorst, *Mies,* 194. Detlef Mertins, *Mies,* 237: Mertins has a chapter that extensively discusses Mies and organicism, 231–279.

31 — Mertins, *Mies,* 237. Also, Phyllis Lambert recalled this in an interview with Mertins, October 1998.

32 — Mertins, *Mies,* 237.

33 — Mertins, *Mies,* 237.

34 — arch.iit.edu/about/history.

35 — George Edson Danforth, *Oral History of George Danforth / Interviewed by Pauline A. Saliga, Compiled Under the Auspices of the Chicago Architects Oral History Project, Ernest R. Graham Study Center for Architectural Drawings, Department of Architecture, the Art Institute of Chicago* (Chicago: Art Institute of Chicago, 1993), 102.

36 — Kevin Harrington, "Order, Space, Proportion—Mies's Curriculum at IIT" in *Mies van der Rohe: Architect as Educator,* eds. Rolf Achilles, Kevin Harrington, and Charlotte Myhrum (Chicago: Illinois Institute of Technology, distributed by University of Chicago Press, 1986), 49–68, published in conjunction with an exhibition of the same title at S. R. Crown Hall, June 6–July 12, 1986.

37 — *Architect and Educator,* 155–166: has a complete list of faculty and graduates from IIT between 1938–1958.

38 — *Architect and Educator,* 4: was dedicated to John Augur Holabird, Sr., FAIA who "as Chairman of its search Committee which brought Mies to Chicago contributed significantly to changing the course of architectural education in America." 4. The catalogue includes a floor plan of the house, "Jacques Brownson Graduate Thesis—A Steel and Glass House."

39 — Don Wrobleski, interview with author, November 28, 2018: Architect Don Wrobleski taught Speyer as a student and recalled that Speyer "knew how people lived, and you could learn from that."

40 — Alan G. Artner, Art critic, "Art Curator A. James Speyer," *Chicago Tribune,* November 11, 1986. In the obituary, the director of the Art Institute of Chicago, James N. Wood was quoted as saying about Speyer: "Jim not only possessed the professionalism and skill of a first-rate curator but he also represented for us in Chicago the ambitions of the entire modernist period. He was a product and a primary source of what we see as Modern, and he realized it as an architect, a curator and in his lifestyle," accessed September 18, 2019, chicagotribune.

41 — Harry Weese, *Oral History of Harry Mohr Weese / Interviewed by Betty J. Blum, Compiled under the Auspices of the Chicago Architects Oral History Project, the Ernest R. Graham Study Center for Architectural Drawings, Department of Architecture, the Art Institute of Chicago, rev. ed.* (Chicago: Art Institute of Chicago, 2001), 23.

42 — Weese, *Oral History,* 21.

43 — Weese, *Oral History,* 21.

44 — Weese, *Oral History,* 209

45 — Bertrand Goldberg, *Oral History of Bertrand Goldberg / Interviewed by Betty J. Blum, Compiled Under the Auspices of the Chicago Architects Oral History Project, Department of Architecture, the Art Institute of Chicago* (Chicago: Art Institute of Chicago, 2001), 17.

46 — Goldberg, *Oral History,* 110.

47 — Goldberg, *Oral History,* 154.

48 — Letitia Baldrige, *Home: The Burlington House Awards, American Interiors* (New York:

Viking Press, 1972), 10: featured the Epstein House.

49 — *Conversations with Mies van der Rohe,* ed. Moises Puente (New York: Princeton Architectural Press. 2008), 40–41.

50 — Schulze and Windhorst, *Mies,* 242.

Katherine Dummer and Walter T. Fisher House

1 — Henry-Russell Hitchcock Jr., "A House in Winnetka," *The Arts* 16, no. 6 (February 1930): 403.

2 — H. Ward Jandl, John A. Burns, and Michael J. Auer, *Yesterday's Houses of Tomorrow: Innovative American Homes 1850–1950* (Washington, DC: National Trust for Historic Preservation Press, 1991), 157 and *Architectural Record* 66, no. 5 (November 1929): 461.

3 — Morgan Fisher, email to architect Stuart Cohen, March 12, 2010.

4 — Fisher, email. Prior to marrying Howard, Marion had worked for the US Bureau of Indian Affairs.

5 — Howard Fisher, "The Modern Dwelling," in *The Hound & Horn: A Harvard Miscellany* 2, no. 4 (Summer 1929), 385–86. In this illustrated essay for a student publication, Howard Fisher advocated modernism in the arts. He noted that the playroom was given the best location with sun throughout the day. The playroom, terrace, and porch (with the lavatory and coat closet) constitute a combination specifically designed for the use of a small nursery school run by Katherine Fisher.

6 — "The Home of Mr. and Mrs. Walter T. Fisher: Winnetka, Illinois: Howard T. Fisher, Designer," *House Beautiful,* March 1930, 317.

7 — Jandl, Burns, and Auer, "L2H40: The Promise of Prefabrication" in *Yesterday's Houses,* 158.

Anne Green and Henry Dubin House

1 — Henry Dubin, "Residence of Henry Dubin, Highland Park, Illinois: A Battledeck Floor House, Dubin & Eisenberg, Architects," *Architectural Forum* 55, no. 1 (August 1931): 227. Arthur D. Dubin, *Oral History of Arthur Detmers Dubin / Interviewed by*

Betty J. Blum, Compiled under the Auspices of the Chicago Architects Oral History Project, the Ernest R. Graham Study Center for Architectural Drawings, Department of Architecture, the Art Institute of Chicago, rev. ed. (Chicago: Art Institute of Chicago, 2003), 124: Index: Dubin, Anne [Green] (mother of Arthur).

2 — Henry Dubin, "Welding Extensively Employed in Steel House," *Welding Journal* 11 (January 1932): 4.

3 — Le Corbusier, *Toward an Architecture*, trans. John Goodman (London: Frances Lincoln, 2008), 87: in 1927, Le Corbusier defined a house as a "machine for living in." (The translation is of the 1928 printing of his manifesto by the same title, *Vers une architecture.* The translation has an Introduction by Jean-Louis Cohen.)

4 — Arthur D. Dubin, *Oral History,* 60–61: Arthur quoted from an article cited by Betty Blum (see page 47) from "Art on the Make," *Chicago Daily News,* June 17, 1933.

5 — Arthur Dubin, *Oral History,* 47.

6 — Peter Dubin, telephone interview by author, April 14, 2017. Note that Charles-Édouard Jeanneret is the birth name of Le Corbusier.

7 — Henry Dubin, "Welding Extensively Employed," 4.

8 — Henry Dubin, "Battledeck Floor House," 223.

9 — Henry Dubin, "Welding Extensively Employed," 7: Dubin notes that "Marine and railroad architecture have far outdistanced building construction."

10 — Henry Dubin, "Battledeck Floor House," 227.

11 — Arthur Dubin, *Oral History,* 55.

12 — "Battledeck House," Johnson Lasky Kindelin Architects, Projects, accessed February 17, 2018, jlkarch.com.

Rosalie Brown and Robert H. Morse House

1 — For a recent overview of the house, see Lisa Napoles, "1932 Morse House, Lake Forest," in Robert Bruegmann ed., *Art Deco Chicago: Designing Modern American* (Chicago: Chicago Art

Deco Society in collaboration with the Chicago History Museum, 2018), 200–03.

2 — *Pioneers in Industry: the Story of Fairbanks, Morse & Co., 1830–1945* (Chicago: Fairbanks, Morse & Co., 1945).

3 — The founder, architect William Carbys Zimmerman (1856–1932), studied architecture at MIT and arrived to Chicago in 1880. His office was located at Steinway Hall (64 E. Van Buren St.) where progressive architects ranging from Frank Lloyd Wright and Dwight Perkins had studios. See bio in Stuart Cohen and Susan Benjamin, *North Shore Chicago: Houses of the Lakefront Suburbs* (New York: Acanthus Press, 2004), 322.

4 — Richard Teller Crane, *History of Crane Co.* (Chicago: Crane, 1921). *Crane Co. 1855–1975: The First 120 Years* (Bloomfield, CT: Crane Co., 1975) The Newberry Library hosts the Crane Co., records (1920–1955).

5 — National Register of Historic Places, Robert Hosmer Morse House, Lake Forest, Lake County, Illinois, National Register #00000947.

Irene Tipler and Paul McCurry House

1 — Paul McCurry, *Interview with Paul Durbin McCurry / Interviewed by Betty J. Blum, Compiled under the Auspices of the Chicago Architects Oral History Project, the Ernest R. Graham Study Center for Architectural Drawings, Department of Architecture, the Art Institute of Chicago,* rev. ed. (Chicago: Art Institute of Chicago, 2005), 9.

2 — McCurry, Interview, 47.

3 — McCurry, Interview, 83.

4 — "Irene Bell Tipler McCurry," *Chicago Tribune,* April 8, 2005.

5 — "Maximum of Light for an Architect's Home: House of Paul D. McCurry in Chicago," *American Home,* January 1938, 17–19.

6 — McCurry, Interview, 82.

7 — McCurry, Interview, 82.

8 — McCurry, Interview, 87.

9 — McCurry, Interview, 88.

10 — Margaret McCurry and Marian Tweedie, interview by

author, November 26, 2018. Paul and Irene McCurry's daughters provided much of the information on the house and living there.

Vine Itschner and Herbert Bruning House

1 — "Architect Stages 1-Man Design Job in Chicago House," *Architectural Record* 83 (February 1938): 32, archives now digitized at architecturalrecord.com, as quoted in Robert Boyce, *Keck & Keck* (New York: Princeton Architectural Press, 1993), 57.

2 — Boyce, *Keck*, 57.

3 — Boyce, *Keck*, 57: Keck designed the house, superintended its construction, and saw it through to completion, assisted by (brother) William Keck and Robert Bruce Tague, his two draftsmen.

4 — Keck's first building designed in what came to be called the International Style was the Miralago Ballroom, built in 1928, and located in Wilmette; it burned only three years after it was constructed.

5 — "Wilmette Home Nearing Completion," *Chicago Daily Tribune,* November 8, 1936 reports $30,000 while "Architect Stages," *Architectural Record* reports $54,000 for the structure with a total of $75,000 when including architect's fees, furnishings, and equipment.

6 — The 1940 US Federal Population Census lists Bruning as Vice President of a company that produced surveying instruments.

7 — In addition to the House of Tomorrow and the Crystal House at the Century of Progress, both designed by Keck, see *Floor Plan for the Stran-Steel House Exhibit,* Century of Progress Records, Special Collections and University Archives, University of Illinois at Chicago Library, digitized, accessed February 19, 2019, collections.carli.illinois.edu. Also see the Good Housekeeping Stran-Steel House at users.marshall.edu.

Doris L. and Thomas H. Mullen House

1 — Blair Kamin, "Bertrand Goldberg, 84," *Chicago Tribune,* October 9, 1997.

2 — Jeanne M. Lambin, "The Goldberg Variation," *Positions in Architecture: The Chicago Architectural Journal* 9 (2003): 42.

3 — 1930 and 40 US Federal Population Census, accessed January 14, 2019, ancestry.com: Thomas H. Mullen, born 1904, resident Evanston, IL.

4 — "A Portfolio of Work by Bertrand Goldberg," *Architectural Forum* 84, no. 5 (March 1946): 107.

5 — Alison Fisher, "The Road to Community: The Houses and Housing of Bertrand Goldberg," in *Bertrand Goldberg: Architecture of Invention,* ed., Zoë Ryan (Chicago: Art Institute of Chicago; 2011), 64, distributed by New Haven and London: Yale University Press. Alison Fisher is Associate Curator of Architecture and Design at The Art Institute of Chicago.

6 — Bertrand Goldberg, *Oral History of Bertrand Goldberg / Interviewed by Betty J. Blum, Compiled under the Auspices of the Chicago Architects Oral History Project, the Ernest R. Graham Study Center for Architectural Drawings, Department of Architecture, the Art Institute of Chicago,* rev. ed. (Chicago: Art Institute of Chicago, 2001), 154: Goldberg used mahogany plywood and left it natural, built of freight car units manufactured in Chicago and shipped to Shelter Island, New York.

7 — Goldberg, *Oral History,* 121.

8 — *Architectural Forum* Editors, *The 1940 Book of Small Houses* (New York: Simon and Schuster, 1939), 44–45: The book was meant to serve for the homeowner as a "constant source of reference and guidance throughout the course of his homebuilding program."

9 — Editors, *Small Houses,* 45. Harwell Hamilton Harris, FAIA (1903–1990).

Rosalie Strauss and Gustave Weinfeld House

1 — *The Michigan Alumnus* 37, 698, books.google.com, Medical degree 1924; *Mount Sinai Hospital Annual Reports* (1941, '48, and '52), Mount Sinai Digital Repository, Resident Staff in Pediatrics 1927; "Meeting of the Board of Trustees of the University of Illinois" (July 13, 1932): 86, trustees.uillinois.edu and "Transactions of the Board of Trustees July 13, 1932 to June 15, 1934," University of Illinois at Urbana-Champaign (June 15, 1934): 591, archives.library.illinois.edu, Associate Professor; Gustave F. Weinfeld, MD and Frances B. Floore, "Infant Feeding with Unlimited Amounts of a Concentrated and a Dilute Cow's Milk Formula," *Am Journal Dis Child* 40, no. 6 (December 1930): 1208–14; Gustave F. Weinfeld, "Sino-Auricular Heart-Block in Childhood," *Journal of Pediatrics* 2, no. 5 (May 1933) 559–67; "Pediatrics and Child Psychiatry: A Symposium: Pediatric Training Approaches in Infancy," *American Journal of Orthopsychiatry* 11, no. 3 (1941), 423–29, psycnet.apa.org; "If Habit Training Goes Awry" in *The P.T.A. Magazine, National Parent Teacher* (Chicago: Child Welfare Co., 1947), 11; "Common Causes of Baby's Night Crying and Sleeplessness" in Arnold W. Holmes and Maurice P. Fryefield, eds, *The Family Problems Handbook: How and Where to Find Help and Guidance* (New York: F. Fell, 1952), 104, books.google.com, all accessed February 12, 2019.

2 — Weinfeld, "Self-Demand Feeding and Indulgence in Early Infancy," *Journal of Pediatrics* 31, no. 2 (August 1947): 203–06, sciencedirect.com and "Self-Demand Feeding," *Medical Clinics of North America* 34, no. 1 (1950): 33–40, sciencedirect.com; "Mental Training of the Child," Young Mother's Club, *Wilmette Life,* September 6, 1934, 28, images.ourontario.ca and "Training of Children Discussed by Lecturer," University Women's Club, *Lima News,* January 19, 1939, 6, newspaperarchive.com, all accessed February 12, 2019.

3 — Kenan Heise, "Rosalie Weinfeld, Former Nursery School Head," *Chicago Tribune,* September 28, 1994, accessed February 8, 2019: quotation from Evelyn Baumann, retired clinical social worker. Honors received: May 10, 1974, was proclaimed "Rosalie Weinfeld Day" in Highland Park and in 1987 the Lake County Medical Society voted her "Woman of the Year."

4 — 1940 US Federal Population Census, accessed February 12, 2019, archive.com.

5 — Patrick Steffens, "Sharply Defined Masses: The Forgotten Work of James F. Eppenstein," at Forgotten Chicago: The Weinfeld House and the Eppenstein House are both illustrated in Part 3 at forgottenchicago.com.

6 — *Solar Houses: An Architectural Lift in Living* (Toledo: Libbey-Owens-Ford Glass, 1945), 20 and Thomas Creighton, Frank Lopez, Charles Magruder, and George Sanderson, *Homes Small, Medium, Large* (New York: Reinhold, 1947).

7 — Brian Solomon, *Electric Locomotives* (St. Paul: MBI, 2003), 60–61 and John Gruber, "James E. Eppenstein" in *Streamliners: Locomotives and Trains in the Age of Speed and Style*, ed. Brian Solomon (Minneapolis: Voyageur Press, 2015), 114–16.

8 — Steffens, "Eppenstein," Part 3.

9 — Bonnie Warren, "A Garden District Classic with Stories to Tell," *New Orleans Magazine,* July 2016, shows a dining room table designed by Eppenstein.

Irma Kuppenheimer and Bertram J. Cahn House

1 — William Keck, *Oral History of William Keck / Interviewed by Betty J. Blum, Compiled under the Auspices of the Chicago Architects Oral History Project, the Ernest R. Graham Study Center for Architectural Drawings, Department of Architecture, the Art Institute of Chicago,* rev. ed. (Chicago: Art Institute of Chicago, 2001), 100.

2 — "George Fred Keck Architect: House for B. J. Cahn, Lake Forest, Illinois," *Architectural Forum* 71, no. 1 (July 1939): 13, as quoted in Robert Piper Boyce, *Keck & Keck* (New York: Princeton Architectural Press, 1993).

3 — The mechanical windows were priced at $40,000. Keck, *Oral History,* 109.

4 — "George Fred Keck," 13.

5 — James Ford and Katherine Morrow Ford, "George Fred Keck, Architect: House for B. J. Cahn, Lake Forest, 1937," in *The Modern House in America* (New York: Architectural Book Publishing, 1940). Republished as James Ford and Katherine Morrow Ford, *Classic Modern Homes of the Thirties: 64 Designs by Neutra, Gropius, Breuer, Stone and Others* (Mineola, NY: Dover, 1989), 66. In their preface, James Ford and Katherine Morrow Ford extend their appreciation and guidance

in the selections of much of the material in the book to Professor Walter Gropius, chairman of the Department of Architecture of the Graduate School of Design of Harvard University, and to Dr. Sigfried Giedion, general secretary of the International Congress of Modern Architecture, 7.

Josephine Topp and De Forest S. Colburn House

1 — Bertrand Goldberg, *Oral History of Bertrand Goldberg / Interviewed by Betty J. Blum, Chicago Architects Oral History Project, the Ernest R. Graham Study Center for Architectural Drawings, Department of Architecture, the Art Institute of Chicago,* rev. ed. (Chicago: Art Institute, 2001), 104. Cubist architecture never achieved the popularity of cubist painting and sculpture popularized by Pablo Picasso and George Braque. It did, however, flourish in Prague from about 1912 until the beginning of the First World War in 1918.

2 — Le Corbusier, *Toward an Architecture,* trans. John Goodman (London: Frances Lincoln, 2007), 87: in 1927, Le Corbusier defined a house as a "machine for living in." (The translation is of the 1928 printing of his manifesto by the same title, *Vers une architecture.* The translation has an Introduction by Jean-Louis Cohen.)

3 — Elizabeth A. T. Smith, "Space, Structure, Society: The Architecture of Bertrand Goldberg," in *Bertrand Goldberg: Architecture of Invention* ed., Zoë Ryan (Chicago: Art Institute of Chicago, 2011), 22, distributed by Yale University Press. The North Pole Mobile Ice Cream Shop, that consisted of a central mechanized core from which the roof was suspended, was designed by Goldberg and Black as a prefabricated unit that could be disassembled and easily transported by truck to warm places in the winter and to the north in the summer. It dates from 1938.

4 — Goldberg, *Oral History,* 96. For more on William T. Priestley, FAIA (1907–1995) see his interview in the Chicago Architects Oral History Project, with some overlap regarding the visit on page 6.

5 — Goldberg, *Oral History,* 93.

6 — Louise Bargelt, *Chicago Daily Tribune,* n.d., clipping in the collection of the current owner, architectural photographer, Howard Kaplan.

7 — "Listed Among Nation's Finest Buildings" clipping from unknown and undated newspaper as well as an article in *House & Garden* 75, no. 6 (June 1939): 40, "Among the residences chosen for this exhibit by the Committee on Education of the American Institute of Architects is the attractive home shown. This home, designed for D. S. Colburn of Highland Park, Illinois by Gilmer V. Black has concrete *walls, floors, and roof.* It exemplifies the beauty concrete can help achieve for any style of home, modern or traditional."

8 — Domestic Interiors Special Issue *Architectural Forum* 67, no. 4 (October 1937): 364.

Caroline Sinclair and Philip Will Jr. House

1 — "100 Years of Significant Buildings, 4: Schools," *Architectural Record* 120, no. 3 (September 1956): 237–38: Crow Island School, Winnetka, Illinois, 1939–40, (Tied for twelfth). Crow Island School received the AIA 25-year Award in 1975 for a design of enduring significance.

2 — Lawrence Bradford Perkins, *Oral History of Lawrence Bradford Perkins / Interviewed by Betty J. Blum, Compiled under the Auspices of the Chicago Architects Oral History Project, the Ernest R. Graham Study Center for Architectural Drawings, Department of Architecture, the Art Institute of Chicago,* rev. ed. (Chicago: Art Institute of Chicago, 2000), 62. The firm Perkins + Will global continues the legacy of its founders, perkinswill.com.

3 — Debbie Fry and Robyn Beaver, eds., *Perkins + Will: 75 Years* (Victoria, Australia: Images Publishing, 2010).

4 — Lawrence B. Perkins, "Philip Will Jr." [1906–1985], *New York Times,* October 25, 1985.

5 — Jennifer Komar Olivarez, "Perkins and Will" in *Encyclopedia of Twentieth Century Architecture, Volume 3, P-Z,* ed. R. Stephen Sennott (New York: Fitzroy Dearborn, imprint of Taylor & Francis, 2004), 997–99. Will retired to Venice, Florida in 1980 and died there in 1985.

6 — Perkins, *Oral History,* 42.

7 — Special Issue: "101 New Houses," *Architectural Forum* 71, no. 4 (October 1939).

Madeleine Michelson and Philip B. Maher House

1 — Michigan Avenue is sometimes referred to as "Boul Mich." City Planner Daniel Burnham envisioned Chicago as Paris on the Prairie. Alice Sinkevitch and Laurie McGovern Peterson, eds., *AIA Guide to Chicago Third Edition* (Urbana, Chicago and Springfield: University of Illinois Press, 2014), 134–35, 181: source for dates of buildings in text.

2 — James Ford and Katherine Morrow Ford, *Classic Modern Homes of the Thirties* (Mineola, NY: Dover, 1989). The book was originally published as *The Modern House in America* (New York: Architectural Book, 1940). The other Chicago area houses included in the book are George Fred Keck's Herbert Bruning House and B. J. Cahn House. William F. Deknatel's Walter J. Kohler Jr. House is also included but located in Kohler, Wisconsin.

Dorothy Miller and Paul Schweikher House

1 — Robert Paul Schweikher, *Oral History of Robert Paul Schweikher / Interviewed by Betty J. Blum, Complied under the Auspices of the Chicago Architects Oral History Project, the Ernest R. Graham Study Center for Architectural Drawings, Department of Architecture, the Art Institute of Chicago* rev. ed. (Chicago: Art Institute of Chicago, 2000), 125.

2 — Paul Schweikher, telephone interview by author, October 10, 1986.

3 — Schweikher, interview by author.

4 — Peter Blake to Michael Devine, September 12, 1986, State Historic Preservation Office, Illinois.

5 — Will Bruder to Michael Devine, October 8, 1986, State Historic Preservation Office, Illinois.

6 — Schweikher, *Oral History,* 124.

7 — Schweikher, *Oral History,* 124.

8 — Schweikher, *Oral History,* 109.

9 — Schweikher, *Oral History,* 111.

10 — Schweikher, 26; Todd Wenger, Executive Director, and Sarah Welcome, Program Coordinator, Schweikher House Preservation Trust, email to author, February 15, 2019.

11 — Schweikher, interview by author.

12 — I thank Dan Fitzpatrick, Historian, The Schweikher House, for providing detailed information about the additions.

13 — "House in Rural Illinois Features a Plan of Marked Simplicity Vigorously Translated into Structure and Detail," *Architectural Forum* 86, no. 5 (May 1947) and "Casa de Paul Schweikher," *Nuestra Arquitectura* 213, no. 4 (Abril 1947) [Buenos Aires].

14 — David Stout, "Alexander Langsdorf, 83, Plutonium Pioneer," *New York Times,* obituary, May 26, 1996.

15 — Sandie Shumaker, email to author, March 22, 2016.

16 — Ralph Rapson to Michael Devine, October 2, 1986, State Historic Preservation Office, Illinois and the Art Institute of Chicago, Ryerson and Burnham Libraries.

Ellen Borden and Adlai E. Stevenson II House

1 — John Barlow Martin, *Adlai Stevenson of Illinois: The Life of Adlai E. Stevenson* (Garden City, NY: Doubleday, 1976), 130.

2 — H. Ward Jandl, John Burns, and Michael Auer, *Yesterday's Houses of Tomorrow: Innovative American Houses, 1850–1950,* (Washington DC: Preservation Press, National Trust for Historic Preservation, 1991), 161: Howard Fisher describes General Houses' approach to prefabrication. E. Todd Wheeler, *Interview with E. Todd Wheeler / Interviewed by Betty J. Blum, Compiled Under the Auspices of the Chicago Architects Oral History Project, the Ernest Graham Study Center for Architectural Drawings, Department of Architecture, the Art Institute of Chicago* (Chicago: Art Institute of Chicago, 2003), 21.

3 — Wheeler, *Interview,* 21.

4 — Wheeler, *Interview,* 21

5 — Adlai Stevenson III, interview with author, March 26, 2003: There is a great story about Stevenson's legendary wit. The

best-known photograph of Stevenson, taken during his 1952 presidential campaign, showed him on the platform at Flint, Michigan, his legs crossed, with a hole in his shoe. He was working on a speech when a photograph was taken that received the Pulitzer Prize. Porter McKeever, *Adlai Stevenson: His Life and Legacy, a Biography* (New York: William Morrow, 1989), 287: When Stevenson found out about the award, he sent a postcard to the photographer: "Congratulations. I'll bet this is the first time anyone ever won a Pulitzer Prize for a hole in one." (Some of his campaign buttons featured a shoe with a hole in it.)

Lucile Gottschalk and Aaron Heimbach House

1 — "A Portfolio of Work by Bertrand Goldberg," *Architectural Forum* 84, no. 5 (March 1946): 107–15. See also Alison Fisher, "The Road to Community: The Houses and Housing of Bertrand Goldberg," in *Bertrand Goldberg: Architecture of Invention,* ed., Zoë Ryan (Chicago: Art Institute of Chicago; 2011), 62–97, distributed by New Haven and London: Yale University Press. See also Gary Gand, *Julius Shulman: Chicago Midcentury Modernism* (New York: Rizzoli, 2010), 46–53.

2 — 1940 US Federal Population Census, accessed April 3, 2019, archive.com: lists Aaron Heimbach (30) as "doctor" in "private practice," Lucile (27) as "medical/social" working at a "hospital," and their son (5) residing at 11356 So. Lothair Ave, Cook County, prior to relocating.

3 — Tom Hawley, email reply to author, May 15, 2019.

Kathryn Dougherty and Lloyd Lewis House

1 — "Biography of Lloyd Lewis," Lloyd Lewis Papers, 1886–1985, Bulk 1905–1949, The Newberry Library, Modern Manuscripts, Chicago, mms.newberry.org; "Lloyd Lewis: An Outstanding Figure in the American Literary World," lecture brochure, Traveling Culture collection MSC0150, University of Iowa Libraries, digital.lib.uiowa.edu; both accessed January 10, 2019.

2 — Wright often positioned his living spaces on an upper level. He started doing this during his Prairie-school years in the late

nineteenth to early twentieth centuries.

3 — Plywood was a manufactured material that Wright used enthusiastically.

4 — See Dorothy Miller and Paul Schweikher House (p. 98) for his response to apparent similarities.

5 — For further information about Wright and his relationship with Taliesin apprentices see memoirs by apprentices such as Edgar Tafel, *Years with Frank Lloyd Wright, Apprentice to Genius* (New York: Dover, 1979) and Curtis Besinger, *Working with Mr. Wright: What It Was Like* (New York and Melbourne, Australia: Cambridge University Press, 1995).

6 — Lloyd Lewis Papers Finding Aid, Photographs, Sheep ranching in Colorado and Utah, ca. 1925–1930, accessed January 10, 2019, mms.newberry.org.

7 — Richard H. Brown, "Lloyd W. Lewis: A Chicago Journalist," *Encyclopedia of Chicago,* accessed January 10, 2019, encyclopedia.chicagohistory.org.

8 — "Luncheon to Honor the Memory of Lloyd Lewis, Held at the Sherman Hotel," press release photograph, May 20, 1950, in the possession of author.

Charles Dewey Jr. House and Beach House

1 — "Charles Dewey Jr., Investment Advisor," *New York Times,* May 2, 1974, accessed November 5, 2018, nytimes.com.

2 — The entry *William Pereira* attributes his work as an architect and production designer for Paramount and RKO as being during "the same period he designed the Lake County Tuberculosis Sanitarium (1938)," (sic) accessed January 21, 2019, laconservancy.org.

3 — "William A. Ganster and William L. Pereira: Lake Country Tuberculosis Sanatorium, Waukegan, Illinois," in *Built in USA 1932–1944,* ed. Elizabeth Mock (New York: Museum of Modern Art, 1944), 93, with a photograph by Hedrich Blessing, accessed PDF March 9, 2019, moma.org. "Landmark Nomination Form," City of Waukegan, Historic Preservation Commission, for the Lake County Tuberculosis Sanatorium cites its architects as "William

A. Ganster and Offices of W. L. Pereira, Associated Architects," and a press release for the Architecture Section of Fifteenth Anniversary Exhibition, *Art in Progress,* Museum of Modern Art, May 24th to October 8th, 1944, Exhibition List, Built in USA: 1932–44 lists "William A. Ganster and William L. Pereira: Lake County Tuberculosis Sanatorium, Waukegan, Illinois. 1939," both accessed March 23, 2019, drupal. docomomo-us.org. See also Marjorie Candler and William Ganster House (p. 126).

4 — "Home Projects Announced for Chicago Area: 4000 Lots to be Marketed in Evanston," *Chicago Daily Tribune,* June 6, 1937.

5 — George Nelson and Henry Wright, *Tomorrow's Houses: How to Plan Your Post-War Home Now* (New York: Simon and Schuster, 1945). George Nelson was consultant editor of the *Architectural Forum* when he co-authored this book with Wright.

6 — Nelson, *Tomorrow's Houses,* 9.

7 — His most famous building is likely the forty-eight-story 1972 Transamerica Pyramid building in San Francisco.

8 — *Hal Pereira* (1905–1983) biography imdb.com and Steven Jacobs, *The Wrong House: The Architecture of Alfred Hitchcock* (Rotterdam, Netherlands: 010, 2007), 284: about *Rear Window,* "For months, Hitchcock, Pereira, and MacMillan Johnson did nothing but plan the design of what was to become the largest set ever built at Paramount," books.google.com, both accessed January 20, 2019. William Pereira in 1943 received an Academy Award for Special Effects, *Reap the Wild Wind,* laconservancy.org.

Marjorie Horton and Winston Elting House

1 — Stuart Cohen, *Inventing the New American House: Howard Van Doren Shaw, Architect* (New York: The Monacelli Press, 2015), 235.

2 — Victor Elting, *Recollections of a Grandfather* (Chicago: A. Kroch, 1940), 171.

3 — For a historical overview of Walden see Kim Coventry, Daniel Meyer, Arthur H. Miller, *Classic Country Estates of Lake Forest:*

Architecture and Landscape Design, 1856–1940 (New York: Norton, 2003), 79–86. Further information was obtained from Arthur Miller, email to author, May 8, 2019. Harriet Hammond McCormick died in 1921 and Cyrus McCormick Jr. died in 1936; his subsequent spouse, Alice Holt McCormick had the main house demolished in 1955.

4 — "House in Lake Forest, IL.," *Architectural Forum* 72, no. 1 (January 1941), 44–46.

5 — Betty Blum, "A Regale of Tales," *Inland Architect* 28, no. 6 (November–December, 1984): 36–41, the article mentions tensions between the two former partners. John Zukowsky ed., *Architecture in Context: The Avant-Garde in Chicago's Suburbs: Paul Schweikher and William Ferguson Deknatel* (Chicago: Graham Foundation for Advanced Studies in the Fine Arts and Art Institute of Chicago, 1984). The likely overstatement of Schweikher's quality was reinforced by the fact that Elting was not explicitly mentioned in the subtitle of the exhibition catalogue publication.

6 — Among the numerous high-profile publications their work is featured in during the postwar years is Henry-Russell Hitchcock and Arthur Drexler, *Built in USA: Post-War Architecture* (New York: Museum of Modern Art, 1952) published in conjunction with an exhibition of the same name held January 20–March 15, 1953 at the Museum of Modern Art. (Schweikher and Elting's Louis C. Upton House in Paradise Valley, Arizona (1950) is featured on pages 100–01). An Argentinian journal dedicated an entire issue to Schweikher and Elting: *Nuestra Arquitectura* 213, no. 4 (Abril 1947) [Buenos Aires]. The Marjorie Horton and Winston Elting House and the Dorothy Miller and Paul Schweikher House and Studio (p. 96) are included in the works featured. Dan Fitzpatrick, Historian, The Schweikher House, email reply to author, January 31, 2020. Schweikher established a practice with Theodore "Ted" Lamb in 1934, joined by Winston Elting in 1938. Both Schweikher and Elting were discharged following the war in 1945 (each having attained the rank of Lieutenant Commander in the Navy) and reconvened their

practice until 1953. (Lamb had died in 1943 when his PanAm plane crashed into the Targus River near Portugal; he was en route to the American Embassy in London to lead an Office of Civil Defense commission related to the impact bombing has on different types of buildings. "Crash of a Boeing 134A Clipper off Lisbon: 24 Killed," Bureau of Aircraft Accidents Archives, baaa_acro.com and "Theodore Warren 'Ted' Lamb," findagrave.com, both accessed January 31, 2020).

7 — Meyric Rogers, "The Work of Schweikher and Elting," (Chicago: Renaissance Society, 1949), 1, published in conjunction with the exhibition *Schweikher and Elting, Architects* held March 21–April 14, 1949 at the Renaissance Society at the University of Chicago, accessed May 8, 2019, renaissancesociety.org.

Marjorie Candler and William Ganster House

1 — A 1944 publication cites "William A. Ganster and William L. Pereira: Lake County Tuberculosis Sanitorium, Waukegan, Illinois," in *Built in USA 1932–1944*, ed. Elizabeth Mock (New York: Museum of Modern Art, 1944), 93, with a photograph by Hedrich Blessing, accessed PDF March 9, 2019, moma.org. Diana Dretske, "Tuberculosis Sanitorium," lakecountyhistory.blogspot.com, updated March 22, 2019. "William L. Pereira" entry accessed March 23, 2019, docomomo-us.org. Note that the Lake County Tuberculosis Sanatorium has frequently been spelled Sanitorium.

2 — "William Ganster, 70, Shaped City Landmarks," *Lake County News-Sun,* January 30–31, 1988: "An award winning architect, Ganster won a gold medal in 1949 from the Philadelphia Art Alliance for designing the former Lake County Tuberculosis Sanatorium," assessed March 23, 2019, docomomo-us.org. See also, "Charles Dewey Jr. House and Beach House" (p. 118).

3 — Mitchell Stephens, "History of Television," *Grolier Encyclopedia,* accessed November 10, 2018, nyu.edu: "The number of television sets in use rose from 6,000 in 1946 to some 12 million by 1951. By 1955

half of all US homes had black and white sets."

4 — PFC Auctions, Chanel Islands, Guernsey, provenance notes for auction, accessed October 10, 2017, pfcauctions.com.

5 — Eve Kahn, "Fallingwater Working Blueprints up for Auction Sept. 27," *Architect: The Journal of the American Institute of Architects,* September 20, 2012, accessed October 10, 2017, architectmagazine.com, also cites from PFC Auctions. Hope's Windows was "the upstate New York manufacturer of Fallingwater's steel ribbons and casements."

6 — Dennis Peterson, interview by author, October 2, 2018: Dennis remembers Hennighausen saying that he had attended a couple of seminars given by Wright and had shaken his hand.

Minna Green and Hugh Duncan House I

1 — James C. Peebles and William C. Knopf Jr., "Products and Practice: Solar heating," *Architectural Forum* 76, no. 8 (August, 1943): 6–7, 114. A detailed summary of the report issued by IIT mechanical engineering professor James C. Peebles and graduate student William C. Knopf Jr.

2 — Robert Boyce, *Keck & Keck* (New York: Princeton Architectural Press, 1993), 78: The study, according to Robert Boyce, didn't take into account such unexpected variables as the lack of control for the radiant heated floor, lack of caulking around door and window frames because of labor shortages, and higher wind velocity than expected. Boyce pointed out that news articles about the Duncan House in both the architectural and lay press greatly increased solar architecture's popularity, and the Keck office was receiving more job requests than it could handle. Anthony Denzer, *The Solar House: Pioneering Sustainable Design* (New York: Rizzoli, 2013), 24–25: discusses the Duncan House I and points out other problems, including those related to heat infiltration and loss.

3 — Hugh Dalziel Duncan, *Culture and Democracy: The Struggle for Form in Society and

Architecture in Chicago and the Middle West during the Life and Times of Louis H. Sullivan* (Totowa, NJ: Bedminster Press, 1965, reissued by Piscataway, NJ: Transaction Publishers, 1989) and "The Chicago School: Original Principles" in *Chicago's Famous Buildings,* ed. Ira J. Bach (Chicago: University of Chicago Press, 1980), 1–12. Minna Green Duncan, "An Experiment in Applying New Methods in Field Work," *Social Casework* 44, no. 4 (April 1963): 179–84. Charles Elkins, "'Son of Burke,': The Hugh Dalziel Duncan Collection at Morris Library," *ICarbS* 5, no. 1 (1985): 45–60.

Ellen Newby and Lambert Ennis House

1 — John Sergeant, *Frank Lloyd Wright's Usonian Houses: Designs for Moderate Cost One-Family Homes, the Case for Organic Architecture* (New York: Watson-Guptill, 1984), 199: Appendix E "Taliesin Memorabilia, Charter Applicants."

2 — "William F. Deknatel, Architect: House for Walter J. Kohler Jr.," *Architectural Forum* 71 no. 1 (July 1939), 50–53.

3 — Helen Koues, "Functional Modern at Its Best," *Good Housekeeping* 110, no. 4 (April 1940): 138: in the *Good Housekeeping*'s "Better Living" House Studio section, Architecture, Building, & Furnishings, 137–38; now digitized through the Albert R. Mann Library, Home Economics Archive: Research, Tradition and History (HEARTH), Ithaca, NY, Cornell University, October 30, 2018, dlxs2.library.cornell.edu.

4 — Geoffrey Baker and Bruno Funaro, "Windows Hung Outside Frame," in *Windows in Modern Architecture* (New York: Architectural Book Publishing, 1948), 80–81.

5 — Henry-Russell Hitchcock and Philip Johnson, "André Lurçat: Hotel Nord-Sud, Calvi, Corsica, 1931" in *The International Style* (New York: Norton, 1966), 173, originally published in 1932 under the title *The International Style: Architecture since 1922.*

6 — *Architectural Forum* 86, no. 3 (March 1947): 84–86.

7 — John Zukowsky, ed., *Architecture in Context: The Avant-Garde in Chicago's

Suburbs: Paul Schweikher and William Ferguson Deknatel* (Chicago: The Graham Foundation for Advanced Studies in the Fine Arts and Art Institute of Chicago, 1984). Published in conjunction with an exhibition and lectures of the same title, organized by John Zukowsky, Curator of Architecture, with Betty Blum, Project Coordinator, *100 Chicago Architects 1920–1970,* Oral and Video History Recording Project.

Adele Bretzfeld and Willard Gidwitz House

1 — Jane King Hession, Rip Rapson, and Bruce N. Wright, *Ralph Rapson: Sixty Years of Modern Design* (Afton, MN: Afton Historical Society Press, 1999), 56.

2 — The New Bauhaus evolved into the Institute of Design and, in 1949, it became part of the Illinois Institute of Technology.

3 — *Modern Architecture International Exhibition* (New York: Museum of Modern Art, 1932), 166–67. Published in conjunction with an exhibition of the same title organized and presented at the Museum of Modern Art, February 10, to March 23, 1932, accessed March 13, 2019, moma.org.

4 — Hession, *Sixty Years,* 48: Rapson doesn't specify the exact houses he visited.

5 — Hession, *Sixty Years,* 56.

6 — Hession, *Sixty Years,* 57 and "Circulating Exhibitions 1931–1954, *Bulletin of the Museum of Modern Art* 21 no. 3/4, Circulating Exhibitions 1931–1954 (Summer 1954): 23, accessed March 10, 2019, jstor.org/stable/4058235.

7 — Other architects invited by Entenza, who was editor of *Arts & Architecture,* to participate included Charles Eames, Richard Neutra, and Eero Saarinen.

8 — Gary Gand, "Ralph Rapson," in *Julius Shulman: Chicago Midcentury Modernism* (New York: Rizzoli, 2010), 68.

Eleanor Knopp and Henry P. Glass House

1 — Carma R. Gorman, "Henry P. Glass and World War II," *Design Issues* 22, no. 4 (Autumn 2006): 4–26, accessed October 5, 2004, jstor.org and Harry P. Glass, "Harry P. Glass, FIDSA Interview,"

by Victoria Matranga, October 18, 2001, accessed October 5, 2004, idsa.org.

2 — Gorman, "Glass," 6.

3 — Gorman, "Glass," 16.

4 — *Architectural Forum* 87 (October 1947): 114–120. As Glass was not a licensed architect, he collaborated with registered architects for his architectural work through the 1960s. In 1946, he took on a major architectural project for Kling Studios, a commercial art and photography company, for a new building at the corner of Fairbanks from Ontario to Ohio streets. He designed the interior layout, offices and fixtures with architects and engineers Friedman, Alschuler and Sincere.

5 — Victoria Matranga, Design Programs Coordinator for the International Housewares Association an authority on the history of industrial design in Chicago, visited with Henry and Elly in their home. She conferred with their daughter Anne Karin Glass to offer insights and information for this essay. Henry (1911–2003) and Elly (1915–2010) lived in this home until their passing. Some of his designed products are held in the permanent collection of the Art Institute of Chicago. His papers are at the Ryerson & Burnham Libraries there and at the Chicago History Museum.

Florence Pass and Erne Frueh House I and II

1 — Robert Bruce Tague, *Oral History of Robert Bruce Tague / Interviewed by Betty J. Blum, Complied under the Auspices of the Chicago Architects Oral History Project, the Ernest R. Graham Study Center for Architectural Drawings, Department of Architecture, the Art Institute of Chicago* rev. ed. (Chicago: Art Institute of Chicago, 2005), 3.

2 — Tague, *Oral History,* 6.

3 — Evan Osnos, "Florence Frueh, Authority on Art Glass," *Chicago Tribune,* March 9, 2000, accessed November 15, 2019, chicagotribune.com.

4 — Erne R. and Florence Frueh, *Chicago Stained Glass* (Chicago: Loyola University Press, 1983) (second edition; Chicago: Wild Onion Books, 1998). Illustrated

with photographs taken by Erne Frueh. Other co-authored scholarly works includes Erne R. and Florence Frueh, *The Second Presbyterian Church of Chicago. Art and Architecture* (Chicago: The Church, 1978) and "Frederic Clay Bartlett: Chicago Painter and Patron of the Arts," in *Chicago History* 8, no. 1 (Spring 1979): 16–19. This issue of the magazine of the Chicago Historical Society featured as its theme "The Art Institute of Chicago: A Centennial Perspective."

5 — Tague, *Oral History,* 29.

6 — The house was featured with a title "Living-Dining" in a section entitled "Today's House Client is Practical," in *Architectural Record* 116, no. 5 (November 1954):174–176. See also Stuart Cohen (with introduction by Stanley Tigerman), *Chicago Architects* (Chicago: Swallow Press, 1976), 103. In this catalogue Cohen wrote: "Tague's Frueh house in Highland Park of 1949 is an interesting work which stands between the houses of the new prairie style and the structurally modulated and panelized residential work of Keck and Keck during the 1940s and 1950s and Mies van der Rohe's residential projects of the 1950s."

7 — Jeffrey Plank, *Crombie Taylor: Modern Architecture, Building Restoration, and the Rediscovery of Louis Sullivan* (Richmond, CA: William Stout, 2009), 51–52. Robert Bruce Tague, *Oral History,* 28: Although Tague was not a graduate of the Institute of Design, he credits having met Taylor through the Institute.

8 — Tague, *Oral History,* 28.

9 — See Abigail Foerstner, "Images Record Original Splendor of Sullivan Architecture," July 22, 1994, *Chicago Tribune,* chicagotribune.com; Lois Marie Fink, "Roosevelt University: In the Chicago Auditorium Building," *College Art Journal* 19, no. 4 (Summer 1960): 363–370; Biography for the Crombie Taylor Papers, Ryerson and Burnham Archives, The Art Institute of Chicago; and Heidi Pawlowski Carey, "Auditorium Building," Encyclopedia of Chicago, encyclopedia.chicagohistory.org, all accessed November 17, 2019.

10 — See also Crombie Taylor

and Jeffrey Plank, *The Early Louis Sullivan Building Photographs* (San Francisco: William Stout Publishers, 2001).

11 — John Vinci, "Remembering Jim Speyer" in *A. James Speyer: Architect, Curator, Exhibition Designer* (Chicago: The Arts Club of Chicago, distributed by the University of Chicago Press, 1997) published in conjunction with an exhibition organized by Dorthea Speyer and John Vinci of the same title at the Arts Club of Chicago, September 17–November 1, 1997; Carnegie Museum of Art, the Heinz Architectural Center, December 4, 1997–March 22, 1998; and National Technical University of Athens, School of Architecture, Spring 1998.

12 — Yasuhiro Ishimoto (with Kenzo Tange and Walter Gropius), *Katsura: Tradition and Creation in Japanese Architecture* (New Haven: Yale University Press, 1960).

13 — Lynette Stuhlmacher, "Chapter News" from Docomomo US/Chicago in *Docomomo US News* (Fall 2006): 7, "We have also lent our advocacy support to significant modern works … such as the Frueh House … designed by Robert Bruce Tague in 1948," and Plank, *Crombie Taylor,* 303.

Maggie Sheahan and Le Roy Binkley House

1 — Lisa Brunke, interview by author, Chicago, October 31, 2018.

2 — "Roy 'Bud' Binkley," Architects + More, chicagobauhausbeyond.org, accessed March 15, 2019: John Black Lee remembered working with Binkley there.

3 — Brunke, interview.

4 — Ann Elizabeth Binkley [Rand Ozbekhan] studied with László Moholy-Nagy at the School of Design and with Ludwig Mies van der Rohe, receiving her BS in 1945 from Illinois Institute of Technology and working in Mies's office after the war. Liz Titus, "One of the 10 Best Houses of 1953," Weston Historical Society, entitles her article with the recognition from *Interiors* magazine about the house that Ann designed with Paul Rand, her spouse at the time, and references the article "A House to Live With:

Paul Rand, One of America's Great Graphic Designers, Builds a Home," *Esquire,* August 1953. After the birth of a daughter, Ann Rand established herself in the 1950s with imaginative and witty children's books, including *Listen! Listen!* and *Sparkle and Spin,* illustrated by the playful designs of Paul Rand, who received international acclaim for the iconic corporate logos he designed for IBM, UPS, ABC, Enron, and Westinghouse.

5 — Steven Heller, "Gene Federico, 81, Graphic Designer, Dies," *New York Times,* September 10, 1999: was also an advertising executive and art director; he died at his Pound Ridge home on September 8th. "Helen Lesser Federico," *New York Times,* July 22, 2012: was a graphic designer, painter, and illustrator, who at one time was an associate art director under Paul Rand at William Weintraub Agency. She worked independently after her move to the Pound Ridge house, where she died on July 19, 2012; both accessed March 13, 2019, nytimes.com. *Modern in Pound Ridge: 20th Century Architecture + Lifestyle* exhibition, 2017, Pound Ridge Historic Society. Douglas P. Clement, "Emerging from the Shadows: An Exhibition Sheds Light on Pound Ridge's Trove of Mid-Century Houses," *Modern Magazine,* August 8, 2017, accessed March 14, 2019, modmag.com. John Black Lee was the managing architect.

6 — Responding to a title search request to identify who commissioned the house from Roy Binkley, Sara Krasne, Archives Manager, Westport Historical Society found that Ernest Herrmann bought the site in July 1957, with a note in the land records for an approval of plans with Country Estates Builders & Supplies. "Appeals Granted," *Westport Town Crier and Herald,* May 9, 1957, 13: the notice grants Herrmann a "variance of the front yard requirement to permit the construction of a dwelling on Burritt's Cove." *Westport Town Crier and Herald,* August 8, 1957: "Ernest Herrmann will build a $35,000 home on Burritts Landing. The house will have six rooms, three baths, a fireplace, a garage and warm air heat." After Ernest's death, his

widow, Marcia Peterson, sold the house in 1971 and left Binkley's original drawings and blueprints for subsequent owners, which the Allens now have in their possession.

7 — "House by Le Roy Binkley, Architect," *Arts & Architecture* 73, no. 4 (April 1956): 24 and "Small House by Roy Binkley, Architect," *Arts & Architecture* 75, no. 10 (October 1958): 31.

Ruth van Sickle and Albert Sam Ford House

1 — Timothy Samuelson, "Bruce Goff in Chicago," in Pauline Saliga and Mary Woolever eds., *The Architecture of Bruce Goff 1904–1982: Design for the Continuous Present* (New York and Munich: Art Institute of Chicago and Prestel-Verlag, 1995), 46–55. Also, The Art Institute of Chicago, "Bruce Goff: Ford House," September 27, 2017, video for its installation *Past Forward: Architecture and Design at the Art Institute,* accessed March 20, 2019, youtube.com.

2 — Nancy Smith Hopp, *Warm Light, Cool Shadows: The Life and Art of Ruth Van Sickle Ford* (Aurora: Pen Works Press, 2011).

3 — "The Round House," *Life* 30, no. 12 (March 19, 1951): 70–75. Photographs by Eliot Elison, noted African American photojournalist, who in 1939 became the first staff photographer for the Museum of Modern Art, among many other accomplishments. Ruth van Sickle Ford papers, 1924–1986, Archives of American Art, Smithsonian Institution, overview notes "a brochure about the Umbrella House" in the collection, accessed April 11, 2019, aaa.si.edu. "Ruth van Sickle Ford," accessed April 10, 2019, foxvalleyarts.org.

4 — Jen Graves, "When a Building Makes You Who You Are: Leo Berk Goes Home Again," April 12, 2011, *The Stranger,* accessed March 21, 2019, thestranger.com. For Leo Saul Berk's works of art, see leoberk. com.

5 — Sidney K. Robinson, "Bruce Goff: Ford and Price Houses," *Friends of Kebyar* 32.1, no. 85 (2017): 36–42. See theme issue dedicated to "Bruce Goff's Ford House: Living in Joyful Order," in *Friends of Kebyar* 30.3,

no. 82 (Winter 2015), 64–72. Sidney Robinson, "Residential Masterpieces: Bruce Goff, Ford House, Aurora, Illinois, USA, 1949–50," *GA Houses* 68 (November 2001): 64–79, editor Yoshio Futagawa [English and Japanese translation].

6 — National Register of Historic Places Registration Form # 16000056 lists "Sam and Ruth van Sickle Ford House." The Art Institute of Chicago, Architecture and Design gallery has the Bruce Alonzo Goff, "Ruth and Sam Ford House, Aurora, Illinois, Floor Plan," with Ruth's name primary, accessed March 20, 2019, artic. edu.

7 — Landmarks Illinois, accessed October 4, 2019, landmarks.org.

Marian Short and Stanley G. Harris Jr. House

1 — John Vinci, "Remembering Jim Speyer" in *A. James Speyer: Architect, Curator, Exhibition Designer* (Chicago: The Arts Club of Chicago, distributed by the University of Chicago Press, 1997) 1–5, published in conjunction with an exhibition organized by Dorthea Speyer and John Vinci of the same title at the Arts Club of Chicago, September 17–November 1, 1997; Carnegie Museum of Art, the Heinz Architectural Center, December 4, 1997–March 22, 1998; and National Technical University of Athens, School of Architecture, Spring 1998.

2 — A. James Speyer, *Oral History of A. James Speyer / Interviewed by Pauline Saliga, Complied under the Auspices of the Chicago Architects Oral History Project, the Ernest R. Graham Study Center for Architectural Drawings, Department of Architecture, the Art Institute of Chicago* rev. ed. (Chicago: Art Institute of Chicago, 2001), 61–65. For some references to James Speyer from his art-dealer sister in Paris, see Dorthea Speyer, *Oral History Interview with Dorthea Speyer, 1976 June 28* [by Paul Cummings], Archives of American Art, Smithsonian Institution, accessed February 20, 2019, aaa.si.edu. James Speyer designed her Galerie Dorthea Speyer in 1968.

3 — Alan G. Artner, art critic, "Art Curator A. James Speyer," *Chicago Tribune,* November 11, 1986.

Wilhelmina Plansoen and Edward Dart House I

1 — "Wilhelmina Plansoen Dart," *Chicago Tribune*, October 18, 2018.

2 — Susan Dart, *Edward Dart Architect* (Evanston, IL: Evanston Publishing, 1993) 128–29. Richard Bennett was chairman of the department of architecture when Dart entered Yale.

3 — Matthew Seymour, "Edward Dart: Preserving the Works of a Mid-Century Architect" (MS thesis, School of the Art Institute of Chicago, Historic Preservation Program, 2011), 10: Shaw had a distinguished career in the Chicago area designing country houses and was arguably the finest Midwest eclectic architect of his generation.

4 — Today, Schweikher's home and studio are owned by the Village of Schaumburg and serve as a house museum. At the time that Dart applied for the job with Schweikher, the firm was Schweikher and Elting.

5 — Dart, *Edward Dart*, 139.

6 — Dart, *Edward Dart*, 138.

7 — Dart, *Edward Dart*, 143.

8 — "House: Barrington, Illinois, Edward D. Dart, Architect," *Progressive Architecture* 36, no. 12 (December 1955), 87–91, archive of *Progressive Architecture* now digitized at USModernist Library, accessed February 20, 2019, usmodernist.org.

9 — Dart, *Edward Dart*, 152–53.

10 — "Wilhelmina Plansoen Dart."

Edith Farnsworth House

1 — For accounts targeted at general audiences see the forthcoming book by journalist Alex Beam, *Broken Glass: Mies van der Rohe, Edith Farnsworth, and the Fight Over a Modernist Masterpiece* (New York: Penguin Random House, 2020) and *Farnsworth House,* a film written and directed by Richard Press currently in production with Maggie Gyllenhaal playing Edith Farnsworth and Ralph Fiennes playing Mies.

2 — Plano had a population of 2154 in 1950 according to the Census of Population and Housing compared to Chicago, which measured 3,620,962 Census of Population and Housing, accessed December 2,

2019, census.gov.

3 — See for example Alice T. Friedman, *Women and the Making of the Modern House: A Social and Architectural History* (New York: Abrams, 1998), 129–59, and Nora Wendl, "A Story of Sex and Real Estate, Reconsidered," *Thresholds* 43, annual issue (Spring 2015): 20–32, 347–361, is the Journal of the Department of Architecture, MIT; the issue Scandals was edited by Nathan Friedman and Ann Liu.

4 — Maritz Vandenberg, *Farnsworth House: Ludwig Mies van der Rohe* (London: Phaidon, 2003), 24. See the account given in "The Farnsworth Saga: 1946–2003" in Franz Schulze, Edward Windhorst, *Mies Van Der Rohe: A Critical Biography, New and Revised Edition* (Chicago: University of Chicago Press, 2014), 248–273.

5 — See my introduction "Modern Houses for Modern Living in Chicago" (p. 10) and Monica Penick, *Tastemaker: Elizabeth Gordon, House Beautiful, and the Postwar American Home* (New Haven: Yale University Press, 2017), 115–128. Elizabeth Gordon, *House Beautiful*, April 1953, 129.

6 — House Issue, *Architectural Forum* 95, no. 4 (October 1951): 155.

7 — House Issue, 160. Note that although the Glass House was built earlier than the Farnsworth House, Mies had designed the Farnsworth before Johnson designed his own house.

8 — For detailed construction drawings see *Farnsworth House, Plano 1945–1950* (Tokyo: ADA Edita, 2000); see also Neil Jackson, *The Modern Steel House* (London: Routledge, 2016), 65–76. For details about flooding see Wright Water Engineers, Inc., "Farnsworth House Flood Risk and Conceptional Mitigation Evaluation, 14520, River Road, Plano, Illinois, May 15, 2013," cites the Historic American Building Survey (HABS): 5, Farnsworth House, accessed January 5, 2019, farnsworthhouse.org: "… regional development and climatic changes have significantly impacted the house by altering the relationship with its site."

Rachel Brin and Ralph Helstein House

1 — Michelle Benoit, "One Architect, Three Approaches: Bertrand Goldberg's Early Experiments with Prefabrication, 1937–1952," *MAS Context* Repetition, 21 (Spring 2014): 161: "Goldberg himself refers to the Snyder Residence as his last house, but it should be noted that he completely redesigned the house for Ralph Helstein in 1955 (which was originally completed before the Snyder Residence)—technically making it the last single-family home designed by Goldberg."

2 — After a dedicated battle by preservationists to prevent its demolition, the nine-story Northwestern University Prentice Hospital Building was demolished by its owners in 2014. Wim de Wit, "Marina City," in *AIA Guide to Chicago* 3rd ed., eds. Alice Sinkevitch, Laurie McGovern Petersen (Urbana, Chicago, Springfield: University of Illinois Press, 2014), 72–73: provides the date 1967.

3 — Tim Samuelson, "Hyde Park & Kenwood Issue: Beyond Robie House: A Tour of Some of the Neighborhoods' Lesser-Known Architectural Gems," *Chicago Reader,* March 4, 2010.

4 — "Anti-Semitism in Minneapolis History," Minnesota Public Radio's *NPR News,* October 18, 2017, accessed April 17, 2018, mprnews.org.

5 — "Ralph Helstein, 76, is Dead; Headed Packinghouse Union," *New York Times,* February 15, 1985.

6 — "Rachel B. Helstein," *Chicago Tribune,* May 16, 2008.

7 — Nina Helstein, interview by author, March 21, 2015: Nina Helstein noted that Rachel had considerable input and that her parents' house couldn't have happened without "the support of my mother."

8 — Helstein, interview: Ms. Helstein, Rachel and Ralph Helstein's daughter, said that Goldberg expressed this to her parents.

9 — Bertrand Goldberg, *Oral History of Bertrand Goldberg / Interviewed by Betty J. Blum, Compiled Under the Auspices of the Chicago Architects Oral History Project, Department of Architecture, the Art Institute of Chicago* (Chicago: Art Institute of

Chicago, 2001), 97–98.

10 — Goldberg, *Oral History,* 152.

11 — "Rachel B. Helstein."

12 — "Ralph Helstein, 76, is Dead; Headed Packinghouse Union." About Helstein's life see, Cyril Robinson, *Marching with Dr. King: Ralph Helstein and the United Packinghouse Workers of America* (Santa Barbara: Praeger, 2011).

13 — Bruce Fehn, "Marching with Dr. King: Ralph Helstein and the United Packinghouse Workers of America," *Annals of Iowa* 71 (2012): 365. Dr. Martin Luther King Jr. was first president of the SCLC, the African American civil-rights organization.

14 — Nina Helstein, interview by author, July 23, 2015.

Elizabeth Castle and Robert Muirhead Farmhouse

1 — Mr. and Mrs. Robert Muirhead, letter to Frank Lloyd Wright, Spring Green Wisconsin, October 14, 1948. The six-page letter is in the collection of Michael and Sarah Petersdorf, owners of the house, and is stamped "Copyright The Frank Lloyd Wright Foundation, 1990." The Petersdorfs allowed the author to read the letter.

2 — "Lloyd Lewis House," *Architectural Forum,* 75, no. 1 (July 1941): the photographer was Kenneth Hedrich of Hedrich-Blessing (HB06485j-Chicago History Museum).

3 — Although the workroom is noted as a garage with a garage door on the plans, it has never been used for vehicles.

4 — Muirhead Farmhouse accessed March 19, 2019, muirheadfarmhouse.com.

Doris Curry and Jacques Brownson House

1 — Associated architects for the civic center included Loebl Schlossman & Dart, Bennett, SOM, and C.F. Murphy (supervising architect). "Jacques C. Brownson," Faculty History Project, University of Michigan Library, The Michigan Alumnus, 14, accessed April 3, 2019, lib. umich.edu: commercial projects included Continental National Insurance Building and Hektoen Institute for Medical Research. "Public Building Commission of Chicago Minutes of the Rescheduled Meeting of the

Board of Commissioners Held on March 9, 2010," accessed April 3, 2019, pbcchicago.com: adopted Resolution No. 7775, honoring Jacques Calman Brownson, who had served as managing architect of the Chicago Public Building Commission.

2 — Blair Kamin, "Daley Center Architect, Jacques Brownson, Dies at 88," February 21, 2012, accessed April 3, 2019, chicagotribune.com, which included a quotation from Paul Gapp, "Building on Tradition," *Chicago Tribune,* Sunday magazine, March 31, 1991, 11: placing it with "such icons as the X-braced John Hancock Center, the corncob-shaped tower of Marina City, and Mies' foremost temple of steel and glass, Crown Hall at IIT."

3 — See Jacques Calman Brownson, *Oral History of Jacques Calman Brownson / Interviewed by Betty J. Blum, Compiled Under the Auspices of the Chicago Architects Oral History Project, the Ernest R. Graham Study Center for Architectural Drawings, Department of Architecture, the Art Institute of Chicago* (Chicago: Art Institute of Chicago, 1996), 23.

4 — "Here is the Home That Millions Want … The Popular Mechanics Build-It-Yourself House," *Popular Mechanics* 87, no. 4 (April 1947): 105–13, 252, 256, 260, 264. Second part by James R. Ward in *Popular Mechanics* 87, no. 5 (May 1947), 168–74.

5 — The "modified Cape Cod house" is still extant in Aurora.

6 — "Here is the Home That Millions Want": 109. Brownson is quoted as saying: "I hope you like my house: I sure do. It measures up to the dreams I had overseas a year and a half ago. Frankly the house is the biggest thing that has ever happened to Doris and to me. It was a challenge from the beginning to end, but I assure you that no man could have greater pride than we have in having constructed our own home with our own hands."

7 — The lot purchased by Brownson was part of a parcel of land that was subdivided and sold by the Reckitt family and was located adjacent to the Fabyan Forest Preserve. In 1907 Frank Lloyd Wright remodeled

the Fabyan Villa—known as "Riverbank" estate.

8 — *Architectural Record: Record Houses of 1956,* Special Issue, *Architectural Record* 119, no. 6 (Mid-May 1956): 206–07.

9 — Brownson, *Oral History,* 120–21: Brownson went on to say, "The other two, the Farnsworth House and the Johnson house, are different. Johnson went to a small adjacent building to sleep. He had a kitchen and the other kinds of things in it, but the glass house itself was a completely open public space, but yet he went to the other one for the more private aspects of his life. In Mies's case, in the Farnsworth House, Edith Farnsworth could do all of her activities, anything she wanted. Her house was a private house, and she could live in it any way she wanted to. She slept there, she prepared food there, she did gardening out of there, and she did all the kinds of things. But as I say, the Geneva House was two houses, and if you look at the plan, you'll see it very clearly."

10 — Jacques C. Brownson, "A Steel and Glass House," (MS thesis, Illinois Institute of Technology, 1954), iv, held in the University Archives and signed by Ludwig Hilberseimer as adviser.

11 — "Jacques C. Brownson," Faculty History Project.

12 — "Glass House is Suspended From Steel Frames," *Record Houses of 1956,* 206–07.

13 — "Exposed Steel Frames Modular Illinois Home," *Record Houses of 1956,* 157–61.

14 — Anne Douglas, "Geneva Residence A Blend of Steel, Glass and Brick," *Chicago Tribune* Sunday, July 12, 1953, 32–33; "With Steel Components Like These You Can Build A Home," *House & Home* 7–8 (December 1955): 138–51. The Brownson House is discussed and illustrated under the rubric of "Dwellings" in Oswald W. Grube, Peter C. Pran and Franz Schulze, *100 Years of Architecture in Chicago: Continuity of Structure and Form Tribune* (Chicago: J. Philip O'Hara, 1976), 115–33.

Maxine Weil and Sigmund Kunstadter House

1 — Robert Piper Boyce, *Keck & Keck* (New York: Princeton Architectural Press, 1993), 107, 155: The Sidney C. Wohl House, 1946, is the first design in which

William Keck's name appears with Fred Keck's name.

2 — Stuart E. Cohen, *Chicago Architects: Documenting the Exhibition of the Same Name Organized by Laurence Booth, Stuart E. Cohen, Stanley Tigerman, and Benjamin Weese* (Chicago: Swallow Press, 1976).

3 — Nory Miller, "Fred Keck at 81, 'Hit of Show' after 56 years," *Inland Architect* 20 (May 1976): 6.

4 — Stanley Tigerman, "Inlandscape: Into the Pantheon," *Inland Architect* (January/February 1981).

5 — Press Release Index, "Press releases from 1957," January 16, 1957, 35–37 and "Press Releases From 1971," November 19, 1971, 223–24, and the Art Institute of Chicago's "1956 Acquisitions" lists Mr. & Mrs. Sigmund Kunstadter, artic.edu. "The Art Institute of Chicago Forty-First Annual Report for the Year 1919," 44: Sigmund's father, Albert Kunstadter, was also a Life Member; "List of Images" in *American Art* (Chicago: Art Institute of Chicago, 2008), 10 and 169, accessed March 13, 2019, artic.edu: credits restricted gift of Mr. And Mrs. Sigmund W. Kunstadter for Stuart Davis, *Ready-to-Wear,* 1955, oil on canvas and features it as reflecting "the energy and optimism of the prosperous postwar years, conveyed through its animated rhythms, bold shapes, and lively red, white, and blue color scheme. With its flat, abstract motifs that suggest items such as scissors, ribbons, and fabrics, the painting mirrors a new facet of America's fashion industry in the 1950s: the emergence of ready-to-wear clothing for middle-class consumers. Davis's jaunty composition exemplifies the resurgence after World War II of abstraction in the service of personal expression, reversing the more conservative, realist tendencies of Regionalism, which had held sway during the prior decades." William C. Seitz, *Mark Tobey* (New York: Museum of Modern Art, 1962), 75, exhibitions calendar, moma.org: in collaboration with Cleveland Museum of Art and AIC, *Above the Earth,* 1953, tempura, gift of Mr. & Mrs. Sigmund Kunstadter, and a correspondence folder for "Kunstadter, Sigmund" appears

in the Finding Aid for Chicago art conservator, Louis Pomerantz Papers, Archives of American Art, Smithsonian Institution, si.edu, all accessed March 13, 2019.

6 — Boyce, *Keck & Keck,* 101–02.

7 — Boyce, *Keck & Keck,* 104: Although Fred Keck had been a member of the AIA but resigned because the organization had an anti-modern bias and never rejoined, his brother William was a member.

8 — "Events," Art Institute of Chicago's Society for Contemporary Art, April 14, 1956, "Kunstadter, Maremont, and Zurcher Collection Tour," accessed March 15, 2019, scaaic.org: reference to works by Mark Tobey and Paul Klee.

9 — Andy Cross, AICP, Senior Planner, City of Highland Park, IL, email to author, March 27, 2019: included references to the "City of Highland Park, Illinois, Urban Architectural and Historical Survey," the "Historic Preservation Commission, Highland Park, Illinois, Landmark Nomination Form," and documentation of new construction year and demo range years.

Isabella Gardner and Robert Hall McCormick III House

1 — In 1955 Mies also designed a house for Rose Drapkin and Morris Greenwald in Weston, Connecticut. See Barry Bergdoll, et al., *Mies van der Rohe: McCormick House* (Elmhurst: Elmhurst Art Museum, 2018). Thanks to Hubie Greenwald for his assistance.

2 — For a history of prefabrication see Colin Davies, *The Prefabricated Home* (London: Reaktion, 2005). Barry Bergdoll and Peter Christensen eds., *Home Delivery: Fabricating the Modern Dwelling* (New York: Museum of Modern Art, 2008). Gilbert Herbert, *The Dream of the Factory-Made House: Walter Gropius and Konrad Wachsmann* (Cambridge, MA: MIT Press, 1984).

3 — Thomas M. Slade, 'The Crystal House' of 1934," *Journal of the Society of Architectural Historians* 29, no. 4 (December 1970), 350–53. *Stran-Steel Corporation, Homes for Modern Living* (Detroit: Stran-Steel 1934).

4 — Bruce Brooks Pfeiffer ed., *Frank Lloyd Wright Usonian Houses* (Tokyo: A.D.A. Edita, 2002).

5 — Founded in Chicago by Harriet Monroe in 1912, *Poetry* is the oldest monthly devoted to verse in the English-speaking world, accessed May 18, 2019, poetryfoundation.org. Monroe was the sister-in-law of Chicago architect John Wellborn Root and wrote his biography, entitled *John Wellborn Root: A Study of his Life and Work* (Boston: Houghton Mifflin, 1896), accessed May 18, 2019, books.google.com.

6 — Ray W. Fick, letter to Mr. D. Neil Bremer (Executive Director Elmhurst Art Museum), October 11, 2007, 2, accessed May 18, 2019, 150southcottagehilave.net

7 — De Stefano + Partners is now Lothan Van Hook De Stefano Architecture LLC; Principal James "Jim" De Stefano received his BArch from IIT's College of Architecture.

Walter Frazier and William Moulis House

1 — Kim Coventry and Arthur Hawks Miller, *Walter Frazier: Frazier, Raftery, Orr & Fairbank Architects, Houses of Chicago's North Shore, 1924–1970* (Lake Forest: Lake Forest-Lake Bluff Historical Society, 2009), 103.

2 — Coventry, *Frazier,* 12.

3 — Dorothy Raley, ed. *A Century of Progress Homes and Furnishings* (Chicago: M. A. Ring, 1934), reprint (Delhi, India: Facsimile Publisher, 2018), 4.

Frances Landrum and Ben Rose House

1 — Lesley Jackson, "United States: Ben Rose," in *Twentieth-Century Pattern Design: Textile and Wallpaper Pioneers* (New York: Princeton Architectural Press, 2002/2nd ed 2011), 109–10, 112, 160: Ben had studied painting at the School of the Art Institute of Chicago from 1939–41. Tom Rybarczyk, "Ben Rose, 88," *Chicago Tribune,* November 28, 2004, notes that Frances Landrum was his classmate at the Chicago Art Institute.

2 — Lisa Skolnik, "Coming up Roses: A Family Lives out Their Dream in a Modern Box on the North Shore," *Chicago Tribune Sunday Magazine,* February 20,

2005, accessed July 10, 2018, chicagotribune.com.

3 — Tom Rybarczyk, "Textile Designer Built a Legacy," *Chicago Tribune,* November 25, 2004: In the 1950s Ben Rose won more than seven Good Design Awards from the Museum of Modern Art. He also received recognition for this wallpaper and drapery patterns from the American Institute of Decorators. At the time of his death, Rose was described as "one of the foremost commercial textile designers of his day."

4 — "Patterns Are Smaller for Fall Fabrics," *Chicago Daily Tribune,* July 31, 1949. ProQuest Historical Newspapers, *Chicago Tribune* (1849–1986), accessed July 10, 2018, proquest.com.

5 — Christa C. Mayer Thurman, "Ben Rose," in *Rooted in Chicago: Fifty Years of Textile Design Traditions, special issue, Museum Studies* 23, no. 1 (Chicago: Art Institute of Chicago, 1997).

6 — The car collection was auctioned by Christies in Spring 1997 at Lyndhurst in Tarrytown, New York. See "Christie's Pedigree Motor Car Auction Coming to Lyndhurst," *Half Moon Press,* April 1997, accessed July 10, 2018, hudsonriver.com.

7 — Frances Landrum Rose, interview by author, May 2000.

Susanne Weese and Robert Drucker House

1 — Harry Weese, *Oral History of Harry Mohr Weese / Interviewed by Betty J. Blum, Compiled under the Auspices of the Chicago Architects Oral History Project, the Ernest R. Graham Study Center for Architectural Drawings, Department of Architecture, the Art Institute of Chicago,* rev. ed. (Chicago: Art Institute of Chicago, 2001), 105.

2 — George Fred Keck's early houses, many located in the Indian Hill Estates area near where the Drucker House was later constructed, were designed in the Tudor Revival style, which was popular in the 1920s.

3 — Kitty Baldwin Weese, *Harry Weese Houses* (Chicago: Chicago Review Press, 1987), 56: This book by Harry's wife focuses on his residential architecture. The Drucker House is illustrated and

described along with his many other houses.

4 — Susanne [Weese Drucker] Frank, Interview by author, January 2015.

5 — Weese, *Oral History,* 21. Robert Bruegmann and Kathleen Murphy Skolnik, *The Architecture of Harry Weese* (New York, London: Norton, 2010), 25.

6 — Weese, *Oral History,* 257.

7 — Kamin, Blair, "Harry Weese, Visionary Architect known as 'Chicago's Conscience,'" *Chicago Tribune,* November 1, 1998.

Elizabeth Hunt and John W. Moutoussamy House

1 — Stephen A. Kliment, AIA "The Trailblazers," in *AIA Architect* 13 (November 10, 2006). See also "Architect John W. Moutoussamy," *Chicago Tribune,* May 9, 1995; "John W. Moutoussamy, 73, Award-Winning Architect," *Chicago Sun-Times,* April 10, 1995.

2 — Jeanne Moutoussamy-Ashe, email to author, November 6 and December 12, 2019, Elizabeth Moutoussamy earned her degree in the 1980s. "Moutoussamy, Elizabeth (Hunt)," *Chicago Tribune,* February 15, 2006, accessed September 24, 2019, chicagotribune.com.

3 — For a thorough overview see Krisann Rehbein, "At Home in Chatham: A Bounty of Mid-Century Modern on the South Side, Where the African-American Elite Once 'Strutted Their Stuff,'" in *New City Design,* November 19, 2015, accessed September 24, 2019, design. newcity.com. Also, "Lawrence E. Smith Jr.," *Chicago Tribune,* May 18, 2000, accessed September 24, 2019, chicagotribune.com.

4 — K. Roderick O'Neil, *A Portfolio of Modern Houses* (Chicago: Architectural Drafting Bureau, 1949).

5 — Arthur D. Dubin, *Oral History of Arthur Detmers Dubin / Interviewed by Betty J. Blum, Complied under the Auspices of the Chicago Architects Oral History Project, the Ernest R. Graham Study Center for Architectural Drawings, Department of Architecture, the Art Institute of Chicago* rev. ed. (Chicago: Art Institute of Chicago, 2003), 89 and 93.

6 — Moutoussamy-Ashe, email to author, November 6, 2019, clipping: "Wanted: Money to Lend—Home Loan Demands Rise on South Side," *Chicago Daily News,* June 24, 1955, 47.

Margaret Montgomery and Howard Raftery House

1 — Kim Coventry and Arthur Hawks Miller, *Walter Frazier: Frazier, Raftery, Orr & Fairbank Architects, Houses of Chicago's North Shore, 1924–1970* (Lake Forest: Lake Forest-Lake Bluff Historical Society, 2009).

2 — Kimberly Lyons, email to author, May 21, 2019.

Priscilla Huffard and H.P. Davis Rockwell House I

1 — From my note 6 in Marjorie Horton and Winston Elting House: Schweikher established a practice with Theodore "Ted" Lamb in 1934, joined by Winston Elting in 1938. After the war Schweikher and Elting reconvened their practice until 1953. (Lamb had died in a 1943 plane crash.)

2 — April 28, 1947: 77–82.

3 — Karen Reimer ed., *Centennial: A History of the Renaissance Society 1915–2015* (Chicago: Renaissance Society, 2015), accessed November 26, 2019, renaissancesociety.org. See also Meyric Rogers, "The Work of Schweikher and Elting," (Chicago: Renaissance Society, 1949) published in conjunction with the exhibition *Schweikher and Elting, Architects* held March 21–April 14, 1949 at the Renaissance Society at the University of Chicago, accessed May 8, 2019, renaissancesociety.org.

4 — Susan Wagner, *A History of the Village of Flossmoor, 1851–1974* (Flossmoor: Flossmoor Historical Committee, 1974). Elise D. Kabbes and Mary GiaQuinta, *Flossmoor, Illinois* (Charleston, SC: Arcadia, 1999).

5 — Robert Paul Schweikher, *Oral History of Robert Paul Schweikher / Interviewed by Betty J. Blum, Complied under the Auspices of the Chicago Architects Oral History Project, the Ernest R. Graham Study Center for Architectural Drawings, Department of Architecture, the Art Institute of Chicago* rev. ed. (Chicago: Art Institute of Chicago, 2000), 201.

6 — "Central Court Adds Space to Illinois House: Schweikher and Elting, Architects; Mr. and Mrs. H. P. Davis Rockwell, Owners," *Architectural Record* 119, no. 6 (Mid-May 1956): 121–25, accessed August 25, 2019, chicagoarchitect.com.

7 — Monica Pidgeon and Theo Crosby, eds., *An Anthology of Houses* (New York: Reinhold, 1960), 126–128.

8 — Pidgeon, *Anthology,* 126.

9 — Pidgeon, *Anthology,* 126.

10 — Schweikher, *Oral History,* 201. Additional details to be found in Rockwell House II (p. 232).

Alice Lieberman and J. Marion Gutnayer House

1 — Glenn Gutnayer, son of J. Marion, interview by author, December 26, 2018.

2 — Michael Wilkinson, AIA, found this reference among Gutnayer's papers when his firm was hired to renovate the house in 2009. Dennis Rodkin, "Man of the House, House of the Man," *Chicago Architect* (August, 2011): 34.

3 — J. Marion Gutnayer, "Gutnayer and Associates, Inc, Master Builders," brochure: illustrates his custom homes, many of which were built on Chicago's North Shore, especially in Wilmette, and also shows examples of his firm's commercial and industrial work. Anne and Reed Stevens, current owners of the Gutnayer house, loaned the brochure, written materials, photographs, and drawings of the house to the author.

4 — "Gutnayer and Associates, Inc.: J. Marion Gutnayer, Architect, American Institute of Architects, AIA," brochure: illustrates projects for hotels and apartment buildings, including a high-rise on Lake Shore Drive in partnership with L. Solomon, who later formed the firm Solomon, Cordwell, Buenz. The brochure also has a drawing of the "atelier & Domus" that Gutnayer designed for Jacques Lipchitz.

5 — Gutnayer's copy of Wright's book is in the collection of the current homeowner.

6 — Glenn Gutnayer provided a copy of "Trustee's Inventory of Art, 10/26/2010" to the author.

7 — "The First Witness," *Chicago Sun-Times,* n.d.: much of the information on Gutnayer's escape from Poland is taken from this clipping. Ray Lindahl, Arch. '53, The University of Illinois at Navy Pier: Professor Josef-Marion Gutnayer, *Illinois Technograph* 66, no. 2 (November 1950): 13, 28, accessed February 20, 2019, archive.org.

8 — Anne Hayden Stevens, email to author, May 13, 2019: With the purchase came all of the contents (including Gutnayer's studio, drawings, and papers, which Anne, an artist, cataloged with the assistance of area experts and historic societies). The Stevenses donated Gutnayer's archive to historical societies in Wilmette, Highland Park, Glenview, and Evanston. Materials related to Chicago projects went to the Art Institute of Chicago Ryerson & Burnham Libraries. Documentation and letters related to the restitution of Gutnayer family artworks stolen by the Dutch Nazi Pieter Menten, who facilitated the looting of Jewish art collections during World War II were scanned and saved.

Kitty Baldwin and Harry Weese House

1 — Kitty Baldwin Weese, *Harry Weese Houses* (Chicago: Chicago Review Press, 1987), 11.

2 — K. B. Weese, *Houses,* 74.

3 — The Miller House is a National Historic Landmark.

4 — K. B. Weese, *Houses,* 74.

5 — Harry Weese, *Oral History of Harry Mohr Weese / Interviewed by Betty J. Blum, Compiled under the Auspices of the Chicago Architects Oral History Project, the Ernest R. Graham Study Center for Architectural Drawings, Department of Architecture, the Art Institute of Chicago,* rev. ed. (Chicago: Art Institute of Chicago, 2001), 23 and 124. Examples cited by Weese were I. M. Pei and Louis Skidmore. When asked how his ideas were influenced by Mies, Weese referenced a savings and loan he designed in Holland, Michigan.

6 — Weese, *Oral History,* iv.

7 — Robert Bruegmann and Kathleen Murphy Skolnik, *The Architecture of Harry Weese* (New York, London: Norton,

2010), 75: Breugmann states that Weese's work has a great deal in common with the work of his contemporary native Chicagoans Bertrand Goldberg, Edward Dart, and Walter Netsch.

8 — Bruegmann, *Weese,* 75.

9 — Bruegmann, *Weese,* 94.

10 — "Harry Weese," Architects + More, Chicago Bauhaus and Beyond, accessed February 17, 2019, chicagobauhausbeyond.org.

Ruth Koier and Laurence Sjoblom House

1 — Laurence R. Sjoblom: *Undergraduate Study Chicago Circle 1971–1972* (Chicago: University of Illinois, 1971), 143: Mathematics, Assistant Professor and "University of Illinois at Chicago Circle Undergraduate Study 1975–76," *Chicago Circle Bulletin* 9, no. 5 (April 25, 1975), 331: Mathematics, Associate Professor, accessed March 24, 2019, archive.org.

2 — Nancy Sjoblom, interview by author, September 17, 2019: sister-in-law Nancy Sjoblom is in possession of Patti Sjoblom's ledger, which documents that the couple chose to work with Jean and John Wehrheim but does not provide a rationale for their decision or details about the relationship between the clients and the architect.

3 — Jennifer Sjoblom, interview by author, July 31, 2018 and email to author, September 16, 2019.

4 — Anne Douglas [Bayless], "Great Home is a Bargain," *Chicago Tribune,* January 8, 1972.

5 — Ada Louise Huxtable, "The Last Profession to be Liberated by Women," *New York Times,* March 13, 1977.

6 — Nancy Poore, "Woman Architect Cashes in on Design Talent," *Chicago Tribune,* March 13, 1966 and Despina Stratigakos, *Where are the Women Architects?* (Princeton and Oxford: Princeton University Press in association with Places Journal, 2016), 14.

7 — Thirty years ago architect Cynthia Weese, FAIA, designed the kitchen of the author's home (the former Ruth Danielson and Hilmer V. Swenson House designed by Lawrence Perkins in 1941), and it remains a handsome functional work space.

8 — "Mom Finds Time to Design, Build Houses," *Chicago Tribune,* Sunday, October 30, 1955.

9 — "College of Du Page to Hold Course in House Planning," *Chicago Tribune,* December 4, 1969.

10 — *Chicago Women Architects: Contemporary Directions* (Chicago: Chicago Women in Architecture, 1978). Published in conjunction with the exhibition of the same title at Artemisia Gallery, Chicago, January 10–February 4, 1978.

11 — Stratigakos, *Where are the Women Architects?,* 15.

12 — Kenan Heise, "Mary Ann Crawford, 87, Architect," *Chicago Tribune,* December 30, 1988.

13 — Stuart E. Cohen, *Chicago Architects: Documenting the Exhibition of the Same Name Organized by Laurence Booth, Stuart E. Cohen, Stanley Tigerman, and Benjamin Weese* (Chicago: Swallow Press, 1976). Harry Francis Mallgrave, David J. Goodman, *An Introduction to Architectural Theory: 1968 to the Present* (Hoboken, NJ: Wiley-Blackwell, 2011): notes that the *Chicago Architects* exhibition ran concurrently and counter to the traveling German show "100 Years of Architecture in Chicago," that "honored the Chicago School at the turn of the century and the Miesian tradition after 1938," to which Cohen and Tigerman were "protesting the narrowness of this historical selection (thereby omitting many Chicago modernists during the intervening years)." Two important transitional exhibitions followed: "Seven Chicago Architects," Richard Gray Gallery, 1977 and "Exquisite Corpse," Walter Kelley Gallery, 1978.

14 — "Paying Homage to Women in Architecture," *Inland Architect* (December 1977), 20, clipping in the collection of author; Jennifer Dunning, "A Retrospective of Women Master Builders at Work," *New York Times,* February 25, 1977: Curated by Susana Torres, the exhibition also included "an informal 'open wall' space for drawings by women architects in each area that this traveling exhibition will visit."

15 — Among those featured in the *Chicago Women Architects* exhibition were Gunduz

Dagdelen Ast, Carol Ross Barney, FAIA, Kirsten Peltzer Beeby, Pao-Chi Chang, Marion Mahony Griffin, Po Hu Shao, Jeanne Kane, Gertrude Lempp Kerbis, FAIA, Janet A. Null, Kathryn Quinn, Fredericka M. Rosengren, Cynthia Weese, FAIA, and Margaret Young.

Donald Wrobleski House

1 — Don Wrobleski, interview by author, December 15, 2018, which provided much of the information for this essay.

2 — "Great Union of Site, Plan," *Better Homes and Gardens 1968 Home Building Ideas* (Des Moines: Meredith, 1968), 54; Gary Gand, "Don Wrobleski" in *Julius Shulman: Chicago Midcentury Modernism* (New York: Rizzoli, 2010), 178–83, and Don Wrobleski, interview by author, November 28, 2018.

Joan Henderson and George E. Johnson Sr. House

1 — See "George Johnson," interview by Timuel D. Black Jr., in *Bridges of Memoir: Chicago's First Wave of Black Migration* (Evanston: Northwestern University Press, 2003), 343–387: Johnson attributed his success to the mentorship he received from S. B. Fuller, an African American entrepreneur who had arrived in Chicago in 1928 and eventually founded the Fuller Products Company. See Mary Fuller Casey, *S. B. Fuller: Pioneer in Black Economic Development* (Jamestown, NC: Bridge Master Press, 2003).

2 — Neil Genzlinger, "Joan Johnson, Whose Company Broke a Racial Barrier, Dies at 89," *New York Times,* September 10, 2019, nytimes.com; Jake Wittich, "Joan Johnson, co-founder of Trailblazing Black Hair Care Company, Dies at 89," September 9, 2019, *Chicago Sun-Times,* chicago.suntimes.com; and Konstantin Roropin and Doug Criss, "Joan Johnson, Who Co-Founded the Black Hair Company that Made Afro Sheen, Has Died," CNN, September 9, 2019, cnn.com, all accessed November 10, 2019.

3 — For a thorough overview see Krisann Rehbein, "At Home in Chatham: A Bounty of Mid-Century Modern on the South Side, Where the African-American Elite Once 'Strutted

Their Stuff,'" in *New City Design,* November 11, 2015, accessed September 24, 2019, design. newcity.com. See "Chatham" in Encyclopedia of Chicago, accessed November 11, 2019, encyclopediachicagohistory.org.

4 — "Your Chicago: Chatham," 2 CBS Chicago, December 7, 2012, accessed November 10, 2019, chicago.cbslocal.com.

5 — See Mahalia Jackson with Evan McLeod Wylie, *Movin' on Up* (New York: Hawthorn Books, 1966).

6 — See "Small Urban House by Louis H. Huebner, Architect," *Arts & Architecture* 71, no. 10 (October 1954): 30. "Louis H. Huebner," *Chicago Tribune,* January 28, 1995, accessed November 21, 2019, chicagotribune. com. On Park Ridge see parkridgehistorycenter.org and "Park Ridge, IL," *Encyclopedia of Chicago,* accessed November 22, 2019, encyclopedia. chicagohistory.org.

7 — Kalo Foundation of Park Ridge has had ownership of the Iannelli Studios Heritage Center since 2011, accessed November 22, 2019, kalofoundation.org.

8 — "Frank F. Cole," *Chicago Tribune,* September 13, 1968, accessed November 22, 2019, newspapers.com.

9 — Huebner & Henneberg would go on to design an addition to the Johnson Products Co. Inc. Off. & Mfg. Bldg completed in 1969. See groundbreaking photos in *Jet,* (Oct. 7, 1971): 16.

10 — Unbuilt project "House by Louis H. Huebner, architect," *Arts & Architecture* 72, no. 9 (September 1955); "House by Louis H. Huebner, architect," *Arts & Architecture* 73, no. 10 (October 1956): 28; "House by Louis H. Huebner, architect" *Arts & Architecture* 74, no. 5 (May 1957): 28; "House by Louis H. Huebner, architect," *Arts & Architecture* 75, no. 10 (October 1958): 30, 33; "House by Louis H. Huebner, architect," *Arts & Architecture* (May 1960): 26–27; the first publication with both architects appears in "Winter Vacation House by Huebner and Henneberg, architects," *Arts & Architecture* 78, no. 1 (January 1961): 18–19; "House by Huebner and Henneberg, architects," *Arts*

& Architecture 80, no. 8 (August 1963): 29.

11 — "House by Huebner and Henneberg, architects," *Arts & Architecture* 78, no. 6 (June 1961): 24–25.

12 — Corinne J. Naden and Ashyia N. Henderson, "Johnson, George E. 1927–" accessed November 19, 2019, encyclopedia. com: in the mid-1970s, the Johnsons were reported as owning in addition to their home in Glencoe, vacation homes in Paris and Jamaica, a farm, and cattle ranches in Mississippi. Robert A. Sideman, "Where Are All the Black People," in *African Americans in Glencoe: The Little Migration* (Charleston, SC : The History Press, 2009), 81–84; Sideman, email to Susan Benjamin, November 24, 2019; Cook County Assessor's Office, accessed November 24, 2019, cookcountyassessor.com; "Glencoe: An Early North Shore African American Community," *Shorefront Journal,* March 25, 2013, accessed November 19, 2019, shorefrontjournal. wordpress.com; "Brentwood Avenue," March 25, 2013, redfin. com. Teresa Wiltz, "Jerrold Wexler, 68, Giant in Real Estate," November 8, 1992, *Chicago Tribune,* chicagotribune.com and Bruce Lambert, "Jerrold Wexler, 68; Chicago Developer Who Built Empire," *New York Times,* November 12, 1992, accessed November 10, 2019, nytimes. com, both accessed November 27, 2019.

13 — Pamela Martin Orr, emails to author, December 9, 2019.

14 — Lee Bey, *Southern Exposure: The Overlooked Architecture of Chicago's South Side* (Evanston: Northwestern Press, 2019).

Priscilla Huffard and H.P. Davis Rockwell House II

1 — See for example, "Mies's One-Office Office Building," *Architectural Forum* 110 (February 1959), 95: Mies van der Rohe's unrealized project for the Bacardi Corporate Headquarters in Cuba (1959) adopts a similar structural partis: "On eight massive, tapered cast concrete pillars will rest an enormous monolith of post-tensioned reinforced concrete, a true plate, its girder edge floating heavily on pin joins which accept no horizontal thrust."

2 — "Brenner, Danforth, Rockwell, Architects," *Arts & Architecture* 82, no. 8 (August 1965): 15–17.

3 — See Monica Pidgeon and Theo Crosby ed., *An Anthology of Houses* (New York: Reinholt, 1960), 126–28. "H. P. Davis Rockwell House, Flossmoor, Illinois," *Architectural Record* 119, no. 6 (Mid-May) 121–25, accessed August 25, 2019, chicagoarchitect.com.

4 — George Danforth, *Oral History of George Danforth / Interviewed by Pauline Saliga, Complied under the Auspices of the Chicago Architects Oral History Project, the Ernest R. Graham Study Center for Architectural Drawings, Department of Architecture, the Art Institute of Chicago* rev. ed. (Chicago: Art Institute of Chicago, 2003), 65: he continues, "Downstairs are the bedrooms for the children, when they were there, before they left, and the services. That's all back in the cliff and it opens out to the south. It's quite free all the way around. You come in through a very wooded area into the garage, which is just vertical siding of cypress, and there's a pool and then the house."

5 — "Architects' Own Houses," *Architectural Record* 138, no. 3 (September 1965): 178: continues with, "All exterior concrete is exposed aggregate, except for the roof edge-beam. And for unity, the same aggregate is used for terrazzo in the upper floor and as loose gravel in the forecourt north of the house. Wall paneling and cabinets are Burmese teak. A pool at the edge of the wood adjoins a garage and bathhouse."

6 — John Vinci, "John Vinci, FAIA, Remembers Harry P. Davis (Deever) Rockwell, 1926–2014," *Chicago Architect,* August 12, 2014.

7 — "H. P. Davis Rockwell" in Gary Gand, *Julius Shulman: Chicago Midcentury Modernism* (New York: Rizzoli, 2010), 188–99.

Ming Djang and Chung Kuo Liao House

1 — "Chung Kuo Liao, 89," *Chicago Tribune,* June 21, 2001, accessed November 10, 2019, chicagotribune.com.

2 — "Y. C. Wong, 79, Chicago Architect," *Chicago Tribune,* August 30, 2000,

accessed November 10, 2019, chicagotribune.com.

3 — "Death Notice: R. Ogden Hannaford," *Chicago Tribune,* August 30, 2008, accessed November 10, 2019, chicagotribune.com and "R. Ogden Hannaford," *Chicago Sun-Times,* August 30, 2008.

4 — Werner Blaser, *After Mies: Mies van der Rohe – Teaching and Principles* (New York: VNR, 1977), 291.

5 — Interview with Yau Chun Wong, *Oral History of Yau Chun Wong / Interviewed by Betty J. Blum, Compiled under the Auspices of the Chicago Architects Oral History Project, the Ernest R. Graham Study Center for Architectural Drawings, Department of Architecture, the Art Institute of Chicago* (Chicago: Art Institute of Chicago, 1995), 26.

6 — From the 1960s–70s onwards, a number of Chicago-based architects in younger generations explored the role that classicism and history could play in modern architecture. See Jay Pridmore and, I. W. Colburn, *Emotion in Modern Architecture* (Lake Forest, IL: Lake Forest College Press, 2015); Edward Keegan, "Modern Classicism in Chicago, 1970–1990s," *Classicist* no. 16 (2019): 50– 57. Guest editors: Stuart Cohen and Julie Hacker.

7 — "Two Projects by Yau Chun Wong, Architect," *Arts & Architecture* 83, no. 12 (January 1967): 20–21. See also "Doctor's Home and Clinic Utilize Prestressed Concrete," *PC Items* 13, no. 2 (February 1967), published monthly by the Prestressed Concrete Institute (PC), editor Edward D. Dionne.

8 — "Two Projects," 20–21.

9 — "Atrium Houses by Y. C. Wong," *Arts & Architecture* 79, no. 4 (April 1962): 12–13. Werner Blaser, *After Mies. Mies van der Rohe: Teaching and Principles* (New York: Van Nostrand Reinhold Company, 1977), 218–221. "Town Houses by Y. C. Wong," *Arts & Architecture* vol, 79, no. 4 (April 1962): 12–13. See also Susan O'Connor Davis, *Chicago's Historic Hyde Park* (Chicago: University of Chicago Press, 2013), 239.

10 — A J Latrace, "Get an Exquisite, Minimalist Mid-Century Modern Home for Just

$450K," *Chicago Magazine*, June 28, 2018, accessed November 26, 2019, chicagomag.com: Eleanor Lieberman's father was the Graymoor developer.

11 — See Josephine Minutillo, "Casina by Alfred Swenson Pao-Chi Chang Architects," *Architectural Record* 197, no. 1 (January 2009). Chang's spouse, Alfred Swenson, who obtained a Master of Science in Architecture in 1968 and served as Associate Professor at IIT from 1966 to his retirement. The duo formed Alfred Swenson Pao-Chi Chang Architects. They co-authored *Architectural Education at IIT 1938–1978* (Chicago: Illinois Institute of Technology, 1980).

12 — After Mies's death, he established (with Mies's grandson) the firm Fujikawa, Conterato, Lohan & Associates in 1968. Blair Kamin, "Joseph Y. Fujikawa, 81," *Chicago Tribune,* January 30, 2004, accessed November 25, 2019, chicagotribune.com. Fujikawa designed a modest modernist house in Winnetka; see Sally Schneiders, "Winnetka Modernist Joe Fujikawa," *Winnetka Historical Society Gazette* (Spring 2018), accessed November 25, 2019, winnetkahistory.org. For more on Fujikawa see: William S. Shell, *Impressions of Mies: An Interview on Mies van der Rohe: His Early Chicago Years 1938–58, with former students Edward A. Duckett and Joseph Y. Fujikawa* (Chicago: n.p., 1988); "January 23, 1949—Joseph Fujikawa Named Best New Talent," January 23, 2016, accessed November 25, 2019, connectingthewindycity. com: Fujikawa placed first in a MoMA-sponsored nation-wide architectural competition for new talent. Joseph Y. Fujikawa, *Oral History of Joseph Fujikawa / Interviewed by Betty J. Blum, Compiled under the Auspices of the Chicago Architects Oral History Project, the Ernest R. Graham Study Center for Architectural Drawings, Department of Architecture, the Art Institute of Chicago rev. ed.* (Chicago: Art Institute of Chicago, 2003). Joseph Y. Fujikawa, "Joseph Fujikawa in Conversation with Kevin Harrington," transcript/cassette, April–May 1996, Mies and His American Colleagues Oral History Project, Canadian Centre for Architecture, accessed November 25, 2019, hip.

cca.qc.ca and "Joseph Fujikawa in Conversation with Phyllis Lambert," cassette, August 18, 1997, Canadian Centre for Architecture, Montreal, Quebec, Canada. Thomas Dyja, *The Third Coast: When Chicago Built the American Dream* (New York: Penguin, 2014), 209.

13 — John Matuszak, "An American Family: Bea Takeuchi, 92, Carries on Creative Spirit," *Herald-Palladium* (Michigan), May 6, 2013, accessed May 20, 2019, heraldpalladium.com: Arthur Takeuchi's sister shares the experiences her family faced during the war. Their father, Kijiro Takeuchi, emigrated from Japan around 1917 and started a small newspaper in Japanese, *The Great Northern Daily News* or *Taihoku Nippo* in Seattle. He died in 1934 before having to witness his wife and their children who were born in America face interment. Kōjirō Takeuchi, Beikoku *Seihokubu Nihon Iminshi: A History of Japanese Immigrants in the Northwestern United States* (Seattle: Taihoku Nipposhō, 1929; reprinted with a new preface by Arthur S. Takeuchi and explanatory remarks by Eizaburō Okuizumi (Tokyo: Yūshōdō Press, 1994).

14 — Werner Blaser, *After Mies. Mies van der Rohe: Teaching and Principles* (New York: Van Nostrand Reinhold Company, 1977). See Kevin Harrington, "Order, Space, Proportion: Mies's Curriculum at IIT," in *Mies van der Rohe, Architect as Educator, eds.* Rolf Achilles, Kevin Harrington, and Charlotte Myhrum (Chicago: Illinois Institute of Technology, 1986), 49–68, Mies van der Rohe Centennial Project.

15 — Gregory C. Randall, *America's Original GI Town: Park Forest, Illinois* (Baltimore: John Hopkins University Press, 2003). See also "Park Forest, IL," Encyclopedia of Chicago, accessed November 25, 2019, encyclopedia.chicagohistory.org: it was incorporated as a village in February 1949.

Sheila Adelman and David Haid House

1 — Dwight H. Perkins designed his house in collaboration with his spouse Lucy Fitch Perkins for the interiors and Jens Jensen for the landscape. Philip Will Jr. designed his house. For an

overview of architecture, see Jack Weiss, Stuart Cohen, Kris Hartzell, and Laura Saviano, *Evanston: 150 Years 150 Places: Design Evanston Celebrates Evanston's Notable Architecture* (Evanston: Design Evanston, 2013). Barbara J. Buchbinder-Green ed., Margery Blair Perkins, *Evanston: A Tour through the City's History* (Evanston: Evanston History Center, 2013). (Margery was married to architect Lawrence (Larry) Perkins, who was part of the team that designed Crow Island School (1940) in Winnetka, and the couple made Evanston their home.)

2 — Record Houses of 1971 issue, *Architectural Record* 149, no. 6 (Mid-May 1971), 48–49: his award reads, "Architectural Record Award of Excellence for House Design presented to David Haid, Architect for his own house selected as a Record House for outstanding architectural excellence in planning and design and presented in Record Houses of 1971 as one of the nation's most significant houses of the year." In addition, the Chicago Chapter of the American Institute of Architects and the Chicago Association of Commerce and Industry presented the 1970 Single-Family Residence Distinguished Building Award to the Haid Residence.

3 — David Haid, Project Brief, David Haid and Associates (Joseph Frank Archive).

4 — Jon Anderson, "David Haid, Award-Winning Architect," *Chicago Tribune*, March 13, 1993, accessed May 18, 2019. See also Serena Keshavjee ed., *Winnipeg Modern: Architecture, 1944–1975* (Winnipeg: University of Manitoba Press, 2006).

5 — "Sheila Haid (née Adelman)," *Winnipeg Free Press*, September 18, 1999, 53, winnipegfreepress. com and *Chicago Tribune*, August 19, 1999, chicagotribune.com, both accessed May 18, 2019. She received her BA from the University of Manitoba and her master's in psychology from the University of Toronto.

6 — Reyner Banham, "In the Neighborhood of Art," *Art in America* 75 (June 1987): 124–29; reprinted in Mary Banham, Paul Barker, Sutherland Lyall, and Cedric Price, comps., *A Critic Writes: Essays by Reyner Banham*

(Los Angeles: University of California Press, 1996), 270–75.

7 — Stephen Fox, email reply to author, May 18, 2019. See also Ron Witte, ed., *Counting: In Honor of Anderson Todd's 90th Birthday* (Houston: Rice School of Architecture, 2011).

8 — *Modern Steel Construction* 8, no. 3 (Third Quarter 1968): 13, the Abraham Lincoln Oasis received the 1969 Architectural Awards of Excellence issued by the American Institute of Steel Construction.

9 — Joe Frank, "David Haid's Archive," in *Midwest Architecture Journeys,* ed. Zach Mortice with introduction by Alexandra Lange (Cleveland: Belt Publishing, 2019), 60–65.

Donna Parr and Charles Walgreen III House

1 — "Our Past," Walgreens, accessed May 1, 2019, walgreens. com.

2 — Clarence Krusinski, interview by author, April 23, 2013 formed the basis for a significant amount of information used in this essay.

3 — It was an entry for the Friedrichstrasse skyscraper competition in Berlin, see Dietrich Neumann, "Three Early Designs by Mies van der Rohe," *Perspecta* 27 (1992): 76–97, accessed February 20, 2019, repository.library.brown.edu.

4 — "Prize-Winning Home Lets Sun Come In," *Chicago Tribune,* Home Guide North, June 10, 1972.

5 — Susan Benjamin and Gwen Sommers Yant, Benjamin Historic Certifications, "Historic Resource Evaluation, 1313 East Westleigh Road, Lake Forest, IL, June, 2013." Dennis Rodkin, "At Lake Forest House Sale, Less is Less," *Chicago*, June 4, 2012, chicagomag.com.

Margaret Berman and Paul Lurie House

1 — James L. Nagle, telephone interview by author, September 1, 2001.

2 — "Midwest Modern," *Residential Architect* (March 1999): 58.

3 — James L. Nagle, telephone interview by author, August 23, 2001.

4 — Nagle, interview, August 23, 2001: The other design types

within Nagle's musical analogy include the "Pops" house, like popular music, which borrows from the vernacular culture in form and/or material and the "Jazz," which describes the informality and asymmetry of some of the houses. Nagle makes a reference to a 2001 interview at the Graham Foundation for Advancement in the Fine Arts, Chicago where he had discussed the pluralistic approach of his work with Richard Solomon.

5 — "Residence Evanston," *Inland Architect* (April 1975): 27, Peter C. Pran and Franz Schulze, "Build Me a City: A New Exhibition Tells Us Why Chicago is 'The Most Important City in the History of Modern Architecture,'" *Chicago Sun-Times Midwest Magazine*, April 25, 1976, and "Private Residence, Evanston, Illinois, USA/Architects Booth & Nagle," *A + U Architecture and Urbanism* (December 1976): 92.

6 — Oswald W. Grube, Peter C. Pran, and Franz Schulze, translations and additional text by David Norris, *100 Years of Architecture in Chicago: Continuity of Structure and Form* (Chicago: Follett Publishing, 1978), 117–18.

7 — The Chicago Architecture Foundation was originally named the Chicago School of Architecture Foundation but became the Chicago Architecture Foundation when confusion over the name caused people to believe it was a school. Paul, along with Wayne Benjamin, Richard Wintergreen, and Jim Schultz were the original founders. James Nagle served as president of the board of the organization in the 1970s.

Dawn Clark and Walter Netsch House

1 — For an online version of a paper originally published during his last year at SOM by Walter Netsch, "Field Theory Architecture," in 1979, see "Unraveling One Architect's Kaleidoscopic Design Theory in 9 Projects" at medium.com.

2 — Walter A. Netsch, *Oral History of Walter Netsch / Interviewed by Betty J. Blum under the Auspices of the Chicago Architects Oral History Project, the Ernest R. Graham Study Center for Architectural Drawings, Department of Architecture, the*

Art Institute of Chicago rev. ed. (Chicago: Art Institute of Chicago, 2000), 238.

3 — See "Netsch House, Chicago, Ill. Netsch," *Progressive Architecture* 57, no. 8 (August 1976): 46, for his field theory as it relates to this house.

4 — Anthony Jones, *The Netsch House: Living with Art,* photographers Jay Wolke, Patty Carroll, and William Lukes (Chicago: Anthony Jones, 2015), 28.

5 — Netsch would later design similar diagonal stairs for the Art Institute of Chicago, East Wing.

6 — At one of their art auctions, the author purchased a lithograph.

7 — Netsch, *Oral History,* 227.

8 — Netsch, *Oral History,* 1: in her introductory paragraph, interviewer Betty J. Blum paraphrases Netsch's previous comment about Wright's advice.

9 — Jones, *Netsch House,* 12.

Arlene and Richard Don House

1 — Stanley Tigerman, interview by author, January 2, 2019: formed the basis for a considerable amount of information used in this essay.

2 — Mara Tapp, "Can Stanley Tigerman Play Nice?: The Legendarily Combative Architect is Trying to Keep His Cool as He Works Toward What May be the Crowning Achievement of His Career," *Reader,* November 20, 2003, accessed January 3, 2019, chicagoreader.com.

3 — Stanley Tigerman, *Stanley Tigerman: Buildings and Projects, 1966–1989,* ed. Sarah Mollman Underhill (New York: Rizzoli, 1989), 42. The house is also illustrated in Stanley Tigerman, *VERSUS: An American Architect's Alternatives* (New York: Rizzoli, 1982), 76: includes an illustration of the house. Articles about the house appeared in *House and Garden* (July 1976), *Progressive Architecture* (August 1976) and *Inland Architect* (March/April 1984), accessed January 3, 2019, tigerman-mccurry.com.

Ruth Nelson and Robert J. Freeark House

1 — Victoria Post Ranney, *Olmsted in Chicago* (Chicago: Open Parks Project, 1972).

2 — Thorncroft housed teachers for the Coonley Estate's private school.

3 — The Freeark House is discussed and illustrated under the rubric of "Dwellings" in Oswald W. Grube, Peter C. Pran, and Franz Schulze, *100 Years of Architecture in Chicago: Continuity of Structure and Form* (Chicago: J. Philip O'Hara, 1976), 115–33; Ante Glibota and Frédéric Edelmann, eds., *Chicago: 150 Years of Architecture 1833–1983* (Paris: Paris Art Center), 208.

4 — See discussion in the Coda (p. 288) of this book.

5 — Robert Sharoff and William Zbaren, *John Vinci: Life and Landmarks* (Evanston: Northwestern University Press, 2017). Vinci and Kenny were the architects for the reconstruction of the Louis Sullivan Stock Exchange Room at the Art Institute of Chicago.

6 — Lawrence Kenny returned to New York City for a year in 1974 before returning there in 1977, accessed July 19, 2019, lkarc.com. Kenny, email to author, November 16, 2019.

7 — John Vinci, email to author, November 18, 2019.

8 — John Vinci, *Oral History of John Vinci / Interviewed by Betty J. Blum, Compiled under the Auspices of the Chicago Architects Oral History Project, the Ernest R. Graham Study Center for Architectural Drawings, Department of Architecture, the Art Institute of Chicago* (Chicago: Art Institute of Chicago, 2002), 37.

9 — Vinci, *Oral History,* 51.

10 — Vinci, *Oral History,* 50.

Iris Smith and Paul Goldstein House

1 — Stanley Tigerman, interview by author, January 2, 2019, revealed that when he was a young boy, he was enamored with Mondrian and told his mother he wanted to meet him. Stanley's mother took him to New York and arranged for her son to meet the artist, who had immigrated to New York from the Netherlands after World War II. Until he arrived at Yale and studied under the chairman of the school's art department, Josef Albers, Tigerman painted in the manner of Mondrian.

2 — Iris Goldstein, email correspondence with author, May 17–18, 2019. Iris Goldstein studied sculpture with Leonard Baskin at Smith College and received her MFA in drawing and painting at the School of the Art Institute of Chicago. She is a former President of ARC Gallery, a woman-run, non-profit cooperative gallery and Educational Foundation in Chicago. She reviewed the essay for accuracy.

3 — Stanley Tigerman, "One: Mies van der Rohe-Influenced, Chicago School Contextual Phase 1963–1981," in *VERSUS: An American Architect's Alternatives Stanley Tigerman* (New York: Rizzoli, 1982), 15.

4 — Tigerman's website and archive at Yale both list the project with this name, which may have been, in part, for the client's privacy.

5 — *House and Garden* (September 1975), *Architectural Record* (September 1976), *A + U* (July 1976), and *L'Architecture d'Aujourd'hui* (August/September 1976), accessed January 3, 2019, tigerman-mccurry.com.

Coda

Michelangelo Sabatino

Revising the Modern House in Chicago

Museum of Contemporary Art
(opened in 1967) at original
location, 237 East Ontario Street,
with Time-Life Building under
construction (c. 1968-69).

A tipping point in the complex story of modern houses in Chicago occurs just after the temporal bookend of *Modern in the Middle,* in 1976, the year that the United States of America celebrated its bicentennial. Hosted during the same year, in the lobby of the Corten-steel 30-story Time-Life Building (1969) designed by Harry Weese, the exhibition *Chicago Architects* (and accompanying catalogue) served as a catalyst for questioning prevailing notions about modern architecture in and outside Chicago.[1] While the focus was not predominantly on the role of houses in shaping this understanding, the debate it generated about the existence of multiple strains of modern architecture gave architects newfound freedom to diversify their approach to designing houses. Architect and theorist Stanley Tigerman, cocurator with architect and historian Stuart Cohen, dubbed the exhibition "A *Salon des Refuseés.*"[2]

Chicago Architects was meant to counter the narrative framework of another prominent exhibition, *100 Years of Architecture in Chicago: Continuity of Structure and Form,* being held simultaneously at the Museum of Contemporary Art Chicago on East Ontario Street.[3] *Chicago Architects* was polemical insofar as the curators went out of their way to include a number of overlooked yet talented architects whose best work, as it turns out, tended to be residential architecture, ranging from Howard Van Doren Shaw and David Adler to Andrew Rebori and Barry Byrne. It offered a local perspective of the city's recent architectural past that sought to reject the teleological narrative of a singular modern movement espoused during the 1930s by the influential critic Nikolaus Pevsner, whose militant account *Pioneers of the Modern Movement* began with Arts and Crafts only to reach its

Cover, *Chicago Architects* exhibition traveled to NYC and Cambridge, Massachusetts before opening in Chicago (1976).

Cover, *100 Years of Architecture in Chicago* (1976).

289

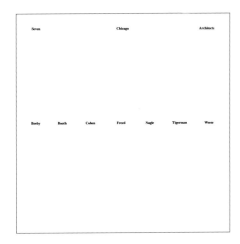

true expression with the machine-based aesthetic of the International Style.[4] With his *Modern Movements in Architecture* published in 1973, American critic Charles Jencks promoted pluralism (*movements* instead of movement) over doctrinaire attitudes and eventually became one of the earliest and most prominent advocates of so-called postmodernism."[5] Since the early 1970s, some of the more interesting architects looked to postmodernism as a condition more than a mere style; they sought to recover a narrative dimension of architecture without rejecting the spatial complexity and formal inventions of the modern movement.

In Robert Venturi's *Complexity and Contradiction in Architecture* published in 1966, he playfully quipped "less is a bore" in response to the "less is more" expression associated with but not coined by Mies.[6] Two years prior to this groundbreaking publication, which he described as a "Gentle Manifesto," Venturi had completed the Vanna Venturi House (1964) for his mother in the Philadelphia suburban neighborhood of Chestnut Hill.[7] Nothing could be further away from the spatial and structural purity of the Edith Farnsworth House (p. 162) that Mies designed a little more than a decade earlier than Venturi's green-stucco wood-frame house with its pitched roof alluding to a giant classical pediment. Although Mies was still alive when the Vanna Venturi House was completed and the book appeared (published by the Museum of Modern Art), it was clear that a number of architects (and their clients) in America and beyond were seeking to diversify and pluralize the assumed tenets of the modern movement with important implications for the built environment. In Chicago the Alice and William McLennan House (1959) in Lake Forest was an early outlier as discussed in Jay Pridmore's study on architect *I. W. Colburn: Emotion in Modern Architecture* (2015).

Cover, *Seven Chicago Architects* (1976) left.

Cover, *Five Architects* (1975) right.

Chicago Townhouse Competition exhibition (1978).

Two of the twentieth century's most significant architects closely associated with Chicago died during a decade of transformation in American society. Frank Lloyd Wright died in 1959 and Mies van der Rohe died in 1969, a year after the retrospective exhibition on his work opened at the Art Institute of Chicago, curated by A. James Speyer.[8] As demonstrated through a careful analysis of the modern houses discussed in *Modern in the Middle*—beginning with the Katherine Dummer and Walter T. Fisher House (1929, p. 58) and near the end the Ruth Nelson and Robert J. Freeark House (1975, p. 258)—both Wright and Mies exerted a complex influence on different generations of architects practicing in Chicago who sought to combine lessons learned about architecture from both.

Shortly after the critical success of *Chicago Architects,* the four co-organizers of the exhibition—Stanley Tigerman, Stuart Cohen, Laurence Booth, and Benjamin Weese—invited three other architects—Thomas H. Beeby, James Ingo Freed, and James Nagle—to join them as members of the Chicago Seven. Eventually the all-male seven became eleven with the addition of Gerald Horn, Helmut Jahn, Kenneth Schroeder, and Cynthia Weese, the only woman in the group. The Chicago Seven label for this group of architects was inspired by the group of seven political activists (also known as the Chicago Seven) who were arrested (and subsequently went on trial) during the dramatic Democratic National Convention held in Chicago in August of 1968. The Chicago Seven architects helped promote a greater interest in context and history at a time when American cities were grappling with a host of new demands, including urban renewal, preservation, adaptive reuse, and the pressing need for more attention to be paid to urban design and comprehensive planning. Yet, the idea of a group of architects coming together to protest the status quo of orthodox modernism was launched when Arthur Drexler, Museum of Modern Art curator and director of the Department of Architecture and Design, convened a meeting (Committee of Architects for the study of the Environment) that eventually led to the publication of *Five Architects* (1972) that included the work of Peter Eisenman, Michael Graves, Charles Gwathmey, John Hejduk, and Richard Meier.[9] The group came to be identified as the New York Five.

Significantly, the New York Five, like the Chicago Seven who were also identified with the city where they all practiced, launched their careers with a series of innovative houses ranging from Richard Meier's Carole and Fred Smith House in Darien, Connecticut (1967) to Peter Eisenman's Florence and Richard Falk House II (1970) in Hardwick, Vermont. Not long after the publication of *Five Architects*, Robert A. M. Stern, offered an alternative and complementary version to the "whites," the name that came to be associated with the New York Five because they tended to design all-white buildings, with his own version of the "grays," a group of architects with whom Stern identified including Charles Moore and Robert Venturi that were also working to expand the preconceived notion of the modern in a different way by looking to context, the vernacular tradition, and history.[10]

Three other significant exhibitions consolidated the visibility of the Chicago Seven and demonstrated the importance these architects placed on residential architecture as a way to explore ideas that could counter the powerful corporate lobby that favored Mies and Miesian office towers (Skidmore, Owings & Merrill, which Frank Lloyd Wright derogatorily dubbed the "Three Blind Mies").[11] The first exhibition *Seven Chicago Architects,* held at the Richard Gray Gallery (established in 1963 on Michigan Avenue) between December 10, 1976–January 10, 1977, featured residential proposals for rural or suburban sites that would remain unbuilt—such as Beeby's beautifully illustrated "The House of Virgil," and Cohen's "Kindergarten Chats," to Nagle's Le Corbusier-inspired "The Sun Dial House"—but simultaneously questioned and expanded the structural determinism and antihistory biases of the International Style.[12]

Graham House (1968). Chicago.

Garden patio view of Nagle House (1978). Chicago.

Graham House courtyard with
sculptures.

Siegel House (1976) renovated
by Gordon Gill in 2015. Chicago.

In 1977 the Graham Foundation hosted the symposium "State of the Art of Architecture" that brought together "whites" and "grays" (and others) in dialogue with the Chicago Seven.[13] Shortly after a number of initiatives shifted attention away from the single-family house to that of the townhouse, a type that was becoming increasingly important as families began to return to Chicago neighborhoods, leaving behind the villages and cities that had been the sites of so many of the modern houses discussed in this book. A second exhibition entitled *Chicago Seven: The Exquisite Corpse* held at the Walter Kelly Gallery (December 17, 1977–February 16, 1978) presented proposals for townhouses by Beeby, Booth, Cohen, Freed, Jahn, Nagle, Tigerman, and Weese.[14] The exhibition *Chicago Seven Plus 11* was held at the Graham Foundation in 1978, and featured the work of participants from the Walter Kelly Gallery show in addition to the winners of a townhouse competition launched by the Chicago Seven.

The first tangible evidence that architects were leading the way through example by moving back to Chicago's neighborhoods can be seen in a handful of single-family houses: the cast-in-place concrete Jane Abend and Bruce Graham House (1968, renovated by Dan Wheeler of Wheeler Kearns Architects in 2006) and the Dawn Clark and Walter Netsch House (1974, p. 252), both designed as single-family, multistory urban houses for the Lincoln Park neighborhood of Chicago.[15] As Lincoln Park became increasingly desirable because of its affordability and proximity to the Loop, Chicago Seven architects followed SOM lead designers Graham and Netsch by designing compact dwellings that offered all the convenience of the suburbs including garages: see for example Booth & Nagle's Janis Fey and Dr. Saul Siegel

House (1976, renovated by Gordon Gill of Adrian Smith + Gordon Gill Architecture, 2015) and the Ann Steinbaugh and James Nagle House (1978).[16]

With his collage *The Titanic* (1978), showing Mies's S. R. Crown Hall sinking into Lake Michigan, Tigerman offered yet another witty provocation to Mies's former students, whose work continued to dominate the city nearly a decade after his death, despite the efforts of the Chicago Seven. With the exception of James Ingo Freed, all the rest of the original members of the group of Chicago Seven architects studied at schools outside of Chicago—ranging from Cornell (Beeby and Cohen), MIT (Booth), Harvard (Nagle, Weese), and Yale (Tigerman)—and consequently brought their new "outsider" perspectives to bear on the architectural practice and discourse during the 1970s and beyond.[17] While there was steadfast adherence to the Miesian approach to materials and structure among the graduates of IIT, it was hardly as blind a copying exercise as some might have assumed. Two graduates

Opposite: Mies van der Rohe Exhibition at The Art Institute of Chicago (April 27–June 30, 1968).

Stanley Tigerman's photomontage *The Titanic* (1978).

who would go on to form Mies's successor firm (Fujikawa, Conterato, Lohan & Associates) designed their own houses based on a loose interpretation of Miesian architecture for themselves: the Emily Wandasiewicz and Bruno Conterato House (1968) in Geneva and the split-level Grace Yamada and Joseph Fujikawa House (1971, p. 296) in Winnetka, both realized in reinforced concrete with brick infill walls and flat roofs stood in contrast to neighboring wood frame and brick clad houses.[18] Fujikawa revealed to Betty Blum: "Yes. It took me a while, but I did it about fifteen years ago; built a house, finally. What a traumatic experience!"[19]

A number of other significant houses by IIT-trained architects reveal how the Miesian principles were transformed over time: IIT graduates Ron Krueck and Keith Olsen (both Bachelor of Architecture, 1970 and formed Office of Krueck & Olsen Architects) designed the Steel and Glass House for David Meitus (1981), located on a former urban-renewal site just south of Lincoln Park; this spatially complex two-story house absorbs cues from the Ray Kaiser and Charles Eames House and Studio (Pacific Palisades, CA) and juxtaposes sensuous interiors with off-the-shelf components.[20] During that same period David Hovey, who graduated from IIT (Bachelor of Architecture, 1969, and Master of Science in Architecture, 1971) went on to found the award-winning Design-Build firm Optima and designed both the Eileen Sheehan and David Hovey House I in Winnetka (1982; demolished) and the Barbara and Douglas Hoekstra House in Homewood (1984).[21] These houses exploited the economy of prefabricated steel construction while offsetting a machine-age appearance with the addition of playful color accents and signature castellated beams.[22]

During the 1970s through the 1990s, a number of Chicago architects increasingly turned to research, writing, and curating exhibitions as a means to stimulate discourse in the architectural profession and to engage with a larger public to think about modern architecture. California native John Entenza directed the Graham Foundation for Advanced Studies in the Fine Arts between 1960–71, succeeded by Carter H. Manny Jr., (IIT's Master of Science in Architecture, 1948) who remained in the role from 1971–93. During their tenures Entenza and Manny supported a number of initiatives that would create opportunities for debate about the nature of the modern (and contemporary) house. Important advocates included the appointments of Paul Gapp as architecture critic for the *Chicago Tribune* (1972–92) and John Zukowsky as the inaugural curator of the Department of Architecture at the Art Institute in 1981 (Design was added in 2005), the second in the country after MoMA in 1932. The establishment of the Pritzker Prize of Architecture in 1979 by the Hyatt Foundation based in Chicago (with Philip Johnson as the first laureate)

and the rebirth of the Chicago Architectural Club in 1979 (with its affiliated "yearbook" published as *The Chicago Architectural Journal* (volumes 1–8 from 1981–89)

Opposite, top to bottom:

Conterato House (1968) from street. Geneva.

Conterato House living area with Hugo Weber portrait of Mies van der Rohe (1961).

Fujikawa House (1971) from street. Winnetka.

Fujikawa House from rear garden.

Right: Living area of David Meitus Steel and Glass House (1981). Chicago.

provided important visibility for the culture of architecture in the region.[23] The Chicago Institute for Architecture and Urbanism (CIAU) was established in 1988 by the SOM Foundation and located in the Charnley House (1892) that they purchased and rehabilitated. The short-lived think-tank (1988–2003) directed by Harvard-trained John Whiteman was meant to promote architectural research by way of lectures, exhibitions, and a publication series. The Charnley-Persky House has served as the headquarters for the Society of Architectural Historians since 1995 when they relocated from Philadelphia.[24] During Cynthia C. Davidson's tenure as editor (1983–1990) of *Inland Architect,* she energized the historic periodical before it eventually ceased publication.

Together with these initiatives aimed at raising awareness of modern, contemporary, and historic architecture of Chicago, two international exhibitions continued to highlight changes in approach to the design of modern houses: *New Chicago Architecture: Beyond the International Style* (1981), co-organized by the Museo di Castelvecchio and the Graham Foundation, was followed by *Chicago: 150 Years*

of Architecture, 1833–1983 curated by Ante Glibota and Frédéric Edelmann held in Paris in 1982–83; this exhibition later traveled to Chicago where it was displayed at the Museum of Science and Industry in 1985–86.[25] Subsequent major exhibitions (and accompanying scholarly catalogues) at the Art Institute of Chicago such as Chicago Architecture, 1872–1922: Birth of a Metropolis (1988), and Chicago Architecture and Design, 1923–93: Reconfiguration of an American Metropolis (1993) did much to increase understanding of Chicago's multifaceted domestic, residential, and commercial buildings.[26] In anticipation of the twenty-first century, the Renaissance Society at the University of Chicago hosted the thematic exhibition Turn of the Century Home (1994), featuring the house designs of several generations of Chicago-based architects that contributed to the ongoing debate about what is the future of the single-family house. [27] Participants included architects of different generations such as Dirk Lohan (Devon House, 1992) and Cynthia Weese (A House in the Woods, 1984).

Hovey House I (1982) with castellated steel beams. Winnetka, demolished.

Opposite top: Hoekstra House (1984) under construction. Homewood.

Opposite bottom: First and second floor plans, Larson House (1978). Evanston.

SECOND FLOOR PLAN

FIRST FLOOR PLAN

Although the 1970s to the 1990s witnessed a boom in townhouses, a number of architects continued to design single-family modern houses in Chicagoland. Evanston had long attracted a number of distinguished modern architects, including William Deknatel, Bertrand Goldberg, David Haid, Keck & Keck, James Nagle, and Philip Will Jr.[28] A number of modern houses designed in Evanston during the 1970s and 80s that took into account the issues raised by critics who argued in favor of a more inclusive and eclectic approach: Susan Breckenridge and George A. Larson House (1978) designed by Larson, an accomplished architect, interior designer, and author, elegantly adapts to a small lot with an open-air garden room in the front and a side entrance. The Evelyn and Charles

Wilson House by Kenneth A. Schroeder (with Richard Whitaker and Lloyd Gadau, 1975) brings West Coast architectural sensitivity to Evanston. The house that George Schipporeit, dean of IIT College of Architecture from 1983–89, designed for himself and his spouse Alice Butler in 1984 eschews modern transparency in favor of sculptural exuberance. The Eileen Sheehan and David Hovey House II in Winnetka brings steel-and-glass construction full circle for a dramatic site over-looking Lake Michigan (1996).[29] Competing with the concentration in Evanston, a small but significant group of modern urban houses were realized in the Chicago neighborhood of Lincoln Park: John Vinci (with Max Gordon) designed the elegant

Front facade Wilson House (1975). Evanston.

Front facade Manilow House (1989). Chicago.

brick-clad two-story Susan Rosenberg and Lewis Manilow House (1989) and Tadao Ando's reinforced concrete Fred Eychaner and Ken Lee House (1997) creates a oasis of tranquility in an otherwise bustling neighborhood that has seen a remarkable transformation since the early days in which architects like Bruce Graham and Walter Netsch first designed their own houses.

This selective group of modern houses realized after 1975 through to the late 1990s must be understood against the backdrop of the thoughtful provocations advanced by the original Chicago Seven; this said, the houses reveal that despite changing times a number of architects continued to identify with some of the most Miesian qualities of modern architecture especially as it related to new building materials, technology, and spatial layout. In choosing to conclude with twentieth century-houses, those realized in the first two decades of the twenty-first century have not been discussed insofar as the primary aim of *Modern in the Middle* is to

View across reflecting pool of Fred Eychaner and Ken Lee House (1997) with adjacent Wrightwood 659 (2018) just visible on the upper right. Chicago.

focus on the complex history of modern (not contemporary) houses in Chicago. While the school that Mies led at IIT continues to thrive long after his death, the School of Architecture at Taliesin, founded by Wright, will close in 2020. As new graduates from schools in and outside of Chicago continue to shape contemporary practice, it will be up to future generations of critics and historians to write the history of twenty-first century Chicago houses against the backdrop of a remarkable design legacy as well as the challenges to the future of architecture such as equity, diversity, and sustainability.

Chicago: Moving Modern Forward

Serge Ambrose, Susan S. Benjamin, Michelangelo Sabatino

The recent history of the two residences on the front and back covers of *Modern in the Middle*—the Maxine Weil and Sigmund Kunstadter House (p. 180) by Keck & Keck and the Edith Farnsworth House (p. 162) by Ludwig Mies van der Rohe—reveals the challenges associated with preserving Chicago's modern houses. Both were completed in the early 1950s, and both received acclaim from the architectural community. In addition to sharing the same years of completion, as coincidence would have it, 2003 was an important year in the history of both houses. The Kunstadter House, located in Highland Park, was demolished and replaced with a new house. That same year, Lord Peter Palumbo's decision to sell the Farnsworth House (with the assistance of Sotheby's New York) propelled it

to the center of a dramatic private-public fundraising campaign to ensure that it would not be purchased and possibly relocated outside of Illinois. Fortunately, the Farnsworth House was saved thanks to a collaborative effort with Landmarks Illinois (then Landmarks Preservation Council of Illinois), the National Trust for Historic Preservation, and the Friends of the Farnsworth House who purchased it at auction for $7.5 million and shortly thereafter opened it to the public. During the years of his ownership, Palumbo oversaw preservation initiatives (together with Dirk Lohan) over the years in response to flooding damage to the Farnsworth House, a risk that continues to this very day.

Due to its association with the urban renewal movement and the proliferation of concrete, steel, and glass buildings that often failed to take context into account, modernism faced a backlash from the late 1960s well into the 1980s. This growing anti-modern bias was also bolstered by the parallel rise of so-called postmodernism.

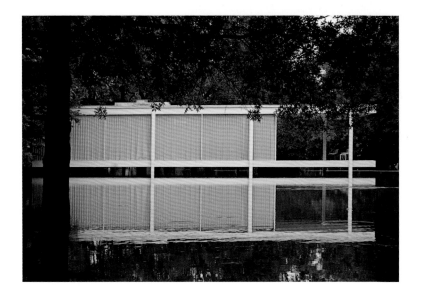

This bias gradually began to dissipate during the 1990s when a number of iconic houses in America underwent significant preservation efforts by public and private stakeholders such as the Ise Frank and Walter Gropius House in Lincoln, Massachusetts and the Richard Neutra-designed Liliane Kaufmann and Edgar J. Kaufmann Desert House in Palm Springs, California. A commitment to the preservation of modern historic buildings has increased substantially over the years through: the efforts of not-for-profit advocacy organizations, the rise of preservation programs in universities, and municipalities establishing preservation ordinances. The social cache associated with modern residential architecture has also increased as midcentury design has gained visibility in popular culture thanks to American period films such as Tom Ford's *A Single Man* (2009) and television series such as *Mad Men* (2007–15). Shelter magazines like *Atomic Ranch, Dwell,* and *Domino* along with retailer Crate & Barrel, founded in Chicago in 1962 by Gordon and Carol Segal in the city's Old Town neighborhood, promote well-designed products for the home. Design Within Reach (established in 1998 in San Francisco by Rob Forbes) has made modern classics and contemporary design available to new generations of consumers.

Despite ongoing threats of demolition due to increasing land values and other factors, the preservation of significant late-nineteenth and early-to-mid-twentieth-century houses in the United States has gained considerable traction among nonprofit organizations and private owners over the past decades in parallel with efforts directed toward civic, commercial, and religious buildings. Jump-started with the National Trust for Historic Preservation (founded in 1949), followed by the game-changing National Historic Preservation Act (NHPA) of 1966 (which established the National Register of Historic Places), much progress has been made in America in changing perceptions about the importance of preserving the built environment.[1] Over the past decades a number of houses discussed in *Modern in the Middle* have been included in the National Register of Historic Places for Illinois: Lewis House (listed in 1982, p. 112), Schweikher House (listed in 1987, p. 96), Morse House (listed in 2000, p. 68), Stevenson II House (listed in 2003, p. 104), and Farnsworth House (listed in 2004, p. 162). The Robie House (landmarked in 1963), Glessner House (landmarked in 1976), Farnsworth House (landmarked in 2006), and Stevenson House (landmarked in 2014) are part of an even more selective list of sites designated as National Historic Landmarks in Illinois.

A turning point in the preservation of twentieth-century houses in Chicago occurred in 1957, when the leaders of the Chicago Theological Seminary decided to proceed with the demolition of Frank Lloyd Wright's Robie House (1910) in Hyde Park in order to build a married students' dormitory in its place.[2] Were it not for the vocal protests of Wright himself (who was eighty-seven at the time) along with a local and international community of architects, historians, and preservationists, the house, recognized as a masterpiece of American (and Prairie) residential design, would no longer be standing.[3] Poet Carl Sandburg equated the proposed demolition of the Robie House to a "Nazi book burning."[4] During the very same years that the Robie House was being saved from the wrecking ball, the iconic Villa Savoye

Original Crate & Barrel retail store in Old Town / Lincoln Park neighborhood. Closed.

Opposite top: John Anderson, "Designs for Living," in *Playboy* (July 1961).

Opposite bottom: Laura Hieronymus and Frederick C. Robie House (1910) photo c. 1950s.

(1931) on the outskirts of Paris lay nearly in ruins. Were it not for Le Corbusier's protests—who, like Wright, defended his work—the Villa Savoye would not have survived. Over the years it has undergone extensive preservation campaigns, and in 1964 was designated in France as a historic monument while Le Corbusier was still alive. It, like many other modern houses in Europe, is open to the general public.[5]

Frank Lloyd Wright, more than most American architects, has been the object of concerted educational and preservation efforts aimed at making his buildings accessible to the general audience. The relocation of Wright's Usonian, designed for Charlotte Swart and Loren Pope, the Pope-Leighey House (1941) to avoid demolition and reopening to the public in 1965 established an important precedent in American preservation history. The establishment, in Chicago, of both the Frank Lloyd Wright Trust (formerly known as the Frank Lloyd Wright Home and Studio Foundation) in 1974 and the Frank Lloyd Wright Building Conservancy in 1989, is apt recognition of the impact Wright had upon the city that served as a springboard for his national and international reputation. The Foundation owns the Frank Lloyd Wright Home and Studio in Oak Park and

operates tours and programs out of this venue, as well as the Emil Bach House, the Robie House, the Rookery Light Court in Chicago, and Unity Temple in Oak Park.[6] The Conservancy's mission extends beyond Chicago to "facilitate the preservation and maintenance of the remaining structures designed by Frank Lloyd Wright through education, advocacy, and technical services."[7] Thanks to the efforts of these two organizations and the network of volunteers, Wright's houses (and other buildings) continue to receive sustained attention by general and specialized audiences.

In 1965, nearly a decade after the threatened demolition of the Robie House, another iconic residence—the Glessner House (1886) designed by Henry Hobson Richardson as part of the Prairie Avenue enclave of Chicago's elite—was listed for sale and faced an uncertain future.[8] In 1966, a group of architects, educators, and professionals created the Chicago School of Architecture Foundation (currently the Chicago Architecture Center).[9] Its headquarters was originally established in the Glessner House, though now located in the Mies van der Rohe-designed One Illinois Center on the Chicago River.[10] Funds to purchase the Glessner House were raised by individuals and architectural firms.[11] Today, the Glessner House and the Robie House are part of a growing local network of house museums founded in 2011—*At Home in Chicago*.[12] Several of Chicago-area modern houses are in the public realm and have been converted into house museums: in addition to the Farnsworth House, there are the Schweikher House (1938), the Isabella Gardner and Robert Hall McCormick III House (1952, p. 184) by Mies van der Rohe and the Stevenson II House (1936) designed by Perkins, Wheeler & Will in Libertyville that serves as the Adlai Stevenson Center on Democracy.

While preservation of the Robie House and the Glessner House are two success stories, the same cannot be said about the fate of a number of Adler and Sullivan-designed houses during the dangerous years before preservation began to be taken seriously in Chicago.[13] The 1960 demolition of the Laura Davis and Henry Babson Estate (1907) designed by Sullivan with landscape architect Jens Jensen in the Frederick Law Olmsted and Calvert Vaux-designed Village of Riverside is a case in point.[14] In 1953, the estate was sold to developer Walter S. Baltis, the house demolished, and the property was subdivided into forty residential lots. Architectural

Richard Nickel photograph of Glessner House for sale (summer 1966).

Babson House under demolition and for sale sign advertising "Baltis Built Homes" development site c. 1953.

photographer and preservation advocate Richard Nickel led a documentary campaign of Sullivan-designed houses and public buildings, which began in the mid-1950s (when he was studying at IIT under Aaron Siskind) and lasted until his untimely death in 1972.[15] The Helen Douglas and James Charnley House (1891–92), designed by Sullivan with the assistance of his then junior draftsman Frank Lloyd Wright, has fared better.[16] It was purchased from private owners by Skidmore, Owings & Merrill and restored in the mid 1980s to serve as the SOM Foundation and Chicago Institute for Architecture and Urbanism headquarters. In 1995 philanthropist Seymour Perksy purchased the house and donated it to the Society of Architectural Historians (which became its international headquarters). Renamed the Charnley-Perksy House, it was designated a National Historic Landmark in 1998.

A remarkable (if unconventional) example of preservation and continuing use of modern houses involves the Mies-designed McCormick III House (1952), relocated in 1994 from its former site to become a part of the Elmhurst Art Museum campus. An even more ambitious relocation involves several of Chicago's Century of Progress International Exposition model houses from the "Home and Industrial Arts" exhibit (1933–34). In 1935, after the fair closed, five of the houses—Armco-Ferro House, Cypress Log Cabin, Florida Tropical House, House of Tomorrow, Wieboldt-Rostone House—were moved along the coast of Lake Michigan via barge to Beverly Shores, Indiana as part of a business scheme to attract future buyers to a residential development

by Robert Bartlett.[17] After the development was complete, the historic modern houses were sold to private owners and eventually purchased by the Indiana Dunes National Park and renamed the Century of Progress Architectural District (added to the National Register of Historic Places in 1986). In recent decades a partnership between Indiana Landmarks and the Indiana Dunes National Park offers private parties a long-term lease in exchange for covering the cost of restoring and maintaining these houses. This agreement requires the lease holders to open the houses to visitors once a year. The George Fred Keck-designed House of Tomorrow, designated in 2016 as a National Treasure by the National Trust for Historic Preservation, is the last to await "rebirth" with a plan to return its lost historic exterior to the architect's original vision.[18] Over the past decade, retired engineer J. Christoph Lichtenfeld and his spouse Char have meticulously preserved and rebuilt much of the Armco-Ferro Porcelain Enamel Frameless Steel House located next to the House of Tomorrow.

While the history of Keck's House of Tomorrow is well-known, many other significant modern houses, like the ones discussed in this book, have not acquired iconic status and as such are threatened by the very fact that they are out of the public spotlight and vulnerable to the pressures of land values and changing tastes. One important preservation vehicle is through municipal oversight. The City of Chicago has a Commission on Chicago Landmarks which recommends landmark designation of buildings, sites, and districts that it deems valuable; it also oversees alterations and potential demolitions to the city's individually designated landmarks and to the numerous houses in its landmark districts.[19] The commission was spearheaded in the late 1950s by Chicago City Council Fifth Ward Alderman Leon M. Despres in response to the Robie House controversy.[20] Twentieth-century residential buildings designated Chicago Landmarks include: Andrew Rebori's Fisher Studio Houses (1936, designated in 1996) and Mies van der Rohe's 860–880 Lake Shore Drive Apartments (1951, designated in 1996). Many of the Chicago area suburbs also have preservation ordinances, but a number only have advisory review over alterations that could potentially destroy the character of designated landmarks. Some local governments have a demolition delay that can be instituted for buildings that have landmark potential. There are modern houses scattered throughout the Chicago metropolitan area that are not recognized because research on their significance has not yet been undertaken due to sometimes difficult access to archival materials. Some communities, however, are undertaking comprehensive surveys

Relocation of McCormick House to Wilder Park (future site of Elmhurst Art Museum).

Construction of new basement (2005) for the Century of Progress Armco-Ferro House (1933).

Opposite top: Frank F. Fisher Studio (1936) Chicago Landmark.

Opposite right: Harriet Davis and Louis Ancel House (1961) Glencoe Landmark designed by Edward Dart.

of their buildings—including modern ones—to evaluate their significance. For example, Lake Bluff has recently completed a survey of 1950s–70s subdivisions. Beginning in 2006, Illinois Statewide advocacy group Landmarks Illinois and the School of the Art Institute of Chicago's Graduate Program in Historic Preservation have collaborated on a multiyear effort to survey recent past non-residential architecture in the Chicago metropolitan area. Although it does not include houses, the survey is ongoing and does focus on suburban buildings ranging from 1935 to 1975.[21] A similar effort is ongoing in Los Angeles: Survey LA (Los Angeles Historic Resources Survey) promises to provide a model for comprehensive approaches to identifying historic resources including houses and housing.[22]

Local landmarking can provide protection, but it is a common misconception that national landmarking (being listed on the National Register of Historic Places) offers similar measures of protection or can

prevent demolition. For example: the Elizabeth Lamb and Alfred A. Schiller House by Schweikher & Elting (addition by Keck & Keck) in Glen Ellyn (1954; 1964) was listed in 2008 only to be demolished in 2016. Modern houses completed before 1970 have crossed the "Fifty-Year Rule" threshold established by the National Register of Historic Places. Unless it can be proven that a modern house has special significance, beyond the normal criteria for listing, it cannot be designated. Exceptions do exist: for example, the Schweikher House (1938) and Studio (1949) in Schaumburg was listed on the National Register of Historic Places when it was less than fifty years old because of its extraordinary architectural and cultural significance. Physicist Alexander Langsdorf Jr. and his spouse artist Martyl Suzanne Schweig Langsdorf (designer of the Doomsday Clock emblem in 1947) bought the house from Schweikher and lived in it for many decades before the City of Schaumburg became its owner.

To promote preservation, tax incentives are available for owners of houses listed on the National Register and (where there is an appropriate ordinance) owners of local landmarks. The Illinois State Historic Preservation Office (SHPO) administers a Property Tax Assessment Freeze program for owner-occupied residential properties. In order to qualify, the building must be renovated in accordance with the US Secretary of the Interior's Standards for Rehabilitation and must have eligible expenses equal to or exceeding 25 percent of the County Assessor's fair cash value. Numerous houses across the Chicago region have been rehabilitated thanks to this tax incentive. One example, the Harriet Davis and Louis Ancel House in Glencoe designed by Edward Dart in 1961 received Landmarks Illinois' Richard H. Driehaus Foundation Preservation Award in 2011. The owners Ellen Kimmel and David Muslin who initially purchased it as a "tear-down," grew to understand its significance and invested in its preservation.

Chicago is rich with educational and advocacy organizations that promote awareness about its architecture and cultural heritage. The Chicago Architecture Center's mission is to educate the general public about the built and natural environment and offer tours to sites in Chicago and suburbs by volunteer trained docents. The Chicago Art Deco Society promotes the preservation of 1920s–40s architecture and design through lectures and publications.[23] The Historic Resources committee of the Chicago chapter of the American Institute of Architects (AIA) offers educational programs geared toward members of the architectural profession who are interested in the preservation and adaptive reuse of historic buildings.[24]

Landmarks Illinois is a statewide not-for-profit "dedicated to saving historic places that matter."[25] It has been instrumental in leading policy initiatives to create historic rehabilitation financial incentives and providing professional guidance and pro-bono services to historic building owners, public officials, and community advocates. Landmarks Illinois also holds historic easements on properties throughout Illinois. The organization was founded in 1971 by a handful of people who banded together in an effort to save Dankmar Adler and Louis Sullivan's Chicago Stock Exchange Building, which was demolished in 1972. The Stock Exchange Trading Room was reconstructed with some original materials and installed in a new wing of the Art Institute of Chicago in 1976–77.[26] Landmarks Illinois annually hosts the Richard H. Driehaus Foundation Preservation Awards and calls attention to threatened historic sites with its Most Endangered Historic Places in Illinois program, and honors civic and cultural leaders who have made a positive impact on Illinois through its Legendary Landmarks Celebration. The organization provides grants to nonprofit organizations, maintains an online historic resources

Chicago Bauhaus and Beyond gathering in 2019.

directory, produces feasibility and adaptive reuse studies for historic properties, and provides technical assistance on restoration/rehabilitation projects. The organization was a critical partner in providing funding and leadership in the campaign to save the Farnsworth House.

Preservation Chicago is an advocacy organization, founded in 2001 by a group of individuals and friends interested in preserving Chicago's rich architectural heritage and its built environment. Preservation Chicago defends, protects, and helps to promote Chicago's irreplaceable historic landmarks, buildings, and neighborhoods. The organization creates an annual Chicago 7 Most Endangered List and works with stakeholders, elected officials, and community members toward creative reuses and preservation through outreach, education, and partnership. With the shared mission of preserving historic buildings, Preservation Chicago, with its focus on the city, and Landmarks Illinois, with its statewide scope, complement each other.[27]

In a city that tends to focus perhaps too much on Frank Lloyd Wright and Ludwig Mies van der Rohe, a group of interested individuals founded Chicago Bauhaus and Beyond (CBB) in 2004 to celebrate modern architecture and design with an emphasis on the 1930s–70s. Chicago Bauhaus and Beyond's members include collectors, dealers, architects, designers, curators, architectural historians, and enthusiasts. Programs feature home tours, gallery openings, and visits to collections. The founders, musicians Joan and Gary Gand, with realtor Joe Kunkel, created Chicago's first book to focus on modern residential architecture as seen through the lens of *Julius Shulman: Chicago Midcentury Modernism,* written by Gary Gand.[28] The Gands own a house designed by Keck & Keck. Co-founders of Forgotten Chicago Jacob Kaplan and Serhil Chrucky, with others, document aspects of Chicago's built environment, including historical, and broaden access through the website to encourage an appreciation for preservation.

Docomomo US/Chicago is a regional chapter of Docomomo US and serves the greater Chicago area, including neighboring counties in Wisconsin and Indiana and the greater state of Illinois. Docomomo is the international organization for the **do**cumentation and **co**nservation of buildings and sites of the **mo**dern **mo**vement. Founded in 1990 in the Netherlands, Docomomo has active chapters in forty-five countries. The US chapter was founded in 1995 at the first Preserving the Recent Past Conference that was held in Chicago. Docomomo's mission is to increase awareness of modern-movement buildings, sites, and allied arts realized during the twentieth century through education, documentation, conservation, and advocacy. Docomomo works together with local, state, regional, and other preservation and conservation organizations and with governmental agencies to enhance public and professional appreciation and education about our modern built and cultural heritage. Docomomo US maintains an online register of twentieth-century structures and sites in the US. Docomomo US/Chicago sponsors lectures, host tours, and curates symposia in order to increase the awareness of the modern buildings and sites in our city and its surrounding communities.[29]

The Association for Preservation Technology International (APT) has a local Western Great Lakes Chapter that was founded in 2009 by preservation architect Bob Score at the direction of APT International. Membership comprises architects, engineers, contractors, and conservators who specialize in the technical aspects of building restoration. It offers hands-on workshops, craftsman demonstrations, lectures, conferences, and symposia. This important resource for preservation has been enhanced by research in the field and publications supported by The Getty Conservation Institute.[30] Their Conserving Modern Architecture Initiative (CMAI) has sponsored the conservation of iconic residential buildings such as the Charles and Ray Eames House and Studio (Case Study House No. 8; 1949) in the Pacific Palisades area of Los Angeles.

The expertise required to operate within different scenarios of preservation—from architectural history and planning to the rehabilitation, restoration, and reconstruction of historic buildings—is taught at many American universities. In 1964, James Marston Fitch established the first graduate preservation program in the US at the Columbia University Graduate School of Architecture, Planning and Preservation. Many other schools, including the University of Pennsylvania (Philadelphia), Cornell University (Ithaca, New York), the University of Southern California (Los Angeles) and Belmont College, a 2-year program, (St. Clairesville, Ohio) currently offer degrees in historic preservation.[31] In 1993, Professor Donald Kalec, in consultation with noted preservation architects in Chicago, established a Master of Science degree in Historic Preservation at the School of the Art Institute of Chicago. The program was led for many years by Vince Michael, PhD, followed by the current director, Anne T.

Doris Kaplan and Howard R.
Conant House (1953) Glenview
designed by Richard Barancik,
restored and expanded in 2004
by Margaret McCurry.

Sullivan, FAIA, and attracts a talented group of regional preservation professionals with expertise in their respective fields as teaching faculty. Many graduates of the program remain in Chicago to work in a variety of preservation disciplines, including stewarding tax incentives for preservation, writing landmark nominations, preparing Historic American Buildings Survey (HABS) documentation, working in preservation advocacy for government agencies, or providing hands-on preservation skills as contractors, craftspersons, or conservators.

Houses less than fifty years old or even somewhat older present a special challenge, especially those in private hands, since they are often not perceived as "historic enough" and thus unworthy of rigorous approaches to preservation. In the realm of domestic architecture, the desire to "update" kitchens and bathrooms often takes precedence over retaining historic materials and features. Original clients of modern houses, those who commissioned the houses in *Modern in the Middle* and made decisions on design and choice of materials, are among the least likely to make drastic changes because they want to retain their home's authenticity and the memory of their time there. When modern houses change owners, however, the risk of insensitive alterations can increase exponentially. Fortunately there are a number of important modern houses in Chicago's metropolitan area that have changed ownership over the years but serve as a testament to dedicated individuals who have either carefully preserved and renovated them or have simply served as attentive stewards. Examples include the Ruth van Sickle and Albert Sam Ford House (1949) designed by Bruce Goff in Aurora that is currently owned by architectural historian Sidney Robinson; the Lucile Gottschalk and Aaron Heimbach House (1939, p. 108) designed by Bertrand Goldberg in Blue Island: and the Frances Landrum and Ben Rose House (1954, p. 190)

by A. James Speyer in Highland Park, currently under renovation by Baranski Hammer Moretta & Sheehy. The home of architect Walter and Dawn Clark Netsch (1974) in Lincoln Park was recently renovated under the direction of Brian Lee at SOM; and Margaret McCurry restored and thoughtfully added onto the Doris Kaplan and Howard R. Conant Sr. House (1953) by Richard Barancik. The April 2019 "Record Houses" issue of the *Architectural Record* featured a story on Frank Lloyd Wright's 1958 Margaret Soos and Louis B. Fredrick House in Barrington Hills. The new owner hired architect John Eifler, who undertook a careful restoration/ rehabilitation.[32]

Chicago is part of a growing network of cities in America that are taking the heritage of modern residential architecture seriously. High-profile efforts include those in Cape Cod (Cape Cod Modern House Trust), Sarasota (Sarasota Architectural Foundation), and Palm Springs (Palm Springs Preservation Foundation and Modernism Week). Significantly, Philip Johnson's Glass House (1949)—like its progenitor the Farnsworth House—are both part of the portfolio of modern houses owned and operated by the National Trust for Historic Preservation. In parallel to these efforts, numerous informative books on modern architecture, containing a considerable amount of material on significant houses of the period, continue to be published.[33]

Yet, threats of demolition still abound. Recently, citizen groups in the city of Evanston have warded off proposed demolition of the Hildur Freeman and Harley Clarke Mansion (1927) by architect Richard Powers (with landscape architects Jens Jensen and Alfred Caldwell). The Keck & Keck-designed Elizabeth Iglehart and Edward McCormick Blair House (1955) in Lake Bluff, however, was demolished in 2016, and the property was marketed for development shortly afterwards. On a positive note, after languishing and deteriorating for many years, Keck & Keck's 1948 Mildred Rees and Abel Fagen House in Lake Forest was purchased by architect Christopher Enck, who is meticulously restoring it; his plan is to sell the house to an owner who will cherish it.

As authors we hope that *Modern in the Middle* will showcase houses and their architects that have faded from the awareness of historians, preservationists, and the general public to ensure that lesser-known houses as well as the modern icons are preserved for posterity and enjoyed by different generations of homeowners.

Mildred Rees and Abel Fagen House (1948) Lake Forest, designed by Keck & Keck.

Notes

Coda: Revising the Modern House in Chicago

1 — Stuart E. Cohen with introduction by Stanley Tigerman, *Chicago Architects: Documenting the Exhibition of the Same Name Organized by Laurence Booth, Stuart E. Cohen, Stanley Tigerman, and Benjamin Weese* (Chicago: Swallow Press, 1976) published in conjunction with the exhibition *Chicago Architects* at the Time Life in May 1–June 20, 1976: note that Susan Benjamin contributed research to the catalogue and that she would later co-author two books with Stuart Cohen. See also Penelope Dean, "That '70's Show," in Alexander Eisenschmidt with Jonathan Mekinda, eds., *Chicagoisms: The City as Catalyst for Architectural Speculation* (Zurich: Park Books, 2013), 22–37. Blair Kamin, "Adding up the other Chicago 7," *Chicago Tribune,* October 2, 2005, accessed November 28, 2019, chicagotribune.com. Ross Miller, "Architecture after Mies," *Critical Inquiry* 6, no. 2 (Winter 1979), 271–289.

2 — Cohen, *Chicago Architects*, 8–9.

3 — Stuart Cohen, conversation with author, November 30, 2019: revealed that the choice of the lobby of the Time-Life Building was strategic insofar as it was within walking distance from the Museum of Contemporary Art at 237 E. Ontario Street, so the curators hoped that both exhibitions would be viewed together. It was based on an exhibition (and accompanying catalogue) originally curated and edited by Oswald W. Grube, *100 Jahre Architektur in Chicago: Kontinuität von Struktur und Form* for Die Neue Sammlung in Munich, Germany, 1973. Oswald W. Grube, Peter C. Pran, Franz Schulze, *100 Years of Architecture in Chicago: Continuity of Structure and Form* (Chicago: J. Philip O'Hara, 1976) published in conjunction with an exhibition of the same title presented by Stephen Prokopoff as artistic director and Peter C. Pran as consultant at the Museum of Contemporary Art, which was also hosted in conjunction with the celebrations and activities surrounding the United States Bicentennial in 1976.

4 — Nikolaus Pevsner, *Pioneers of the Modern Movement: From William Morris to Walter Gropius* (London: Faber, 1936). For a discussion about the limitations of the *Chicago Architects* exhibition, which included work only by men and the counter response by Chicago's women architects, see Susan Benjamin's "Ruth Koier and Laurence Sjoblom House," (p. 220).

5 — Charles Jencks, *Modern Movements in Architecture* (Garden City, NY: Anchor, 1973); Jencks, *The Language of Post-Modern Architecture* (New York: Rizzoli, 1977); Jencks, "Postmodern and Late Modern: The Essential Definitions," *Chicago Review* 35, no. 4, (1987): 31–58.

6 — Robert Venturi, *Complexity and Contradiction in Architecture* (New York: Museum of Modern Art, 1966), 25: has recently been republished as a two-volume set that includes symposium contributions: Martino Stierli ed., *Robert Venturi's Complexity and Contradiction at Fifty* (New York: Museum of Modern Art, 2019). Although "less is more" is credited to Mies, in reality it was Philip Johnson who used it in his 1947 catalogue. See Fritz Neumeyer, *The Artless Word: Mies van der Rohe on the Building Art* (Cambridge, MA: MIT Press, 1991), xi–xxii.

7 — Frederic Schwartz ed., *Mother's House: The Evolution of Vanna Venturi's House in Chestnut Hill* (New York: Rizzoli, 1992).

8 — A. James Speyer with Frederick Koeper, *Mies van der Rohe* (Chicago: Art Institute of Chicago, 1968) published in conjunction with the exhibition *Ludwig Mies van der Rohe Retrospective* organized by A. James Speyer first held at the Art Institute of Chicago, April 27–June 30, 1968.

9 — Republished as *Five Architects: Eisenman, Graves, Gwathmey, Hejduk, Meier* (New York: Oxford University Press, 1975). (With contributions by Colin Rowe, Kenneth Frampton and Philip Johnson).

10 — Robert A. M. Stern, "The Doubles of Post-Modern," *Harvard Architecture Review* 1 (Spring 1980), 74–87.

11 — During those years two SOM-designed towers transformed Chicago's skyline: John Hancock Center (1969) and Sears Tower (1973). Lake Point Tower (1968) by John Heinrich and George Schipporeit also contributed to a renewed and bold skyline during the same years.

12 — Richard Gray wrote: "The work of the architect, like that of any artist, is an expression of a unique vision and a personal philosophy. The Imprint of the artist's will and an original and meaningful conception are what qualify his work as art." *Seven Chicago Architects Presented by the Richard Gray Gallery (Beeby Booth Cohen Freed Nagle Tigerman Weese)* (Chicago: Richard Gray Gallery, 1976).

13 — Participants included Helmut Jahn, Stuart Cohen, Craig Hodgetts, Michael Graves, Frank Gehry, Jim Freed, Tom Beeby, Larry Booth and Charles Jencks. See Stanley Tigerman, "The State of the Art of Architecture: 2015 vs. 1977," (originally appeared in the September/October 2015 issue of *Chicago Architect*) accessed December 1, 2019, design. newcity.com.

14 — See "The Chicago Seven, plus one, design an 'exquisite corpse' to create a row of post-modernist townhouse," *Architectural Record* 163, no. 7 (June 1978), 39; see also "Introduction" in Alexander Gorlin, *The New American Town House* (New York: Rizzoli, 2000).

15 — See Daniel Kay Hertz, *The Battle of Lincoln Park: Urban Renewal and Gentrification in Chicago* (Cleveland: Belt Publishing, 2018).

16 — James Nagle et al., *Houses: The Architecture of Nagle, Hartray, Danke, Kagan, McKay, Penney* (New York: Edizioni Press, 2005), 70–71. Jay Pridmore, *Total Performance Architecture. The Work of Booth Hansen* (San Francisco: Oro Editions, 2015).

17 — James Ingo Freed not only studied at IIT but also served as Dean from 1975–78; Thomas "Tom" Beeby taught at IIT from 1973–80.

18 — Susan Benjamin, ed., *Winnetka Architecture: Where Past is Present* (Winnetka: Winnetka Historical Museum, 1990), 45.

19 — Joseph Fujikawa, *Oral History of Joseph Fujikawa / Interviewed by Betty J. Blum, Compiled under the Auspices*

of the Chicago Architects Oral History Project, the Ernest R. Graham Study Center for Architectural Drawings, Department of Architecture, the Art Institute of Chicago rev. ed. (Chicago: Art Institute of Chicago, 2003), 13. See also citations in note 10 in my "Ming Djang and Chung Kuo Liao House" (p. 236).

20 — Franz Schulze, *Krueck Sexton: Architects* (New York: The Monacelli Press, 1997). James Steele, *Eames House: Charles and Ray Eames* (London: Phaidon, 1994).

21 — Cheryl Kent ed., *The Nature of Dwellings: The Architecture of David Hovey* (New York: Rizzoli, 2004), 154–65: 166–81.

22 — With the Centre Pompidou in Paris completed in 1977, Renzo Piano and Richard Rogers introduced brilliantly colored architectural elements that tempered the seriousness of the machine-age aesthetic. In Chicago Helmut Jahn would follow suit with his James R. Thompson Center (1985). Jahn, Helmut, conversation with author, June 13, 2018.

23 — Paul Gapp, *Paul Gapp's Chicago: Selected Writings of the Chicago Tribune's Architecture Critic* (Chicago: *Chicago Tribune*, 1980). John Zukowsky, "Exhibitions & Observations on Blueprints, Bricks, and Mortar," in *Masterpieces of Chicago Architecture* (New York: Rizzoli, 2004), 10–22. Martha Thorne, ed., *The Pritzker Architecture Prize: The First Twenty Years* (New York: Harry N. Abrams in association with the Art Institute of Chicago, 1999); Stanley Tigerman, "Significant Events Leading to the Revival of the Chicago Architectural Club," *Chicago Architectural Journal* vol. 2, 1982 (New York: Rizzoli, 1982), 175–77.

24 — See "Dialogue: John Whiteman," *Design Book Review* 15 (Fall 1988), 12–14; Four books were published under the auspices of the CIAU: John Whiteman, *Divisible by 2* (Cambridge, MA: MIT Press, 1990); Ben Nicholson, *Appliance House* (Cambridge, MA: MIT Press, 1990); Mario Gandelsonas, *The Urban Text* (Cambridge, MA: MIT Press, 1991); Richard Burdett, Jeffrey Kipnis, and John Whiteman, eds., *Strategies in Architectural*

Thinking (Cambridge, MA: MIT Press, 1992). See also Dylan Landis, "Old Gold Coast," *Chicago Tribune*, October 23, 1988, accessed December 4, 2019, chicagotribune.com.

25 — Maurizio Casari and Vincenzo Pavan eds., *New Chicago Architecture: Beyond the International Style* (New York: Rizzoli, 1981) published in conjunction with an exhibition of the same title organized by Maurizio Casari, Vincenzo Pavan, and Peter Pran, held at the Chicago Art Institute, May 19– August 17, 1983, held in Verona September 11–October 31, 1981. See Ante Glibota and Frédéric Edelmann, eds., *Chicago: 150 Years of Architecture, 1833–1983* (Paris: Paris Art Center, 1985) and Ante Glibota and Robert Bruegmann, eds., *A Guide to 150 Years of Chicago Architecture* (Chicago: Chicago Review Press, 1985).

26 — John Zukowsky ed., *Chicago Architecture and Design 1923–1993: Reconfiguration of an American Metropolis* (Munich: Prestel, 1993) published in conjunction with an exhibition of the same title organized by John Zukowsky held at the Art Institute of Chicago, June 12–August 29, 1993. Zukowsky, *Chicago Architecture 1872–1922: Birth of a Metropolis* (Munich: Prestel, 1987; reprint 2000) published in conjunction with an exhibition of the same title organized jointly by John Zubrosky, Henri Loyrette, and Heinrich Klotz, held at the Art Institute of Chicago, July 16– September 5, 1988, the Musée d'Orsay, and the Deutsches Architekturmuseum in Frankfurt.

27 — Jean Fulton and Joseph Scanlan, ed., *Turn of the Century Home* (Chicago: Renaissance Society at the University of Chicago, 1994) published in conjunction with an exhibition of the same title organized by Susanne Ghez, held at the Renaissance Society at the University of Chicago, January 16–February 27, 1994.

28 — Heidrun Hoppe, ed., *Evanston: 150 Years 150 Places*, second ed. (Evanston: Design Evanston, 2015).

29 — Cheryl Kent, ed., *Ravine Bluff: A House by David Hovey* (n.p.: Silver Fern Inc., 2008): with an essay by David Hovey.

Chicago: Moving Modern Forward

1 — William J. Murtagh, *Keeping Time: The History and Theory of Preservation in America* (New York: John Wiley & Sons, 1997); Daniel M. Bluestone, *Buildings, Landscapes, and Memory: Case Studies in Historic Preservation* (New York: Norton, 2011).

2 — Daniel M. Bluestone, "Wright Saving Wright: Preserving the Robie House, 1957," in *Rethinking Wright at 150*, eds. Neil Levine and Richard Longstreth (Charlottesville: University of Virginia Press, 2020). After pressure was brought to bear, William Zeckendorf of the redevelopment firm of Webb and Knapp was persuaded to purchase the property to use as an office while constructing the University Apartments and the Hyde Park Shopping Center. In 1962, Zeckendorf donated the property to the University. Susan O'Connor Davis, *Chicago's Hyde Park* (Chicago and London: University of Chicago Press, 2013), 342-43, "The Surprising Savior of Wright's Robie House," *Hyde Park Herald,* July 21, 2004, 450.

3 — The Robie House recently re-opened on March 29, 2019 after an $11 million dollar project with preservation efforts led by Chicago-based Gunny Harboe (Harboe Architects).

4 — Davis, 342 fn: "Likens Seminary 'murder' to German book burning," *Hyde Park Herald,* August 28, 1967, 450.

5 — For an overview see Theodore H. M. Prudon, *Preservation of Modern Architecture* (Hoboken, NJ: John Wiley & Sons, Inc., 2008), see in particular "Preservation of Modern Architecture: The Beginning," pp. 2–23. Edward Diestelkamp, "Modern Houses Open to the Public in Europe and America," in The Modern House Revisited (theme issue), *Journal of Twentieth Century Society* 2 (1996), 86–94.

6 — Frank Lloyd Wright Trust, accessed April 19, 2019, flwright.org.

7 — Accessed April 19, 2019, savewright.org.

8 — See William Tyre, *50 Moments: Highlights from the First Fifty Years of the Glessner*

House Museum 1966–2016 (Chicago: Glessner House Museum, 2016). See also John J. Glessner, *The Story of a House—The House at 1800 Prairie Avenue—Chicago* (Chicago: Glessner House Museum, 2011).

9 — Initially, four young men— two architects who worked in Mies' office (Richard Wintergreen and James Schultz), an attorney (Paul Lurie) an investment banker (Wayne Benjamin)—convinced the sellers of the house to halve the price. Then a Board was formed. The expanded group included: Joseph Benson, Irving Berman, Carl Condit, George Danforth, Maurice English, Wilbert Hasbrouck, Phyllis Lambert, Dirk Lohan, Dan Murphy, Richard Nickel, Herman Pundt, Earl Reed, A. James Speyer, Clement Sylvestro, Ben Weese and Harry Weese. In 1979, the organization became the Chicago Architecture Foundation.

10 — Jay Pridmore, *Seeing the City: Celebrating 50 Years of the Chicago Architecture Foundation 1966–2016* (Chicago: Chicago School of Architecture Foundation, 2016). It later became the Chicago Architecture Foundation and is today the Chicago Architecture Center. The Glessner House Museum is now independent and sponsors tours and a variety of events.

11 — The group included: Leon (Hyde Park Alderman) and Marion Despres, Philip Johnson, Phyllis Lambert, C. F. Murphy, Perkins + Will, Skidmore, Owings & Merrill (SOM), Ben Weese, and Harry and Associates.

12 — Daniel Joseph Whittaker, "Chicago House Museums: An Examination of Motives, Origins, and Transformations of the Institution" (PhD diss., IIT College of Architecture, 2018), for Robie see in particular chapter 7. A group of more than twenty former residences—large and small— have banded together to form *At Home in Chicago.* Each house museum, with its distinctive architecture and collections, is a living artifact showcasing the lives of people who shaped or were shaped by the city, see chicagohousemuseums.org.

13 — Richard Cahan and Michael Williams, *Richard Nickel: Dangerous Years: What He Saw*

and What He Wrote (Chicago: CityFiles Press, 2016).

14 — 1940 US Federal Census, Chicago, IL, Ward 43, Block 10: Henry Babson, head, and Laura Davis Babson, wife.

15 — Richard Nickel and Aaron Siskind (with John Vinci and Ward Miller), The Complete Architecture of Adler & Sullivan (Chicago: Richard Nickel Committee, 2010). Sullivan's legacy was in part preserved thanks to architects who trained as modernists such as Crombie Taylor and John Vinci. Taylor undertook the restoration of the Banquet Hall in Sullivan's Auditorium Building during the 1950s whereas John Vinci reconstructed the Chicago Stock Exchange Trading Room in the 1970s. See John Vinci, The Trading Room: Louis Sullivan and the Chicago Stock Exchange (Chicago: Art Institute of Chicago, 1989). Jeffrey Plank, Crombie Taylor: Modern Architecture, Building Restoration, and the Rediscovery of Louis Sullivan (Richmond, CA: William Stout, 2009). Richard Nickel's career documenting the work of Sullivan is described in Richard Cahan, They All Fall Down: Richard Nickel's Struggle to Save American Architecture (Washington, DC: Preservation Press, National Trust for Historic Preservation, 1994). Richard Nickel was killed on April 13, 1974 when he was attempting to salvage ornament from Louis Sullivan's Old Chicago Stock Exchange Building and portions of the building collapsed on him. He is buried in Graceland Cemetery near the tomb of Louis Sullivan. The Richard Nickel archives are at the Ryerson and Burnham Libraries at the Art Institute of Chicago.

16 — Richard Longstreth ed., The Charnley House: Louis Sullivan, Frank Lloyd Wright, and the Making of Chicago's Gold Coast (Chicago: University of Chicago Press, 2004).

17 — Robin A. Carlascio and Theresa K. Badovich, Saving a Century of Progress: From Their Storied Beginnings to Their Rebirth Along the Dunes National Lakes, Journey with the 1933–34 World's Fair Homes and the Leasees Who Restored Them (Crown Point, IN: Amalfi, 2014).

18 — See indianalandmarks.org.

19 — Unfortunately, the Chicago Historic Resources Survey (CHRS) started in 1983 and completed in 1995 "to analyze the historic and architectural importance of all buildings, objects, structures, and sites constructed in the city prior to 1940" has not been recently updated, accessed May 3, 2019, data.cityofchicago.org

20 — Leon M. Despres (with Kenan Heise), Challenging The Daley Machine: A Chicago Alderman's Memoir (Evanston: Northwestern University Press, 2005), 47–57: see "Saving the City's Outdoor Museum."

21 — See "Chicago Style Conducting a Windshield Survey of the Recent Past," Alliance Review (July-August 2008), accessed May 13, 2019, landmarks.org.

22 — Accessed May 4, 2019, preservation.lacity.org.

23 — Members of the organization recently collaborated on Robert Bruegmann, ed., Art Deco Chicago: Designing Modern America (Chicago: Chicago Art Deco Society in collaboration with the Chicago History Museum, 2018). Distributed by Yale University Press, New Haven and London, 2018.

24 — A.I.A. Chicago's committee—the Historic Resources Knowledge Community—that has educational programs geared toward members of the architectural profession who are interested in historic buildings provides programs that are technical; others are of a general historical nature. The programs are set up to share and educate the members of A.I.A Chicago on the subject, with a focus on the services that architects can provide their clients.

25 — "Landmarks Illinois, Who We Are," landmarks.org and Kaitlyn McAvoy, email to author, April 8, 2019.

26 — John Vinci, The Art Institute of Chicago: The Stock Exchange Trading Room (Chicago: Art Institute of Chicago, 1977).

27 — Preservation Chicago, Mission & Vision, preservationchicago.org: Prior to serving as founding board member, Board president and, currently, Executive Director, Ward (2003–2011) was Executive Director of the Richard Nickel Committee and before that project architect and project manager of the firm of Vinci-Hamp Architects (1983–2003).

28 — Chicago Bauhaus & Beyond, chicagobauhausbeyond.org, Gary Gand, Julius Shulman: Chicago Midcentury Modernism (New York: Rizzoli, 2010).

29 — Docomomo US has as its tagline "Moving Modern Forward." Ever since the founding of Docomomo International in 1988 by Hubert-Jan Henket and Wessel de Jonge (Netherlands), a growing awareness of the historic value of modern architecture has brought together academics and professionals in a shared pursuit of documentation and conservation. Architect Dr. Theodore Prudhon, who teaches preservation at Columbia University, is the founding President of Docomomo US and a board member of Docomomo International. Docomomo US will hold its 2020 symposium "Crossroads of Modern America" in Chicago.

30 — See the important Thomas C. Jester, Twentieth-Century Building Materials: History and Conservation (Los Angeles: Getty Conservation Institute, 2014).

31 — There is a national membership organization for preservation programs, NCPE–the National Council on Preservation Education. Their initial "product" was what was called "The Great List," a pull-out section that was published yearly in the National Trust newsletter that listed all the historic preservation programs in the country. Their website serves that purpose now. A number of preservation architects and engineers who practice in Chicago came out of the University of Illinois at Urbana where they offered a Master of Architecture with areas of specialization, including one in Historic Preservation (started by Prof. Walter Creese), and one in Structures, from which many of our leading preservation engineers graduated.

32 — Sarah Amelar, "A Little Known Gem," Architectural Record 207, no. 4 (April, 2019): 54. Melissa Dalton, "Before & After: Frank Lloyd Wright's Rarely Seen Fredrick House is Deftly Restored," Dwell (May 1, 2019), accessed May 15, 2019, dwell.com.

33 — Michael Webb, Modernism Reborn: Mid-Century American Houses (New York: Universe, 2001). A sampling includes Tomorrow's Houses: New England Modernism (New York: Rizzoli, 2011); Cape Cod Modern: Midcentury Architecture and Community (New York: Metropolis, 2014) Midcentury Houses Today: New Canaan, Connecticut (New York: The Monacelli Press, 2014); Long Island Modernism: 1930–1980 (New York: Norton, 2012); Michigan Modern: Design that Shaped America (Layton, UT: Gibbs Smith, 2016) Minnesota Modern: Architecture and Life at Midcentury (Minneapolis: University of Minnesota Press, 2015); Desert Modernists: The Architects Who Envisioned Midcentury Modern (Palm Springs: Palm Springs Modernism Week and Desert Publications, 2015); and Sarasota Modern (New York: Rizzoli, 2006).

Sylvia Valha and Francis J. Benda House

It is not uncommon for homeowners to identify with the architectural personality of their houses. Shortly after our arrival to Chicago (via Houston), my partner Serge Ambrose and I purchased the modernist Sylvia Valha and Francis J. Benda House, designed by architect Winston Elting and completed in 1939. Our house is located west of Chicago in the late-nineteenth-century railroad suburb of Riverside, a village designed by Frederick L. Olmsted and Calvert Vaux in 1869. The house resides on a site bordering the former Laura Davis and Henry Babson Estate (1907) designed by Louis Sullivan and George Grant Elmslie with landscape architect Jens Jensen. Then as now, Riverside is a demonstration of how the relationship with nature should guide the design of livable communities.

The house designed for the Bendas was most likely Elting's first independent residential commission before he formed an architectural partnership with Paul Schweikher. This flat-roofed house, a rarity in Riverside, is an example of what

Front facade of Benda House (1939) in winter, 2020.

could be described as "gentle" modernism in architecture built during the latter half of Franklin Delano Roosevelt's New-Deal era. Elting, an architect who trained at Princeton and the École des Beaux-Arts, conflated cues gleaned from northern European modern architecture of the late 1920s and '30s (Dutch, English, and German) with approaches to construction and materiality typical of Chicago (as seen in the load-bearing, three-wythe, common brick exterior walls). Although the house is characterized by emerging modern attitudes to site, space, and materiality—exemplified by south-facing large picture windows and modern materials such as glass block—an appreciation for hand craftsmanship and its "design-with-

Rear garden view of Benda House in winter 2020.

nature" qualities distinguish it from the so-called machine-age aesthetic and the International Style typical of the period in Europe.

Serge took the lead on the preservation-restoration of the house. Having trained as both an architect and engineer, he combined design, technical, and construction skills to solve a wide range of issues that arose during the multi-year process. Some key interventions involved returning the kitchen to its original layout and curating the interiors to the original period aesthetic. Serge's oversight of the Benda House project was informed by his deep knowledge of modern architecture and materials. Having spent time living in a number of different cites (Miami, Singapore, Jakarta), Serge is particularly interested in the ways in which variations of climate and materials impact both vernacular and architect-designed buildings. Since 2017 he has served as Chair of the Chicago chapter of Docomomo US and volunteered on the Riverside Historical Commission (2015–18).

Having trained as an architect, historian, and preservationist in Italy before returning to North America to continue my studies (first to Canada and then to the US), I have always considered the built environment as an interwoven fabric in which strands of the past, present, and future coexist. As such, the opportunity to collaborate with Serge while he led the preservation-restoration of our house has greatly enhanced my understanding of the architectural, cultural, economic, and material underpinnings of twentieth-century architecture and the built environment.

Serving on the Board of Directors of Docomomo US and as the inaugural John Vinci Distinguished Research Fellow (IIT College of Architecture) has heightened my awareness of the ongoing challenges to the legacy of the twentieth century. As a historian and preservationist, my teaching, research, and writing is focused on the intersections between culture, technology, and design in the built and natural environment in the Americas and Europe. From my previous books on

preindustrial vernacular traditions and their influence on modern architecture in the Mediterranean, my current research project looks at the transnational forces that have shaped the architecture, infrastructure, and landscape of cities of the Americas ranging from Houston to Chicago. I am most interested in buildings that—like the Benda House—are cosmopolitan in aspiration but grounded in local realities.

Historic photo with awnings (c. 1980).

Elevations and details. Drawing by Winston Elting (1938).

Serge and I are keenly aware of the ways in which advocacy, education, and preservation overlap. We all need to work collectively if our modern architectural heritage is to be safeguarded for future generations. Living in a home that simultaneously provides comfort (a notion that some modernist architects overlooked) and the necessities of modern life such as a two-car garage (a rare feature for 1930s houses) has enhanced our appreciation of historic modernism and reinforces our understanding of the important role it continues to play in contemporary life. Although the process has required equal doses of perseverance, patience, and a bit of obsessive folly, it has proven a worthwhile endeavor and we encourage others to take on similar challenges. —MS

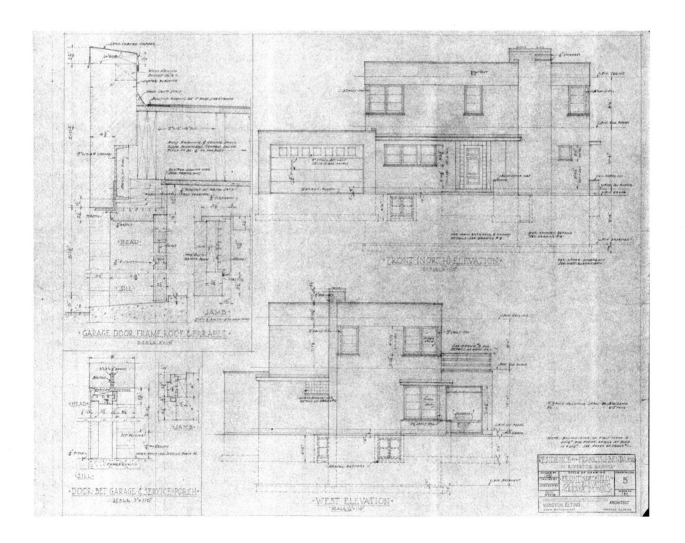

Ruth Danielson and Hilmer V. Swenson House

The Authors and Their Homes: Susan & Wayne Benjamin

Looking back on the over forty-five years I have devoted to historic preservation, I wonder if my interest in architecture had its genesis in childhood. As a little girl growing up in Minneapolis, I drew floor plans of my dreamhouse (complete with an indoor swimming pool) while my friends were making paper dolls. My father, Lou Sinykin, who was a furniture manufacturer, took my mother, Mildred Mark, and me around to showrooms at the Chicago markets, which nurtured my interest in the larger world of design.

After arriving at Brown University in 1960, I began my major in Art History, discovered the joys of studying the history of architecture, and had the good fortune of being mentored by architectural historian William Jordy. I settled in Chicago where I acquired various jobs related to architecture, including stints with the Chicago School of Architecture Foundation (today the Chicago Architecture Center), the Chicago Chapter of the AIA, and the Commission on Chicago Landmarks. I married Wayne Benjamin who was himself an architecture enthusiast (he had been a founder of the Chicago Architecture Foundation, which was formed in 1966 to purchase and preserve H. H. Richardson's Glessner House). After a few years of apartment living, we went house hunting.

In 1973, Wayne and I bought a modernist house in the North Shore suburb of Highland Park, not far from the Dubin House and the site of the Kunstadter House. My interest in modernism began in earnest when we moved into our house designed in 1941 by Larry Perkins of Perkins, Wheeler & Will. Although Larry Perkins and his partner Philip Will received international acclaim for their school designs, beginning with Crow Island School in Winnetka (1940, in collaboration with Eliel and Eero Saarinen), Larry was always fond of our house, and we would have him and his wife Midge over for a glass of sherry, Bach, and conversation. Larry was a man of huge spirit and great ideas; we feel lucky to have known him. Larry's clients for our house were Ruth Danielson and Hilmer V. Swenson, whose advertising company created the "say it with flowers" publicity campaign that brought florists generous returns and established a legendary slogan.

Our redwood-clad house is traditional in its rectangular form. Yet it is protomodern—lacking any reference to historical styles, with an open plan, large corner windows, and a multilevel interior. It is a transitional house, reflecting the early work of a generation of Chicago modernists influenced by both Frank Lloyd Wright and the International Style. Over the more than forty-five years we have lived here, we have restored, reconfigured, and updated the house multiple times without compromising its historic features. That is how we preservationists think. It drove me crazy that the simple living/dining room redwood crown molding had been painted "to make the ceiling look higher." The first thing we did was strip the redwood so that the walls read, as they were intended to, like geometric panels. A little thing, but more was to follow. We remodeled our kitchen, hiring Cynthia Weese who created a kitchen that we still view as perfect; we divided an upstairs bedroom to create private spaces for our two sons; we restored our hall bath without even changing the fixtures. Best of all, we converted the back of our tandem garage into my office (lined with books) to accommodate my passion and vocation.

The opportunity to explore further and write about Chicago's wealth of modern houses began in 1976, when I had the pleasure of assembling a small traveling exhibition on the subject with architects Jim Nagle and Roland Lieber. We became enthralled with George Fred Keck's Crystal House, built for the Century of Progress International Exposition in 1934, and uncovered houses designed by some of the region's great midcentury architects, including Paul Schweikher, Winston Elting, and Bertrand Goldberg. Gorgeous Hedrich Blessing photographs illustrated the selections. Our research turned up buildings that never had received much public attention and in turn contributed to the game-changing exhibition *Chicago Architects,* organized by Stuart Cohen, Stanley Tigerman, Laurence Booth, and Benjamin Weese, which was displayed in the lobby of Chicago's Time Life Building.

By the early 2000s, I devoted myself to historic preservation, founding Benjamin Historic Certifications in 2004, with a focus on writing landmark nominations, preparing Historic American Buildings Survey documentation, and working with developers and homeowners to acquire tax incentives for rehabilitating historic buildings. My opportunity to write books on the regions architecture began around the same time when architect Stuart Cohen and I coauthored *North Shore Chicago, Houses of the Lakefront Suburbs, 1890–1940* and *Great Houses of Chicago, 1871–1921,* published by Acanthus Press in 2004 and 2008 respectively.

Having acquired experience in the field, I am frequently invited to lecture on a variety of topics related to architecture and preservation. A favorite is on the history of the shopping mall along with other lectures that focus on modern residential architecture. Several years ago I team-taught (with Illinois State Historic Preservation Office architects Anthony Rubano and Carol Dyson) a course at the School of the Art Institute of Chicago, "From Lustron to Neon, Preserving the Recent Past."

Modern in the Middle marks the culmination of my fascination with the modernist tradition of the Chicago area. The extensive research undertaken to write about it has allowed me to explore in depth the layers of history that establish the importance of Chicago's modern residential architecture and see it recognized as a significant component of Chicago's rich architectural heritage. The stories of these amazing and often little-known houses need to be told—with the goal that they be better understood, valued for their significance, and preserved. —SSB

Contributors

Serge Ambrose trained as an architect and engineer, earning his Bachelor of Science in Industrial Engineering from the University of Miami and a Master of Architecture from Virginia Polytechnic Institute and State University. He is focused on contemporary design and the conservation of twentieth-century architectural heritage. He has worked on building projects in Florida, Texas, and Illinois. Ambrose has served as Chair of the Docomomo US/Chicago chapter since 2017 and presented projects and research at several Docomomo US symposia and at other conferences. He is a member of the Association for Preservation Technology and served on the Riverside Historical Commission. He is coauthoring, with his partner Michelangelo Sabatino, a forthcoming book about the preservation-restoration of their modernist house in Riverside, Illinois.

Pauline Saliga is executive director of the Society of Architectural Historians, where she oversees strategic planning and fundraising for the Chicago-based international society. Saliga's major initiatives for SAH include the online educational resources SAH Archipedia, the online encyclopedia of U.S. architecture; SAHARA, an online image bank for teaching and research; and a multimedia edition of JSAH.

In a nearly twenty-year curatorial career, with research emphasis in nineteenth- and twentieth-century American architecture and its international influences, Saliga has served as Assistant Curator at the Museum of Contemporary Art in Chicago and Associate Curator in the Department of Architecture at The Art Institute of Chicago. At the Art Institute, she organized numerous oral histories of Mies disciples, as well as exhibitions and catalogues focusing on American and European architecture, including *Fragments of Chicago's Past; Building in a New Spain: Contemporary Spanish Architecture; and Design for the Continuous Present: The Architecture of Bruce Goff, 1904–1982.* Other of her publications include *The Sky's the Limit: A Century of Chicago Skyscrapers* as well as numerous museum catalogs, articles, and reviews.

Acknowledgments

Our book is dedicated to Betty J. Blum, who developed and nurtured the Chicago Architects Oral History Project (CAOHP) at the Ernest R. Graham Study Center for Architectural Drawings, Department of Architecture, the Art Institute of Chicago. The interviews that Betty spearheaded were an invaluable resource on many of Chicago's most accomplished architects and provided us with material that guided our understanding of the work of the talented architects we feature in our book. The program she developed has included other interviewers. We hope that the project extends to include future generations of architects to preserve a record of the individuals behind Chicago's exceptional architecture.

It is with heartfelt appreciation that we thank all those who have assisted and supported us throughout our journey to bring the complex history of Chicago's modern houses to the attention of a general and specialized audience. Without a team effort of numerous institutions, architects, historians, homeowners, journalists, preservationists, and enthusiasts, including colleagues, family, and friends, *Modern in the Middle: Chicago Houses 1929–1975* would still be a dream.

At a time when readers are relying on the internet and electronic media instead of traditional printed matter, we are especially grateful to be published by The Monacelli Press. We owe our commissioning editor Alan Rapp a special thank you for his confidence in our book project and his assistance during the research, writing, and layout stages.

We have been most fortunate to have Nancy Mangum McCaslin as our developmental editor. Not only has she been a thoughtful and careful critic to ensure accuracy and consistency but, because of her professionalism, has contributed information from her own careful research. Nancy understands the important role that spouses/partners have played in residential architecture, and they are credited with their contributions throughout our book. Bud Rodecker and Alyssa Arnesen, of the talented communication design practice Thirst based in Chicago, provided expertise and patience during the process of designing the book. We thank our copyeditor Laurie Manfra.

We especially wish to thank Pauline Saliga, executive director of the Society of Architectural Historians, who wrote the foreword and from the beginning encouraged our publication. Pauline brings an important perspective on the extent of research and analysis of modern architecture that preceded our work on this book.

Columbia University's Barry Bergdoll, who is the Meyer Shapiro Professor of Art History and Archaeology, suggested *Modern in the Middle* as the title for our book. The play on middle was enticing, from the moment he suggested it. The houses featured in our book were constructed in America's heartland, the middle of our country. The clients were largely middle or upper middle class. Many houses in the book contain influences by Frank Lloyd Wright and Ludwig Mies van der Rohe—expressing an architectural middle ground. "Middle"—with all its many connotations and associations—has been a guiding concept for us.

From the outset we aimed to make *Modern in the Middle* a visually compelling and informative book. A grant from the Fred Eychaner Fund made the costs associated with research, writing, and publication possible. The AIA Chicago Foundation, with the support of its Board, acted as fiscal agent. Zurich Esposito, executive vice president of AIA Chicago, has been encouraging our endeavor from the moment he learned about the possibility of a book on the subject being published. Joan Pomeranc, program director at AIA Chicago, has continuously been supportive. A number of board members of the AIA Chicago Foundation, including Lisa Di Chiera, Roberta Feldman, and Mary K. Woolever, provided valuable feedback during initial conversations about the book. Special thanks to Jim McDonough and Brad White at the Alphawood Foundation for their support of our book. Additional funding for this project was provided by former dean Michelangelo Sabatino through the Rowe Family College of Architecture Dean Endowed Chair and the John Vinci Distinguished Research Fellowship at the Illinois Institute of Technology.

Two Chicago institutions played significant roles because of their extraordinary collections and talented staff: the Chicago History Museum and the Art Institute of Chicago. Because of his faith in the project, Russell L. Lewis Jr., former executive vice president and chief historian at the Chicago History Museum (who passed away in 2019) gave us unlimited access to the treasure trove of Hedrich Blessing photographs in the museum's collection. We wish Russell were still alive to see *Modern in the Middle* come to fruition. Angela Hoover, rights and reproductions manager at the CHM, was always there to provide us access to photographs. Olivia Mahoney, retired senior curator at the museum, continuously provided insights, knowledge, and support. Lesley A. Martin, an extraordinary research librarian at the museum Research Center, helped us locate images and information when material wasn't easily attainable.

At the Art Institute of Chicago, Nathaniel Parks, Tigerman McCurry Art and Architecture archivist of the Ryerson and Burnham Libraries, provided us with images from the collection of photographs taken by Richard Nickel and other key photographers. From the Department of Architecture and Design, Lori Boyer former manager of collections sought out the beautiful drawings we requested, Alison Fisher, Associate Curator, provided information on Bertrand Goldberg and was always supportive, as was Zoë Ryan, John H. Bryan Chair and Curator. In New York, Paul Galloway, collection specialist in the Department of Architecture & Design at the Museum of Modern Art, and Jennifer Belt, permissions director at Art Resource, were very helpful.

The majority of images in the book are archival, taken by the talented photographers working at the legendary studio Hedrich Blessing. Jon Miller, former president of Hedrich Blessing, provided time and advice on the selection of images. Other contemporary photographers provided images foremost among them Bill Zbaren, who photographed our respective houses and prepared images for the book before printing. James Caulfield, Dave Burke Harris for Skidmore Owens & Merrill, and Steve Hall also provided beautiful photographs.

Although we have relied upon archives and libraries for much of the research, a special thanks goes to the individuals who have worked to make available digital editions of magazines and journals, including *Arts & Architecture, Architectural Forum,* and *Architectural Record.* In particular the USModernist Library and the Assoc. for Preservation Technology have played an important role in our access to historical publications.

We wish to thank former and current homeowners, who have played an important role in safeguarding their homes and who have shared their stories of proud ownership with us, which we list with the name of the house. These include Sue Bush (Fisher), Lydia Henkins (Dubin), Bruce Grieve (Morse), Margaret McRaith (Mullen), Martyl Langsdorf (Schweikher), Tom Hawley and Tom Mantel (Heimbach), Kathryn and James Govas (Elting), Tim Smith (Dewey Jr.), Eileen and Dennis Peterson (Ganster), Sidney Robinson (Ford), Barry Alberts (Ennis), Rian and Leon Walker (Gidwitz), Kimberly and Joseph Lyons (Raftery), Elizabeth Moulis (Frazier-Moulis), Fran and Ben Rose (Rose), Sue Weese Drucker Frank (Drucker), Toyea Knazze (Moutoussamy), Charles Baumann (Brownson), Pamela and Michael Orr (Johnson),

Claudine and Giorgio Lostao (Deever Rockwell II), Elizabeth Solaro and Joe Frank (Haid), Mark Smithe and Will Forrest (Netsch), Margaret and Paul Lurie (Lurie), Iris Goldstein (Goldstein), Gail and Tom Hodges and George Larson (Larson). Gordon Gill (Siegel), Doug Hoekstra (Hoekstra), Eileen and David Hovey (Hovey I and II), Goran and Marianne Strokirk (Meitus), Megan and Frank Beidler (Glore), Christoph and Char Lichtenfeld (Armco-Ferro), Jennifer Nickerson (Lieberman), Fred Eychaner (Eychaner Lee), Susan Manilow (Manilow).

Others graciously provided images and information on their own houses, ones they grew up in or that are/were in their families, including architects Margaret McCurry and Marian Tweedie (McCurry), architect Don Wrobleski (Wrobleski), Lisa Brunke (Binkley), Howard Kaplan (Colburn), Nancy Stevenson (Stevenson), Mike and Sarah Petersdorf (Muirhead), and Anne Stevens (Gutnayer), Jeanne Moutoussamy-Ashe (Moutoussamy), Jennifer Sjoblom and Nancy Sjoblom (Sjoblom) Rachel Helstein (Helstein), David Nelson (Deever Rockwell I), Kim Freeark (Freeark), Elizabeth Fujikawa (Fujikawa), Jim and Kathleen Nagle (Nagle), and Paul Conterato (Conterato).

Many professionals have contributed time and made suggestions about the content and ways to shape the text. Special thanks go to Nancy Eklund Later for making valuable suggestions to Susan for the book early on. We have had a number of insightful discussions with architects including Laurence "Larry" Booth, Peter Dubin, Chris Enck, Heidi Granke, Gunny Harboe, Tom Jacobs, Ronald Krueck, Dirk Lohan, Kathy and Jim Nagle, Keith Olsen, Kenneth Schroeder, Stanley Tigerman, John Vinci, Cynthia Weese, Dan Wheeler, Paul Young, and Todd Zeiger. Landscape architect Ernest Wong provided information about the Liao House designed by his father, Y. C. Wong. Stuart Cohen shared information on Chicago architecture in the 1970s and the genesis of the exhibition *Chicago Architects*. Architectural writers and historians who have also offered insights over time include Daniel Bluestone, Robert Boyce, Robert Bruegmann, Thomas Dyja, Dan Fitzpatrick, Iker Gil, Kevin and Elaine Harrington, Sandy Isenstadt, Pamela G. Kirschner, Vicki Matranga, Jonathan Mekinda, Arthur Miller, Annie Moldafsky, Lisa Napoles, Jay Pridmore, Sidney Robinson, Robert Sharoff, Terry Tatum, Gwendolyn Wright, and David Van Zanten.

Special thanks to William Tyre, curator and program director of the Glessner House, who provided a key photograph of the house when it was for sale and to

Todd Wenger, executive director of the Schweikher House Preservation Trust, who redrew floor plans of the Schweikher House for our book. Scott Mehaffey, executive director of the Farnsworth House, provided us with a fascinating tour of stunning houses located in Chicago's south suburbs of Flossmoor and Olympia Fields. John McKinnon, executive director of the Elmhurst Art Museum, assisted with research about the McCormick House. Geneva preservation planner Mike Lambert, with Elizabeth Safanda, arranged for visits to special houses in his community, including the Jacques Brownson House. Katherine Hamilton-Smith, director of public affairs and development at Lake County Forest Preserves, shared her extensive knowledge of the Stevenson Farm as we toured the Stevenson House together. John Waters, preservation programs manager of the Frank Lloyd Wright Preservation Conservancy, provided information and insights into the design of Wright's Usonian houses, especially the Kathryn Dougherty and Lloyd Lewis House. Architect Clarence Krusinski shared information on his design for the Walgreen House. John Zukowsky, retired founding curator of Architecture at the Art Institute of Chicago, provided an overview of the Chicago Architects Oral History Project undertaken in his department.

Chicago-based individuals who work to inform the public about modern and contemporary architecture and have helped build a culture of preservation include: Blair Kamin (*Chicago Tribune*), Joan and Gary Gand and Joe Kunkel (Chicago Bauhaus & Beyond), Lou Zucaro (Modern Illinois), Serge Ambrose (Docomomo US/Chicago), Ward Miller (Preservation Chicago), Bonnie McDonald and Lisa di Chiera (Landmarks Illinois), and Matt Crawford (City of Chicago, Landmarks Division). In Springfield, architects Anthony Rubano, Carol Dyson, Darius Bryika, and Anna Margaret Barris of the Illinois State Historic Preservation Office support the preservation of modern architecture.

Susan wishes to personally thank numerous supportive friends and family. These include Gwen Sommers Yant, Jeanne Sylvester, Andrew Elders, Liz O'Brien, Paul Bergmann and Jan Gibson, Carolyn and Walker Johnson, Louise Holland, Nan Greenough, Craig White, Lisa Temkin, Michael and David Benjamin, Nicole Brock, and many more. Susan's husband, Wayne, has been encouraging her for years to write this book, knowing of her passion for the subject, and has consistently supported her through all of the inevitable trials and tribulations of making a dream become reality.

Michelangelo wishes to personally thank Fred Eychaner for his ongoing support and above all for his commitment to excellence in architecture, past and present. He also wishes to thank students, staff, and faculty of IIT's College of Architecture (CoA) for their help throughout the research and writing process: Marcos Petroli (PhD candidate), Andrew Jiang (BArch), and Abhinaya Iyer (BArch) assisted with sourcing images. Staff members Chris Manuel, Dina Taylor, and Amber Lochner provided logistics and encouragement when needed. Kim Soss (Graham Resource Center) and Mindy Pugh (IIT university archivist) also provided assistance. Although Reed Kroloff (current Dean of the CoA) started his appointment when the book was well into production, he supported the effort upon his arrival. Michelangelo also wishes to thank Susan and Wayne Benjamin for sharing insights with him and his partner Serge during a memorable visit to Crow Island School in Winnetka the first summer after arriving in Chicago in 2015. The seeds of our future collaboration were planted during that tour and meeting. Finally, and most importantly, goes a special thank you to Serge for coauthoring the essay on preservation "Chicago: Moving Modern Forward" and for his assistance throughout the entire process of writing the book. The research necessary for the preservation-restoration of our modernist house led by Serge has offered many opportunities for productive overlap.

Although the focus of our book is Chicago, across the US and beyond, a number of public and private organizations as well as individuals work daily to promote and protect the legacy of twentieth-century modern houses. For this team effort across geographies and languages, we offer a collective thank you for your commitment and endurance in the face of ongoing challenges.

Susan S. Benjamin and Michelangelo Sabatino

Credits

All reasonable efforts have been made to ascertain and obtain licenses to use third party images and materials.

Courtesy of:

Abraham Lincoln Presidential Library, Adlai Stevenson II Collection **107 bottom.**

Abraham Lincoln Presidential Library, Elizabeth Stevenson Ives Collection **105 left.**

Serge Ambrose and Michelangelo Sabatino Collection **322, 323.**

Architectural Book Publishing Co., Inc. **23 left-right, 25 top.**

The Architectural Forum **13 top, 25 bottom, 67 left, 95 bottom, 123 top.**

Architectural Forum Editors, *The 1940 Book of Small Houses* (Simon and Schuster, 1939) **81.**

The Architectural Press **15 top.**

Architectural Record (Courtesy BNP Media) **15 bottom, 24 bottom, 146 middle-left.**

Stanley D. Anderson Archives and Paul Bergmann **106 top-bottom.**

The Art Institute of Chicago, Architecture and Design Department: 1988.411.6-1988.411.10 **65 top,** 1984.741.21 **133 top.**

The Art Institute of Chicago, Ryerson and Burnham Archives:

— Baldwin Kingrey Collection: (Ferenc Berko photographer) 200601_131205_005 **22 top-left.**

— Irving W. Colburn Papers: 200210_200204-001 **291 top.**

— Crombie Taylor Papers: 20105_191206-001 **146 middle-right,** 20105_191206-003 **149.**

— General Collection: *Architectural Forum* (John Skara,

photographer) 000000_190304-001 **64,** 000000_190304-002 **66,** *Architectural Record* 000000_190304-007 **58,** 000000_190304-012 **59 left,** 000000_190304-005 **59 right,** 000000_190304-011 **60 top,** 000000_190304-008 **60 bottom,** 000000_190304-006 **61,** 000000_190304-009 **62.**

— Bruce Goff Archive: 199001_170816-002 **152,** 199001_191209-003 **153,** 199001_180817-001 **154,** 199001_170816-003 **155 top.**

— Bertrand Goldberg Archive: 200203.081229-135 **109,** 200203.081229-140 **169.**

— Historic Architecture and Landscape Image Collection: (J. W. Taylor, photographer) 16473 **40,** 2437 **41,** M080750b **65 bottom** M080751b **67 right.**

— Richard Nickel Archive: 201006_190304-001 **145,** 201006_190304-003 **147,** 201006_190304-002 **148,** 201006_190304-005 **232,** 201006_190304-007 **233 top,** 201006_190304-008 **233 bottom,** 201006_190304-009 **234,** 201006_190304-010 **235 right,** 201006_200225-001 **306–07,** 201006_110815-022 **307 top.**

— A. James Speyer Collection: 199706_200114-002 **20 bottom,** (Richard Nickel photographer) 199706_190304-002 **156,** 199706_190304-004 **157 top,** 199706_190304-001 **157 bottom,** 199706_190304-011 **193,** (Harry Callahan photographer) 199706_190304-007 **190,** 199706_190304-008 **192 top,** (Tom Yee photographer) 199706_190304-005 **192 bottom-left,** 199706_190304-010 **192 bottom-right,** (Tom Yee photographer) 199706_190304-006 **195 top.**

— Tigerman McCurry Archive: 201703_190304-007 **256,** 201703_190304-008 **257 top,** 201703_190304-010 **257 bottom,** 201703_190304-002 **262,** 201703_190304-004 **263,** 201703_190304-005 **264,** 201703_190304-006 **265,** 201703_191216-001 **291 bottom.**

The Art Institute of Chicago / Art Resource, NY **294, 294–95.**

Arts & Architecture © Courtesy Travers Family Trust **237.**

Susan Benjamin **52, 212, 250, 311;** Susan Benjamin Collection **104, 107 top, 104.**

Brick Manufacturers' Association of America (1933) **18.**

Lisa Brunke **150 left-right, 151.**

Jacques Brownson, MS Thesis 1954, Illinois Institute of Technology University Archives **177.**

Bulletin of the Atomic Scientists (June 1947) **103 right.**

Photography by James Caulfield © 2019 **13 bottom, 39.**

Chicago History Museum: ICHi-015955 **38 right,** ICHi-173909 **45,** ICHi-173907 **220,** ICHi-173908 **221 left,** ICHi-173904 **221 top-right,** ICHi-173905 **221 bottom-right,** ICHi-173906 **222,** ICHi-173902 **223,** ICHi-173903 **225.**

Chicago History Museum, Hedrich-Blessing Collection: HB-19312-c **10,** HB-09789-a **17,** HB-06184-h2 **19 bottom,** HB-05554-c **20 top,** HB-19545-a **21 top-left,** HB-09280 **22 top-right,** HB-03929-c **26,** HB-05253-d **27 top,** HB-07630-r **27 bottom,** HB-13809-j5 **30,** HB-04414-1i **38 left,** HB-04414-1h **42,** HB-04414-g6 **43,** HB-04414-5d3 **44,** HB-044142-k **46,** HB-25252-d8 **49,** HB-28204-y4 **50,** HB-33664-v **51,** HB-35339-h **68,** HB-35339-d

70 bottom, HB-35339-f **71,** HB-04382-c **76,** HB-04382-n **77 left,** HB-04382-p **77 right,** HB-04871-a **78,** HB-04871-i **79 top,** HB-04871-b **79 bottom,** HB-04871-k **80 left,** HB-04871-j **80 right,** HB-03343-i **82,** HB-03343-h **83 top,** HB-03343-a **83 bottom,** HB-04781-x **84,** HB-04781-p **85,** HB-04969-b **86 top,** HB-04969-d **86 bottom,** HB-04781-o **87,** HB-04781 **88,** HB-04781-m **89 top,** HB-04781-d **89 bottom,** HB-04868-a **92,** HB-04868-f **93 left,** HB-04868-e **93 right,** HB-04811-d **94,** HB-04811-m **95 top,** HB-09276-a **96,** HB-09276-e **97,** HB-09276-q **98 left,** HB-09276-h **98 right,** HB-09276-p **100,** HB-09276-c **101,** HB-09276-f **102,** HB-09276-k **103 left,** HB-08164-g **108–09,** HB-08164-d **110,** HB-08164-b **111,** HB-06485-o **112,** HB-06485-a **113,** HB-06485-i **114 left,** HB-06485-f **114 right,** HB-06485-h **116,** HB-06485-j **117 top,** HB-05321-b **118,** HB-04936-e **119,** HB-05321-n **120,** HB-05321-l **121 bottom,** HB-05659-a **122,** HB-05659-h **123 bottom,** HB-05659-d **124 left,** HB-05659-n **124 right,** HB-056559-j **125,** HB-14162-a **126,** HB-14162-j **127 left,** HB-14162-m **127 right,** HB-14162-p **128,** HB-14162-r **129 bottom,** HB-06703-x **130,** HB-06703-a2 **129 top,** HB-06703-n **131 bottom,** HB-09279-l **132,** HB-09279-k **133 bottom,** HB-09279-b **134 left,** HB-09279-c **134 right,** HB-09279-i **135,** HB-11508-d **136,** HB-11508-p **137,** HB-11508-q **138,** HB-11508-j **139 left,** HB-11508-g **139 right,** HB-12283-o **140,** HB-12283-p **141,** HB-12283-q **142,** HB-12283-b2 **143,** HB-13744-g **144,** HB-15347-a **158,** HB-15347-c **159 right,** HB-15347-k **160,** HB-15347-g **161 left,** HB-15347-l **161 top-right,** HB-15347-i **161 bottom-right,** HB-14490-d **162-63,** HB-14490-j **164,** HB-14490-m **165,** HB-14490-f **166,**

HB-14490-k **166-67**, HB-15588-a **168**, HB-15588-f **170 top**, HB-15588-c **170 bottom**, HB-15588-j **171**, HB-15588-h **172**, HB-15588-l **173 left**, HB-15588-n **173 right**, HB-16244-i **180**, HB-16244-b **181**, HB-16244-j **182 top-left**, HB-16244-m **182 top-right**, HB-16244-a **182 bottom**, HB-16244-h **183 top**, HB-16244-f **183 bottom**, HB-15690-b **184**, HB-15690-f **185 top**, HB-17555-a **186**, HB-17555-c: **187**, HB-18583-a **188**, HB-18583-c **189 left**, HB-18583-g **189 right**, HB-38426-m2 **191**, HB-38426-b **194**, HB-38426-l2 **195 bottom**, HB-19367-b **199 top**, HB-19367-a **199 bottom**, HB-18584-h **204**, HB-18584-c **205 left**, HB-18584-a **205 right**, HB-18930-a **206**, HB-18930-d **208**, HB-18930-c **209**, HB-18930-b **210**, HB-18930-h **211**, HB-22311-c2 **216**, HB-22311-f **217 left**, HB-22311-k **217 right**, HB-22311-l **218 left**, HB-22311-v **218 right**, HB-22311-p **219 left**, HB-22311-d **219 right**, HB-27821-c **235 left-bottom**, HB-27821-b **235 left-top**, HB-28781-c **236**, HB-2878-1d **238**, HB-28781a2 **239**, HB-32031-m **241 top-right**, HB-32031-q **241 bottom**, HB-32031-p **242**, HB-32031-i **243 top**, HB-32031-x **243 bottom**, HB-34323-f **244**, HB-34323-e **245 top**, HB-34323-d **245 bottom**, HB-3432-3c **246**, HB-34323-b **247**, HB-13810-m **302**, HB-31384-a **304**, HB-19312-b **305 bottom**, HB-1931-2b **305**, HB-03929-a **309 top**, HB-13711-f **314-15**.

Chicago Daily Tribune, June 12, 1932 **16 bottom**.

Gorman Child, The Newberry Library, Chicago **12**.

Stuart E. Cohen, *Chicago Architects* (Swallow Press, 1976) **90**, (Idaka photographer) **146 top**, **289 top**.

Paul Conterato **296 top**, **296 upper-middle**.

Arina Dähnick photographer **37**.

Photograph Robert Damora © Damora Archive **19 top**.

Hugh Dalziel Duncan, *Culture and Democracy* (Bedminster Press, 1965) **32**.

Alan Dunn (George Schipporeit Family) **31**.

Ebony, Johnson Publishing Company **33 top**.

Wolf Von Eckardt, *Mid-Century Architecture in America* (John Hopkins University Press, 1961) **16 top left**.

Elbert Peets Papers, #2772. Division of Rare and Manuscript Collections, Cornell University Library **29**.

Eliot Elisofon/The LIFE Picture Collection/Getty Images **155 bottom**.

Farnsworth House / National Trust for Historic Preservation **303 bottom**.

Joseph Frank Collection **240**, **241 top-left**.

Geneva History Museum, Jacques Brownson photographer **176–179**.

Gordon Gill and © Connor Steinkamp Photography **293 bottom**.

Jeff Goldberg / Esto **301**.

Mel Gray and Scott Mehaffey **35 bottom**.

Richard Gray Gallery **290 top left**.

Bruce and Laureen Grieve **69**.

© 1960 Homer Grooman, published by the Chicago Association of Commerce and Industry (Chicagoland Chamber of Commerce) **54–55**.

Oswald W. Grube, Peter C. Pran, and Franz Schulze, *100 Years of Architecture in Chicago: Continuity of Structure and Form* (Follett, 1978) **249**, **289 bottom**.

Steve Hall photographer **312–13**.

Darris Lee Harris photographer **309 bottom**.

Ruyell Ho photographer **248**, **251 top**, **251 bottom**.

Reprinted with permission of *House Beautiful* (Hearst Magazines) **34**.

© Timothy Hursley photographer **297**.

Anthony Jones, *The Netsch House: Living with Art* (2014) **253 top-bottom**, **254 left**, **255 top-bottom**.

Howard Kaplan photographer **91 left**; Howard Kaplan Collection **91 right**.

Marvin Koner and Daniel Rubin photographers **305 top**.

Joe Kunkel, Baird & Warner, and Jamie Zimpelmann, VHT Studios **35 top**.

George A. Larson **299 bottom**.

Sheila Lewis photographer and Elmhurst History Museum **308 left**.

Courtesy Photo © MCA **288**.

Margaret McCurry **72**; (Gerald Young photographer) **73 left-right**, **74 left-right**, **75**.

Digital Image © The Museum of Modern Art / Licensed by SCALA / Art Resource, NY **16 top right**, **21**, **36**, **157**, **163**, **185**.

George Nelson and Henry Wright, *Tomorrow's House: How to Plan Your Post-War Home Now* (Simon and Schuster, 1945) **121 top**.

Optima, Inc. and Bill Timmerman photographer **298**.

Optima, Inc. and David Hovey photographer **299 top**.

Oxford University Press **290 top right**.

Michael and Sarah Petersdorf **174**, **175**.

Maurizio Casari and Vincenzo Pavan, eds., *Beyond the International Style: New Chicago Architecture* (Rizzoli, 1981) **290 bottom**.

Pineapple Labs **296, middle lower**, **296 bottom**.

Press Release historic image **117 bottom**.

Progressive Architecture 36, (December, 1955) **159 left**.

Monica Pidgeon and Theo Crosby, *An Anthology of Houses* (Reinhold, 1960), **207**.

Felicity Rich, 2002. Vincent L. Michael, *The Architecture of Barry Byrne: Taking the Prairie School to Europe* (University of Illinois Press, 2013), **109**, **53**.

Riverside Historical Commission **28**.

Rolscreen Company / Pella: **70 top**.

SMNG Architecture and Ron Gordon photographer **300 top**.

SOM | © Dave Burk Harris **252**, **254 right**.

Anne Stevens **213**, **214 top-bottom**, **215**.

Nancy and Adlai Stevenson III **105 right**.

William Allin Storrer, *The Frank Lloyd Wright Companion* (University of Chicago, 1993) **115**.

© Hiroshi Sugimoto, Courtesy Fraenkel Gallery, San Francisco **11**.

Edgar Tafel, *Years with Frank Lloyd Wright, Apprentice to Genius* (Dover, 1979) **47**.

Jane Thompson, *Design Research* (Chronicle Books, 2010) **21 top right**.

© Philip A. Turner photographer **292 bottom**.

The Walgreen Drug Stores Historical Foundation **33 bottom**.

William Tyre, Glessner House Museum **306–07**.

University of Illinois, School of Architecture, adaptation by Todd Wenger, Schweikher House Preservation Trust **99**.

Vinci Hamp Architects **259 top**, Vinci Hamp Architects and Bob Thall photographer **258**, **259 bottom**, **260–261**.

Kitty Baldwin Weese, *Harry Weese Houses* (Chicago Review Press, 1987) **196**, **197**, **198**, **199 right**.

Wheeler Kearns Architects and Monica Rosello photographer **292 top**, **293 top**.

Russel Wright Papers, Department of Special Collections at Syracuse University Library **24 top**.

Donald Wrobleski **226**, **227 left-right**.

Jim Zanzi **303 top**.

William Zbaren photographer **200–01**, **202-03**, **228–231**, **300 bottom**, **320–21**, **324–25**.

Todd Zeiger, Indiana Landmarks **308 right**.

Lou Zucaro **311**.

John Zukowsky, *Mies Reconsidered: His Career, Legacy, and Disciples* (Art Institute of Chicago/ Rizzoli, 1986), Hedrich Blessing, gift of Edward Duckett, Appendix I **48**.

Select Resources

Archives & Libraries

The Art Institute of Chicago, Ryerson & Burnham Libraries, Ryerson & Burnham Archives: Department of Architecture

Chicago History Museum Archives and Manuscripts Collection, Research Center

Illinois Institute of Technology, Graham Resource Center, Paul V. Galvin Library, University Archives and Special Collections

The Museum of Modern Art, New York

Web Resources

USModernist® Library

APT Building Technology Heritage Library

Houses (USA and Chicago)

82 Distinguished Houses from Architectural Record. New York: F. W. Dodge, 1952.

Architectural Forum Editors. *The 1936 Book of Small Houses.* New York: Simon and Schuster, 1936.

Architectural Forum Editors. *The 1938 Book of Small Houses.* New York: Simon and Schuster, 1937.

Architectural Forum Editors. *The 1940 Book of Small Houses.* New York: Simon and Schuster, 1939.

Baker, Geoffrey, and Bruno Funaro. *Windows in Modern Architecture.* New York: Architectural Book Publishing, 1948.

Barber, Daniel A. *A House in the Sun: Modern Architecture and Solar Energy in the Cold War.* New York: Oxford University Press, 2016.

Benjamin, Susan, and Stuart Cohen. *North Shore Chicago: Houses of the Lakefront Suburbs, 1890–1940.* New York: Acanthus, 2004.

Bergdoll, Barry, and Peter Christensen, eds. *Home Delivery: Fabricating the Modern Dwelling.* New York: Museum of Modern Art, 2008.

Cheek, Richard. *Selling the Dwelling: The Books that Built America's Houses, 1775–2000.* New York: Grolier, 2013.

Clark, Clifford Edward Jr. *The American Family Home, 1800–1960.* Chapel Hill: University of North Carolina Press, 1986.

Denzer, Anthony. *The Solar House: Pioneering Sustainable Design.* New York: Rizzoli, 2013.

Ford, James, and Katherine Morrow Ford. *The Modern House in America.* New York: Architectural Book Publishing, 1940. Republished, *Classic Modern Homes of the Thirties: 64 Designs by Neutra, Gropius, Breuer, Stone and Others.* Mineola, New York: Dover, 1989.

Ford, Katherine Morrow, and Thomas H. Creighton. *The American House Today: 85 Notable Examples Selected and Evaluated.* New York: Reinhold, 1951.

Frampton, Kenneth, and David Larkin, eds. *American Masterworks: The Twentieth-Century House.* New York: Universe, 2002.

Friedman, Alice T. *Women and the Making of the Modern House: A Social and Architectural History.* New York: Abrams, 1998.

Friedman, Bernard. *The American Idea of Home: Conversations about Architecture & Design.* Austin: University of Texas Press, 2017.

Goldstein, Barbara, ed. *Arts & Architecture: The Entenza Years.* Cambridge, MA: MIT Press, 1990.

Hayden, Dolores. *Building Suburbia: Green Fields and Suburban Growth, 1820–2000.* New York: Pantheon, 2003.

Hennessey, William J. *America's Best Small Houses.* New York: Viking, 1949.

Hitchcock, Henry-Russell, and Arthur Drexler. *Built in USA: Post-War Architecture.* New York: Museum of Modern Art, 1952.

Howe, Jeffery. *The Houses We Live In: An Identification Guide to the History and Style of American Domestic Architecture.* London: PRC, 2003.

Isenstadt, Sandy. *The Modern American House: Spaciousness and Middle-Class Identity.* New York: Cambridge University Press, 2006.

Jacob, Mary Jane, and Jacquelynn Baas, eds. *Chicago Makes Modern: How Creative Minds Changed Society.* Chicago: University of Chicago Press and School of the Art Institute of Chicago, 2012.

Jandl, H. Ward, John A. Burns, and Michael J. Auer. *Yesterday's Houses of Tomorrow: Innovative American Homes 1850–1950.* Washington, DC: National Trust for Historic Preservation Press, 1991.

Kassler, Elizabeth Bauer Mock. *Built in USA: 1932–1944.* New York: Museum of Modern Art, 1944.

Leslie, Thomas. "'Insulation with Vision': The Development of Insulated Glazing, 1930–1980." *Journal of Preservation Technology* 49, no. 4, (2018): 23–31.

Matranga, Victoria K. "Clear as Glass: The Libbey-Owens-Ford Window to Better Living." In *The Alliance of Art and Industry: Toledo Designs for a Modern America,* edited by Dennis P.

Doordan, 176–93. Toledo: Toledo Museum of Art, 2002.

Miller Lane, Barbara. *Houses for a New World: Builders and Buyers in American Suburbs, 1945–1965.* Princeton: Princeton University Press, 2015.

Nelson, George, and Henry Wright. *Tomorrow's Houses: How to Plan Your Post-War Home Now.* New York: Simon and Schuster, 1945.

Pearson, Clifford A., ed. *Modern American Houses: Four Decades of Award Winning Design in Architectural Record.* New York: Harry N. Abrams in Association with *Architectural Record,* 1996.

Penick, Monica. *Tastemaker: Elizabeth Gordon, House Beautiful, and the Postwar American Home.* New Haven: Yale University Press, 2017.

Phaidon Editors. *The American House.* London: Phaidon, 2001.

Rogers, Kate Ellen. *The Modern House, U.S.A.: Its Design and Decoration.* New York: Harper & Rowe, 1962.

Simon, Maron J., with Libbey-Owens-Ford Glass Company. *Your Solar House.* New York: Simon and Schuster, 1947.

Smith, Elizabeth A. T. *Blueprints for Modern Living: History and Legacy of the Case Study Houses.* Los Angeles: Museum of Contemporary Art, 1989.

Stern, Robert A. M., David Fishman and Jacob Tilove. *Paradise Planned: the Garden Suburb and the Modern City.* New York: The Monacelli Press, 2013.

Stevenson, Katherine Cole, and W. Ward Jandl. *Houses by Mail: A Guide to Houses from Sears, Roebuck and Company.* Washington, DC : Preservation Press, 1986.

Thornton, Rosemary. *Sears Homes of Illinois*. Charleston, SC: The History Press, 2010.

Thornton, Rosemary, and Dale Patrick Wolicki. *Montgomery Ward's Mail-order Homes. A History and Field Guide to Wardway Homes*. Portsmouth, VA: Gentle Beam Publications. 2010.

Upton, Dell. *Architecture in the United States*. Oxford: Oxford University Press, 1998.

Walter, Lester. *American Homes: The Landmark Illustrated Encyclopedia of Domestic Architecture*. New York: Black Dog and Leventhal, 2014.

Wright, Gwendolyn. *Building the Dream: A Social History of Housing in America*. Cambridge, MA: MIT Press, 1981.

Wright, Gwendolyn. *USA: Modern Architectures in History*. London: Reaktion, 2008.

Art, Design, Interiors, Literature, and Photography

Achilles, Rolf. *Made in Illinois. A Story of Illinois Manufacturing Published in Honor of the Illinois Manufacturers' Association Centennial*. Chicago: Illinois Manufacturers' Association. 1993.

Auscherman, Amy, and Sam Grawe and Leon Ransmeier eds. *Herman Miller. A Way of Life*. London: Phaidon, 2019.

Brunetti, John. *Baldwin Kingrey: Midcentury Modern in Chicago, 1947–1957*. Chicago: Wright, 2004.

Cahan, Richard, and Michael Williams, *Richard Nickel's Chicago: Photographs of a Lost City*. Chicago: Cityfiles Press, 2006.

Clark, Robert Judson. *Designing in America: The Cranbrook Vision, 1925–1950*. New York: Abrams, in association with the Detroit Institute of Arts and the Metropolitan Museum of Art, 1983.

Colomina, Beatriz, and AnnMarie Brennan, and Jeannie Kim eds. *Cold War Hothouses: Inventing Postwar Culture from Cockpit to Playboy*. New York: Princeton Architectural Press, 2004.

Darling, Sharon S. *Chicago Furniture: Art, Craft & Industry, 1833–1933*. New York: Chicago Historical Society, in association with Norton, 1984.

Ford, James, and Katherine Morrow Ford. *Design of Modern Interiors*. New York: Architectural Book Publishing, 1942.

Friedman, Marilyn F. *Selling Good Design: Promoting the Early Modern Interior*. New York: Rizzoli, 2003.

Friedman, Marilyn F. *Making America Modern: Interior Design in the 1930s*. New York: Bauer and Dean, 2018.

Gand, Gary. *Julius Shulman: Chicago Midcentury Modernism*. New York: Rizzoli, 2010.

Ganz, Cheryl. *The 1933 Chicago World's Fair: A Century of Progress*. Urbana: University of Illinois Press, 2008.

Genauer, Emily. *Modern Interiors Today and Tomorrow*. Cleveland and New York: World Publishing, 1942.

Harris, Neil. *Chicago by the Book: 101 Publications that Shaped the City and Its Image*. Chicago: University of Chicago Press, 2018.

Hedrich, Jack O. *Oral History of Jack O. Hedrich / Interviewed by Betty J. Blum, Chicago Architects Oral History Project*. Chicago: Art Institute of Chicago, 2006.

Hedrich, William C. *Oral History of William C. Hedrich / Interviewed by Betty J. Blum, Chicago Architects Oral History Project*. Chicago: Art Institute of Chicago, 2006.

Hiss, Tony, and Timothy Samuelson. *Building Images: Seventy Years of Photography at Hedrich Blessing*. San Francisco: Chronicle Books, 2000.

Kennedy, Elizabeth. *Chicago Modern, 1893–1945: Pursuit of the New*. Chicago: Terra Museum of American Art, 2004.

Lutz, Brian. *Knoll: A Modernist Universe*. New York: Rizzoli, 2010.

Mileaf, Janine, and Susan F. Rossen, eds. *The Arts Club of Chicago at 100: Art and Culture 1916-2016*. Chicago: Arts Club of Chicago, 2016.

Piña, Leslie A. *Dunbar: Fine Furniture of the 1950s*. Atglen, PA: Schiffer, 2000.

Raley, Dorothy, ed. *A Century of Progress Homes and Furnishings*. Chicago: M. A. Ring, 1934, Delhi, India: Facsimile Publisher, 2018.

Reimer, Karen, ed. *Centennial: A History of the Renaissance Society 1915–2015*. Chicago: Renaissance Society, 2015.

Schrenk, Lisa D. *Building a Century of Progress: The Architecture of Chicago's 1933–34 World Fair*. Minneapolis: University of Minnesota Press, 2007.

Sharp, Robert V., and Elizabeth Stepina, eds. *1945 Creativity and Crisis: Chicago Architecture and Design of the World War II Era*. Chicago: Art Institute of Chicago, 2005.

Sobieszek, Robert A., ed. *The Architectural Photography of Hedrich-Blessing*. New York: Holt, Rinehart and Winston, 1984.

Taft, Maggie, and Robert Cozzolino, eds. *Art in Chicago: A History from the Fire to Now*. Chicago: University of Chicago Press, 2018.

Thompson, Jane, and Alexandra Lange. *Design Research: The Store that Brought Modern Living to American Homes*. San Francisco: Chronicle Books, 2010.

Todd, Dorothy, and Raymond Mortimer. *The New Interior Decoration*. New York: Scribner's, 1929.

Thurman, Christa C. Mayer. "Rooted in Chicago: Fifty Years of Textile Design Traditions." The Art Institute of Chicago. *Museum Studies* 23, no. 1 (1997).

Valley, Matt. "The Crate and Barrel Story." *National Real Estate Investor* June 01, 2001.

Warren, Lynn, ed. *Art in Chicago, 1945–1995*. Chicago: Museum of Contemporary Art, 1996.

Zukowsky, John. *Chicago Architecture and Design, 1923–1993: Reconfiguration of an American Metropolis*. Munich: Prestel, 1993.

Zukowsky, John. *Chicago Architecture 1872–1922: Birth of a Metropolis*. Munich: Prestel, 1987, reprint 2000.

Overview (Chicago)

Bach, Ira J. *Chicago's Famous Buildings*. Chicago: University of Chicago Press, 1980. (5th edition, Franz Schulze and Kevin Harrington: Chicago: University of Chicago Press, 2003).

Bach, Ira J., with Susan Wolfson. *A Guide to Chicago's Historic Suburbs on Wheels and on Foot (Lake, McHenry, Kane, DuPage, Will & Cook Counties)*. Chicago: Swallow Press, 1981.

Bey, Lee. *Southern Exposure: The Overlooked Architecture of Chicago's South Side*. Evanston: Northwestern University Press, 2019.

Benjamin, Susan. *Winnetka Architecture: A Guide to Timeless Styles*. Winnetka: Winnetka Historical Museum, 1990.

Berger, Philip, ed. *Highland Park: American Suburb At Its Best*. Highland Park: Highland Park Landmark Preservation Committee, 1982.

Bruegmann, Robert, ed. *Art Deco Chicago: Designing Modern America*. Chicago: Chicago Art Deco Society in collaboration with the Chicago History Museum, 2018, distributed by Yale University Press.

Buchbinder-Green, Barbara J., and Margery Blair Perkins, eds. *Evanston: A Tour through the City's History*. Evanston: Evanston History Center, 2013 (1st ed. 1984).

Cummings, Kathleen Roy. *Architectural Records in Chicago: A Guide to Architectural Research Resources in Cook County and Vicinity*. Chicago: Art Institute of Chicago, 1981.

Davis, Susan O'Connor. *Chicago's Historic Hyde Park*. Chicago: University of Chicago Press, 2013.

Dyja, Thomas. *The Third Coast: When Chicago Built the American Dream*. New York: Penguin, 2014.

Gapp, Paul. *Paul Gapp's Chicago: Selected Writings of the Chicago Tribune's Architecture Critic*. Chicago: Chicago Tribune, 1980.

Harris, Neil, and Michael Conzen, *The WPA Guide to Illinois: The Federal Writers Project Guide to 1930s Illinois*. New York: Pantheon, 1983; WPA Federal Writers' Project. *Chicago and Suburbs, 1939* (reprint with preface by Paul Gapp). Evanston: Chicago Historical Bookworks, 1991.

Harris, Neil, and Teri J. Edelstein. *Chicago Apartments: A Century of Lakefront Luxury*. Chicago: The University of Chicago Press, 2020.

Kamin, Blair. *Why Architecture Matters: Lessons from Chicago*. Chicago: University of Chicago Press, 2001.

Keating, Ann Durkin. *Building Chicago: Suburban Developers and the Creation of a Divided Metropolis*. Urbana: University of Illinois Press, 2002.

Keating, Ann Durkin, ed. *Neighborhoods and Suburbs: A Historical Guide.* Chicago: University of Chicago Press, 2008.

Larson, George A., and Jay Pridmore. *Chicago Architecture and Design.* New York: Abrams, 1st edition 1993, 3rd ed. 2018.

Mayer, Harold M., and Richard C. Wade with Glen E. Holt. *Chicago: Growth of a Metropolis.* Chicago: University of Chicago Press, 1969.

Pacyga, Dominic A., and Ellen Skerrett. *Chicago, City of Neighborhoods: Histories & Tours.* Chicago: Loyola University Press, 1986.

Peltason, Ruth, and Grace Ong Yan. *Architect: The Pritzker Prize Laureates in their Own Words.* New York: Black Dog & Leventhal, 2017.

Pridmore. Jay. *Seeing the City: Celebrating 50 Years of the Chicago Architecture Foundation 1966–2016.* Chicago: Chicago Architecture Foundation, 2016.

Saviano, Laura, Stuart Cohen, Kris Hartzell, Jack Weiss, and Heidrun Hoppe, eds. *Evanston: 150 Years 150 Places,* 2nd ed. Evanston: Design Evanston, 2015.

Sinkevitch, Alice, and Laurie McGovern Petersen, eds. *AIA Guidebook to Chicago.* Urbana, Chicago, and Springfield: University of Illinois Press, 2014.

Szucs, Loretto Dennis. *Chicago & Cook County: A Guide to Research.* Salt Lake City: Ancestry, 1996.

Tisher, William H., ed. *Midwestern Landscape Architecture.* Urbana: University of Illinois Press, 2000.

Waldheim, Charles, and Katerina Rüedi Ray, eds. *Chicago Architecture: Histories, Revisions, Alternatives.* Chicago: University of Chicago Press, 2005.

Zukowsky, John, and Martha Thorne. *Masterpieces of Chicago Architecture.* New York: Rizzoli in association with the Art Institute of Chicago, 2004.

Oral Histories

Compiled under the Auspices of the Chicago Architects Oral History Project, the Ernest R. Graham Study Center for Architectural Drawings, Department of Architecture, the Art Institute of Chicago include the following architects referenced in *Modern in the Middle:*

Jacques Calman Brownson, George Danforth (H. P. Davis Rockwell), Arthur Detmers Dubin (Henry Dubin), Joseph Fujikawa, Bertrand Goldberg, Myron Goldsmith, Bruce Graham, Edward Humrich, Fred George Keck, Gertrude Kerbis [Lempp], Paul McCurry, James Nagle, Walter Netsch, Lawrence Perkins (Philip Will Jr.), [Robert] Paul Schweikher (Winston Elting), A. James Speyer, Gene Summers, Robert Bruce Tague, Stanley Tigerman, John Vinci, Benjamin Weese, Harry Weese, Y. C. Wong, and Edward Todd Wheeler.

Monographs

David Adler
Salny, Steven N. *The Country Houses of David Adler: Interior by Frances Elkins.* New York: W. W. Norton, 2001.

Thorne, Martha, ed. *David Adler, Architect: The Elements of Style.* New Haven: Art Institute of Chicago in Association with Yale University Press, 2002.

Laurence Booth
Pridmore, Jay. *Total Performance Architecture: The Work of Booth Hansen.* San Francisco: Oro Editions, 2015.

Barry Byrne
Vincent, L. Michael. *The Architecture of Barry Byrne: Taking the Prairie School to Europe.* Urbana: University of Illinois Press, 2013.

Alfred Caldwell
Blaser, Werner. *Architecture and Nature: The Work of Alfred Caldwell.* Basel: Birkhäuser Verlag, 1984.

Domer, Dennis, ed, *Alfred Caldwell: The Life and Work of a Prairie School Landscape Architect.* Baltimore: John Hopkins University Press, 1997.

I. W. Colburn
Pridmore, Jay. *I. W. Colburn: Emotion in Modern Architecture.* Lake Forest: Lake Forest College Press, 2015.

Stuart Cohen
Cohen, Stuart, and Julie Hacker. *Transforming the Traditional: The Work of Cohen & Hacker.* Mulgrave, Victoria: Images Publishing, 2009.

Edward Dart
Dart, Susan. *Edward Dart Architect.* Evanston: Evanston Publishing, 1993.

Seymour, Matthew. "Edward Dart: Preserving the Works of a Mid-Century Architect." MS thesis, School of the Art Institute of Chicago, Historic Preservation Program, 2011.

George Edson Danforth
Robertson, Donna Robertson. *George Edson Danforth 1916–2007.* Chicago: College of Architecture -Illinois Institute of Technology, 2007.

William Ferguson Deknatel
Zukowsky, John, and Betty Blum. *Architecture in Context: The Avant-Garde in Chicago's Suburbs: Paul Schweiker and William Ferguson Deknatel.* Chicago: Graham Foundation for Advanced Studies in the Fine Arts and Art Institute of Chicago, 1984.

Howard T. Fisher
John A. Burns. "K2H40: The Promise of Prefabrication." In *Yesterday's Houses of Tomorrow: Innovative American Homes 1850 to 1950,* edited by H. Ward Jandl, John A. Burns, and Michael J. Auer. Washington, DC: Preservation Press, 1991, 156–67.

Walter Frazier J. (Howard Raftery)
Coventry, Kim, and Arthur Hawks Miller. *Walter Frazier: Frazier, Raftery, Orr & Fairbank Architects, Houses of Chicago's North Shore, 1924–1970.* Lake Forest: Lake Forest-Lake Bluff Historical Society, 2009.

Henry P. Glass
Gorman, Carma R. "Henry P. Glass and World War II." *Design Issues* 22, no. 4 (Autumn, 2006): 4–26.

Bruce Goff
De Long, David G. *Bruce Goff: Toward Absolute Architecture.* New York: Architectural History Foundation, 1988.

Henderson, Arn. *Bruce Goff: Architecture of Discipline in Freedom.* Norman: University of Oklahoma Press, 2017.

Saliga, Pauline, and Mary Woolever, eds. *The Architecture of Bruce Goff 1904–1982: Design for the Continuous Present.* New York: Art Institute of Chicago and Prestel Verlag, 1995.

Bertrand Goldberg
Ragon, Michel. *Goldberg: Dans La Ville/On the City.* Paris: Paris Art Center, 1985.

Ryan, Zoë, ed. *Bertrand Goldberg: Architecture of Invention.* Chicago: Art Institute of Chicago, 2011, distributed by Yale University Press.

Myron Goldsmith
Blaser, Werner. *Myron Goldsmith: Buildings and Concepts.* New York: Rizzoli, 1987.

Bruce Graham
Adams, Nicholas. *Skidmore, Owings & Merrill.* Milan: Electa Architecture / Mondadori Electa S.p.A, 2006.

Graham, Bruce. *Bruce Graham of SOM.* New York: Rizzoli, 1989.

David Hovey
Kent Cheryl. *The Nature of Dwellings: The Architecture of David Hovey.* New York: Rizzoli, 2004.

Edward Humrich
Roth, Thomas Charles. "The Architecture of Edward Robert Humrich." MA thesis, University of Illinois at Chicago, 1993.

Jens Jensen
Jensen, Jens. *Siftings.* Baltimore: John Hopkins University Press, 1990.

Johnston, Jane L., ed. *A Force of Nature: The Life and Work of Jens Jensen. A Collection of Essays.* Chicago: Chicago Dept. of Cultural Affairs, 2002.

George Fred Keck
Boyce, Robert Piper. *Keck and Keck.* New York: Princeton Architectural Press, 1993.

Menocal, Narciso G. *Keck & Keck, Architects.* Madison: Elvehjem Museum of Art, University of Wisconsin-Madison, 1980.

Krueck and Sexton
Dixon, John Morris. *Krueck and Sexton: From There to Here.* Mulgrave, Victoria, Australia: Images Publishing, 2017.

Tracey, Timothy and Franz Schulze. *Krueck + Sexton: Architects.* New York: The Monacelli Press, 1997.

Ludwig Mies van der Rohe
Achilles, Rolf, Kevin Harrington and Charlotte Myhrum. *Mies Van Der Rohe: Architect as Educator.* Chicago: Mies Van der Rohe Centennial Project, Illinois Institute of Technology, 1986, distributed by University of Chicago Press.

Blaser, Werner. *After Mies: Mies van der Rohe, Teaching*

and Principles. New York: Van Nostrand Reinhold, 1977.

Mertins, Detlef. *Mies*. New York: Phaidon, 2014.

Lambert, Phyllis ed., *Mies in America* (Montréal: Canadian Centre for Architecture, 2001).

Neumeyer, Fritz. *The Artless Word: Mies van der Rohe on the Building Art*. Cambridge: MIT Press, 1991.

Schulze, Franz, and Edward Windhorst. *Mies van der Rohe: A Critical Biography, New and Revised Edition*. Chicago: University of Chicago Press, 2012.

Speyer, A. James, with Frederick Koeper. *Mies van der Rohe*. Chicago: Art Institute of Chicago, 1968.

Swenson, Alfred, and Pao-Chi Chang. *Architectural Education at IIT, 1938–1978*. Chicago: Illinois Institute of Technology, 1980.

Tegethoff, Wolf. *Mies van der Rohe: The Villas and Country Houses*. New York: Museum of Modern Art, 1985.

John W. Moutoussamy
Kliment, Stephen A., FAIA. "The Trailblazers." In *AIA Architect* 13 (November 10, 2006).

James Lee Nagle
Nagle, James, and Stanley Tigerman. *Houses: the Architecture of Nagle, Hartray, Danker, Kagan, McKay, Penney*. New York: Edizioni Press, 2005.

Walter Netsch
Jones, Anthony. *The Netsch House: Living with Art*. Chicago: Anthony Jones, 2015.

William L. Pereira
Robertson, Colin M. *Modernist Maverick: The Architecture of William L. Pereira*. Reno: Nevada Museum of Art, 2013.

Steele, James. *William Pereira*. Los Angeles: University of Southern California Architectural Guild Press, 2002.

Lawrence Perkins (Philip Will Jr.)
Fry, Debbie, and Robyn Beaver, eds. *Perkins + Will: 75 Years*. Mulgrave, Victoria, Australia: Images Publishing, 2010.

Ralph Rapson
Hession, Jane King, Rip Rapson, and Bruce N. Wright. *Ralph Rapson: Sixty Years of Modern Design*. Afton, MN: Afton Historical Society Press, 1999.

Andrew N. Rebori
Tatum, Raymond Terry. "A Catalogue Raisonné of the Work of Andrew Nicholas Rebori." MS thesis, Columbia University, 1985.

Draper, Joan E., and Raymond T. Tatum. "The Buildings of Andrew Nicholas Rebori." *Chicago Architectural Journal* 4 (1984): 14–24.

Paul Schweikher (Winston Elting)
Rogers, Meyric Reynold. *The Work of Schweikher and Elting*. Chicago: Renaissance Society, 1949.

"Schweikher y Elting," theme issue. *Nuestra Arquitectura* 213, no. 4 (Abril 1947): 110–42.

"Recent Work by the Office of Paul Schweikher and Theodore Warren Lamb Associated Architects." *Architectural Forum* 71, no. 5 (November 1939): 351–66.

George Schipporeit
Windhorst, Edward. *George Schipporeit: Architect, Educator, Urbanist*. Chicago: Illinois Institute of Technology Architecture, 2014.

A. James Speyer
Vinci, John. *A. James Speyer: Architect, Curator, Exhibition Designer*. Chicago: The Arts Club of Chicago, 1997, distributed by the University of Chicago Press.

Gene Summers
Blaser, Werner ed., *Gene Summers Art / Architecture*. Basel: Birkhäuser, 2003.

Crombie Taylor
Plank, Jeffrey. *Crombie Taylor: Modern Architecture, Building Restoration, and the Rediscovery of Louis Sullivan*. Richmond, CA: William Stout, 2009.

Stanley Tigerman
Mollman, Sarah. *Stanley Tigerman: Buildings and Projects, 1966–1989*. New York: Rizzoli, 1989.

Petit, Emmanuel, ed. *Schlepping through Ambivalence: Essays on an American Condition*. (New Haven: Yale University Press, 2011).

Tigerman, Stanley. *Versus: An American Architect's Alternatives*. New York: Rizzoli, 1982.

Tigerman, Stanley. *Designing Bridges to Burn: Architectural Memoirs*. Chicago: Oro Editions, 2010.

John Vinci (Lawrence Kenny)
Sharoff, Robert, and William Zbaren. *John Vinci: Life and Landmarks*. Evanston: Northwestern University Press, 2017.

Harry Weese
Weese, Kitty Baldwin. *Harry Weese Houses*. Chicago: Chicago Review Press, 1987.

Bruegmann, Robert, and Kathleen Murphy Skolnik. *The Architecture of Harry Weese*. New York: Norton, 2010.

Frank Lloyd Wright
Gutheim, Frederic, ed. *In the Cause of Architecture Frank Lloyd Wright*. New York: Architectural Record Books, 1975.

Levine, Neil. *The Architecture of Frank Lloyd Wright*. Princeton: Princeton University Press, 1996.

Levine, Neil. *The Urbanism of Frank Lloyd Wright*. Princeton: Princeton University Press, 1996.

Sergeant, John. *Frank Lloyd Wright's Usonian Houses: Designs for Moderate Cost One Family Homes*. New York: Whitney Library of Design, an imprint of Watson-Guptill, 1984.

Storrer, William Allin. *The Architecture of Frank Lloyd Wright: A Complete Catalog*. Chicago: University of Chicago Press, 2017.

Advocacy & Preservation

Birnbaum, Charles A. *Preserving Modern Landscape Architecture II: Making Postwar Landscapes Visible*. Washington, DC: Spacemaker Press, 2004.

Bluestone, Daniel M. "Wright Saving Wright: Preserving the Robie House, 1957." In *Rethinking Wright at 150* edited by Neil Levine and Richard Longstreth. Charlottesville: University of Virginia Press, 2020.

Carlascio, Robin A., and Theresa K. Badovich. *Saving a Century of Progress: From Their Storied Beginnings to Their Rebirth Along the Dunes National Lakes, Journey with the 1933–34 World's Fair Homes and the Leasees Who Restored Them*. Crown Point, IN: Amalfi, 2014.

Cunningham, Allen, ed. *Do.Co.Mo.Mo. Modern Movement Heritage*. New York: Routledge, 2012.

Diestelkamp, Edward. "Modern Houses Open to the Public in Europe and America." "The Modern House Revisited," *Journal of the Twentieth Century Society 2* (1996): 86–94.

Hertz, Daniel Kay. *The Battle of Lincoln Park: Urban Renewal and Gentrification in Chicago*. Cleveland: Belt Publishing, 2018.

Heuvel, Dirk, ed. *The Challenge of Change: Dealing with the Legacy of the Modern Movement*. Amsterdam: IOS Press, 2008.

Jester, Thomas C., ed. *Twentieth-Century Building Materials: History and Conservation*. Los Angeles: Getty Conservation Institute, 2014.

Matz, Jeffrey, and Lorenzo Ottaviani, Cristina A. Ross, and Michael Biondo. *Midcentury Houses Today: New Canaan, Connecticut*. New York: The Monacelli Press. 2014.

Prudon, Theodore H. M. *Preservation of Modern Architecture*. Hoboken, NJ: John Wiley, 2008.

Webb, Michael. *Modernism Reborn: Mid-Century American Houses*. New York: Universe, 2001.

Index

Funding for this project
was provided by the Fred
Eychaner Fund and by former
dean Michelangelo Sabatino
through the Rowe Family
College of Architecture Dean
Endowed Chair and the John
Vinci Distinguished Research
Fellowship at the Illinois
Institute of Technology.

Library of Congress Control
Number: 2020934128
ISBN 978-1-58093-526-5

10 9 8 7 6 5 4 3 2 1

Printed in China
Design by Bud Rodecker, Alyssa
Arnesen, and Logan Doyle, Thirst

The Monacelli Press
65 Bleecker Street
8th Floor
New York, New York 10012

www.monacellipress.com